Reconfiguring Racial Capitalism

MINGWEI HUANG

Reconfiguring Racial Capitalism

SOUTH AFRICA
IN THE CHINESE CENTURY

DUKE UNIVERSITY PRESS
Durham and London
2024

© 2024 DUKE UNIVERSITY PRESS
Designed by A. Mattson Gallagher
Typeset in Minion Pro by Westchester Publishing Services

Library of Congress Cataloging-in-Publication Data
Names: Huang, Mingwei, [date] author.
Title: Reconfiguring racial capitalism : South Africa in the
Chinese century / Mingwei Huang.
Description: Durham : Duke University Press, 2024. | Includes
bibliographical references and index.
Identifiers: LCCN 2024005740 (print)
LCCN 2024005741 (ebook)
ISBN 9781478031031 (paperback)
ISBN 9781478026792 (hardcover)
ISBN 9781478059998 (ebook)
Subjects: LCSH: Chinese—South Africa—Johannesburg—Economic
conditions. | Foreign workers, African—South Africa—
Johannesburg—Economic conditions. | Capitalism—Social aspects—
South Africa—Johannesburg. | Chinese diaspora—Economic aspects.
| Shopping malls—South Africa—Johannesburg. | South Africa—
Emigration and immigration—Economic aspects. | South Africa—
Race relations—Economic aspects. | BISAC: SOCIAL SCIENCE /
Ethnic Studies / African Studies |SOCIAL SCIENCE /
Anthropology / Cultural & Social
Classification: LCC DT1768.C55 H83 2024 (print) | LCC DT1768.C55
(ebook) | DDC 305.8951/068—dc23/eng/20240430
LC record available at https://lccn.loc.gov/2024005740
LC ebook record available at https://lccn.loc.gov/2024005741

Cover art: Photograph by the author.

For my parents

CONTENTS

It often surprises people to learn that I am an Americanist. This book started as an American studies project. I set out to research Afro-Asia and trace radical traditions between African and Asian diasporas. By happenstance, I was funded for a research trip to South Africa. At the outset, I hoped to find continuities between the Afro-Asian solidarities of the era of the Bandung Conference and the BRICS alliance between the People's Republic of China (PRC) and South Africa, even though the apartheid state was not part of the watershed colonial conference. I was intent on understanding how ordinary people renewed the spirit of anticolonial friendship and solidarity in an era of neoliberal globalization and empire centered on China's relationship with the Global South. On my first visit to South Africa, the social vibrancy of the China Mall, the Chinese wholesale outlet examined in this book, captivated me. The mall became my fieldwork site, and I became an ethnographer. Initially, I read the mall as a space of conviviality and hybridity, but over subsequent fieldwork trips, the racialized dynamics of exploitation exposed my romance with solidarity and cosmopolitanism. I turned to the lingua franca of American studies—racial capitalism, settler colonialism, cultures of imperialism, exceptionalism, and intimacy—to make sense of a different Afro-Asia.

China's return to the African continent in the twenty-first century is one of the most storied global developments of our time. In African countries, China, it seems, is suddenly everywhere: in new expressways, construction sites, international terminals, industrial zones, mining concessions, pipelines, residential complexes, wholesale malls, and small shops. This book grew out of a desire to complicate the dominant narrative of Chinese neocolonialism in a milieu of popular and academic writing on China-Africa engagements. *Colonialism* and *racism* are divisive terms in the study of China and Africa. I have been interrogated for my use of these terms, in claims that they are too Americanist or ahistorical to apply to China. I also find myself defensive when hearing scholars invoke neocolonialism as self-evident and singling out China as a bad global actor. And yet, for many South Africans and southern Africans I met at the mall, the actions of Chinese state companies, expatriates, and entrepreneurs are not that dissimilar from racism and colonialism in recent lifetimes. These experiences are at least similar enough to raise the comparison. Ethnography makes concrete how ordinary Chinese and African actors experience, understand, and negotiate power relations and difference at various scales, and it complicates grand narratives such as the "Chinese scramble in Africa" or "south-south cooperation." And yet, these tropes are so entrenched in popular discourse, even commonsensical, that it is difficult to dislodge them. Why is European colonialism the main framework to make sense of China's economic presence in Africa? What is it about this historical conjuncture that makes *race* and *empire*, as analytical terms, so loaded? In this book, I arrive at a similar conclusion as those with whom I take issue: there is something colonial, racial, and specifically anti-Black about Chinese capitalist projects in Africa. But I do so through a different line of argument and engagement with these terms. Through a longer historical reframing, I wager that Chinese migrants act within the global structural parameters of white supremacy, anti-Blackness, capitalism, and colonialism that they have not made but nevertheless inherited and further perpetuate. This is not to let Chinese migrants off the hook, but recognizes how colonizing capacities are produced within broader histories of domination. I am wary of how my arguments might come across to readers looking for ethnographic confirmation of what they thought they already knew. There is an ambivalence that runs throughout the book that reflects the challenge of writing about interminority relations without losing sight of histories of domination and flattening the complexity of colonialism, empire, race, and capitalism.

In lieu of neocolonialism, I found racial capitalism to be a generative analytic for Sino-African engagements. This project is shaped by the revival in the study of racial capitalism since the reissuing of Cedric Robinson's landmark *Black Marxism* ([1983] 2000), a chronicle of the Black radical tradition that is often credited with coining the term *racial capitalism* and has undeniably transformed the study of capitalism. A generation of scholars have built on Robinson's work and, as I do in this book, extend the analytic of racial capitalism to other historical, geographic, and disciplinary contexts. As the study of racial capitalism has been institutionalized and expanded, the term risks losing its analytical specificity and political power (Burden-Stelly, Hudson, and Pierre 2020). My engagement with racial capitalism builds on the long-standing intellectual and political work of Black studies and traditions of Black internationalist engagement with China and Afro-Asian solidarity. In examining racial capitalism from South Africa, I engage with South African theorists such as David Hemson, Martin Legassick, and Bernard Magubane, contemporaries of Robinson whose Marxist analysis of race and capitalism under apartheid influenced his thinking. Scholars are returning to this South Africanist radical tradition to revive racial capitalism's radical potential and resituate the term in the historical conditions of its theorization. Racial capitalism—and its interconnections with empire and colonialism—is vital for understanding the colonial, racial, and capitalist oppression of the global majority in the twenty-first century.

My thinking is indebted to the comparative concerns, theoretical vocabularies, and interdisciplinary and transnational methods of American studies and critical ethnic studies. And yet, well after the postnational and transnational turns in American studies, China is still largely off the map. As Petrus Liu (2022) urges, any materialist analysis, including the study of racial capitalism, must grapple with the transformations of global political economy accompanying the rise of China. China cannot remain relegated to area studies while Americanist scholarship, a form of area studies itself, maintains the universal status of "theory." In the US academy from where I write, we need to deprovincialize social theory to better understand and transform a world in which the United States is not the center of gravity but the PRC and the Global South. As China moves from global margins to the center, Chinese racial formations and anti-Black racism are increasingly salient in and beyond China. As the PRC expands its military bases in the Atlantic and Indian Oceans, the South China Sea, and the Taiwan Strait, movements for sovereignty and democracy in Hong Kong and Taiwan swell. Xi Jinping's government faces criticism for authoritarianism, ethnoracial oppression, and the surveillance and detention of Muslim Uyghurs in Xinjiang—a placename that means "new frontier." We are now three decades into the Chinese Century. Its racial and imperial forms are still emergent, but it has also sedimented enough to theorize.

ACKNOWLEDGMENTS

I wrote most of this book in the isolated years of 2020 and 2021. I kept a sticky note on my computer: "Tell them about us." These words came from Oscar, a Zimbabwean street vendor whom I met at the China City mall in February 2020, the last time I would be in Johannesburg for several years. Oscar came from a long line of migrants to Johannesburg and took great interest in my book and its argument about racial capitalism. He is one of many people whose structural analysis of their reality informed my thinking and writing. When I was stuck, his words reminded me of my purpose: to share the experiences and worldviews of ordinary people with readers and students. My first thanks go to the hundreds of African and Chinese people I met in South Africa, most of whom do not prominently appear in these pages but informed my research. This book is possible because they generously invited me into their shops and homes, let me tag along on outings, and shared their lives with me.

At the University of Minnesota (UMN), the American Studies Department gave me extraordinary freedom and support to pursue a project that moved perhaps too far from traditional sites, even after the postnational and transnational turns. Jigna Desai was my first reader and taught me how to think critically about knowledge production and act promiscuously with interdisciplinarity. Karen Ho brought me into the anthropology of capitalism through a feminist lineage and trained me as an ethnographer. I couldn't have asked for a more dynamic duo of advisers. I was fortunate to work with two Afro-Asian scholars: Yuichiro Onishi introduced me to Cedric Robinson's *Black Marxism* in a directed reading of Afro-Asian radical texts, and Elliott Powell's cultural analysis was necessary for doing Afro-Asian studies differently. Aren Aizura and Lorena Muñoz mentored me in queer approaches to informal economies and transnational mobilities. Since the beginning, Jamie Monson was a generous reader who brought me into China-Africa studies. To the members of my longest-running group chat—Alix Johnson, Vivian Lu, Susan MacDougall, Eda Pepi, and Megan Steffen—I'm so grateful for your friendship, wisdom, and wit. Jen Hughes, Lars Mackenzie, Lydia Pelot-Hobbs, Olivia Polk, Sarah Records, Evan Taparata, Madison Van Oort, and Shana Ye were excellent co-travelers in the final years of grad school, in Minneapolis and beyond.

Every project has an origin story. When I first arrived in Johannesburg in 2013, Christopher J. Lee casually mentioned that "someone should do an ethnography of the China Mall from top to bottom." The next day, Philip Harrison and Yan Yang took me on an impromptu driving tour of the city's two Chinatowns and its Chinese malls. That was the day this book started. I am indebted to Yoon Jung Park for her generosity in sharing academic contacts to help me get started and her leadership of the Chinese in Africa / Africans in China Research Network. Jamie and Yoon have been instrumental in building the China-Africa field and bringing up a generation of scholars. In South Africa, conversations with scholars, journalists, and artists shaped my imagination and thinking: Gilles Baro, Brittany Birberick, Keith Breckenridge, Siân Butcher, Sharad Chari, Sarah Duff, Nicky Falkof, Kimon de Greef, Pamila Gupta, Will Hanke, Ufrieda Ho, Mehita Iqani, Megan Judge, Charne Lavery, Dorothee Kreutzfeldt, Dilip Menon, Sarah Nuttall, Cobus van Staden, Tim Wright, and Tanya Zack. Your ideas are peppered throughout this book. Special thanks to Mark Lewis, who has graciously allowed me to include his work in this book. Mark, your photographs always take me back to Joburg. I greatly appreciate Kenneth Hlungwane at Museum Africa and Gabriele Mohale at the Historical Papers Research Archive at the University of Witwatersrand (Wits) for assistance with archival research.

The Program in Women's, Gender, and Sexuality Studies at Dartmouth College has been a welcoming home with supportive colleagues, past and present, foremostly Misty de Berry, Laura Edmondson, Eng-Beng Lim, Annelise Orleck, Julia Rabig, Aanchal Saraf, Sachi Schmidt-Hori, Anna Storti, Patricia Stuelke, MT Vallarta, Dennis Washburn, Sa Whitley, and

Melissa Zeiger. Bevan Dunbar makes the world go round. Eng-Beng has been a dream intellectual interlocutor and fierce champion for me. I have been buoyed by the mentorship and solidarity of Kimberly Juanita Brown, Hazel Carby, Sienna Craig, Trica Keaton, Jodi Kim, Tish Lopez, Bethany Moreton, Abby Neely, Naaborko Sackeyfio-Lenoch, Jesse Shipley Weaver, and Pamela Voekel. Thank you to Eman Morsi for convening vital spaces for intellectual community, including a weekly catered writing group and the South-South Forum. My first few years in the woods were with my "fast and furious" family: Kelly Chung, Rebecca Clark, Summer Kim Lee, Yumi Lee, Golnar Nikpour, and Lakshmi Padmanabhan. It has been a joy to think and organize with Bench Ansfield, Nataliya Braginsky, Jorge Cuéllar, RL Goldberg, Jane Henderson, Matt Hooley, Najwa Mayer, Tyler Monson, and Yiren Zheng. Coteaching with Jorge, a friend and comrade, has been pedagogically transformative. This book is a product of the Consortium for Studies in Race, Migration, and Sexuality (RMS), a profoundly impactful but short-lived institutional formation for comparative and relational ethnic studies. I did my best thinking in RMS spaces. So much becomes possible when minoritized faculty and students come together to experiment with radical knowledge making across disciplinary silos and institutional hierarchies. Finally, I am constantly renewed by my students, who theorize the world in sophisticated ways and speak truth to power; everything I love about my job is because of them.

Over the past decade, numerous people have read, heard, or commented on portions of the book. At my manuscript workshop, Rebecca Biron, Iyko Day, Eng-Beng Lim, Lisa Rofel, and Jesse Shipley Weaver gave me the push I needed at the end to go bigger and bolder. Thank you to Lisa Armstrong, Kiran Asher, Laura Briggs, Allison Cool, Nicky Falkof, Patricia Hayes, Mimi Thi Nguyen, Jeanne Penvenne, Lisa Rofel, Carlos Rojas, Louisa Schein, Lynn Thomas, and Cobus van Staden for commenting on drafts. As an interdisciplinary scholar who works across three continents, my work has benefited from engagement with myriad audiences at academic conferences and institutions: the Five Colleges Women's Studies Research Center, the Open University, Rutgers University, the University of Washington, the University of Western Cape, the University of Virginia, and Wits. At Dartmouth, my colleagues in the Department of African and African American Studies, Leslie Center for the Humanities, RMS, and the Society of Fellows enthusiastically workshopped this project at critical moments. It has been wonderful to come up with a cohort of Afro-Asia and China-Africa scholars: Miriam

Driessen, Ruodi Duan, Zifeng Liu, Vivian Lu, Kaneesha Parsard, Neelofer Qadir, Maria Repnikova, Cheryl Mei-Ting Schmitz, Derek Sheridan, Maya Singhal, and Duncan M. Yoon.

This book is possible because of much institutional support. Sixteen months of fieldwork in South Africa were funded by a Social Science Research Council Dissertation Proposal Development Fellowship; the UMN College of Liberal Arts Graduate Research Partnership Program; the UMN Interdisciplinary Dissertation Fellowship, hosted at the Interdisciplinary Center for the Study of Global Change; a UMN Doctoral Dissertation Fellowship; a Wenner-Gren Foundation for Anthropological Research Dissertation Fieldwork Grant; and a Wenner-Gren Post-PhD Research Grant. In South Africa, the Centre for Indian Studies in Africa at Wits provided an institutional home. Thank you, Dilip, for creating a vibrant space based in a capacious vision of the Indian Ocean and for welcoming me at Wits. When the COVID-19 pandemic hit, like many anthropologists, I had to quickly rethink my research. Thank you, Danchen Xu, for being a diligent research assistant, assembling a social media archive, and checking my translations. At Dartmouth College, Charlotte Bacon's knack for breaking down research projects was critical for securing resources and imagining my work as a book. I have greatly benefited from the Mellon Faculty Fellowship and the efforts Michelle Warren and Israel Reyes have led to create institutional support structures for junior faculty of color and women of color, as well as providing Mellon funds

I am deeply appreciative of the editorial expertise and labor of many individuals. I am one of few authors who knew Elizabeth Ault before she began her illustrious career as an editor. Liz hosted a party during my recruitment visit for graduate school. I learned a lot about how to teach writing as her teaching assistant, and later a lot about writing a book. How amazing it is to have our professional lives intertwine in this way. Thank you to Benjamin Kossak for being a fantastic editorial assistant, and the staff and board at Duke University Press for publishing provocative, interdisciplinary books that I have admired for so long. Craig Willse helped me find myself as a writer after graduate school, which no writing guide can teach. A huge thanks to Erin Davis, Ihsan Taylor, and colleagues at Westchester Publishing Services and Ideas on Fire for meticulous editing and indexing. I am indebted to two anonymous readers for seeing the book's arguments and interventions more clearly than I could. Your comments pushed me to deepen my ethnographic analysis and explicitly situate whiteness, which has made this a stronger book.

I am blessed to have a wonderful community of friends and family cheering me on. Thank you to Kristin for making the big move to Vermont with me. We are forever family. Romain, it has been a real joy to have a partner to think about my work with. During the pandemic, I took up swimming again. The pool has been an unexpected source of writing company, including Adrian, who has imparted much wisdom during our brief but energizing chats, and Barbara, a former editor and pedagogically inspiring coach. I will never forget how my sister Beth came all the way to South Africa to visit me during my hardest time. A pragmatically minded, uncompromising organizer, Beth is a political role model. Beth and Justin, I am ever grateful for your hospitality during the final stretch of writing. My parents, Hong and Jiahe, instilled in me a great sense of determination. Sent to the countryside during the Cultural Revolution, my parents never took education for granted. They immigrated to the US Midwest in the early 1980s and endured much hardship for me to have the life that I have. My proclivity to talk to strangers comes from my mom, and dedication to study from my dad. I did not follow the trajectory they initially imagined for me, but I thank them for having the faith that I could make my own way.

Introduction

THEORIZING IN THE CHINESE CENTURY

Even though the "Chinese century" may seem more imminent and inevitable than ever . . . "China" remains a shifting and elusive sign at once close and unreachable, familiar and alien, backward and too far ahead.

Mei Zhan, *Other-Worldly*, 2009

The challenge is to what degree, and in what ways, can we think alongside the unthought, just as relations of study are likewise relations of difference, non-correspondence, and incommensurability.

Manu Vimalassery, Juliana Hu Pegues, and Alyosha Goldstein, "Colonial Unknowing and Relations of Study," 2017

In 2013, during my first foray into fieldwork, I met Dominic, a Zimbabwean migrant in his early twenties, working at a busy electronics shop in Cape Town, South Africa. The shop was in a China Mall, the moniker for Chinese wholesale malls that have become ubiquitous in South African cities. These China Malls are destinations for bargain hunters and southern African migrants who have few employment options without papers. Every day Dominic and Victor, from Nigeria, installed and repaired budget speakers and media players imported from China. Dominic knew little about electronics before arriving in South Africa and was proudly self-taught. While Dominic and Victor worked the floor and warehouse, Tai Jie, a middle-aged woman from Shandong, sat behind the counter. Her sister, the first in their family to come from China, was back home on a visit. Upon meeting me, Tai Jie showed me surveillance footage of a recent store break-in and intimated that Dominic and Victor were involved. Such stereotyping of Black employees as criminals was common in how Chinese traders talked about their experience in Africa. But Dominic viewed Tai Jie in a different light. Since she spoke little English, the two communicated by pointing at images in electronics catalogs. In their makeshift communication, Dominic picked up some Mandarin and "fell in love with the language." He sought out local Chinese friends and was saving up to attend night classes at a nearby language school. As a sign of commitment, he even had his name in Chinese characters tattooed on his neck. Our exchange outside the shop was brief but revelatory. Regarding the Chinese newcomers, Dominic said to me, "They come with nothing here, now they are conquering the world. I want to know how they are doing it . . . within months they are . . . driving big cars, wearing big clothes. I want to know how." He admired how "penniless" Chinese made it "big." In his three years working for Tai Jie and her sister, Dominic had received higher-paying offers to work elsewhere but stayed to study the strategies of Chinese entrepreneurs. "The Chinese rule the world," and he wanted a "head start." "I want to know a lot about them. I want to know how they make it. Why they are so strange." Although working for low pay in the present, Dominic strove to get ahead in an increasingly Sinocentric world.

Since the turn of the millennium, the steady arrival of Chinese migrant entrepreneurs, tourists, business travelers, infrastructure projects, companies, banks, and commodities has been transforming African metropolises. Johannesburg—fondly known as Joburg, Jozi, and Egoli (the last of which is isiZulu for "City of Gold")—is a city undergoing dramatic transformation. Since the discovery of gold in the Witwatersrand, or Rand, in 1886, South Africa reigned as the world's largest producer of gold over the entire twentieth century. For a century, African laborers recruited from South Africa's

Native Reserves or neighboring colonies excavated the precious metal from the bowels of the earth. The mineral revolution made South Africa into the economic powerhouse it is today. As gold levels were inevitably depleted, the mining belt underwent several metamorphoses, first becoming a hub for factories and later warehouses and wholesale centers. Today along the central mining belt there are a dozen Chinese wholesale malls. Since 2010 the People's Republic of China (PRC) has been South Africa's top trading partner. In 2020 South Africa was the second largest African buyer of Chinese goods, with US$25 billion in total trade.[1] Known for their bargains, the China Malls attract working-class families, hawkers, and entrepreneurs from all over the city and the region, from Angola to Zimbabwe. The malls are a consumer paradise of abundance and variety, offering plastic toys, fast fashion apparel, luxury knockoff bags, jewelry, sneakers, wedding dresses, headscarves, wigs, electronics, furniture, party goods, and herbal medicines.

With over four hundred shops and stalls, "China City," the mall where I conducted fieldwork, is a dense site of Sino-African interactions that pulsates with the unmistakable frenetic energy of Joburg. A microcosm of the city's migrant communities, the mall is a multilingual space comprising Chinese, Indian, and Pakistani traders and workers; Malawian and Zimbabwean shopworkers; Nigerian and Black South African security guards; and contingent workers and informal economic actors who facilitate the transnational movement of people, goods, and money. China City is at once a place of sanctuary and exploitation, cosmopolitan mixing and rigid boundaries. It shines with the novelty of China and yet is deeply of Johannesburg. The mall sits atop an exhausted gold reef and is near where gold was discovered, the serendipitous sighting that catalyzed everything that followed: white settlement, industrial capitalism, Indigenous dispossession, and racial apartheid. China City emblematizes the longer histories of colonialism and racial capitalism that underly, quite literally, the twenty-first-century global transformations at the heart of this book.

Reconfiguring Racial Capitalism: South Africa in the Chinese Century examines the entanglements of Chinese and South African pasts, presents, and futures from the perspectives of ordinary people like Dominic and Tai Jie. As capitalism's center of gravity has shifted to the PRC over the past three decades, the movement of capital from the PRC to South Africa and the Global South presents a novel formation of power made possible by the debris of Euro-American empire and racial capitalism. China City is the ordinary yet remarkable place that inspires my palimpsestic approach, an analysis attuned to multiple erasures, inscriptions, and timescales that coexist within a social formation or place. The *mining belt mall* is a metaphor for the central argument of this book: Chinese racial and imperial forms overlay Euro-American ones, not burying or displacing them but building on and interacting with the traces of ongoing "posts-"—of apartheid, colonialism, and socialism—that sediment.[2]

This story also takes place in Johannesburg's Cyrildene Chinatown, the newer of the two Chinatowns in Johannesburg and the epicenter for three hundred thousand Chinese migrants—expatriates, sojourners, immigrants, transmigrants, and entrepreneurial migrants by other names—in South Africa. These newcomers, who do not aim to stay for the long term, join a smaller multigenerational community of settled immigrants from mainland China, Hong Kong, and Taiwan who established Johannesburg as the oldest and largest Chinese diasporic community in Africa. Despite this lengthy history of Chinese presence in South Africa, a distinct shift happened in the late twentieth century. Migrant traders were in South Africa precisely because of the "rise of China." Beginning with China's reform and opening policies in 1978, the privatization of national industries, commercialization of the rural economy, and exploitation of labor propelled rapid capitalist development and created immense class and regional inequalities in its wake—a process of "post-socialist primitive accumulation" (Xiang 2014). Peasants, low-wage urban workers, laid-off state workers, and other people left behind by economic reform could achieve a stabler, more prosperous material future in China by temporarily migrating to the emerging economies of Africa, Asia, and Latin America. Whereas Chinese entrepreneurs choose Johannesburg from a range of Global South destinations, the same is not true for southern African migrants whose connection to Johannesburg is forged through the colonial migrant labor system. Johannesburg is a destination for generations of southern African men who journeyed to the City of Gold and continue migrating for economic opportunity. Although African and Chinese migrants are both racialized foreign nationals with precarious legal status, they are these things to different degrees. While both groups face routine police harassment, only southern Africans face deportation and the most virulent forms of xenophobic violence. The difference goes back to how southern Africans and Chinese were incorporated into the racialized political economy of the Rand and the world economy, which enables Chinese migrant traders to exploit southern African migrant workers today. African and Chinese actors are brought together through world-historical forces, and they bring different aspirations, visions of global futures, and racial ideologies to their daily encounters.

Reconfiguring Racial Capitalism is an ethnography of an epoch in the making, of non-Western racial formations attuned to forms of "minority-to-minority relationality" (Shih and Lionnet 2005), and of lateral modes of power that are difficult to name because they transpire between peripheries and across intellectual silos. The configurations of migration, exploitation, and extraction that I describe invite us to consider racial, capitalist, and imperial formations more expansively and to recalibrate understandings of race, racial capitalism, and colonialism when dislodged from their more familiar historical, geographical, and disciplinary contexts and unanchored from the white West. Theorizing in the Chinese Century examines transformations and continuities in *race, racial capitalism, colonialism*, and *empire*. It requires deprovincializing these key words and radically revising how we understand them. Whether ideas and categories formulated within the historical conditions of Euro-American modernity can be applied to the Sino-African context raises the recurring binary of China and the West. China has been frequently figured as outside Euro-American liberalism and modernity—the West's paradigmatic other (Eng, Ruskola, and Shen 2011; Liu 2015). Chinese political economy has been aptly described as "illiberal" (Vukovich 2019), the experimental adaptation of neoliberalism as nonnormative (Rofel 2007), and its partial loss of sovereignty as semicolonial. "China" is an elusive sign, far off in the future or stuck in the past, making it hard to grasp (Zhan 2009, 27). Modifying universalist concepts with "Chinese" or "Chinese characteristics" relies on essentialized notions of culture, ethnicity, and nation for historical explanation (Dirlik 1997). Equally inadequate is turning to Chinese exceptionalism, whereby China "by definition can speak only to and of itself" (Lewis and Hsieh 2017, 46). The theoretical task is to discern what is "distinctly Chinese" or "generically modern," while challenging Orientalist assumptions about Chinese difference (Pieke 2014). "Chinese difference" and the difference it makes need to be continuously interrogated.

My ethnography reframes a dominant popular and academic narrative, that of the Chinese "scramble for Africa" and conventional formulations of Chinese neocolonialism in two ways. First, the scramble narrative reductively scripts Chinese capital as a totalizing force with a singular logic—a monolithic "China Inc." (Hirono and Suzuki 2014)—penetrating African markets (Gibson-Graham [1996] 2006; Sylvanus 2013, 67). This narrative treats China as "an externalised, separate, and self-contained 'Other,'" an agent of change disembedded from the local historical contexts where it acts (Franceschini and Loubere 2022, 5). Instead, I insist on the heterogeneous, embedded, contingent character of Chinese capitalist projects in African countries (and especially South Africa) that cannot be reduced to a monolithic "Chinese capitalism" or "Chinese capital" (C. K. Lee 2017). In Sino-African contexts, transnational capitalism is not a stable structure but a dynamic assemblage of African and Chinese social and kinship networks, moral economies, cultural ethos, and embodied processes (Appel 2019; Bear et al. 2015; K. Ho 2005; Rofel and Yanagisako 2019; Tsing 2000). Second, I problematize abstractions of China–Africa flows as a generic global capitalism, alternatively reframing Chinese capitalist projects as racial capitalism with distinct colonial entanglements and features.

Scholars of racial capitalism working across disciplines and fields—including African studies, Asian American studies, Black studies, Marxist political economy, and Native and Indigenous studies, to name a few that I engage—have powerfully demonstrated that race plays a central, not supplemental, role in capitalism. Historical features of capitalism, race and racialization processes emerged in the crucible of slavery, capitalism, colonialism, liberalism, and white supremacy.[3] The history of capitalism is a history of racial capitalism, and race is intrinsic to capitalism's most fundamental workings. As Jodi Melamed elaborates, "Capital can only be capital when it is accumulating, and it can only accumulate by producing and moving through relations of severe inequality among human groups." Racism, among other "antimonies of accumulation," create and maintain the severe inequalities necessary for accumulation (2015, 77). Capital requires social differentiation to create value, and it produces racial, national, gender, and sexual difference to create surplus populations and spaces (R. A. Ferguson 2004; Hong 2006; Liu 2022; Lowe 1996). Capitalism also abstracts these differences to turn differentiated laborers into commensurable units of labor power (Day 2016, 9). Race acts as a "social script of equivalences [through which] 'value' is created" (Lowe 2015, 83). Capitalism simultaneously mobilizes the differences of race and gender to exploit workers and create commensurable units of labor power, drawing processes of social differentiation and capital accumulation more tightly together. As the study of racial capitalism has flourished in Black studies, racial capitalism has been grounded in Euro-American racial formations and histories of enslavement and colonialism in the New World. Destin Jenkins and Justin Leroy challenge the taken-for-granted centrality of the North Atlantic in scholarship on racial capitalism, asking in what other global contexts might racial capitalism be useful (2021, 16). In the era of emerging postcolonial economies of the Global South, new configurations of race, capitalism, and colonialism are underway. An analysis of racial capitalism is necessary for understanding the contemporary dynamics of global extractive industries, land grabs, Asian foreign investment ("Asian capital"), and the superexploitation of migrant labor across south–south and south–east circuits (Hoang 2022; Koshy et al. 2022).

Scholars of settler colonialism have insisted that capitalism is intertwined with race *and* colonialism. Extending the analytic of racial capitalism to colonial racial capitalism, scholars connect contemporary regimes of predatory accumulation with histories, legacies, and ongoing processes of settlement, colonization, and racialization (Byrd et al. 2018; Day 2016; Koshy et al. 2022). South Africa's history of racial capitalism and settler colonialism has been critical to this reformulation. In their introduction to *Colonial Racial Capitalism*, Susan Koshy, Lisa Cacho, Brian Jordan Jefferson, and Jodi A. Byrd note that "we can push Robinson's analytic of racial capitalism back to the significance of the term's South African settler colonialist origins to examine how Indigenous dispossession is not the precondition for racial capitalism to emerge but always has been part of its very structure" (2022, 5). In South Africa, a settler colonial mode of accumulation enshrined the political economy of apartheid that South African Marxists named racial capitalism, which Cedric Robinson expanded on in *Black Marxism* (Robinson [1983] 2002, see also Biermann and Kössler 1980; Burden-Stelly, Hudson, and Pierre 2020; Hudson 2018; Kelley 2017; White 2020). In the 1970s, South African scholars, Black consciousness activists, and South African Communist Party members from multiple intellectual and political traditions theorized racial capitalism as the inextricable relationship between capitalism and apartheid (Chari 2021). The term countered liberal arguments that the overt racism of Afrikaner nationalism and the apartheid state was illogical to capitalism in South Africa. As they insisted, racism was not extraneous but endemic to capitalism, and racial oppression would not end with economic growth (Alexander [1983] 1985; Legassick and Hemson 1976; B. M. Magubane 1979). The term racial capitalism emerges from the specific, even unique context of South Africa, thus making its broad circulation somewhat curious (White 2022). If all capitalism is colonial racial capitalism, Chinese capitalist projects in the settler colony South Africa are no exception. Racial capitalism is malleable in its modes of production, accumulation, and racial subjugation, incorporating minoritized people and peripheral regions to sustain itself (Jenkins and Leroy 2021). This incorporation is dynamic. Chinese practices of racial capitalism in South Africa have developed along specific trajectories of race and capitalism in China and map onto settler colonial relations, colonial legacies, and racial capitalist geographies in South Africa and southern Africa as a whole. *Reconfiguring Racial Capitalism* returns to South Africa as a key site for theorizing novel patterns of racial accumulation and exploitation in the Chinese Century.

Nested within this study of racial capitalism is an inquiry into race itself: how race is constituted in the collision of Chinese and South African racial histories, categories, and ideologies and theorized across American, African, and China studies. Studying race in the Sino-African context grapples with the *globality of race* in three ways. First, it provincializes race as a concept specific to historical, global, and epistemological contexts and destabilizes its coherence. Deprovincializing race means theorizing it beyond debates coded in Western (specifically US) terms and the universalization of a singular historic tradition. Only then can there be "scholarship that truly demarginalizes the margins while decentering the center" (Z. Magubane 2004, 196). Second, the globality of race refers to the ways in which race maps onto modern global space (Ferreira Da Silva 2015, 33), from the "West and the Rest" and "Europe and its others" to Du Bois's twentieth-century global color line. Third, a global approach to race also insists on the transnational construction of racial meanings and identities (Ferreira Da Silva 1998; Karl 2002; Z. Magubane 2004; Pierre 2013). As a method, ethnography rejects a priori formulations of what race means. By theorizing concepts from the inside-out and bottom-up, ethnography is especially attuned to the incommensurabilities of race. An ethnography of racial formation examines the processes by which race acquires social, cultural, and political meaning and how these meanings are ideologically deployed through practices and institutions (Pierre 2012). It attends to the *how* of racialization, which refers not to social situations with racial dimensions but the processes by which social life is racially ordered and the order maintained (Goldberg 2009).

Building on these ethnographic and transnational approaches to race, I examine how racial meanings such as Chineseness, Blackness, and whiteness map onto the global space of China, Africa, and the West that gesture to a regime of global racial power that exceeds the terms of white supremacy. I investigate how racial lexicons are defined through transnational circulation between China and South Africa and intertwined with gender, ethnicity, sexuality, citizenship, labor, and quality (*suzhi*). What I call race is never only about race but its intersections with other categories that amplify its force and forms. I also wrestle with multiple, layered histories of race, colonialism, and capitalism and racial vocabularies that do not neatly overlay or align. Side by side, and concurrent but not the same, they are *adjacent*, a heuristic I develop in chapter 3. Adjacency helps us think relationally across histories, areas, and fields. Incommensurability is not an impasse but an invitation to "think alongside the unthought" (Vimalassery, Pegues, and Goldstein 2017, 1051). In the remainder of this introduction, I give an overview of macrohistorical contexts, theoretical questions, and ethnographic sites, as well as the structure of this book.

The Long Twenty-First Century

Reconfiguring Racial Capitalism proceeds through multiple scales, from centuries and continents to individual biographies and everyday encounters to capture the granular and quotidian ways world-historical forces manifest in ordinary people's lives. The chapters that follow delve into specific histories, but first I give an overview of tectonic shifts in historical capitalism relevant to this conjuncture. "The Chinese Century"—like "China" or the "Rise of China"—is an expression that can never capture the contested geographies, histories, and visions bracketed within it. It is shorthand for a multipolar world that orbits around China. The Chinese Century is an American neologism, coined in the early 2000s as the PRC overtook the United States as the world's premier economic power (Fishman 2004; Stiglitz 2015).[4] The moniker suggests a linear progression from British, to American, to Chinese hegemony from the nineteenth to twenty-first centuries. The Chinese Century conjoins Chinese economic ascension with US imperial decline. While the United States began the globally unpopular War on Terror, the PRC emerged on the world stage: the 2001 entrance into the World Trade Organization, the 2008 Olympics in Beijing, and the 2013 launch of the Belt and Road Initiative, a multitrillion-dollar infrastructure project larger than the Marshall Plan, to create a New Silk Road across Africa, Asia, Europe, Latin America, the Middle East, and Oceania. American discourses about the Chinese Century and the PRC's neocolonial exploits in Africa extend a Cold War legacy of treating China as a threat to be known, contained, and harnessed for US economic and imperial interests.[5] Throughout this book, I treat the Chinese Century as a world-making project in formation, one of several competing global visions amid interimperial realignments (Rofel and Rojas 2022). The Chinese Century is provisional, incomplete, and aspirational, more of an idea and global horizon than totalizing geopolitical reality. South Africa is not a generic place where the Chinese Century unfolds but is an active force in its transformation.

While the Chinese Century seems to have emerged only in recent decades, from a *longue durée* perspective it signals the world economy coming full circle. From the fifteenth to twenty-first centuries, as Giovanni Arrighi periodizes, historical capitalism has systemically evolved through successive cycles of accumulation broken into "long centuries" of Genoese, Dutch, British, US, and Chinese hegemony. Each denotes a transition between world powers and a shift in the center of global accumulation processes (Arrighi 1994, 2007; Braudel 2009). The New Asian Age marks the cyclical return of modern Chinese empire in the age of neoliberal globalization, not a new phenomenon as understood in Eurocentric economic historiography. From 1500 to 1800, a Sinocentric international order, not a Western one, organized the early modern world economy (Frank 1998). European merchants arrived in South China with silver from the Americas to trade for silk and ceramics. With its trade networks and tributary system, imperial China was the final sink for the world's silver. In the late eighteenth century, Asia and Europe began to trade places. Europe amassed wealth through colonial conquest and slavery in Africa and the Americas and gunboat-secured "free" trade with Asia. Following the Opium Wars, the Qing state was forced to cede Hong Kong to Britain and grant extraterritoriality to Western merchants and missionaries who looted ports, evaded tariffs, and inflicted racial terror with impunity (Driscoll 2020; Li 2008; Lowe 2015). China's coasts supplied contract labor and the commodities necessary for the development of liberal free trade and settlement of New World colonies. Chinese victimization by Japanese and Western powers became the basis for Han nationalism, which paved the way for the 1949 revolution that split China into the PRC and the Republic of China. Mao Zedong's domestic program of class struggle developed the modern social, political, and technological infrastructure for China's integration into the globalizing world economy from the 1980s onward, in turn catalyzing the current trading of places (Li 2008).

From a long historical perspective, Africa and other Asian nations supplied the land, labor, and raw materials for the expansion of capitalism. South Africa played a key role through its gold. The nation is a colonial palimpsest, with overlapping histories of Dutch, Dutch-descended Afrikaner, and British settlement, as well as white supremacy. The Cape of Good Hope marks the point where the Atlantic Ocean flows into the Indian Ocean. Since the arrival of the Dutch East India Company in 1652 and the British in 1795, the Cape connected maritime routes for Dutch mercantile capitalism and the British slave trade (until the latter's abolition in 1833). The Cape was home to the Kimberley diamond fields, which laid the infrastructure for the subsequent gold rush. The colonies that became the Union of South Africa in 1910—including the Cape's diamond fields, Natal's sugar estates, and the Transvaal's gold mines—created fortunes for British mining houses and financiers. With gold as the world's currency standard for most of the twentieth century, Johannesburg's mines played a central role in the global expansion of capitalism. Within this sweeping history of Afro-Asian connection, I am interested in the dramatic change of China and South Africa's places in the world through one point of inflection. In the early twentieth century, Chinese were brought to the Rand on British ships to work alongside African laborers. At the turn of the millennium, the Chinese returned as capitalists and exploiters of southern African labor.

Sino-African worlds are produced through the convergence of two ascendant moments of the late 1990s and early 2000s: the "rise of China" and "Africa rising." As country and a continent, respectively, China's and Africa's uneven incorporation into the capitalist world economy has entangled Chinese and African futures, prompting Achille Mbembe to pose "Africa as a Chinese question" (2021, 34). In response to a crisis of overaccumulation of capital in the United States, global productive forces have shifted to China, subsequently leading to China's spectacular economic boom and a crisis of overaccumulation (Harvey 2003). Africa now functions as a spatial fix for overcapacity in China (C. K. Lee 2017). The influx of foreign investment to the continent has fueled rapid but unequal economic growth with higher incomes and new consumer markets, including demand for Chinese goods. Crucially, China, with its large geographical area and population, has historically functioned as the last major reserve for global capitalist accumulation. Compounding capitalism-driven climate catastrophe, the mobilization of this last reserve portends the terminal crisis of capitalism as we know it (Li 2008). I situate ordinary African and Chinese actors at this twenty-first-century moment of capitalism as capital exhausts its global frontiers and reserves.

Today's promise of Sino-African engagements harkens back to the Afro-Asian and Third World solidarities of the Bandung era, a period of anticolonial solidarities marking the 1955 gathering of leaders from Africa, Asia, and the Middle East in Bandung, Indonesia. The apartheid state was not represented at Bandung, but like many twentieth-century Black revolutionaries, South African freedom fighters found inspiration in the armed struggle sweeping Algeria, Cuba, and the PRC. African National Congress (ANC) members studied the writings of Mao, peasant revolutions, and the student-led anti-imperialist May Fourth Movement. Walter Sisulu and members of the Spear of the Nation, the armed wing of the ANC, visited the PRC to acquire military equipment and training (Meredith 1998). South African poet Dennis Brutus visited for political inspiration (Yoon 2022). In the other direction, Mao sent a cable to South Africa voicing concern over the apartheid regime's impact on Chinese merchants (Snow 1988, 70). These lesser-known solidarities and exchanges destabilize statist narratives of African-Chinese engagements and point to submerged radical traditions. Decades after the rise and fall of anticolonial nationalisms, the global consciousness and political imagination of the Bandung era remain a force in people's lives (C. J. Lee 2010). African and Chinese state appeals to south-south cooperation breathe new life into the unfinished project of decolonization, even though these appeals are mostly rhetorical. In the way Mao claimed to lead the Third World toward decolonization, Xi Jinping claims to lead the emerging economies of the Global South, most notably BRICS (the bloc of Brazil, Russia, India, China, and South Africa, expanded to include Argentina, Egypt, Ethiopia, Iran, Saudi Arabia, and the United Arab Emirates in 2024). China's place in and of the Global South is ambiguous, somewhere between Global North and Global South, semiperiphery and core. China's southern collaborations redirect southern surpluses to southern destinations (Arrighi 2007). But the triumphalism of China over the West papers over the PRC's fraught relationship with Hong Kong, Taiwan, and autonomous regions and its expansionist ambitions in the Global South. This book sits with the many layered histories, moods, narratives, and emancipatory possibilities of the twenty-first century—of postcapitalist, decolonial futures—while critiquing the way histories of anticolonial struggle cover for regional hegemony and capitalist extraction.

Racism without Whiteness, Colonialism without the West

Since the formal end of apartheid in 1994, xenophobia has impeded South Africa's vision for a multiracial democracy. In a stroke of historical amnesia, virulent xenophobic violence has been directed toward Black foreign nationals, southern Africans who labored on farms, mines, factories, and domestic households and contributed to South Africa's liberation struggle. Colonialism and apartheid continue to manifest as anti-Blackness and xenophobia. In 2008, sixty-two people—mostly Malawians, Mozambicans, and Zimbabweans—were killed in xenophobic attacks (Hassim, Kupe, and

Worby 2008). When I returned to China City in 2015, a second wave of xenophobic violence swept through the country after a Somali shop owner fatally shot a Black South African teenager in the southwestern township of Soweto. After months of turmoil, the country stood on the brink of national emergency. In the majority migrant space of China City, fear of imminent violence was palpable. A xenophobic attack did not require much imagination. The previous year, after a slate of immigration restrictions was passed, one of China City's two white tenants feared that the mall could be razed to the ground in a repeat of the events of 2008. As the situation in 2015 worsened, shopworkers—nearly all Malawian and Zimbabwean foreign nationals, many of whom were Soweto residents—exercised precautions traveling to and from work. Some stopped going to work altogether, and a few chose emergency repatriation. Without other options, most continued to work, praying for their own safety. The atmosphere was dark. Workers watched videos of gruesome beatings and killings on their phones. Frank, a security guard, told me, "I don't want to die in a foreign land. I will die in my father country. I will die in Nigeria."

Chinese traders monitored the situation on the social media platform WeChat. They paid close attention to the looting of foreign-owned businesses and described the tumult as riots (*baoluan*). Chinese shopkeepers in cities and townships were occasionally caught up in the mix but not targeted like their Bangladeshi, Indian, Pakistani, and Somali counterparts. Chinese migrants also consumed images of vigilante violence but took them as proof of African "savagery." Chinese traders understood that southern African employees were the most vulnerable, but that also led to feelings of their own immunity: if a single Chinese national were harmed, they believed the Chinese consulate could pressure the South African government to protect them. As one person expressed it, China's investment in Africa buffered the Chinese from resentment toward Black foreign nationals: "When Africans want to eat, they go to China." China's global stature set the traders apart from other racialized migrants, including racially adjacent South Asian traders. While the xenophobic attacks were a matter of life and death for China City's African workers, the Chinese traders were more concerned about employee absences and property loss.

At the height of the unrest in late April 2015, rumors of a mob traveling from Durban to Johannesburg spread through social media. The China Malls near the inner city closed early as a precaution, and China City went on lockdown. I was near the entrance to a shop when someone ran in announcing, "They're here, they're here!" Word quickly spread that a group of men had reached the mall's gates, and traders and workers, including myself, hid in the dark behind locked doors, a fleeting moment of solidarity through shared vulnerability. The lockdown ended after it was revealed that a Malawian worker mistook a group of running contingent workers as a mob. On the ride home to Cyrildene Chinatown, my fellow passengers praised the loyal employees who helped to secure their shops and cursed the disloyal ones who bolted. One passenger crassly speculated that the lockdown was a stunt, perpetrated so that "lazy" workers could go home early. In the following weeks, local Chinese leaders seized an opportunity to raise the profile of the mainland Chinese community in South African politics. Prominent businessmen, including China City's developer, donated to relief efforts and organized a bus to take one hundred Chinese traders to participate in a citywide march against xenophobia. African workers, however, had to stay at work. After the unrest was quelled, the state reenergized its efforts to curb "illegal immigration." After a Chinese factory was raided, a Chinese association called attention on social media to hefty fines bosses would pay for employing undocumented African migrants—namely, "illegal workers [heigong] from neighboring countries" (Nanfei 365, 2015a, my translation). In China the term heigong refers to undocumented workers, but in South Africa it racializes undocumented African workers as Black. This event impressed on how I think about lateral relations of power. How do we grapple with racialization, global racial power, and anti-Blackness when white bodies and Western discourses are largely absent? What difference does "China"—with its current stature and past subjugation—make?

Race and racism have been long ignored in China because of the myth of a monoracial society and an emphasis on ethnic (minzu), not racial, difference. Further clouding critical inquiry is a zero-sum logic whereby Han Chinese are the victims of Euro-American racism as the originators of race and racism, and therefore cannot themselves be racist. Contemplating Chinese racism and empire is challenging because of multiple racial vocabularies and dramatic role reversals between China and the West in a relatively compressed period. Chinese people have been subjugated to Western imperialism and racism, but since the turn of the century, the PRC has become a regional hegemonic, sub-imperial, or even neocolonial force in Africa, the Asia Pacific, the Caribbean, and Latin America (K.-H. Chen 2010). Additionally, scholars have questioned if race and racism mean the same thing in Chinese and Western contexts. Core to the West's domination of the non-West, race has been reproduced over centuries through

Euro-American empires, liberalism, and global white supremacy (Beliso-De Jesús and Pierre 2019; Lowe 2015; Pierre 2012). Imperialism introduced the construct of race to new places where race, or a concept by another name, was retooled within existing epistemologies of difference, hierarchy, and exclusion (Goldberg 2009, 3–4). And yet, race does not exclusively belong to the West to dominate the non-West. Racial ideas, unmoored from their "Western origins," can still serve as conduits for power in "non-Western" settings. Such is the case in Chinese racial thought that combines premodern ideas of social difference akin to race with Western racial ideas that circulated through missionaries, Chinese students in the West, and the Japanese translation of Western texts (Fennell 2013; S. Lan 2017). Even as some features might be recognizably Western, Chinese racial thought cannot be reduced to a Western import (Dikötter [1992] 2015). Chinese racial ideas—of color, class, civilization, human, animal, beast, and slave—emerge from a composite of premodern and modern Chinese *and* Western racial thought. Regardless of irreducible differences between Chinese and Western racial ideas, race has a social existence in China. Racial ideas are configured and mobilized in particular ways in Sino-African contexts.

Questions concerning race and empire have played out fiercely within China-Africa studies, a multidisciplinary field that emerged alongside the renaissance of China's engagements with African nation-states and African migration to Chinese cities. The debate is political and theoretical: whether the terms *racism* and *neocolonialism* apply to China and how to define them. Often assertions of Chinese racism problematically assume that the Chinese racialize and Africans are racialized; like the colonizer and colonized, the former is powerful and the latter powerless. Indeed, Chinese migrants are racialized as "the Chinese," but this does not negate how Chinese enact racism toward racial others.[6] An analysis of race in Sino-African contexts must contend with multiple directionalities, levels, and scales of racialization (Huynh and Park 2018) and the mutuality of Sinophobia, xenophobia, and anti-Black racism within local and global configurations of racial power. To break out of limiting binaries, scholars have triangulated African, Asian, and Euro-American racial identities and categories (Castillo 2020; S. Lan 2017; C. J. Lee 2021; Monson 2013; Monson and Rupp 2013). Whiteness and the West are the "dominant absences" of Sino-African relations, the silent interlocutors of interminority dynamics that are exonerated when they drop out of the frame (Palumbo-Liu 1994).

Investigating what race means in a Sino-African context requires multiple contextual frames and vantage points, and even so, there is something that exceeds "race." Race has distinct meanings, genealogies, and histories in China and South Africa. There is no single word for it in the Chinese language. In modern Chinese racial thought, race has indexed China's place in the world. Before the arrival of Europeans, a hierarchy of skin color already existed in China. During the late Qing and Republican eras, Han racial identity, envisioned as a common patrilineal line and territory, was invented as a nationalist response to Japanese and Western imperialism. Chinese intellectuals, inspired by Darwinian and Spencerian evolutionary theories, turned consciousness of skin color and genealogical thinking into a theory of race as a breed of lineage, or *zhongzu*, the term closest to *race*. These thinkers divided the world into a hierarchy of white and yellow at the top, red or brown in the middle, and Black at the bottom (Dikötter [1992] 2015). In the Mao era, ethnicity (*minzu*) was introduced as a state category of difference that intersects with gender and class to confer status and modernity (Schein 2000). Transracial solidarity of the peoples of Africa, China, and Latin America against Western racism and imperialism was official state discourse (Fennell 2013). Since the 1980s, racial discourses took a nationalist turn. In a reversal of Maoist discourse, Chinese universities were rocked by anti-Black racism against African students. Given state restrictions on family planning, serology and eugenics regained popularity. As China's place in the world has dramatically changed over the past century, so have racial meanings and mappings of China and Chineseness, Africa and Blackness, and the West and whiteness.

Whereas race and racism have been ambiguous in China, South Africa has been treated as a textbook—even exceptional—case. Under early twentieth-century segregation and apartheid, policing racial boundaries was the cornerstone of social, political, and economic life. From 1948 to 1994, the Nationalist Party installed four official categories: White, Coloured, Asiatic (Indian), and Native (Bantu or African). Race was a fundamentally unstable biological and cultural construct tied to color, class, and status; its hybridity made racial categories open to commonsensical interpretation (Posel 2001, 59). Racial classifications determined where one could live, study, work, and move around in the city and with whom one could be intimate or marry. Racial classifications were elastic, and racial boundaries porous, but apartheid meant the "social absolutization of race" (Goldberg 2009, 301). In the postapartheid era, despite the principle of nonracialism and democratic rule, race continues to shape life chances through the imbrication of race, class, and citizenship and lasting segregation of geographies and institutions. Despite the messiness of mapping out multiple genealogies and histories of "race," it is indispensable to naming and analyzing power in Sino-African relations. Culture, language, nation, and ethnicity all fall short.

Of special interest is Chinese anti-Blackness, a ubiquitous yet under-theorized pillar of Sino-African engagements. Anti-Blackness is a condition for the perpetuation of global capitalism, not a secondary effect, and thus key to understanding global racial capitalism (Bledsoe and Wright 2019). Anti-Blackness is analytically necessary to theorizing race in postcolonial Africa and global racial ideologies (Pierre 2013). Without specifically naming anti-Blackness, its dynamics get lost in discussions of anti-Asian/anti-Black racism that make them commensurate under white supremacy. As Afropessimists have defined it, anti-Blackness is the absolute negation of Black life, the ontological condition of Black nonbeing and suffering in the afterlife of slavery. Slavery is a relational dynamic and structure of violence, not a historical era or event. Blackness is the constitutive outside of humanity; it is universal and singular and nonanalogous with the colonialism and racism that non-Black people of color experience (Sexton 2010; Sharpe 2016; Costa Vargas and Jung 2021; Wilderson 2020, 2021). Chinese racial discourses combine Chinese and Western racial ideas to engender specific forms of anti-Blackness that complicate how we understand it as a global phenomenon. I inquire into what anti-Blackness means in a Chinese context in which racial slavery has been relatively limited, and Blackness is in translation. Black (*hei*), which refers to both the color and the racial category, signifies the sinister, dark, hidden, shadowy, and illegal (Sautman 1994). Black is associated with undocumented Black labor (*heigong*), black or illicit markets, and the "slave race" (Shih 2013). Throughout the book, I denote Chinese Blackness as *hei* as a reminder of its unstable meaning in translation. Chinese anti-Blackness may overlap with its Euro-American counterpart but remains distinctive. But this does not mean that Chinese anti-Blackness is outside the structure. Despite *hei*'s situational meanings, Chinese discourses reproduce anti-Blackness in global discursive contexts (Sheridan 2023). It is necessary to theorize Chinese anti-Blackness on its own terms, and comparatively and relationally.

I diverge from Afropessimist theories of anti-Blackness and arrive at its globality differently. In a critique of Afropessimism's core texts, Annie Olaloku-Teriba interrogates the assumption of Black as a stable, coherent category with global generalizability (2018, 105). Black becomes emptied of its historical specificity and subsumes African and slave (Olaloku-Teriba 2018). As Iyko Day (2016) further problematizes, the irreducibility of slavery and exceptionality of anti-Blackness foreclose a comparative, relational, and dialectical analysis of race, colonialism, and capitalism. Building on these generative critiques, I treat anti-Blackness as historically contingent, not transhistorical, and as globally heterogeneous, not a unified totality. Anti-Blackness is not wholly apart from how white supremacy, settler colonialism, slavery, indenture, and imperialism have unfolded concurrently across continents and peoples. To be clear, I do not offer a genealogical study of Chinese anti-Blackness. I give an account of twenty-first-century Chinese articulations of *Blackness* and *Africanness*—terms that are interchangeable in contemporary Chinese racial discourses (K. Huang 2020)—to understand anti-Blackness as a varied global phenomenon. Although anti-Blackness is rooted in European colonialism, slavery, and white supremacy, in the era of China's global ascendance, its ever-expanding structure enlists Chinese subjects into racial projects in South Africa, where anti-Blackness has been foundational.

Mirroring debates on race and racism, dominant characterizations of Chinese neocolonialism in Africa have launched definitional debates that are theoretical, methodological, ideological, and historiographic. Imperialism, neocolonialism, and empire are often used polemically and analytically in ahistorical and inaccurate ways.[7] Duncan M. Yoon (2023) insightfully points out that although there are similarities between Chinese investment and Western neocolonialism in African countries, they cannot be conflated. What is often called Chinese neocolonialism is a different form of extraction and exploitation that nevertheless triggers the collective trauma of European colonialism. Ching Kwan Lee (2017) proposes "global China" to name the geopolitical formation of power of transnational Chinese state capital. Indeed, the PRC does not act in Africa as an imperial power with military bases and foreign direct rule, but it acts within a system of capitalist imperialism that combines "the politics of state and empire" with "molecular processes of capital accumulation in space and time" (Harvey 2003, 26). The Chinese Century is a Sinocentric imperial vision with unique forms of global expansion, influence, presence, and power that we have not yet properly named. What is coalescing into Chinese empire, provisionally speaking, manifests in the molecular movements of capital across uneven geographies of development long made by empires "proper," and in the case of South Africa, ongoing processes of settler colonialism and their structures for accumulation. To consider the question of empire differently, the legacies of Euro-American empires provide the material conditions for Chinese capital accumulation in Africa, not the normative criteria to assess China's imperial likeness.

Further complicating these debates, Chinese historiography has traditionally framed China as a victim of Japanese and Western imperialism, and not a modern empire with imperial ambitions and capacities. Today the Chinese state employs the nationalist narrative of a century of colonial humiliation to legitimize its repression of ethnic and religious minorities in Inner Mongolia, Tibet, and Xinjiang. These regions are autonomous in name only; they are colonies settled by Han Chinese during mid-Qing continental expansion and recolonized by the PRC (Byler 2022). The PRC is the "successor and executor of empire" (Shih 2011, 711). On the politics of naming, it is useful to recall that US empire has always hid behind exceptionalism, asserting its unlikeness from Europe's overseas colonies. As Shu-mei Shih urged over a decade ago, "The spectacular rise of China as a superpower perhaps only now compels us to recalibrate existing discourses of empire and postcoloniality" (2011, 709). In the twilight of US and Western supremacy, new theories of (post)colonialism are needed as capital veers east and south. Drawing from ethnographic work on Chinese investment in Vietnam's natural resource industry, Kimberly Kay Hoang states, "This is not a simple story of exploiter/exploited, colonizer/dispossessed, but rather a new tension that is possible only in the aftermath of colonialism and imperialism." It is time to "theorize and conceptualize colonialism outside of overused binaries like East/West, global North/global South, or First World/Third World" (2022, 153). Critically, colonial empires need not be European. In places like Xinjiang, as Darren Byler argues in his ethnography of Uyghur dispossession, we are witnessing "new sequences of capitalist ethno-racialization that are not generated directly by Western powers" (2022, 10). Imperialism, capitalism, and settler colonialism constitute overlapping yet distinct modes of power. They name formations that inevitably adapt, and thus our analysis must be adapted. Chinese imperial and colonial formations may digress from nineteenth- and twentieth-century definitions but may belatedly become "classically twenty-first" definitions (Karl 2020).

I also consider Sino-African capitalist projects through racial capitalism. As Julian Go notes, "if we are to insist on the global character of racial capitalism, we must assume that analysts' racial classifications are global as well" (2021, 41). What is taking shape is not "Chinese racial capitalism" as much as "Chinese capitalism" or "capitalism with Chinese characteristics" that treats capitalist activities in and beyond China as a cultural variation of capitalism's universal core features.[8] Such a construction of "Chinese racial capitalism" assumes a universal paradigm of racial capitalism based in the Euro-American example and ambiguously modified by an essential notion of Chineseness. In the Sino-African context, racial capitalism emerges sui generis with the movement of capital—always global and globalizing, racial and racializing—along south–east axes and distinct rubrics of race. In the dialectics of capital and race, capitalism continuously remakes itself while incorporating the particularities of Chinese racial formations and postsocialist capitalist developments in China, and at the same time, the reorganization of race and economy in postapartheid South Africa.

The complexity of Sino-African realities demands a rejection of ready-made concepts and paradigms, as well as imaginative methodologies that break from the positivist, social scientific approaches that dominate China-Africa studies. Calling for a decolonial transformation of such studies, Christopher J. Lee points out that the European colonial past haunts the present as scholars rely on metanarratives of colonial scrambles and old paradigms, which "can foreclose new methodologies and obscure a more layered set of foundations and archives" (2021, 230). Toward creating new archives and paradigms, I take a palimpsestic approach to the interimperial present. Empires are coforming: as one empire emerges, it enfolds and incorporates others (Doyle 2020). Colonial histories are not flat and linear but form a mat in which "threads meet up, loop each other, and interlock" (Manjapra 2020, 5). The Chinese Century is not a linear progression from or even a superimposition of global hegemony over earlier epochs—the Dutch Golden Age, the British Imperial Century, and the American Century—but overlays them, actively building on and extending them. Imperial forms are recursive as they "*fold back on themselves* and, in that refolding, reveal new surfaces, and new planes" (Stoler 2017, 26, emphasis in the original). History follows a recursive logic that expands and calcifies what came before. Theorizing in a North American settler colonial context, Rob Nichols notes that "recursion is not . . . simple tautology. . . . [R]ecursive procedures loop back upon themselves in a 'boot-strapping' manner such that each iteration is not only different from the last but builds upon or augments its original postulate" (2020, 9). Returning to Arrighi's formulation of long centuries, each hegemonic transition enlarges the spatial and social foundations of capitalism, akin to the Marxian formula for the conversion of money to commodity to more money (M–C–M') on a global scale. Like a palimpsest, each hegemon overlaps with its predecessor and proceeds in a double movement forward and back, resurrecting and reconstituting older regimes in an expanded capitalist world system (Arrighi 1994, 79–80). Along these lines, we might think of the incorporation of China into global structures of racial capitalism, empire, and white supremacy through a similar logic of recursion and double movement. The integration of Chinese difference expands on the Dutch, British, and American centuries with the effect of enlarging the legacies of European empire, settler colonialism, and white supremacy "after whiteness." Through the mining belt mall, I trace how Chinese racial, capitalist, and imperial forms are layered with Euro-American ones. Chinese neocolonialism, as the scramble narrative posits, does not simply replicate twentieth-century colonial modalities of power but intensifies, proliferates, and reconfigures them through recursion.

A Mall at the Center of the World

Located off Main Reef Road—the road's namesake being the gold-rich main reef series that started it all—China City is a symbol of Johannesburg's Chinese future and its gold mining and manufacturing pasts. Surrounding the mall are scrapyards, warehouses, derelict factories, and open mining shafts. China City resembles the megamarkets in Yiwu, China, the "small commodity capital of the world," that attract importers from every continent, including traders at China City. Surrounding the mall are row after row of decommissioned shipping containers—colorful, rust-worn boxes stacked two high that have been repurposed as warehouses and conveniently form a secure perimeter around the premises. Within the labyrinth of hundreds of shops are side corridors, stairwells, and back entrances where one can stumble on lifeworlds hidden in plain sight: an apartment complex, an underground bank, a grocery store, a prayer room, a weeknight cricket game, a vegetable garden, and a feral cat colony. I roamed the mall's corridors first as a visitor and consumer, and then, over the course of a year, as a worker, resident, and dedicated student.

All kinds of economic life flourish on the mall's edges. Outside the gate, a fleet of minibus taxis thrives on the traffic between town and the numerous China Malls in the area. There are long-distance bakkies to take customers and their wholesale hauls beyond city limits, and taxi drivers who have made China City their home base for years. China City's parking lot alone sustains many livelihoods. On busy weekends and holidays, the mall receives around six hundred cars per hour; the two thousand parking spots are full. Dozens of Zimbabwean car guards and car washers in fluorescent vests and blue coveralls adroitly direct traffic in synchronous movements, making a modest fortune from small coins. Informal vendors go around selling food and basic provisions. In a remote corner of the mall, a subcontracted team of recyclers comprising Black South African and Malawian men swiftly sorts through heaps of plastic, cardboard, and recyclable waste generated inside the mall. On the busy corner of Main Reef Road, Zimbabwean hawkers, whom the mall security guards call "robot boys," resell goods from the mall and supply the guards with tips (for cash) on suspicious activity. Whereas other businesses treat them as a nuisance, they are the eyes and ears of China City. From early morning to early evening, over a dozen "container boys," underemployed Black South African men, wait outside the gate to unload containers. This is the final step in a container's monthlong journey from a wholesale market or factory in Guangzhou or Yiwu, to inspection at the Port of Durban, and finally to China City.

A host of services for the mall's hundreds of migrant shopworkers exists on the edges. Cross-border operators offering remittance services to Malawi and Zimbabwe circulate between taxi ranks and the China Malls. Just outside the gate, young Malawian men sell loose cigarettes and fat cakes from plastic bins. Older Black South African women serve *pap* (porridge) and stew from food stalls. Some of the ingredients come from the vegetable garden at the back of the mall, a labor of love between Frank, a Nigerian security guard, and "the gardener," the mall's longtime groundskeeper, an older Black South African man. Frank lovingly cares for the colony of feral cats that sleep beneath shipping containers and roam through the garden. The diverse actors on the mall's edges share a marginal location among Johannesburg's poor and paperless: underemployed and unemployed residents of Black townships, street vendors without permits, and southern African migrants without papers. In the symbiosis of core and periphery, they are indispensable to the mall's daily functioning. These contingent arrangements can last for years, counterintuitively showing that precarious livelihoods and urban life are not always in flux.

This book is based on eighteen months of fieldwork, from 2013 to 2020, which was primarily conducted in Johannesburg and abruptly cut short by the COVID-19 pandemic. The names of all people and places, except for public figures, have been changed. While the specific locations of places I write about matter, I have omitted details about exact locations to protect people engaging in illicit activities, even if they are already open secrets to the state. At China City, I worked as a shop assistant to get an inside look at day-to-day business operations and relationships, splitting my time between Jenny's party goods store and Xiao Li's clothing store. In these shops I experienced the repetitive, cyclical, and seasonal rhythms of "mall time"—that is, having no choice but to sit behind the register hour after hour, day after day—felt most acutely

I.1   A party goods shop at China City. Photo by the author.

I.2   A hidden vegetable garden and feral cat colony. Photo by the author.

I.3   A recycler sorts through China City's waste.
        Photo by the author.

when Jenny returned to Fujian for a month and entrusted me with her store. Although they could sometimes be slow, these hours often went by quickly due to conversations with shopworkers, customers, and security guards and sudden events like a robbery, firing, deportation, or lockdown. For most of the time that I worked at the mall, I lived in Cyrildene Chinatown. I lived in a boisterous household of traders, most of them relatives or hometown acquaintances from Fuqing, a county-level city in Fujian Province famous for entrepreneurial emigration and clandestine migration. The house belonged to Mr. Zheng, a China City tenant and revered community leader of Cyrildene Chinatown, who turned out to be a retired human smuggler. He was my window into migration processes, underground economies, and the network of men who govern the Chinese migrant community in the liminal jurisdiction between the Chinese and South African states.

I.4   A Malawian tailor fashions curtains. Photo by the author.

Every morning I took my seat in the back of a minibus taxi that left Mr. Zheng's house for China City. The vehicle was an old security van, with its logos still intact, and these logos ingeniously shielded passengers from corrupt police and opportunistic thieves who targeted cash-carrying Chinese traders. During each ride I listened to my fellow passengers, most of them workers at Mr. Zheng's businesses, recount their exchanges with customers and employees and share gossip. The taxi afforded more than door-to-door convenience. Taking it was akin to "walking in the city," an opportunity to traverse and see Johannesburg as Chinese migrants did.

In addition to living in Cyrildene Chinatown, for several months I lived at China City's on-site apartments, a gated building that was only for Chinese traders and workers, including those who worked at other China Malls. South Asian traders at China City were turned away and lived elsewhere.

I experienced the mall after dark, with its rhythms of reproductive labor and dramas among family members, business rivals, and nosy neighbors. They welcomed an ethnographer living in their midst, the trade-off being my American English and cultural capital. I threw myself into this world as fully as I could. I joined my Chinese neighbors on trips to casinos, restaurants, karaoke bars, and shopping malls after the workday was over, and I accompanied them to the offices of immigration lawyers and banks.

Most of my interlocutors were the Chinese traders, Chinese shop assistants, and African shopworkers I saw on a nearly daily basis. I conducted fifty semistructured interviews in English and Mandarin, the latter being my first—but rustiest—language. At times the technical parlance and regional dialects of the mall exceeded the Mandarin I grew up with in my household and later relearned in graduate school when I enrolled in a heritage speaker class. I often consulted a dictionary app on my phone, which to my advantage would prompt my interlocutors to explain situational meanings. My nonnative tongue marked my positionality between inside and outside; it was both an asset and limitation that made my fieldwork possible.[9] Sitting in shops and homes, I interviewed Chinese traders about their lives back in China, migration journeys, and business practices. My interactions with African shopworkers and security guards were more constrained. Chinese traders were wary of what observant employees and security guards knew and might say about them. I interviewed workers and security guards in bars, secluded spaces before work, and over the phone in the evening. To capture a variety of perspectives, I interviewed Chinese and South African community leaders, bankers, accountants, real estate developers, mall managers, security guards, customers, and shipping agents. I spent time with car guards, custodians, recyclers, hawkers, container workers, taxi drivers, food vendors, and customers.

Although the subjectivity of the fieldworker is always vexed, it is especially fraught in China-Africa research in which there is a multiplicity of subjects and perspectives captured in the name China, then hyphenated with Africa, a country and a continent. Like the space of the hyphen, the liminal zone where social boundaries are in flux is a privileged epistemic location. For my Chinese interlocutors, my having an ancestral home in Hangzhou and my parents' story of the Cultural Revolution helped place me in a generational story, while my cultural Americanness and citizenship set me apart. Many of my Chinese interlocutors wished to go to the United States, and they asked questions about the cost of real estate, vehicles, and food and the availability of jobs. They marveled at the ease of traveling with a US passport and wondered why I would opt to leave the United States for South Africa.

By luck, I made early connections with influential Chinese businessmen. Their endorsement functioned as an all-access pass at my fieldwork sites and revealed the social authority of the "boss." Being associated with these powerful men quickly legitimized my outside presence, but I was afraid of losing access if I asked too many questions about illicit activities or said the wrong thing about labor or racism. Being ethnically Chinese put me on an inside track for opportunities for participant observation that would be otherwise closed, but I was taken aback by the immediate trustworthiness and nature of inside status. My interlocutors would glibly share racist remarks about African workers and customers, expecting that I believed the same by virtue of skin color. The remarks were pedagogical and normalizing in teaching and enforcing the rules of race. Wanting to hear more, I usually silently went along, a complicit act to uncover what I was after. At its best, ethnography is the coproduction of knowledge and not a one-way transaction. But coproduction is still fraught with complicities and the colonial tradition of Africanist anthropology (Schumaker 2001).

Among my African interlocutors who worked for my Chinese interlocutors, I was "Chinese, but not Chinese *like them*." My Chinese racial positionality aligned me with the power they associated with Chinese migrants, perhaps akin to the colonial anthropologist, but what distinguished me was my Americanness and political orientation in the world. I sympathized with them about their working conditions and asked them about their lives in Johannesburg and back home in Malawi, Nigeria, or Zimbabwe. Our discussions provided the critical language of racial capitalism, colonialism, slavery, xenophobia, and racism. My African interlocutors asked me questions about the United States, inquiring about finding a job in New York City or the uprisings against police violence in Ferguson, Missouri. Recalling Dominic's remark about Chinese "strangeness," African workers were curious about their employers and asked about Chinese food, habits, and language. Raising the stakes, they also asked me to talk to their employers about their pay, believing their bosses might listen to "one of their own." These moments tested my ability to act in solidarity with African workers without compromising my relationships with my Chinese interlocutors, on whom I depended for access, housing, and transportation. I made suggestions when I could but was usually dismissed as an idealistic outsider. The further I distanced myself from my Chinese interlocutors, the closer I became with my African interlocutors, and vice versa; my fieldwork required a constant negotiation between "two sides," and each wanted me to tell a story that was at odds with the other.

My insights about race, gender, and sexuality draw from the ways in which I am interpellated into the identities and relations of power about which I write. As a young woman on my own, I was viewed as nonthreatening and vulnerable, in need of protection from Johannesburg's racial and sexual dangers. I became acutely aware of the racial anxieties surrounding the "Chinese girl," the young, unmarried Chinese wageworker, through the way I approximated her. When I began my fieldwork, what I thought were benign relationships with African men opened me up to gossip and speculation. During my first summer as a visitor at China City, I spent my afternoons with Marcus, Julius, Roger, and Ziggy, a group of Malawian men (about whom there will be more in this book). We would eat lunch and talk while sitting on a narrow bench. The Chinese traders and workers in the vicinity refused to speak to me, because hanging out with these men raised suspicion among the Chinese. One Chinese worker, using a pejorative term for Black people, asked point-blank, "Why do you talk to black devils [*heigui*]?" This kind of interrogation happened several times. Other Chinese women gave me unsolicited warnings about untoward glances. Among South Asian traders, there were rumors that I was a sex worker. Chinese women have been stereotypically associated with illicit and commercial sex, and in this case, sex work was how my fraternizing across racial lines was seen.

As feminist ethnographers have insisted, the boundaries around identities are fluid, contested, and policed. There are negotiations, entrance fees, and embodied costs tied to race, gender, and sexuality (Berry et al. 2017; D. M. Goldstein 2016; Günel, Varma, and Watanabe 2020; Hoang 2015). Elsewhere I have written about a sexual assault that I experienced, an ordinary acquaintance rape except that it happened in "the field" (Huang 2016; Huang et al. 2019). This assault profoundly altered my relationships with my interlocutors in South Africa, and especially the person whom I call Mr. Zheng, who years later apologized for failing to protect me. Sexual assault can undo years of building relationships and uproot research plans overnight. It is also a predictable consequence of the social embeddedness that fieldwork demands. Like fieldwork, sexual assault is about vulnerability, power, and the ethical relationships of consent, which are more complicated than we can ever anticipate from the outset. Over time, my relationship to this story has changed; no longer does it feel urgent to talk about it. I don't want to allow this single story to overshadow my work, an impossible separation of home and field, theory and practice, and public and private. Given the options of self-citation, omission, confession, or disclosure, I raise but don't retell this story to recognize the embodied realities of ethnographic knowledge production, especially about masculinist concepts like capitalism, and the stories that perhaps we all withhold.

The Outline of This Book

Reconfiguring Racial Capitalism offers a palimpsestic methodology for reading the colonial present. In Part I, "Layered Histories," each chapter works through a set of historical entanglements, transnational connections, and untidy conceptual overlays to tease out the recursive logics of history and contextualize Chinese ascendance in the long arc of Euro-American colonial racial capitalism. Chapter 1, "Palimpsest City," traces new Chinese developments back to the discovery of gold in 1886. The chapter examines the making of the mining belt mall, a place that metaphorizes and literalizes the unfolding of the Chinese Century across a topography of colonialism and apartheid. It visits Johannesburg's two Chinatowns, and other important Sino-African spaces in the city, to underscore fragmented geographies of Chineseness and counter notions of a singular Chinese diaspora, stable Chinese identity, or coherent idea of China. Chapter 2, "Sojourner Colonialism," tells the stories of Chinese migrants' lives and migratory routes to South Africa. To complicate the dominant depiction of the Chinese migrant as neocolonial pioneer, I recast the entrepreneurial migrant as a sojourner who engages in an *unsettler* colonial project with distinct spatial and temporal logics. These stories reflect the contradictory transformations of economic reform that produced the Chinese Century and propelled many to the Global South to catch up to the promise of a rising China. Their worldviews are apertures into Sinocentric imaginaries of a changing global hierarchy of Blackness, Chineseness, and whiteness.

Social relations at the mall are shaped by sedimented histories of racialization, settler colonialism, capitalism, and migration. Chapter 3, "Afro-Asian Adjacencies," situates contemporary Chinese migration and Asian racialization within nineteenth- and twentieth-century Afro-Asian and Indian Ocean circuits of migration, cultural exchange, and solidarity. It examines the racialization of the present-day Chinese trader by returning to their predecessor, the ex-indentured Indian "Asiatic" trader, two adjacent figures that have represented the threat of "Asian capitalism" at different moments in South Africa. Through archives, I show how Black/African, Chinese/Asian, and white/European were triangulated across metropole and colony. Colonial racialization is elastic and enduring: one hundred years later, the Chinese trader approximately substitutes for the Indian trader. Chapter 4,

"Afterlives of Gold," turns to the labor dynamics at China City through the history of African migrant labor in the gold mines. At the mining belt mall, the memory and legacies of mining live on in the political consciousness of China City's African migrant workers, most of whom come from countries that sent workers to the Rand. I read the mall through the mine to show how Chinese labor regimes remake key features of the colonial mining industry, such as the devaluation of Black labor (*heigong*), methods of discipline, and forms of social reproduction. The Sino-African color line—a twenty-first-century global color line—is enmeshed with the twentieth-century global color line and Black-white relations, triangulating Chinese and European racial, imperial, and capitalist projects and blurring distinctions between old and new.

Shifting to a biopolitical register, Part 2, "Racial Formations," theorizes Chinese racial formations and anti-Blackness at the scale of the body and the encounter, as well as through affective registers. These racial formations attend to the transnational, historical, and intersectional aspects of racial formation by tracing how language, stereotypes, and imaginaries—Black labor, Black criminality, racial nationalism, and racial contagion—shape meanings of Blackness and Chineseness as they circulate between China and South Africa and articulate with capitalist social relations and colonial residues. Chapter 5, "Criminal Obsessions and Racial Fictions," is about the everyday talk of crime that relationally constructs Chinese migrants and property as the victims of Black crime and legitimates stereotypes and surveillance practices. Extending this analysis of Chinese racial formation and anti-Blackness, chapter 6, "The Erotic Life of Chinese Racism," explores the intimacies of difference and proximities of skin. Fear of contagion and taboos around interracial intimacies provide some of the clearest examples of anti-Black racism, illuminating how Han Chinese racial nationalism, capitalism, and imperialism are intertwined with heteropatriarchy, the valorization of whiteness, and the denigration of Blackness.

Part 3, "Frictions and Futures," returns to the question of colonialism and twenty-first-century global horizons. Inspired by Walter Rodney's *How Europe Underdeveloped Africa*, chapter 7, "Follow the Surplus," traces the outflow of surplus value from South Africa to China and its underdeveloping effects. It details how Chinese sojourners rely on extralegal practices and African laboring bodies to remit profits back home to China, shining a light on the racial frictions of transnational capitalism that are otherwise opaque. Far from celebratory narratives of "Chinese capitalism" or "south–south cooperation," profits are squeezed from the edge of formal economies and racialized surplus populations. At stake in these quotidian practices is what happens when they are scaled up to retrench uneven geographies of accumulation. The epilogue, "Afro-Asian Futures," meditates on "failed" Chinese capitalist projects that highlight their embeddedness in sedimented histories and the non-totality of the Chinese Century.

Ultimately, my purpose is not to coin a more specific typology of colonialism or racial capitalism or offer another grand narrative about Africa, China, and the Global South, but to conceptualize a method for grasping the contingent ways in which race, capitalism, and colonialism come together and force us to ask new questions. My account is punctuated by the uncertainty and ambivalence of holding together multiple perspectives and genealogies. I hope this book provides a different way of seeing the colonial present we inhabit to change it.

PART I

Layered Histories

1

Palimpsest City

A layered history offers a different approach, an approach that recognizes composite meanings and unexpected conjunctures. Unearthing more subtlety and surprise in the past might just help us to envision less predictable and more liberatory futures.

Lynn M. Thomas, *Beneath the Surface*, 2020

Palimpsestuous reading is an inventive process of creating relations where there may, or should, be none.

Sarah Dillon, "Reinscribing De Quincey's Palimpsest," 2005

China Malls shimmer with the afterlives of gold. Since 2000 these malls, wholesale shopping centers for low-cost goods from the People's Republic of

China (PRC), have cropped up along Johannesburg's old mining belt. Where once was gold is now gilt and goods in one mall after the other: China Cash and Carry, China City, China Mall, China Mart, China Shopping Centre, Dragon City, and so forth. Along Main Reef Road, billboards and signs advertise "factory direct goods" and "a taste of China." Colorful shipping containers stacked two high and holding all kinds of plastic wares dot the landscape. When I began my fieldwork, taking taxis from one mall to another along Main Reef Road, one taxi driver, a middle-aged Black South African man, asked my opinion on whether "the Chinese were generally positive or negative." He went on to praise Chinese technology for "regaining gold from gold dust," referring to the trace amounts of precious metal in the grassy mine dumps along our drive. Where I saw low-end Chinese commodities, he saw the detritus of South Africa's gold mining industry and the promising future that China has come to represent. The remains of gold, metaphorical and material, have lingered with me ever since.

Johannesburg, the "elusive metropolis," as Achille Mbembe and Sarah Nuttall term it, captures the ways in which this iconic, ever-surprising African city defies observations of the way things are or ought to be. The dialectic of surface, underground, and edge continually remakes the mining city. Johannesburg eludes categorization "in which it is African (or perhaps not at all, or not enough); European (or perhaps not, or no longer), or even American (by virtue of its embeddedness in commodity exchange and its culture of consumption)" (Mbembe and Nuttall 2008, 25). Today Chinese communities, goods, architectures, and aesthetics have created clusters of Sino-African worlds around the city. These spaces are unique to Johannesburg and feel distinctively Chinese. In Johannesburg, also known as Egoli or iGoli (isiZulu for "City of Gold"), time collapses and anachronisms abound. A lack of linear organization, from past to present to future, makes Johannesburg distinctive. As Bettina Malcomess and Dorothee Kreutzfeld write, "Johannesburg is a city defined by a nostalgia less for the past than the future. The image of the past is adapted to suit the city's image of itself in the present, itself a desire for its own accelerated future" (2013, 18). Johannesburg runs at different speeds. Although urban transformations seem to happen overnight, Tanya Zack and Mark Lewis assert that "change happens in small adjustments and intrusions at many sites in far more incremental ways" (2022, 4). This chapter explores the dramatic but incremental transformation of the City of Gold in the Chinese Century. The Chinese Century is an idea, not a totalizing reality. Chinese world making is patchy; it proceeds through "a dialectic of unified and heterogeneous visions of the world" (Rofel and Rojas 2022, 7). The Chinese Century means different things to ordinary African and Chinese actors. Whereas the taxi driver on one of my early rides in Johannesburg optimistically saw the horizon of Chinese investment in a depleted landscape, Chinese migrants, marginal to what the name China conjures for the driver, search for prosperity oceans away. Despite the newness the Chinese Century evokes, Sino-African worlds do not begin and end with the arrival of Chinese migrants and capital but are layered with the Golden City's pasts, presents, and futures.

Throughout my fieldwork, the new frequently folded into the old. Located off Main Reef Road, the China City mall is near where gold was sighted in 1886. On the corner, Zimbabwean hawkers, whose grandfathers and fathers were gold miners in Johannesburg, sell bundles of bulrushes, decorative wheat-colored reeds with spindly white flowers plucked from mine dumps. The perennials give Johannesburg's landscape its distinctive golden hue. Doubling as remediator plants, they absorb heavy metals from groundwater. Near the lively intersection is an entrance to the subterranean city of abandoned tunnels where *zama zamas*, unlicensed artisanal miners or "survival miners," many of them migrants, risk their lives excavating the deepest remains of gold (Bench Marks Foundation 2024). Southern African artisanal miners, hawkers, and workers at China City are part of a century-long tradition of journeying to the City of Gold. Migrant mine workers played a vital role in the capitalist development of South Africa and the world by digging up the precious metal for the gold-backed international monetary system. China City is embedded in histories of mineral capitalism, geographies of uneven development, and the (un)built environments of gold. The mall is in an industrial township that was once a booming manufacturing area; it remains surrounded by scrapyards, warehouses, and derelict factories. Before that, the area was a gold mine. China City, many of its building materials imported from China, sits atop a gold reef outcrop and mining sands. With old mine shafts and sinkholes all around, the two-story mall occupies the most stable land; the surrounding parking lot and container yard are located precisely where the ground could buckle under the building. More than a hub for commodities, China City is a symbol of global China's futurity and a place built on and surrounded by gold mining's promise and violence.

China City is emblematic of the *mining belt mall*, a place, concept, and analytic site that brings overlapping histories into view. According to Lisa Lowe and Kris Manjapra, China City's peculiarities, its "uncanny materiality," compel us to "feel historically," not in terms of historicity but in a mode of sensing "different kinds of embodied meanings, across time and space" (2019, 42). The mall is a place that encourages us to consider the proximity of geographically and conceptually distant sites and their relations, as well as spatiotemporal entanglements across scales (Lowe 2015). The mining belt mall, like the City of Gold, can be productively read as a palimpsest. A palimpsest is foremost a surface landform, its layers forged by successive geological events that blanket across and alter the landscape (Knight, n.d.). As a literary object and archive, the palimpsest is a multilayered text produced through serial erasures and inscriptions on vellum that accumulates material traces of erasure over time. The palimpsest draws attention to the contemporaneity of entanglements of seemingly unrelated things and invites reading for emergence and submersion (Dillon 2005; Ly 2020). As a metaphor for history, the palimpsest captures multiple modes and temporalities of historical change—sudden events, long-lasting structures, accelerations, and decelerations. Historical times are composed of several distinct but interpenetrating layers, or "sediments of time" (Koselleck 2018). The Chinese Century unfolds in the City of Gold through multiple temporalities of accretion, sedimentation, recursion, and emergence. Chinese racial, capitalist, and imperial forms overlay the social, spatial, and geological legacies of gold mining and apartheid, reconfiguring racial capitalism in the process.

Inspired by the palimpsest, I chronicle the entanglement of Chinese and South African pasts, presents, and futures and investigate how multilayered Sino-African worlds emerge in the collision of *longue durée* histories. I look at two durational sites of world making: Chinese wholesale malls along the mining belt and Johannesburg's two Chinatowns. I engage the mining belt mall as a palimpsest of contemporaneous entanglements—not discrete formations—of Chinese and European world-making projects. Chinese migrants enter a place profoundly shaped by geographies of segregation and extraction and transform one of Johannesburg's most iconic places. I tell an unexpected story of how the China Malls became embedded in the gold reef's cycles of exhaustion and renewal during a time of political transition. While the malls prominently symbolize the "new Chinese" presence and Chinese futurity, there is also a longer history to this presence. South Africa is home to the continent's oldest and largest Chinese diasporic community. I turn to Johannesburg's Chinatowns to illustrate how recent entrepreneurial migrations overlay histories of sojourning and settlement from mainland China, Hong Kong, and Taiwan dating back to the 1870s. Johannesburg's Chinatowns reveal the heterogeneity of Chinese communities that comprise Sino-African worlds and complicate "China" as a singular idea. Not only are places like the mining belt mall, Chinatown, or Johannesburg multilayered, but identities like *Chinese* are too.

Landscapes of Exhaustion and Renewal

Three billion years ago, the Vredefort asteroid collided with the earth to create the largest reserve of gold in the world. The reef and waterways resulting from the collision was named the Witwatersrand (meaning "ridge of white waters" in Afrikaans), also known as the Rand. Uneven layers of ore-bearing conglomerate slowly pushed their way to the surface to reveal the Main Reef series. Commemorating the fiftieth anniversary of the proclamation of the Rand, a publication celebrated the Rand as "the most permanent and continuous gold field in the world" (Letcher 1936, 7). The discovery of gold in 1886 was not the first. Since at least the sixteenth century, Indigenous Africans, Portuguese, Dutch, and British were prospecting and mining for gold in the Cape, Transvaal, and throughout southern and southeastern Africa. European prospectors discovered gold on the Rand in the 1850s, but it was not until 1886 when the vast mineral wealth of the Rand would be declared (Letcher 1936). As the story goes, English prospector George Harrison, after returning from Australia, tripped over gold-bearing rock on a farm on the outcrop of the Main Reef. As a result, an influx of prospectors and investors, first from London, then New York, descended on the Rand. The Johannesburg Stock Exchange was founded one year into the gold rush in a tent off the Main Reef (Lukasiewicz 2017). The forty-mile stretch of Main Reef Road began in the wagon tracks of pioneers. Mining houses financed the construction of the road, which became the primary transport infrastructure across the Rand and the longest road in South Africa (Richardson 1982, 8; Smith 1971, 312). The rapid development of the Rand's goldfields was possible because of the mineral revolution in the Kimberley diamond fields. The De Beers Corporation had already created the mine compound system for the management of labor, and established transatlantic financial networks for capitalization and a corporate infrastructure for future mining houses (Harrison and Zack 2012; Innes 1984; F. Wilson 2001).

During the twentieth century South Africa reigned as the largest gold producer in the world, accounting for 40 percent of the world's gold in the 1940s and peaking at almost 80 percent in 1970, of which at least one-third came from Johannesburg (Harrison and Zack 2012, 559). Generations of men journeyed from southern Africa and South Africa's Native Reserves to Egoli to work as contract laborers. Following the South African War, Chinese indentured laborers were brought to the Rand (1904–10) to resolve a postwar production crisis. Inevitably, as industrial extraction ran its course, gold deposits neared depletion. Accessing lower-grade ore required mining at deeper, more dangerous depths at a higher cost. In the early 1970s, gold production peaked in volume, but profits were marginal because of the fixed price of gold and the high cost of deep-level mining. Decolonization forced changes in labor supply and impacted mining operations. Foreign workers made up 80 percent of South Africa's labor force in 1973. But by the mid-1970s Mozambique, following the collapse of the colonial government, and newly independent Malawi withdrew their labor from the mines. Black South African workers took the place of these workers and formed powerful trade unions that posed new challenges for the industry. From the 1970s to the 1990s, Johannesburg's mines were decommissioned and cleared. Most but not all shafts were sealed, leaving open thousands of derelict mines, a subterranean city of densely connected tunnels, and toxic air, land, and water (Hecht 2023; Olalde 2015). Aboveground, once omnipresent headgear, the towering steel frames for conveying miners and minerals, have mostly disappeared from the cityscape.

While the industry's heyday has passed, the saga of gold did not end with the mine closures, however. South Africa remains a top gold-producing nation. Concurrent with closures, the industry pivoted to the remining of tailings, extracting minuscule but profitable amounts of gold from massive volumes of waste, and developed new technologies to extract deeper-level, lower-grade ore. On the heels of these closures, the South African gold mining industry was hopeful of finding "a second Witwatersrand Basin" (Vorster 1986) and preparing for "the next wave of its life" (du Plessis 1997). The mining of gold, diamonds, platinum, and other minerals has remained a cornerstone of the national economy and a contested site of labor, capital, and the state (Capps 2015). Where mining companies deem insufficiently profitable to mine, artisanal miners, which include retrenched southern African mineworkers, enter abandoned mines to dig with simple tools (Madimu 2022). Meanwhile, China, with its own domestic gold reserves and global mining ventures, has taken South Africa's title as the world's top gold producer, becoming "the world's new Egoli" (Matthews 2008).

The iconography of gold is all over Johannesburg: in the national currency, street names, heritage placards, replicas of corporate buildings, and extant mine shafts where visitors can literally descend into history. To memorialize migrant workers, a mining hostel was turned into the Workers' Museum; single-sex compounds have been converted into affordable family housing (Harrison and Zack 2012). South of the belt are the Apartheid Museum and the Gold Reef City theme park and casino. Built by the same developers and separated by only a parking lot, these sites exemplify gold's contradictory memorialization. While the Apartheid Museum examines the brutality of the mines and commemorates the struggle for liberation, Gold Reef City turns these histories into frontier nostalgia to be consumed (Rankin and Schmidt 2009).

Decades after the mine closures, magnificent yellow mountains of sandy mine waste, or tailings, remain a distinguishing feature of Johannesburg's landscape. Gold mining's legacy continues in the form of silicosis and respiratory conditions, pools of orange acidic water, and the toxic drift of invisible radon gas and noxious particles carried downwind to Black communities (Harrison and Zack 2012; Malcomess and Kreutzfeld 2013; Olalde 2015). South African gold mining's particulate matter, as Gabrielle Hecht characterizes, are "sediments of racial capitalism" (2023, 31). The afterlives of gold unfold as the slow violence of chemical and radiological poisoning that shortens the lives of generations to come (Nixon 2011). These toxic environments exemplify "wastelanding," a term Diné scholar Traci Brynne Voyles (2015) uses to describe the deliberate location of radioactive uranium tailings and abandoned mines near Indigenous communities in the United States. In Johannesburg, two million people live in informal settlements and townships on or near six billion tons of mine waste (Kardas-Nelson 2013, 8). As Hecht underscores, "the profitability of South Africa's vast mining system has depended on treating African bodies as waste dumps for well over a century" (2023, 31). The old mining belt is "surplus ground," the peripheral zones and negative spaces between the urban and suburban that precarious people deemed disposable occupy. The term is a translation of *uitvalgrond*, an Afrikaans word for the triangular plot of supposedly vacant land between farms from where Johannesburg was settled and built (Malcomess and Kreutzfeld 2013, 62). Negative spaces and liminal zones have been central to Johannesburg's landscape and built environment. While the halcyon years of gold mining are over, the surplus ground of the old mining belt has turned into a regional hub for Chinese capital and commodities. With extraction follows exhaustion and ruination. As Anna Lowenhaupt Tsing argues, capital prizes one asset and alienates it from its environment and, "when its singular asset can no longer be produced, a place can be abandoned." Without missing a beat, "the search for assets resumes elsewhere" (2015, 6). A dialectics of exhaustion and renewal, the post–gold mining landscape offers new possibilities for accumulation and accelerated futures.

Driving south on Highway M1, mammoth mine dumps and towering steel equipment lie on one side of the highway, and the sprawling China Malls appear directly on the other. Their sprawling parking lots, colorful container

1.1 Aerial view of Crown Mines. © Aircraft Operating Company of Africa. Courtesy of Museum Africa.

1.2 The Crown Mines area in 2014. Photo by the author.

yards, and industrial buildings incongruously stand out against the ocher-hued veld. Around a dozen Chinese shopping centers are concentrated in industrial suburbs built around what was once South Africa's largest gold mines, the Crown Mines, their namesake being the crown of hills at the center of the Main Reef (Smith 1971, 109). Closed in 1971, Crown Mines was eulogized as a "mining wonder of world," yielding "more gold than a dozen of King Solomon's Mines"; its closure ended "an era of gold-mining unequalled in the history of the world" (Schafer 1971). In 1968 Crown Mines Ltd. created the property subsidiary Rand Mines Property (RMP) to get ahead of depleting gold levels and dropping gold prices and generate revenue from suburbanization (Butcher 2018, 2193). On the eve of its closure, RMP announced plans for a so-called New South, building roads, highways, schools, and warehousing areas "over gold-exhausted lands" (Schafer 1971). Before urban development could begin, the mine dump was cleared, the waste remined for gold, and the land decontaminated, a process that took over thirty years. During the intermittent years of the 1970s, the Crown Mines area was home to artists, musicians, trade unionists, journalists, teachers, academics, leftists, and social misfits who collectively lived in abandoned mine workers' houses until they were evicted when redevelopment took place (Ozynski 1980). By the early 2000s, the area had become ground zero for Chinese private investment.

The mining industry is responsible for Johannesburg's physical and racial landscape. As Mara Kardas-Nelson writes, "Mining is the city's ecosystem: everything can be traced back to the subterranean riches of gold" (2013, 7). Since the first urban plan in 1897, the east–west mining belt functioned as a physical and geological border. Wealthy mining elites and white mine workers lived north of the downward sloping reef; to the south, Black mine workers were exposed to hazardous wind and water downstream. Under the Urban Areas Act of 1924 and the Group Areas Act of 1950, Johannesburg's Black residents were forcibly relocated into southern townships. Soweto was a laboratory for urban racial segregation and a "model apartheid city" (Czeglédy 2003, 23). By the late years of apartheid, Johannesburg became further fragmented following white flight to the northern suburbs. After 1994, progressive planners and activists hoped to redevelop the disjointed, derelict land along the mining belt to "'stich' together the apartheid city" (Butcher 2018, 2186). As the largest owner of land along the mining belt (Harrison and Zack 2012, 566), RMP emerged as a key actor in remaking the environs. It would attempt to "unburden" the city and itself from a century of racial violence, extraction, and their spatial legacies. If the mining belt had made the colonial frontier city and later the apartheid city, it could also be the site of their undoing. City planners strove to get on the right side of history through integrated development, mixed-use smart cities, and shortening the distances between low-income housing and job opportunities (Tomlinson et al. 2003).

In 2020, I interviewed Mark, a planner who began working for RMP and later the property company that spun off from RMP to develop mining-impacted land. An engineer by training, Mark oversaw the planning of Crown City, the industrial area born from the Crown Mines, and was the principal liaison for Chinese investors. Like other progressive planners at the time, Mark nostalgically remembers the late 1990s as a moment of "transitional thinking" and radical potential: "We were looking for a transformed built environment." Crown City had the potential to bring north and south, rich and poor, and Black and white closer along the mining belt. This progressive vision, however, was not supported by shareholders and investors, to whom anything south of the mining belt signified, as he put it, "Black danger." As Mark explained, "These guys who were sitting in the invest[ment] banks were dressed in military gear, dealing with rioters in Soweto. They had come out of the army being employed by their parents and all that nepotistic nonsense in the banks, and now you're asking them to invest close to where they had guns trained on South Africans who are saying change. Change had happened, but they weren't quite ready to move the money." The project failed because "the psyche of the former market did not have the capacity for the jump that was needed." Essentially, it was "too radical for the market." In Mark's narrative regarding 1994, RMP's property subsidiary, which came from a corporate lineage of gold mining, shed its violent past to emerge as an agent of social change on the cutting edge of global markets.

When the Crown Mines closed in 1971, it was unforeseeable that the New South would become a hub for Chinese commodities in thirty years' time. While RMP was courting wary South African investors, planners were also flying to mainland China, Hong Kong, South Korea, and Taiwan to pitch a version of the New South. Two other transitions were happening: a change in South Africa's recognition, from Taiwan, the Republic of China (ROC) to mainland China, the People's Republic of China (PRC), and a shift in the city's planning priorities. By the late 1990s the city government sought to remake Johannesburg into a "globally competitive African world-class city," as detailed in its plan *iGoli2010*. Within a few years, the city's revised plan, *iGoli2030*, was reprioritized to attract foreign direct investment over providing housing and services (Tomlinson et al. 2003, 17–19). The property

1.3 Bulrushes along Highway M1 South. Photo by the author.

subsidiary RMP was similarly navigating the transition and competing visions for the postapartheid city's future. In a turn of events, Mark and his colleagues met interested Chinese investors and returned to Johannesburg with another project altogether—one of wholesale, distribution, and retail markets; he specifically remembered the meeting at which the board decisively changed course by turning to Chinese development. A few years later, the investors Mark met on his East Asia trip bought a building in Crown City at an extraordinary price, putting Chinese buyers on the map and irreversibly changing the central mining belt. Later they bought a large plot and built a water park where colorful inflatable slides and Astroturf sit above strata of grassy reef outcrop and shallow pools lie above toxic water. In the end, "China Malls have been the McDonald's move," Mark explained. "McDonald's ultimately is a very effective property company because they choose locations where there is potential for future value growth," as was the case with fivefold growth in property values along the central mining belt.

Before the China Malls, the earliest wave of mainland Chinese traders sold their goods at flea markets, set up shop on the sidewalk (*baitan*), and ran small shops in the inner city. The tumult in the early years of democracy led to white and Chinese flight from the city center. As a solution, traders

1.4   A Chinese-owned water park on Main Reef Road. Photo by the author.

sought a centrally located, securitized indoor market with small shops and stalls. The first China Mall, Baijia (One Hundred Households), became the prototype. It formed after one hundred traders collectively bought a warehouse along the mining belt and hired their own security guards. The China Mall boom took off as migrant traders kept arriving and demand for Chinese goods soared (Dittgen 2014; Harrison, Moyo, and Yang 2012; Mulaudzi 2014). In a class of their own, entrepreneurs with substantial start-up capital became mall developers. With thousands of potential tenants in search of warehouses, commercial space, and cheap labor, they found an ideal location along the mining belt. The China Malls and mining-impacted land were suited for one another. The malls require horizontal space for container yards, parking lots, and warehouse operations, not vertical density. Mining-impacted land is not intended for large structures; anything too high might sink into the ground. Chinese developers built new malls from the ground up, often with building materials imported from the PRC, in the style of massive Chinese wholesale markets where importers can browse a dizzying selection of factory goods stall by stall. Developers renovated abandoned supermarkets and sleepy shopping centers along the central mining belt and near Cyrildene Chinatown, as well as by Fordsburg, where Indian and

Muslim wholesalers had already created a vibrant wholesale market during the apartheid era. In the story of the mining belt mall, Mark is one of the foremost figures behind the phenomenon; another is Johannesburg's real estate king.

The Real Estate King

Chinese migrants have their own version of a *Forbes* list for ranking local leaders by wealth and power. Mr. Lai was undisputably first in both categories. A billionaire, Mr. Lai owns seven malls in South Africa, including one by the former Crown Mines, and boasts tens of thousands of square meters in underground garage space alone. In early 2020, I visited Mr. Lai's office and electronics factory near the airport on the city's outskirts. His translator, who arrived in 1994 from Hong Kong, gave me a tour of the warehouse and office, where honorific plaques and photographs of Mr. Lai with members of the African National Congress and the Chinese Communist Party crowd the walls. Mr. Lai praised Open Up and Reform, the Chinese Dream, and the "peaceful reunification" of Hong Kong, the PRC, and Taiwan, which had become increasingly contested with antiextradition protests and rising tensions across the Taiwan Strait the previous year. Mr. Lai has reaped the rewards for fidelity to the party line, having served as chairman of prestigious overseas Chinese organizations. When we met in the earliest days of the not-yet-global COVID-19 pandemic, his office was holding a large shipment of masks destined for Chinese hospitals.

Mr. Lai was born in 1960 in a small coastal city in Fujian Province. After high school, he went to Hong Kong to work and started selling TVs and VCRs to a Taiwanese trader in South Africa, his gateway into the burgeoning market for Chinese goods. In 1996, Mr. Lai went to Johannesburg and started his own business importing TVs, speakers, microwave ovens, and other household appliances from factories in Guangdong. There is much lore about how he became a billionaire. Stories of humble origins give credence to the idea that anyone can make it. In one version, he became superrich when South Africans rushed to buy TVs during the 2008 World Cup in Cape Town. In truth, he invested wisely during major financial crises. A biographical statement praises his "decisive decision-making on the South African and Chinese markets." The 1997 Asian Financial Crisis affected the rand and the yuan differently. With the currency difference in his favor, Mr. Lai rolled his profits into Johannesburg real estate and imported goods to sell when the time was right. With his financial crisis windfall, Mr. Lai expanded investment to seven southern African countries and new sectors. The crown jewel of his portfolio is a copper mine in the Democratic Republic of the Congo, a joint venture with the Chinese government and his brother. All of Mr. Lai's siblings are intrepid entrepreneurs: his sister trades stocks in Hong Kong, and another brother runs an electronics factory in a Chilean special economic zone. Mr. Lai's businesses earned magnificent profits through the 2008–9 global financial crisis. Before the crash, he bought a large plot of land in the Crown Mines area to turn into a mall, an acquisition that developers credit for tripling the price of mining belt land. My questions about gold mining surprised Mr. Lai, as most Chinese migrants are unaware of the history of the ground beneath them.

Next door to Mr. Lai's newly constructed, spacious, light-filled mall was once a Department of Home Affairs Refugee Reception Center where the state formerly adjudicated applications for asylum for the province, including southern African migrant workers and street hawkers at the China Malls. The Crown Mines area was selected for its central location and ability to accommodate a large facility for processing a backlog of refugee applications. Due to long application lines, an informal settlement popped up in the vacant lots. White South African business owners claimed that the squatters were a nuisance and successfully petitioned the court to move the center. With Mr. Lai's financial support, they founded the Crown Mines Community Improvement District (CID) and partnered with an urban renewal firm to clean up the "crime and grime," according to a white CID member and property developer I interviewed. The CID ended when Mr. Lai stopped funding it. While he initially capitalized on the 2008 crisis, the downturn in consumer spending eventually caught up with Mr. Lai. Like the boom-and-bust cycles of gold mining, Mr. Lai's spectacular rise tapered off. Competition from Chinese state-owned enterprises has forced him to ramp up production and decrease profit margins. "The entire game has changed, and if you cannot adapt your business model, you will perish," he explained. Although the reception center closed, informal settlements still surround Mr. Lai's mall. As with the unruliness of undermined land, informal settlements don't bother him. They are market externalities.

Mr. Lai's mall offers a neat encapsulation of the palimpsestic nature of Sino-African worlds and their global entanglements. The building lies atop the gold reef that once made American, British, and South African fortunes; later it made Chinese fortunes, financed through the wreckage of a global financial crisis. The mall's proximity to the defunct refugee processing center and informal settlements crystallizes the dependency of Chinese capital on the surplus population of an African precariat and surplus ground. The Sinification of the mining belt resulted from several historical developments, moments of transition, realignment, and renewal long in the making, as well as fortuitous moments that accelerate happenings. After 1994 the gold-exhausted lands would integrate the postapartheid city toward a multiracial democratic future. Alongside that integration, the mining belt became the site for another promise: the global futurity of China and the liberal freedom to consume.

The Age of the China Mall

The China Mall arrived during South Africa's mall boom, a moment when the meanings of race and democracy were being worked out through the democratization of consumption. Consumption has long been intertwined with race, color, class, and gender in South Africa (Iqani 2017; D. James 2014; Posel 2010; Thomas 2020). As historian Deborah Posel notes, "regimes of race have co-produced regimes of consumption" (2010, 172).[1] The regulation of Black consumption was closely linked to the British civilizing mission, and the department store was the pinnacle of colonial modernity, whiteness, and worldliness (Posel 2019). During the segregation era, racial categories were less defined; a minority of affluent, educated, urban, Christianized Africans could access some privileges of white social status through consumption. Material possessions and respectability could distinguish Native from non-Native. Under the racial rigidity of apartheid, limits on consumption were part of the larger project of Black disenfranchisement. In contrast to unlimited consumer choice and material abundance for whites, being Black became associated with certain types of food, furniture, transport, and cosmetics. Goods were intended for different racial markets. Imported European products were reserved for white consumers, while South African–made goods, derided as "Kaffir products," were reserved for Black consumers (Thomas 2020, 80). Statutory restrictions constrained Black purchasing and earning power, and Black entrepreneurs were limited in where and what they could sell. On the outskirts of the city, townships were built with sparse housing stock, small shops, and no financial services to maintain Black South Africans as low-wage laborers, not dignified, aspirational consumers with choices (Posel 2010, 169). Township residents relied on predatory moneylenders for consumer credit (D. James 2014).

In the postapartheid era, Black acquisition took on an emancipatory significance: Black South Africans were now receiving more employment opportunities, higher wages in unionized public sectors, and consumer credit. The 2003 passage of the Broad-Based Black Economic Empowerment Act (B-BBEE or BEE) created a Black elite and a middle-class consumer market. The new consumer identity of the "Black diamond" named the rise of Black conspicuous consumption (D. James 2014). Take, for instance, the 2007 opening of the first Black-owned mall in Johannesburg, Maponya Mall, in Soweto, a historic site of antiapartheid struggle. At the opening, with Nelson Mandela in attendance, owner Richard Maponya situated the mall in this history: "While politicians fought for the liberation of the country, I was fighting for the liberation of our economy." Maponya Mall was "a new monument to South African liberation" (quoted in Posel 2010, 172–73). As township residents previously had few options for shopping, Maponya triumphantly declared, "For the first time, people in Soweto will be able to wake up and walk to a shopping mall" (*Mail and Guardian* 2005).

Shopping malls are important social and cultural spaces in South Africa. In 2017 South Africa had the sixth highest number of malls per capita in the world (Muller 2015). Shopping malls first catered to the English-speaking elite, expanded to the Afrikaner management class, middle-class Coloured and Indian consumers, and lastly the Black middle class.[2] South Africa's American-style shopping malls are multiracial spaces of leisure, consumption, and aspiration, but they remain highly stratified by race and class. As Fred De Vries remarks about the Sandton City mall in Johannesburg, "If the Apartheid Museum is the yin of the new era, then the shopping mall is the yang. The success of Sandton City over the past ten years is an unplanned example of the rainbow nation" (2008, 302). The China Malls offer a wide variety of low-cost everyday goods with the option to barter and buy in bulk. They have become mainstays for working-class and middle-class Black, Coloured, Indian, and white Afrikaner households. The mall is packed at the end of the month when salaries and government welfare checks are dispensed. Reflecting class diversity, visitors arrive via Uber, in minibus taxis, in luxury cars, and on foot. While multiracial democracy has been more of an ideal than reality, China City approximates Desmond Tutu's Rainbow Nation.[3]

The social, cultural, and economic importance of the postapartheid shopping mall does not come without criticism. In the *Sowetan*, Prince Mashele (2018) observes that "our economy has undergone four phases: the age of the farm, the age of the mine, the age of the factory, and the age of the shopping mall." Placing the mall in a 1994 narrative, Mashele (2017) writes, "While we Black people were busy celebrating political freedom after 1994, a new phase in our economy was setting in—the age of the mall." The democratization of mass consumption has coincided with liberalization, financialization, deindustrialization, and democratization. Mashele reminds *Sowetan* readers that malls are owned by whites and almost all goods are imported from China. Among South African trade unions, the availability of goods imported from China is often equated with the loss of manufacturing jobs after 1994. Writing during a period of high unemployment, Mashele (2018) lays out the stakes: "As it was the case under colonialism and apartheid, the black man is still a jobseeker, hoping to be employed by a white man." Toward the redistribution of wealth, Mashele ends with a call to action: "In the age of the mall, we must expect more shops to be looted." The China Malls make goods accessible but don't create jobs in manufacturing or at the malls themselves. These jobs are filled by southern African migrants, not South Africans, which can raise xenophobic resentments. For Mashele and critics of increased trade with the PRC, the freedom that comes with consumption comes at the expense of working-class South Africans and national industries.

Mashele's periodization presents another angle for situating the mining belt mall in South Africa's history of capitalism. From the 1920s to the 1940s, secondary manufacturing to support the mining sector steadily grew. Postwar industrialization, segregation, and urbanization proceeded apace. The new regime of pass laws and the Group Areas Act ensured that those classified as African would remain temporary laborers, not urban residents. Black workers in white-owned factories produced goods that were advertised and sold to Black consumers (Thomas 2020). In the 1970s manufacturing overtook mining as gold mining entered its final decade of world-leading production. As the largest owners of land, mining companies were confronted with the twilight of their industry and turned to property development. Whereas RMP focused on its landholdings south of the mining belt, another company, Bendor Properties, looked north and launched the industrial and commercial township Amalgam.

Established in 1972, Amalgam simultaneously references the metallurgic processes of amalgamation and the racial mixing of people. Amalgam is home to the former Mayfair Gold Mine and near several China Malls. After a geological probe showed that the subsoil had settled and mine dumps contained enough trace gold to be remined, the former scrapyard sites became valuable land overnight (*Rand Daily Mail* 1974b). To advertise new land for sale in Amalgam, Bendor definitively declared, "Industrial land in the Golden City is more precious than the gold itself." The ad narrates this shift: "Since 1949, the price of gold has increased around sixteen times while the price of industrial land in Johannesburg has increased no less than sixty times. The reason is simple, there's a lot more gold than land available in the Golden City" (Bendor Properties 1979). Amalgam's location has always been its selling point. It is a stone's throw from the Central Business District (CBD), new highways, and labor reserves, enclosures created to dispossess Indigenous South Africans of land. Proximity to surplus labor has consistently featured in marketing Amalgam. One Bendor advertisement declares, "It is within walking distance of Riverlea coloured township and directly accessible to the huge Bantu labour force situated at Soweto and other townships. Your labour is available virtually on the doorstep" (Bendor Properties 1972). Proximity to low-cost labor was the effect of segregated labor and housing markets, the placement of Black and Coloured townships near railway lines, and the pass system for regulating Black mobility.

Today southern African migrant workers take established routes to work at the China Malls. Baked into the city's infrastructure, routes linking residential with industrial areas have held up. Zimbabwean workers commute from Soweto to the malls via rail; Malawian workers walk from Brixton and Mayfair, neighborhoods north of the mining belt that were built for white mine workers. Across each economic phase of mine, factory, and mall, Black labor has been recruited for white, and now Chinese, profit. Situating the China Malls in longer histories of labor exploitation and racial segregation and their spatial legacies illustrates how Chinese newcomers benefit from what preceded them. On the mining belt and in an industrial township, the mall powerfully evokes the presence of Johannesburg's mining and manufacturing past. As palimpsest of production and consumption, the mall illustrates how these phases of capitalism are not temporally discrete but run together. Black migrant workers continue to migrate to the City of Gold to work on farms and in mines or factories—and now in its malls.

Susana Draper examines the conversion of prisons and clandestine detention centers into upscale shopping malls and museums in postdictatorship Argentina, Chile, and Uruguay. She examines the superimposition of architectural models of the mall onto prison, the absence of memorial placards, and selective preservation of the prison's original features, calling the transformation an "architectonic of active amnesia" (2012, 3). In both post-apartheid South Africa and postdictatorship Latin America, "malling," the popularization of the shopping mall, signaled the transition to democracy. Malls were spaces to realize newfound neoliberal freedoms to consume. Draper writes, "the process of malling becomes, literally, a sort of malling of history that stages the tensions between past layers, as though they existed

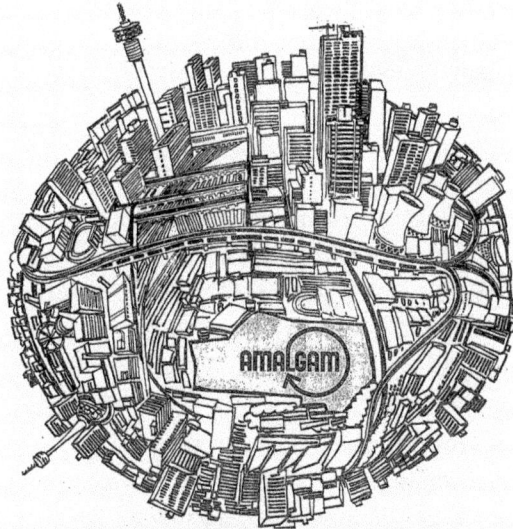

1.5   "Your labour is available virtually on your doorstep." *Rand Daily Mail*, Property News, May 17, 1972. Courtesy of William Cullen Library Historical Papers.

in the architectural unconscious" (2012, 44). The mining belt mall stages different moments of capitalism, which have always been imbricated with racism and colonialism in South Africa. Whereas gold mining is memorialized around the city, its history is largely invisible at the mining belt mall. Like the prison mall, the China Malls, with their postapartheid construction and promise of freedom, enact a similar amnesia. Reading China City as a "new" development part of the Chinese-led future papers over the active legacies of migrant labor regimes, white settlement, carceral enclosures, and underground violence. Like traces of gold buried deep beneath the surface, histories of gold remain alive in the political consciousness, collective memory, and radical traditions of African migrant workers. Reading China City as a palimpsest, the mall literally and figuratively overlays the mining belt, making Chinese investment and entrepreneurial capital the top layer of a sedimented history of colonial racial capitalism while altering the landscape with hypervisible signs of "China." Future inscriptions are yet to come.

Geographies of Chineseness

Chinese world making in Johannesburg extends well beyond the twenty-first-century mining belt mall. Johannesburg has two Chinatowns: First Chinatown, along Commissioner Street in the CBD, and Second (or Cyrildene) Chinatown in the eastern suburb Cyrildene. Where First Chinatown is a symbolic home for Chinese South Africans, Cyrildene Chinatown is for new Chinese migrants. Taken together, they bookend the plural histories of Chinese communities in South Africa and illuminate the diasporic entanglements of Sino-African worlds. Chinese communities have long left their mark on the City of Gold.

Along three quiet blocks of Commissioner Street, Chinese shops, restaurants, and grocers lie between African fabric wholesalers, artist studios, and the Johannesburg Central Police Station, where antiapartheid activists were once detained. Community history is housed in the well-maintained building of the Chinese Association (TCA), previously known as the Transvaal Chinese Association, Johannesburg's longest-running Chinese organization, dating back to the early 1900s. The TCA building is down the street from the former Transvaal United Chinese Club, a majestic modernist mansion with aquamarine tiles where Chinese lived during apartheid. First Chinatown is surrounded by histories of struggle. Down the street is a statue of Nelson Mandela as a young boxer and Gandhi Square. Whereas parts of Chinatown have been maintained as heritage sites, many buildings are in disrepair. The security bars of buildings are rusting, signs are peeling, and shop windows are broken. Graffiti embellishes the facades of grocery stores, herbal medicine shops, and dim sum restaurants. Laundry hangs from the flats above the lived-in Orient House, its name a relic. Beneath a fading hand-painted shop sign someone has tagged NO GOLD. The weathered building surfaces are full of inscriptions that make visible the layered history of Chinese diasporic communities in Johannesburg.

On the city's east side, Cyrildene Chinatown is home to migrants from mainland China who arrived after 2000. The main street, Derrick Avenue, is home to two arches, purportedly the largest Chinatown arches in Africa and financed by Mr. Lai. For a year, Derrick Avenue was my home when I lived with Mr. Zheng, the Chinatown community leader. In only a few blocks, there are the offices of provincial and citywide Chinese associations, a newspaper, and hundreds of grocers, bakeries, clothing shops, restaurants, salons, and travel agencies where Black South Africans and southern Africans work for low wages. With nearly fifty thousand residents, signs of life are everywhere: laundry hung out to dry, satellite dishes, job postings, and ads for Chinese taxis or shops for sale or rent. The cracked sidewalks are sleepy during the day and bustling in the early evening when residents return from the malls. After the sun goes down, residents retreat to their homes. Less visible is the underworld of gambling, sexual commerce, and local gangs.

In 2020, I met Walter Pon on Commissioner Street. He arrived in an old Toyota Corolla with tinted windows, dressed in a suit and sneakers and bespectacled with light-adjusting glasses. He wore a kangaroo lapel pin, a souvenir from visiting his adult children in Australia and New Zealand. Walter is a beloved South African Chinese community leader, chairman of First Chinatown, and one of the few liaisons between the mainland Chinese, Hong Kongese, and Taiwanese who comprise the "Chinese community." As a community elder, he writes obituaries. Going back four generations in South Africa, the Pon family is legendary. His grandfather arrived in the Transvaal in 1898 before the Second South African War and became a shopkeeper in the fledgling Chinatown. His wife was born in Mauritius and raised in East London in the Cape Province. The newlyweds persevered beyond pass laws that prohibited movement across colonial states. While he no longer lives in Chinatown, most of Walter's life unfolded there. On a walking tour, he stood on the street corner and pointed to four buildings where he was born, grew up, and raised his own children. Down the street, the family's grocery store is outfitted with metal bars, security cameras, and signs in English and isiZulu about minimal cash kept on premises. The shop is an informal archive and community center where recent migrations mix with older diasporas. Newspaper stories, plaques, and family photographs adorn the walls. The employees include elderly Chinese women who speak a South African style of old Cantonese, a Black South African man who had been working for

1.6 "No Gold" on Commissioner Street. Photo by the author.

the family for thirty-five years, and a recently employed man from Malawi. Walter and I had dim sum at a restaurant where the owners are newcomers who arrived in 2000 from Enping, the Jiangmen village where many of my interlocutors were from. Walter does not refer to the two Chinatowns as "old" and "new," a distinction that implies obsolescence and replacement. First Chinatown is not a heritage site frozen in the past.

First Chinatown was built by the forefathers of the Chinese diaspora in South Africa, such as Walter's grandfather, who began arriving and settling in the 1870s as independent migrants. Of Cantonese and Moiyeanese descent, most were from Canton (Guangzhou) near the mouth of the Pearl River delta. This early wave of migrants fled natural disaster and war for the fortune of the "gold mountains" in Australia, California, and South Africa (Park 2009). During the period of Asian exclusion laws at the turn of the

1.7　Social proximities in Cyrildene Chinatown. Photo by the author.

twentieth century, Chinese were barred from immigration and economically disenfranchised. As in other white settler colonies, Chinese migrants became shopkeepers, tailors, and butchers. Chinese and Indians were prohibited from owning or renting fixed property except in designated mixed areas, "Asiatic bazaars," and Black townships (Yap and Man 1996, 330). By the 1890s the string of shops along Commissioner Street became the Cantonese Quarter, Chinese Quarter, or Malaikam (a Cantonese adaptation of Malay Camp), an area in the Kimberley diamond fields where Chinese laundrymen, Indian shopkeepers, and Malay transport drivers lived and worked (Yap and Man 1996, 47–48). By the early 1900s there were around one thousand free Chinese in Johannesburg's fledgling Chinatown. Free Chinese were separate from the sixty-four thousand Chinese laborers who made occasional excursions to Chinatown. Despite immigration restrictions, the small community grew as newcomers became the fictive kin of established Chinese and created "paper families." Since its inception, First Chinatown was a vital center for the small, tightly knit Chinese community. Social clubs, language schools, a Chinese press, the Cantonese Club, and the TCA protested anti-Asian ordinances and later the indignities of life under apartheid (Park 2009).

In the 1970s, under the Group Areas Act, the apartheid government attempted to turn the dense commercial and residential Chinese cluster into an official group area for all Chinese in Johannesburg. Chinese residing outside Chinatown would be involuntarily removed and relocated, an idea that community leaders rejected. Historians Melanie Yap and Dianne Leong Man note that "Johannesburg's Chinatown is possibly the smallest in the world because of the Group Areas Act. The awareness of the dangers of grouping themselves and having an area imposed on them made the Chinese repress the tendency shown in Chinatowns elsewhere to move into a vicinity where they could socialize with other Chinese" (1996, 336). Accordingly, Chinatown did not expand during apartheid. In the transitional years of the 1980s and 1990s, crime increased in the inner city and drove many Chinese businesses away. Additionally, the children of shopkeepers moved into the ranks of the professional class and relocated to more affluent suburbs or emigrated to Australia, New Zealand, or North America (Harrison, Moyo, and Yang 2012). As First Chinatown has emptied out over the last thirty years, elders like Walter keep this community history alive.

The diasporic community began to change in the 1980s when the increasingly internationally isolated apartheid state recruited industrialists from Taiwan, another isolated country, to spur development, and at its height, thirty thousand Taiwanese industrialists and entrepreneurs arrived (Hart 2002; Park 2012).[4] In the 1980s and 1990s, geopolitical alignments changed. New entrepreneurs and investors from Hong Kong, the PRC, and Taiwan began coming to South Africa as the older Taiwanese settlers left. Back then, Chinese communities were more porous and dispersed, and there was more mixing between Chinese and Taiwanese. An early cohort of traders from Shanghai and Taiwan occupied ten floors of the Ponte City Apartments, an iconic cylindrical tower in the heart of Johannesburg, and nicknamed it Diaspora University and Shanghai Tower. Then a shift happened. Under Mandela, South Africa changed its alliance from the ROC to the PRC in 1998. The year 2000 marked the largest and most continuous influx of mainland Chinese migrants, becoming the largest group within the Chinese community in South Africa (Huynh, Park, and Chen 2010).

Cyrildene, a historically Jewish and Portuguese suburb on Johannesburg's east side, was built in the 1930s for white families of "moderate means" (*Rand Daily Mail* 1937). As the story goes, in 1995 a Chinese noodle shop opened on Derrick Avenue just as its older ethnic community began to leave (Accone 2006, 266). Chinatown's rapid growth has been described as "a boom out of control" (U. Ho 2013); to control the boom, Chinatown was institutionally formalized with a small governing body, and the Community Police Forum, a collaboration between Chinese leaders and the South African Police Service, was established. For many years, a private security company, notorious for its harsh policing of the CBD, patrolled the area in an armed response vehicle. There has been an attempt to clean Chinatown up with street cleaners, CCTV cameras, and campaigns and crackdowns on gangs, drugs, and littering. As a former police forum leader put it, "Even I don't want to walk down this street, because it stinks. We can't have the arches be beautiful flowers on top of a rubbish dump" (quoted in U. Ho 2013). Chinese South Africans often express frustration when South Africans misrecognize them as mainland migrants and associate them with stereotypes of illegal immigration, cheap goods, poor business practices, and organized crime (Yap and Man 1996). As a Taiwanese South African complained, "The newcomers have been in gold-rush mode and they don't have roots here. . . . They just want to make their money" (U. Ho 2013). The more assimilated, small and diverse community—comprising around ten thousand Chinese South Africans and three thousand Taiwanese—has distanced itself from new migrants, estimated at three hundred thousand and visibly concentrated in Cyrildene Chinatown and the China Malls (Park 2012). The difference is between *settlers* who plant roots and *sojourners* in "gold-rush mode."

Belonging under the umbrella of "Chinese" national or ethnic identity is not a given. Chinese South Africans, a broad category that can include second-, third-, and fourth-generation mainland Chinese, Hong Kongese, and Taiwanese, share a sense of history and fought for their place in the multiracial settler society. Chinese South Africans were initially excluded from the BEE, a postapartheid affirmative action policy for promoting Black economic participation. The category "Black" encompassed "African," "Coloured," and "Indian." Chinese, who were variously categorized as Coloured or Asian, found themselves economically disadvantaged again (Harris 2017). In 2008 the Chinese Association of South Africa appealed Chinese exclusion from the act and won recognition of discrimination under apartheid, becoming eligible for the policy and legally given the designation Black. As the association explained, "The [Chinese] community's struggle has not been about economic opportunism, but about [the] lack of recognition and clearing up of misconceptions of the historical injustices the South African Chinese faced" (quoted in Park 2012). Surviving the racial state, planting roots, and claiming citizenship in the liminal space between Black and white have comprised a distinct Chinese South African identity.

While Chinese South African communities did not identify with new mainland migrants, Chinese migrants saw themselves foremost as Chinese nationals, identifying as Chinese people, nationally (*zhongguoren*) and ethnically (*huaren*), and not overseas Chinese (*huaqiao*), a term they reserve for settled immigrants with roots. Connections between groups happens at the upper echelons of community leaders, such as the coordination of Chinese New Year celebrations across both Chinatowns and a successful legal campaign against anti-Chinese hate speech (U. Ho 2022). This dissonance disrupts assumptions of sameness, continuity, and coethnic solidarity within South African communities of those who speak Cantonese or Mandarin (among other regional dialects) and come from Hong Kong, the PRC, or Taiwan. There is no singular "China" or Chinese diaspora. Chinese and Taiwanese are divided by tensions across the Strait of Taiwan and the One China policy. In sum, Sino-African worlds have been stratified by the colonial, segregation, apartheid, and postapartheid periods. Johannesburg's Chinatowns encapsulate the layered patchwork histories of sojourning and settlement spanning two centuries and mirror the fragments, margins, and centers of Chineseness. Returning to Walter's distinction, it is a mistake to refer to the two Chinatowns as "new" and "old." Rather, they show how Chinese laborers, settlers, and sojourners have left their mark on the Golden City.

Gold's Remnants

Johannesburg is a dynamic city of interpenetrating social and geological layers: the city on the surface and what lies underground. As the Chinese Century unfolds in the City of Gold, "China" and "Chineseness" are not monolithic, totalizing "new" entities that transform the city from the top down or outside in. Rather, Sino-African worlds are palimpsestic, heterogeneous, and fragmented, with pockets all over the city, not only at the China Malls and Chinatown. They are coproduced through histories and relations that are not immediately apparent. These worlds are transnationally shaped by forces at several scales, modes, and velocities of historical change specific to Johannesburg. Sino-African worlds emerge from the collision of epoch-defining transformations: South Africa's mineral revolution and the rise and fall of gold mining over the long twentieth century; geopolitical realignments, economic priorities, democratic freedoms, and urban planning after 1994; and, as chapter 2 examines, the dislocations of China's neoliberal reform driving entrepreneurial migration to Johannesburg and the Global South. Along the mining belt, the China Malls are the products of sedimented histories of European colonial racial capitalism, as well as serendipitous encounters and collaborations of diversely situated actors—property developers, real estate moguls, ordinary Chinese traders, and African workers and consumers—each with different visions of the past, present, and future. Ordinary African and Chinese people, who often do not always see themselves as historical actors, are transforming the city by profoundly changing one of the most defining segments of the Golden City. The mining belt mall is where deep geological time, the memory of gold, and apartheid's spatial and environmental legacies meet the anticipatory future of global China.

2

Sojourner Colonialism

While migration in and of itself does not equate to colonialism, migration to a settler colonial space, where Native lands and resources are under political, ecological, and spiritual contestation, means the political agency of immigrant communities can bolster a colonial system initiated by White settlers.

Dean Saranillio, "Why Asian Settler Colonialism Matters," 2013

In the early 2010s, the figure of the Chinese pioneer in Africa entered global imaginations. In Western liberal journalistic narratives of Chinese neocolonialism, Africa emerged as an economic frontier for daring Chinese entrepreneurs, invoking both the American Wild West and Joseph Conrad's so-called Dark Continent. In *China's Second Continent*, Howard French wagers a land grab: "The continent's rapidly rising population means lots of new mouths to be fed, lots more people to be clothed, devices and appliances and goods of all kinds to be sold. . . . [N]o other big outside players in the world besides the Chinese have fully understood the opportunity this represents" (2014, 44). Reviews of French's book by Ian Johnson (2014) and Alexis Okeowo (2014) reinforce the frame of economic imperialism and settler colonialism. Photojournalist Paolo Woods (2019) similarly articulates, "For the thousands of Chinese who have emigrated in the last decades, Africa holds the promise of a 21st century frontier," with some "selling cheap goods along the burning hot roadsides of some of the poorest countries in the world." Petty traders are read as part of the state project because "the government in Beijing is sending Chinese state companies and adventurous entrepreneurs to Africa." In *China Safari*, Serge Michel and Michel Beuret refer to Chinese migrants as "foot soldiers" of the People's Republic of China (PRC), and these migrants stand out: "To Western eyes the Chinese appear incongruous arrivals on the African scene, like the red and yellow highrises built in the Algerian desert by their construction companies" (Michel and Beuret 2009, 7, 4). In journalistic representations, the "ordinary migrant" is figured as a neocolonial pioneer and symbolizes the novelty, reach, and scale of an emergent Chinese imperial power.

Since the 1990s, Chinese entrepreneurs, workers, and their families steadily arrived in South Africa. When I arrived for my year of fieldwork in 2015, there was constant talk of *huiguo*, a term that refers to temporarily or permanently returning to China. Longtime traders were leaving because of an uptick in armed robberies, a weak foreign currency exchange rate, and decreased consumer spending due to a South African recession beginning in 2013. While most returned to China, some moved northward to the Democratic Republic of Congo, Ghana, or Mozambique, or across the Atlantic Ocean to Argentina. Johannesburg was only one location among many in Africa, the Caribbean, Latin America, and Southeast Asia, as well as transitional economies in eastern Europe (Gao 2017; Hearn 2016; Nyíri 2006; Pieke et al. 2004). Before Johannesburg, some of my interlocutors worked or traded in Cameroon, remote South African towns bordering Swaziland, and South Korea. They had ties to Argentina, Australia, Italy, and Venezuela. Since Aihwa Ong's (1999) study of the flexible citizenship practices of Chinese elites across Hong Kong, Shanghai, Singapore, and Vancouver in the 1990s, Chinese from diverse rural, urban, and class backgrounds have gone to far-flung places in Africa and the Global South. Sociologist Biao Xiang identifies transience as a twenty-first-century mode of global mobility. Transient migration is "against permanency"—"the world of a transient is the world itself" (2017, 1). Migration is not a singular event but rather an open-ended process, way of life, and strategy for accumulation (Pieke et al. 2004). Chinese migrants in Johannesburg exemplify a mode of sojourning across the Global South—of hopping from one emerging market to the next with the goal of returning to China—that is distinctive of the Chinese Century. Unlike the Chinese pioneer, my interlocutors' stories indicate an ambiguous colonial formation based in sojourning, not settling, and driven by markets, not territory, and transience, not permanence. Moreover, ordinary migrants are legally precarious, not embodiments of Chinese state power.

To make sense of Chinese migration and its entanglements with race, empire, and settler colonialism, I turned to the critical framework of Asian settler colonialism. Settler colonialism is a structure and process that "destroys to replace," as Patrick Wolfe has formulated (2006, 388); it entails the theft of land and genocide of Indigenous peoples and social, economic, cultural, and political processes that efface Indigenous sovereignty. Over the eighteenth and nineteenth centuries, British and Boer (Afrikaner) troops fought frontier wars against Khoekhoe, San, and Bantu-speaking Xhosa and Zulu peoples, among others, to establish the colonies comprising South Africa on their land. Divided by ethnicity and language, Indigenous peoples were pushed into Native Reserves and Bantustans or "ethnic homelands" during apartheid. Settler colonialism is distinct from franchise colonialism, such as British and Dutch colonial rule in Africa and Asia, in which the extraction of commodities from mines and plantations, not large-scale settlement, was the objective. Settler colonial critique complicates binaries of settler/Native, settler/migrant, white/nonwhite, and victim/oppressor by recognizing the role nonwhite settlers and racial migrants have played in settler colonialism. As Jodi A. Byrd terms it, "arrivant colonialism" names the coerced, often violent ways nonwhite people arrive in settler colonies and enter their social relations (2011, xxxv). In settler societies, Asian immigrants, some of whom arrived as indentured laborers or fled imperial wars, have been exploited and oppressed as "racial migrants" (Mawani 2009), but as settlers they have politically and economically benefited through rights and inclusion within settler nation-states and "settler accumulation by Native dispossession" (Saranillio 2018, 3). In South Africa, the earliest Chinese were a small group of convict and indentured laborers who were brought to the Cape via the Dutch East India Company in the seventeenth and eighteenth centuries (Huynh, Park, and Chen 2010; Yap and Man 1996). Since the 1870s, Chinese have been independent migrants, temporary sojourners, settled immigrants, and indentured laborers recruited to work alongside Black/Native labor and excluded and exploited by white settler capitalists.[1]

Disenfranchised under apartheid, they have also sought inclusion into the settler nation-state. In 2008 the Chinese South African community won legal recognition as "Black," a category closely related to "African" and "Native," to qualify for the Broad-Based Black Economic Empowerment Act. The win ensured Chinese South Africans had adequate opportunities for employment and small business, and importantly, symbolically recognized their full citizenship in the postapartheid settler colonial society. Returning to the epigraph, Dean Saranillio remarks on Asian settler colonialism, migration to a settler colony, whether Hawai`i or South Africa, "can bolster a colonial system initiated by White settlers" (2013, 286). As Candace Fujikane puts it, Asian settlers are "both active agents in the making of their own histories and unwitting recruits swept into the service of empire" (2008, 7). Contemporary Chinese migration to South Africa is implicated in two colonialisms: the "arrivant" colonialism of earlier Chinese labor migrations and diasporas and the emerging imperial epoch of the Chinese Century. Ordinary migrants are interpolated into these colonial formations despite their loose ties with Chinese South Africans and Chinese state power and explicit lack of intention to settle or reside long-term.

Rather than determine colonial intention—that is, whether Chinese migrants actively, willfully engage in neocolonial practices—I seek to understand how Chinese migrants come to occupy a structural position and colonizing capacity within South Africa. Chinese migrants are racial migrants imbricated in the economic structures of the settler colonialism that fundamentally shaped South Africa. But they do not aspire to put down roots, assimilate, or claim citizenship as Chinese South Africans have. Settling is the antithesis of their purpose. Asian settler colonialism is useful for thinking through a set of positions and relations, but settler colonialism, nor franchise nor "arrivant" colonialisms, do not quite characterize the anomaly of contemporary Chinese entrepreneurial migration. As Manu Vimalassery, Juliana Hu Pegues, and Alyosha Goldstein emphasize, settler colonialism is not a "stand-alone analytic" to be applied across contexts. Rather, "Settler colonial histories, conditions, practices, and logics of dispossession and power must necessarily be understood as relationally constituted to other modes of imperialism, racial capitalism, and historical formations of social difference" (2016). Alternatively, Juliana Hu Pegues (2021) develops the idea of space-time colonialism to understand the messy entanglements of race, empire, and settler colonialism between Asian immigrants and Native Alaskans in colonial Alaska, the "last frontier" of US empire. Space-time colonialism underscores the relational construction of space and time and logics of land and labor that are context specific. Where Chinese sojourning to African "frontiers" confounds classifications of imperialism, colonialism, and settler colonialism, parsing its spatial and temporal dimensions reveals an *unsettler* sojourner colonialism.[2]

With these analytics in mind, this chapter explores the space-times of the Chinese Century from the perspective of the "ordinary migrant" in three registers: Sinocentric understandings of space/geography and time/history; twenty-first-century geographies of accumulation that drive Chinese migration to the Global South; and the spatiotemporal dimensions of entrepreneurial migration. I begin with popular Chinese narratives of sojourning to Africa. A developmental teleology of China leaping ahead and Africa always being behind informs how migrants position themselves within the Chinese Century. Next, I turn to migrants' stories to illustrate how market reforms and rapid economic growth propel ordinary people to Johannesburg. Like other emerging markets in the Global South, Johannesburg becomes a frontier for capital accumulation and a spatial fix for resolving the contradictions of economic reform. Ordinary migrants are driven to South Africa not by a colonizing impulse but by "China's dialectic of development and displacement" (Rojas 2016, 7). Migrants aim to overcome the *temporal* conditions of being left behind, stagnation, and foreclosure in postreform China *spatially* through frontiers, edges, and undergrounds. Their stories reverberate with belatedness, catching up, detours, and dislocation. In the last section of the chapter, I turn to the distinctive mobilities of sojourning. Entrepreneurial migration requires geographic nimbleness amid rapidly changing conditions, which is achieved through clandestine channels to move across borders. I learned about these channels by living with Mr. Zheng, who was formerly South Africa's reigning snakehead (*shetou*), a migration facilitator named after the way snakes slither under fences. These underground mobilities are imperative to the core principles of sojourner colonialism.

Conjuring Africa, China, and the Twenty-First Century

While the Chinese pioneer has entered African and Western imaginations, the African continent has reentered the Chinese imagination in a new global era. Take, for instance, the 2017 blockbuster *Wolf Warrior 2*, which stages a story of Chinese economic and military might and American imperial decline in an unnamed African country beset by a pandemic, civil war, and poverty. The film has been rightfully criticized for its stereotypical representations of Africa and Africans and masculinist Chinese nationalism (Berry 2018; Liu and Rofel 2018). Wolf Warrior is Leng Feng, an ordinary trader with the likeness of a "Chinese Rambo." After being banished from his military station in the Indian Ocean, he starts over as a trader, befriending locals and adopting an African godson in the idealized image of Sino-African friendship and multiracial "global family" (Amar 2021). Throughout the two-hour film, Wolf Warrior battles African rebels and white mercenaries led by an American, Big Daddy. In the final action sequence, Big Daddy asks Wolf Warrior if he is willing to die for the captives, who are all African except for a Chinese American humanitarian worker–cum–love interest. Wolf Warrior righteously responds, "I was born for them." In a final insult, the American villain declares, "People like you will always be inferior to people like me," to which the Chinese hero rebuts, "That's fucking history" before delivering the fatal blow. The film ends with Wolf Warrior leading a peace convoy, marked with a PRC flag. The takeaway is clear: China will no longer be humiliated by Western powers; the PRC is Africa's future, and Africa is critical to the PRC's global stature. As Paul Amar notes, the film "articulated a revised agenda for domination and legitimation that sometimes yearns for, and sometimes spurns, Euro-American notions of imperial race and militarism" (2021, 435). A site of racial and gendered fantasy and adventure, Africa is figured as a timeless space and stage for Chinese imperial ambitions.

Beyond *Wolf Warrior 2*, the African continent has become part of everyday Chinese people's global horizons. Many young, university-educated Chinese, skilled workers and private entrepreneurs, chase their dreams in African countries and then return to China, broadcasting their experiences on overseas Chinese blogs via WeChat. These blogs are replete with photographs and anthropological descriptions of roads, local people, weather, and other mundanities. In a pedagogical manner, they chronicle encounters with the state for would-be travelers: what to expect when arriving at the airport, applying for a visa, or dealing with extortionist police and customs agents. Africa is depicted as a politically unstable, dangerous, economically weak, "backward" continent and a land of economic opportunities, self-cultivation, and dream fulfillment. These stories function as both inspirational and cautionary tales. For instance, a Chinese electrical engineer in Nigeria shared his initial excitement about the high salary and possibility to see the world, but to his dismay, he lived and worked in a walled compound akin to a prison or fishbowl. The "real Africa," he says, was not like the one depicted in *Wolf Warrior 2*. After returning to China, he advised others to decide early whether to settle or return. To indeterminately stay in Nigeria made it harder to eventually return to China, he cautioned: "If you live in this kind of environment with small competition and slow pace for a long time, you will be out of touch after returning to China" (Xing and Xiao 2021, my translation). Chinese expats fall out of custom with the fast pace of market competition. In contrast to the enclosed world of compound life, private entrepreneurs from high social backgrounds in China depict Africa as a business paradise and place for individual, even spiritual, rejuvenation. According to one Huawei executive, in Africa one can "feel the harmony between man and nature, and the greatness of life force" (A. Yan 2019, my translation). Despite class differences between ordinary migrants, elite expats, and state actors, Africa is a global frontier for capital accumulation and a place of respite from the fast pace of life in postreform China.

In scholarship on Chinese migration to Africa and the Global South, ordinary migrants are "pioneering modernizers" attached to China's developmental projects abroad (Nyíri 2006, 86). Ordinary Chinese who migrate to less industrialized or "developed" countries take on the civilizing mission of the modernizing Chinese state, which Pál Nyíri (2006) provocatively calls the "yellow man's burden." In the twenty-first century, "*it is the turn of the Chinese*, with their unique endowments of flexibility and efficiency and now backed by a strong modernizing state, to lead the world to a new, improved version of modernity and capitalism" (Nyíri 2006, 105, emphasis in the original). Since the 2013 launch of the Belt and Road Initiative, the signature infrastructure project of the Chinese Century, the yellow man's burden is as strong as ever. Chinese humanitarian workers, tourists, engineers, construction workers, doctors, entrepreneurs, language teachers, and traders are part of a modernizing mission. For example, the self-anointed Queen of Africa, an entrepreneur in the logistics sector, frames capitalist enterprises as divine calling: "Looking back a hundred years, it was the Europeans and Americans who talked about and directed Africa . . . but history has developed into the 21st century today, and it is groups of Chinese who work hard on the African continent! . . . This is an opportunity given to us by history, and it is also a merit given by the motherland!" (Hao 2019, my translation). Whereas liberal Western observers read Chinese pioneering as neocolonialism, elite Chinese see their capitalist activities in Africa as a higher calling tied to China's triumph over the West and a return to the apex of the global order—in short, a Chinese manifest destiny, a Sinocentric imperial vision of the past, present, and future. While there are important class differences between ordinary migrants, elite expats, and state actors, a developmental teleology of China bounding ahead and Africa falling behind shaped how my interlocutors situated themselves as Chinese sojourners in South Africa. They saw their own quest for upward mobility as congruent with China's global ascendance.

Chinese Mobilities and African Frontiers

Chinese migration to South Africa is driven by economic transformations and changing emigration policies since Deng Xiaoping's succession as leader after Mao Zedong. For some of my interlocutors born in the 1950s to 1990s, their paths were congruent with, but not determined by, the experimental reforms beginning with Open Up and Reform in 1978 and Going Out in 1999. Reform and opening up liberalized foreign direct investment. Special economic zones sprang up for multinational corporations and, subsequently, wealth accumulation and industrial development concentrated in cities along the eastern coast. Under the Going Out policy, the government encouraged Chinese firms to open new markets and invest overseas to "cool off China's overheating, investment-driven economy" (Yeh and Wharton 2016, 287). In what Xiang (2014) calls "post-socialist primitive accumulation," mass privatization created a stark economic divide. Immense wealth accumulation created a superrich class of party elites; a growing urban middle class of gated residential communities, conspicuous consumption, and cosmopolitan lifestyles; and at the bottom, the "floating population" of millions of rural migrant workers (L. Zhang 2001; L. Zhang and Ong 2008). Governmental stances on emigration underwent dramatic change. In the 1940s and 1950s, overseas Chinese were cast as traitorous; since 1978, overseas Chinese became celebrated agents of socialist modernization, diplomacy, and investment (Mohan and Tan-Mullins 2009; Nyíri 2006; Ong 1999). In 1985 emigration policies were relaxed. In this postsocialist terrain of class formation, economic modernization, and newfound mobility, Chinese migrants "go out" (*chumen*) to Johannesburg. While lay accounts see ordinary Chinese migrants as extensions of (or even sent by) the Chinese state, the trajectories of migrants to Johannesburg are not a direct effect of state policies encouraging overseas trade, investment, and emigration. They result from social inequality, economic insecurity, and desiring subjectivities engendered by decades of neoliberal reforms.

My interlocutors hailed from the southeastern coastal provinces Fujian, Guangdong, Jiangsu, and Zhejiang, and as far west as Xinjiang and as far north as Dongbei. But most came from Fuqing, a county-level city in Fuzhou

Prefecture, the administrative capital of Fujian Province, and Enping, a village in Jiangmen, an inland city in Guangdong Province. Globally, Fujianese account for a quarter of overseas Chinese; in South Africa they make up at least two-thirds (McNamee et al. 2012; Park 2009). While both areas have long traditions of overseas migration, reform and opening up intensified them. In 1984 Fuzhou was designated an open coastal city for foreign direct investment. From the late 1970s to the 1990s, rural reform and industrial development destabilized traditional professions such as farming and fishing. Rapid urbanization and population shifts created fierce competition for resources, jobs, and business opportunities and motivated rural–urban migration within China and overseas. Fuqing was revolutionized by an influx of overseas remittances, visible in newly constructed mansions, material goods, and the emergence of a "peasant nouveau riche" (Chu 2010, 81; see also Keefe 2009; and Pieke et al. 2004). Since the mid-1990s, Fuzhou's countryside has become the top source for emigration flows and illicit migration. Moving south along the coast, Jiangmen is celebrated as the Capital of Overseas Chinese. Jiangmen's proximity to Hong Kong, Macao, and the Pearl River delta has made it a port city for imperial trade and a productive base. Today Jiangmen is one of nine cities that are part of the Guangdong–Hong Kong–Macau Greater Bay Area, a regional cluster for high-end manufacturing and information technology.

The economic dislocations and novel class formations of the globalizing market economy and partial dismantling of socialism manifested in gendered, classed, and regional ways, producing differentiated trajectories to South Africa. Some of my interlocutors were university educated and worked in urban offices and state-owned companies. In Johannesburg, they were more likely to have the start-up capital and business know-how to become entrepreneurs. But for most, the limited prospects a middle school or high school education afforded meant that they worked low-wage service jobs in bakeries, gas stations, restaurants, hair salons, shops, and construction sites. Since the 1950s, the household registration system (*hukou*) has classified citizens into rural/peasants and urban/nonpeasants. The system has been at the heart of contemporary rural-urban inequality, most visible in China's "floating population," the millions of illegalized rural migrants who work in cities without social protections or welfare provisions. Many migrants were state-classified peasants relegated to the countryside. Even though migrants would remain workers in Johannesburg, work would be less demanding and potentially better remunerated in foreign currency. Above all, becoming an entrepreneur who was "doing business" was within reach. I commonly heard the phrases "becoming one's own boss" and "getting rich." In an ethnography of Fuqing, Frank Pieke and colleagues explain, "emigration is the most profitable locally accessible opportunity for employment or entrepreneurship" (Pieke et al. 2004, 25). Johannesburg affords higher social status and earnings that migrants cannot achieve in China. As a former peasant from Fuqing explained, whereas he would be mopping floors in the United States, in South Africa he could have a business.

Transnational migration is organized by spatial and temporal logics. Global capitalism expands across geopolitically segregated spaces. As Petrus Liu (2022) argues, capital requires a racialized, geopolitical "constitutive outside"—such as Africa or China's financialized hinterland—as a source of new surplus populations. Both motions—from rural to urban and from China to the Global South—inform Chinese migration to Johannesburg. Entrepreneurial migrants seek out the "virgin territory" of untapped markets. In contrast to highly industrialized countries, African consumer markets provide high demand for low-end goods while business regulations are lax and little start-up capital is required. Heidi Østbø Haugen and Jørgen Carling articulate the spatial logics of this accumulation strategy: "It is on the ever-shifting edge of the diaspora that courageous pioneers make large profits" (2008, 660). Emigration is an accumulation strategy for low-wage workers with entrepreneurial ambitions and established entrepreneurs alike. Chinese entrepreneurial migration also has a distinct temporal component. Entrepreneurial migrants chase after the "first barrel of gold," a popular phrase from the early 2000s that referred to the breakthrough wealth of primitive accumulation (Xiang 2014, 189). The goal is not the limitless acquisition of wealth, but to acquire enough to catch up with China's rapid development and make future entrepreneurial endeavors unnecessary (Xiang 2014, 191). Xiang emphasizes, "The transnational migration projects were always China-rooted and China-oriented, and they enabled one to skip over the present" (2014, 192).[3] Johannesburg is envisioned as a temporary detour in the present on the way to a more secure future in China. A middle-aged woman from Fuqing went to South Africa because China had become too developed (*fada*). Although she came well after South Africa's golden years, there were still more opportunities than in China. In most of my conversations, the present and future in China felt unstable (*bu wending*). The following in-depth profiles of key interlocutors illustrate the ways economic reform, along with an element of chance, shape people's social locations in China, journey to Johannesburg, and sense of belonging in South Africa. No two ordinary migrant stories are the same, and they are anything but ordinary.

2.1 Portrait of a sojourner. Photo by the author.

From *Dagongmei* to *Laobanniang*

In 2014, I worked for Jenny, a quick-witted, ambitious, and fiery petite woman with short hair. From Sanming, an inland mountainous city in Fujian, Jenny arrived in Johannesburg in 2003 when the market for Chinese goods was relatively new. She succeeded in working her way up from being a *dagongmei* to a *laobanniang* (feminized terms for wageworker and boss, respectively). At China City, Jenny wholesaled party goods and novelties imported from Yiwu, a city in Zhejiang famous for its megamarkets. She hired me initially to work part-time after her cousin and business partner returned to Sanming to start a family. The two of us sat shoulder to shoulder behind an enclosed counter for up to forty hours a week. Later, we were next-door neighbors at China City's apartments. Among her friends, Jenny called me "American girl." Before the pandemic hit, we were making plans for me to visit Sanming and Yiwu's wholesale markets. When it was slow, we passed time on our iPhones. Jenny watched a comedy about a rich Beijing family and played *Hay Day*, a game that simulates mall life and her rural childhood: there are crops to be harvested, commodities to be produced, orders to be filled, and ruthless competition. "Shoot, the stuff I wanted is sold out," she cried. Recognizing the irony of playing this game at the shop, she chuckled, "I watch my shop in my sleep. I only know how to watch my shop." Business preoccupied her at every moment.

Born in 1974, Jenny grew up in a governmental unit (*danwei*) where her father was employed. She grew up tending livestock and crops on the family's small plot after school. During summers, she harvested tobacco to sell, her first foray into business: "Even as a small child, I was already making money." Jenny's entrepreneurial savvy came from her father's side. Her paternal uncles were entrepreneurs in Singapore and returned every New Year with red envelopes of money. Jenny graduated high school and entered the workforce when multinational corporations were arriving in Fujian. The early 1990s was an exciting time to be a young person. She and her classmates worked in factories, hoping it would be a ticket to go overseas to the United States. She worked at several factories, but the manual labor was too hard. After she lost her job due to a factory closure, she trained to cut hair, opened a salon, married, and had a daughter. During this time, a mentor called often to report the dazzling earning potential in Italy. Jenny's father fortuitously met a migration broker for South Africa, which could be a stepping stone to Italy. In 2003 Jenny divorced, left her daughter with her parents, and sold her salon to pay the broker. With ten others, she traveled from Fujian to Botswana before crossing the border into South Africa. From this cohort, she was the only one still residing in Johannesburg by the time of my interview with her.

Jenny's early years in South Africa were marked by difficulty, isolation, and dependence. In the early days of Chinatown, the Fuqing Gang was a threatening presence and immigration raids were frequent. Jenny rarely left her apartment and was reliant on a cruel, controlling man for employment and housing. Against his wishes, she covertly took English lessons down the street. Jenny recalled the daily humiliation of going to work. The driver, a Chinese man, forced her to lie flat in the bed of a pickup truck even though there was room in the cab. For several months, she worked for a Chinese wholesaler in Durban, working long hours in the heat and living in a crowded dormitory with other Chinese workers, an experience she likened to "working like a coolie" (*dang kuli*). "It is foolish to think you can get rich [*facai*] overnight," she reflected. "First you have to survive." Jenny and her cousin eventually opened a shop when China City opened. They were among the first to sell party goods. At their best, Jenny and her cousin were importing twenty containers a year, but by the time I met her, business had slowed to three containers. Jenny came to terms with the slowdown as fate: "You are only destined to make so much money in the world. You can never make all the money in the world. Once you accept what is happening, you can be a bit happier and relaxed." She bought a home for her parents, established permanent South African residency, and eventually sold her shop and returned to Sanming, while making occasional trips back to South Africa to maintain permanent residency. But back home she was estranged from her teenage daughter, whom she rarely mentioned in our conversations despite her chattiness. "I didn't raise her, and there isn't much to say to her. I don't want to bring her here. It's too disorderly [*luan*]." Johannesburg, deemed a backward city, was no place for a child to grow up. In contrast, Sanming was changing for the better; every time Jenny returned, the streets she had once known were now unrecognizable. This was a common narrative among Fujianese whose remittances had transformed their hometowns.

Jenny's experience reflects a sense of dislocation. For the many migrants who journey alone, they strain their relations with family and children, whom they migrate to support. It is unclear when one has made enough for the future, and if they will feel at home on return. Her story is also a representative tale of success through eating bitterness. A Mao-era narrative, eating bitterness (*chiku*) is a common way migrants understand their experiences of hard work and sacrifice for their families and country. Jenny understood the social inequality of capitalism in terms of fate and meritocracy. Not everyone can be a millionaire; some people were destined to stay low-wage workers. She believed China lifted itself out of foreign domination and poverty because of the Chinese people's capacity to eat bitterness. Having come of age in the early years of reform, Jenny saw hard work as essential for progress (*jinbu*) and transformation (*gaibian*), whether individual self-development or national development: "If a pot is cracked, you must not throw it out, but work to repair it." The chauvinist belief of Chinese people's developmental capacity informed Jenny's interactions with Afrikaner customers and African employees. A belief in Chinese superiority explained the resentments of rude white customers and justified disciplining of "lazy" African workers. Jenny's worldview reflects a global racial hierarchy of Chinese/China, white/European, and Black/Africa.

Jenny represents a first generation of Chinese women migrant workers in Johannesburg. This generation of young women are often referred to as *dagongmei* (working girls), a Cantonese term that feminizes the act of selling one's labor (*dagong*) with the word for a younger sister (*mei*). *Dagongmei* first described female silk factory workers in nineteenth-century Guangdong; the term reemerged in the post-Mao era as young rural women migrated to work in the urban factories in special economic zones (P. Ngai 1999, 1; H. Yan 2008, 20). In its contemporary usage, the gendered labor identity *dagongmei* encourages single women to become rational market agents of their own self-development (Yan 2008, 10). For Jenny's generation, leaving the countryside for the factory was part of a modern desire to "see the world" (*jian jian shi mian*) and change one's fate (Yan 2008, 26). Among the generation of women workers born in the 1990s, many left low-paid service jobs in Fujian and Guangdong to work in Johannesburg. Often their parents, themselves migrant workers, encouraged them to work abroad for a few years between high school and marriage to "toughen their character." Working abroad and living alone would force young women to acquire the skills required for making a living in China's competitive labor markets, and it would broaden their global horizons as modern cosmopolitan subjects. Like Jenny, young women workers journey alone, start a new life far away, and navigate the gendered vulnerabilities and uncertainties of the future.

The Laid-Off State Worker

I first met Old Cheng when he approached me about working at his shop part-time. Old Cheng is a beloved character at China City. When I met him, he was nearing sixty years old; his back was hunched, and his long hair thinned. Old Cheng left Sanming for South Africa in 2006, the year many traders pinpoint as the moment of market saturation when there were too many migrant traders in Johannesburg. He set out to South Africa with hopes of starting as a worker and becoming an entrepreneur but never made it. Instead he worked for an electronics wholesale store run by a Sichuanese family and lived with them at China City's apartments, a form of employment known as "live with the boss, eat with the boss" (*zu laoban, chi laoban*). These apartments resembled dormitories in Chinese industrial zones, which doubled as convenient accommodation for transient migrant workers and a way to extract longer working days (P. Ngai 1999). Old Cheng and his coworkers slept in bunk beds, four people in each apartment. As the only Chinese employee unrelated to the boss, Old Cheng was tasked with the risky job of picking up cash and dropping off orders in town. The Malawian and Zimbabwean workers empathized with his lowly status and endearingly called him *madala*, a term reserved for male elders that suited his avuncular personality. To other Chinese, coming all this way in old age to work was pitiable.

Born in 1957 during the Great Leap Forward, Old Cheng came of age during the Cultural Revolution. In his first years, the Chinese government relocated his parents from their home in Shandong Province to work on a tree farm in less-developed Sanming. After high school he was sent to the same tree farm for two years of reeducation, a domestic development policy of sending educated urban youth "up to the mountains, down to the villages." My parents have a similar story, having spent their teenage years in the Heilongjiang countryside, and this ingratiated me to Old Cheng. After proving himself to be a good worker, he was enrolled in a governmental work unit and started a family under the stability of the Iron Rice Bowl, a cradle-to-grave Maoist institution of guaranteed lifetime employment and welfare benefits. It organized a way of life, even destiny (C. K. Lee 2007, 124). In the late 1990s, Old Cheng's underperforming factory was privatized. Laid off, he stayed at the work unit with his wife but without a salary *(tingxin liuzhi)*. Old Cheng joined the ranks of millions of laid-off state employees forced to find other work in the private sector—no longer part of Mao's proletariat but instead in flexible labor.[4]

Then in his forties, Old Cheng patched together a living from construction jobs. Later, up until the time he left for Johannesburg, he drove taxis for a private company, logging ten-hour days but netting little after the cost of gas and car rental. With his wife approaching retirement and his son starting college, he needed to support three people at different life stages. "I'm old," he admitted, "I can't endure it." In South Africa, Old Cheng had an aunt who, like Jenny, advanced from worker to entrepreneur. He paid a migration broker to be smuggled into South Africa. At the beginning, the Chinese and South African currencies were close in value; the new work would effectively quadruple his salary. The exchange rate weakened at the same moment South African immigration reforms made work visas difficult to renew. Like many Chinese migrants, Old Cheng was legally caught between states. He tried to make enough to save for the future before running out of time on his visa. While the future was uncertain in China, it was also uncertain in South Africa. If Old Cheng was nostalgic for anything about the socialist past, it was for the stability it had offered. As Ching Kwan Lee writes, "In the age of reform, families face different opportunities and predicaments, depending on idiosyncratic circumstances such as the economic fortune of a spouse or offspring, the availability of start-up capital loans from relatives or friends, the timing of one's retirement or lay-off, knowledge or social connections to get one started in a business venture, and luck. Inequality is painfully visible" (2007, 139). The social inequalities of economic reform pepper Old Cheng's "failed migrant" story. In South Africa, hierarchies of class, region, gender, and quality (*suzhi*) and employment regimes are remade, making it difficult for Chinese workers to overcome the barriers to upward mobility that they faced in China. These class hierarchies also make cross-racial solidarities possible. Old Cheng was at the bottom of the Chinese hierarchy, and this endeared him to his African coworkers.

The story emphasizes that timing is everything. Old Cheng missed "the last bus for the first barrel of gold" (Xiang 2014). A toy wholesaler who was near Old Cheng's age and employed in a work unit in Nanjing emphasized the cruel mercuriality of entrepreneurial migration: "The first one eats crab, the second one drinks some soup, the third one gets nothing." The most successful traders are attuned to the changing tides of markets and ready to move across the world or change business models when profits inevitably plateau.

Chinese Dreamers

My long conversations in English with Joe and Sarah took place in their shop so that they could keep working. Joe's namesake was the character Joey Tribbiani from the TV sitcom *Friends*, the show he credits for teaching him American English. Born into a rural household in Xinjiang in 1975, at the tail end of the Cultural Revolution, he studied railway engineering as his ticket out of working in an agricultural unit. Joe spent a year building tunnels in the western city of Chongqing, but he found the bureaucratic structure of government work unbearable. As he whimsically described his personality, "My character is kind of free." At the age of twenty-two he moved to Beijing, where he sold technical equipment for a Japanese company, met a Taiwanese musician, and changed career paths yet again. He attended music school and started a rock band. Just as he was making money playing shows, the SARS pandemic broke out and music venues closed. Out of work, Joe returned to the music school to work as an English translator, where he met Sarah.

From Hubei, Sarah was born in 1981 into a large rural household. Like Joe, she was determined to escape the countryside and went to college. After graduation, she was assigned to work as a teacher at a private school in Fuqing where she taught children whose parents worked overseas. After Joe and Sarah married, they moved from Beijing to Shenzhen, where Sarah worked for a private firm and Joe at a CCTV camera company. He started as a salesman, was quickly promoted into a technical position with his engineering background, and serendipitously landed a government contract to install cameras at a nuclear power station. Since he was paid upon completion, he took a risk borrowing money from friends to complete the project, but it paid off. A company contact recruited him to service CCTV cameras in South Africa. Joe went to Johannesburg on a work permit, and Sarah joined him later, leaving their son with relatives. Joe landed in Johannesburg when Chinese traders were installing security cameras and few Chinese were in the security camera business; it was a market niche that required a high level of technical knowledge. He wanted to "be his own boss" and split from his business partner. Joe and Sarah sank their savings into a shop at China City selling LED lights, another commodity requiring specialized knowledge. Every risk they took paid off. Sarah began returning home for two months at a time to visit their son and to work in factories in Guangzhou and Shenzhen. Eventually Joe and Sarah decided to settle permanently in Johannesburg. They brought their son over, enrolled him in a predominantly white private school, and bought a house in the quieter suburbs near Cyrildene Chinatown. With the intention to stay, Joe and Sarah represent a new generation of Chinese South Africans in hoping their children will surpass their parents by going to the United States.

Implicit in how Joe and Sarah understood their relation to other Chinese migrants and made choices was the cultivation of quality (*suzhi*), a salient category in the creation of social hierarchies. *Suzhi* is a discourse of human quality that emerged with the Dengist project of cultivating the quality of the overall citizenry—especially those in poor, rural, "backward" areas—to modernize China (Anagnost 2004; H. Yan 2003). In South Africa, Fuqingnese were perceived as having the lowest quality. They were stereotyped for cutthroat entrepreneurialism, rural ways, poor manners, and low levels of formal education. The minority of educated urbanites like Joe and Sarah were deemed to have the highest quality. Quality can be achieved through self-cultivation and becomes naturalized as a universal standard of value (Byler 2022, 91). A "low quality" of people justifies their devaluation as a surplus population and as low-wage workers.

Sarah and Joe embody the ideal self-enterprising Chinese subject carrying the yellow man's burden. I was struck by Sarah's preoccupation with happiness, a popular self-help discourse encouraging citizens to cultivate their productive potentialities (Yang 2013). "Chinese people think, 'First earn money, then you will be happy,'" she generalized. "Chinese people don't know how to be happy." Eating bitterness and deferring happiness for the next generation was the norm. In 2013 Xi Jinping introduced the Belt and Road Initiative and the Chinese Dream—new party policies with a vision for a prosperous, harmonious socialist nation to complement China's leadership role in the world. Dreaming is significant, as "for the first time since Mao's victory in 1949, instead of endless self-sacrifice, Chinese are now encouraged to dream" (Chai and Chai 2013, 97). As ambassadors of the Chinese Dream, Sarah and Joe chased happiness and familial prosperity in South Africa. Carrying the yellow man's burden, they recognized their responsibility to represent the PRC and act with humility and benevolence. They were proud to provide well-paying jobs and consumer goods. In English, Sarah expressed, "For me I thank you, South African people, because these people let me earn money, so I must be very kind to this country, to this country's people. But [only] some Chinese people think this way." Joe and Sarah saw themselves as more cultivated, educated, modern, and forward looking than Fujianese who shortsightedly lived to make money. In Xi's China, "homepatriarchal love" is a sacrificial love for the family, nation, and property that works through a "futuristic and other-place-oriented logic" (C. Y. Zhang 2022, 85). Among Chinese migrants in South Africa, their overseas quest for prosperity and happiness is aligned with the future-oriented Chinese Century and Chinese Dream and heteropatriarchal, nationalist, and neoliberal desires.

Across these stories, Chinese migrants experience the present in South Africa as a detour, while the past and future are in China. They arrive in South Africa with ranging global aspirations, entrepreneurial ambitions, and political views. From rural and urban backgrounds, their trajectories are shaped by yearning for the long-gone stability of the socialist past, the acceleration of urbanization and displacement, and uncertainties about the future. In Johannesburg, migrants can move up in ways they cannot in China, whether from the countryside to city, or from selling one's labor to doing business, but they also experience the material inequalities and precarity that led them to South Africa in the first place. In South Africa, class dynamics and social inequalities from China are remade. Hierarchies of quality, class, gender, and regional and labor regimes, such as the migrant worker dorm, are reinvented. In the City of Gold, migrants try to accumulate enough to stabilize their family's future in China and even to become rich. But success depends on forecasting markets and migration patterns, in addition to the bitter grind of survival, which is gendered and generational. When markets become less profitable, migrants plot their next move, whether returning to China, journeying to another southern location, or indefinitely waiting it out. With the fewest ties, migrant workers are the first to leave. Transitory migrants do not aspire to settle, even if they stay for years by default. They occupy a liminal space through permanent residency status, visas, trips home, and video calls.

Reproductive futurism shapes migrants' horizons and practices. For sojourners, entrepreneurial migration is a China-centered, future-oriented project organized around the heteronormative family unit, a microcosm for the nation. In China, the ability to move up a socioeconomic tier is difficult to effect in one generation but is possible for the next generation. My interlocutors spoke of generational mobility and *fuerdai*, the children of China's nouveau riche who attend prestigious American universities. They invested in education in China or in South African private schools where their children would socialize with white students. As one migrant noted, if it was possible for their generation to make it without a university education, it would not be the same for their children because China and the world had changed. Chinese migrants put their hopes on a better life for their children, even separating from their children to labor for this elusive generational mobility. But separation takes a toll in the form of estrangement. As this paradox plays out among China's rural migrants, Charlie Yi Zhang observes, "many migrants find their family relationships in trouble and sometimes irremediably damaged, contradicting the promissory prospect anchored in heteronormative reproductive futurism" (2022, 105). In South Africa, Chinese migrants struggle to better the futures of their families and country, while becoming more dislocated and estranged from both over time.

These biographies are products of the making of the Chinese Century in recent decades and reflect how ordinary Chinese migrants understand China's place in the world. My interlocutors variously experienced the dislocations of economic reform that catapulted China into the global economy. But instead of becoming jaded with China's accelerated development, they bought into a developmental ideology and heteropatriarchal nationalist vision whereby love for the family is love for the nation, and familial prosperity is national prosperity. As Jenny, Joe, and Sarah expressed, their view of South Africa was shaped by China's global rise, the decline of the West, and the perceived backwardness of the African continent. They identified their upward mobility with China's and their hard work overseas with Chinese people's sacrifice for national development. Ordinary people are compelled by historical forces to take control of their fate and migrate, but migrant mobilities are not linear. Although entrepreneurial migration is China-centered and future-oriented, the future is unclear. Migration does not always lead to prosperity. In fact, it tests family bonds and sometimes ends in failure. Success is not guaranteed on return to China. When I returned to Johannesburg in 2020, I heard anecdotes of several traders who went back to China to start brick-and-mortar businesses, only to find that they could not keep up with the e-commerce boom and, as a result, they returned to Johannesburg's China Malls. They experienced upward mobility not as a linear progression but as a loop, migrating to not migrate in the future, only to return and migrate again. Or they experienced the stasis of not earning what they needed to return to China. Critical to the project of sojourning is a geographic nimbleness to seize market opportunities and hop from place to place, which is achieved through clandestine channels for migration. Extralegal measures are central to staying unsettled.

The Chinatown Boss

Mr. Yu, the owner of China City, offered to find me a place to live. He supplied few details via email but assured me that someone would meet me at the international arrivals terminal at the airport and I would stay with a "good family" at China City's apartment complex. When I landed, there had been a change of plans. I was going to stay with Mr. Zheng, one of Mr. Yu's good friends and an important tenant, who had a spare room in his two-story home in Cyrildene Chinatown and would look after me. Chinese businessmen thicken their relationships by trading favors like this. I would live with Mr. Zheng for nearly a year. As a longtime migration broker and Chinatown boss, Mr. Zheng was central to the making of transnational corridors and the daily governance of migrant communities in gray zones between Chinese and South African states and informal and formal economies.

For many years, Mr. Zheng was Chinatown's manager, its "big boss." He is from Fuqing, a county-level city with a population around one million. Fuqing has an international reputation for its overseas population, human smuggling networks, and the internationally notorious Fuqing Gang. At its peak, the Chinese population in South Africa was officially estimated at three hundred thousand, but the running joke was that there were five hundred thousand from Fuqing alone. Mr. Zheng was the Chinatown boss and a snakehead, an "underworld entrepreneur" part of a diffuse transnational network connecting China and Chinatowns around the world (Keefe 2009, 38). From the perspective of their clients, ordinary people facing inaccessible visa regimes, snakeheads are not seen as criminals but providers of professional services (Pieke et al. 2004, 195). States classify human smuggling activities as organized crime, but migrants see snakeheads as altruistic in the life paths they enable. Chinese human smuggling networks are not highly organized, large-scale transnational syndicates but built from social and familial networks (Zhang, Chin, and Miller 2007). In cities, enclaves of rural migrant workers are informally governed through loosely connected, vertically integrated clientelist networks of state officials, local bosses, and ordinary migrants. The unevenness of state regulation creates vacuums for the privatization of power. There are different kinds of power: the bureaucratic power (*quanli*) of state officials and the de facto community leaders with social and political influence and prestige (*shili*; L. Zhang 2001). In the early 2000s Mr. Zheng had established himself as a community figure in Johannesburg and was elected Chinatown boss by local businessmen to clean up crime. At the time, Fujianese, specifically Fuqingnese, were blamed for petty street crime, gang activity, and kidnappings. With his hometown ties, Mr. Zheng was the front-runner. Under his watch, usury, gambling, and drugs were driven off the streets. He hired a security team to patrol Chinatown and installed surveillance cameras. When I first moved in, the Chinatown office was located inside his house. From the living room window, I could watch grainy black-and-white real-time surveillance footage on the wall-mounted flat screen. It was difficult not to be seduced by this kind of access.

There are two versions of Mr. Zheng's life story as he narrated it to me, each with its ambiguities. In one version, he was a savvy, self-made man and selfless community leader. Born in the late 1960s, he completed one year of middle school before dropping out to work. In his youth he was a mover, plumber, repairman, and construction worker. For a while he made bricks. In his early twenties, he opened a flour mill, franchised several gas stations, and then went into debt. After hearing rumors of US$2,000 monthly wages in South Africa, in 1995, years before South Africa established diplomatic relations with the PRC, he journeyed to Johannesburg. At first he worked for others, selling in flea markets. Back then it was easy to make money. He opened a dozen businesses and started importing containers. He strategically opened shops in areas connected to Johannesburg by highways in "all directions," casting a wide net to reach shopkeepers coming from Kimberley, KwaZulu-Natal, Mozambique, and Mpumalanga. When Mr. Zheng was working around the clock, he drove a cargo truck back and forth to restock his shops, and he would leave his shop in the care of relatives and Black South African employees. Like many Fujianese traders who set up shop in townships referred to as "Black areas" (*heirenqu*), he picked up more Zulu than Afrikaans or English.

While Mr. Zheng was driving his cargo truck, he was also ferrying people from the country's land borders into Johannesburg. This is where the other version of his story begins. Within three days of returning to live in his house for the year, Mr. Zheng invited me to dinner, a farewell before he headed back to Fujian for a few weeks. When I asked biographical questions, one dining companion jeered, "The interview has already started!" When others spoke in Fukienese, he ordered them to speak Mandarin. This kind of code-switching was how I knew Mr. Zheng wanted me to know things about him. With a wry smile, he deliberately said in English, "Some people call me Mafia, but other people call me big brother"—a name for Mafia leaders. Mr. Zheng put his wrists together as if being handcuffed and revealed the reason for the trip: appearing in court. While chain-smoking, he proudly recounted his humble beginnings as a "small snakehead" taking migrants across South Africa's land borders with Botswana, Lesotho, Mozambique, Namibia, and Swaziland before becoming a "big snakehead" with people working for him. The other men egged him on, their faces flushed red from wine and excitement. Mr. Zheng and his business partner organized migration to South Africa until they were arrested in Fujian but his partner informed on him to receive a lighter sentence. By the time I had moved into Mr. Zheng's home, he had completed his sentence, which he paid a fortune to have shortened, and resumed his role as Chinatown boss. After that Mr. Zheng kept a lower profile and tried to repair his reputation. In the unofficial rankings of local leaders, Mr. Zheng used to be in the top three, but after his arrest, he dropped lower in the top ten. His rise and fall, and the two sides to his story, reflect the complicated ways morality is entangled with (il)legality. The Mafia is known as *heisehui*; *heise* means "black," and *hui* means "group." Mafia men show two faces, black and white (*hei bai*). On the white side that I knew, Mr. Zheng was a well-connected community figure and self-made man. The black side, which he kept separate from his homelife, occasionally leaked through. Mr. Zheng's multiple roles exemplify the moral and social capacities of the men who suture legal/illegal and state/nonstate domains.

After his fiftieth birthday Mr. Zheng retired as Chinatown manager and opened a karaoke bar where the state had shut down a Chinese business for tax evasion. Wearing a Louis Vuitton belt and a T-shirt with "Van Gogd [*sic*]" lettered in gold, he gave me a tour of the karaoke bar, which was decorated in a generically Western aesthetic with plastic chandeliers and wall-size paintings. After twenty years in South Africa, he had no interest in relinquishing his PRC citizenship to become a South African citizen; like most of my interlocutors, being a PRC citizen was core to his Chinese identity. Even though Mr. Zheng annually spent several months in his five-story mansion in Fuqing, after so many years away, "everything derailed," reflecting a sense of dislocation and foreclosed future in China. Mr. Zheng was crucial to the sojourner colonial project of the early 2000s. His abiding loyalty to China made him not a settler in identity, even as his long-term residence in South Africa indicated otherwise.

Stealing Passages

During the summers, when school in Fuqing was on break, Mr. Zheng's son and wife would come to stay in Johannesburg. During one of my visits, I spent an afternoon at Mr. Zheng's office. That day, Lily, one of two longtime employees, a couple from Fuqing, was preparing visitor visas to the United States for a family. "Just to visit, not to stay, which would be illegal," she preempted. The brawny, boisterous nine-year-old emptied a Lego set onto the table. The boy ordered me and his mother to locate one piece while he built a battleship. In the back of the ship were seated several figurines, and on the sides were armed figurines defending the passengers from ocean dangers. "These people are being smuggled over [*tamen toudu guo qu*]," the boy gleefully narrated. His mother, in her casual, elegant manner, laughed, a tacit acknowledgment of the open secret about her husband. Bald Head, the second employee, a tattooed ex-car mechanic nicknamed after his short buzzcut, waltzed in. He picked a plastic figurine off the ground and rubbed the boy's head, exclaiming, "You lost a Mafia brother!" Most Chinese arriving in the late 1990s and 2000s entered South Africa without legal authorization in the process of *toudu*, which means to "steal a passage" and is commonly associated with boat smuggling. Estimates of South Africa's Chinese migrant population vary wildly because of clandestine migration.[5]

The arrival of Chinese migrants in the new millennium represents only the most recent layer of a long history of migration. Generations of Chinese, Hong Kongese, and Taiwanese have been coming to and going from South Africa since the 1870s and through a variety of channels. Clandestine migration to South Africa has gone hand in hand with restrictions on Chinese immigration. In the early twentieth century, a slew of anti-Asian legislation prohibited Chinese migration to South Africa. Across settler colonies worldwide, Chinese were highly desired as mobile contract laborers but not as citizens, merchants, or miners (M. M. Ngai 2021). In South Africa, over the first half of the twentieth century, immigration quotas and gender restrictions were put in place to minimize entry and settlement. Chinese were barred from citizenship and subject to a system of pass laws, fingerprints, and certificates. After the National Party took power in 1948, the trickle of immigration that had started in the 1930s was closed, while the newly formed PRC sealed its borders (Park 2009; Yap and Man 1996). Clandestine crossings became the only way to get to South Africa after 1948, but they had a longer history. Generations of Chinese had crossed the Indian Ocean as stowaways; they docked in Durban or Maputo and made the last leg of the journey by train (Yap and Man 1996, 182). In South Africa they assumed the identities of fictive kin of Chinese residents, a phenomenon known as "paper families." Chinese South African writer Ufrieda Ho has one such story. In her memoir *Paper Sons and Daughters*, Ho (2011) recalls a childhood moment of confusion and panic when asked to provide her mother's official birthdate. Growing up in an era of pass laws, Ho reflects on the role that documents played in everyday life. She remembers the tattered piece of paper, a notarized certificate of good standing, that her father carried in his pocket when he rode the train. Under the endless restrictions of apartheid, the small Chinese community flew under the radar and breached the law to economically survive. As Ho recalls, legality was a privilege: "Laws, I realised, were for people who fell into the tight inner circle of society. It became elastic at the edges and it was this edge that people like the Chinese and other nonwhites bounced up against" (2011, 41). Although China's and South Africa's borders have opened, some migration routes and paper practices have held up.

To give an example, in 2015, I met Shimei in Cape Town. From Fuqing, she was a twenty-two-year-old high school graduate and daughter of a construction worker. Her friends left Fuqing for Singapore, South America, and the United States, but she followed her boyfriend, a former classmate, to Cape Town, where his parents ran a shop. He went first, and within a few months, she traveled to reunite with him. They engaged and had a child, but he returned to China, leaving Shimei with his family, working and living at their shop and raising their child on her own. Whenever we spoke about her journey, there was some hesitancy in her voice from the stigma of—and fear of being caught in—illicit migration. I interviewed her in her room behind the shop; while bathing her son, she recounted her journey. The long process began in China with extensive research from friends and family and an introduction to a migration broker, followed by a period of waiting, preparing paperwork, and gathering payment. She arranged her travel with a snakehead for ZAR60,000 and, one month later, flew to Mozambique on a visitor's visa. As Shimei recalled, the plane ride to Mozambique was the easiest leg of the trip: "You just have a meal, go to sleep, and don't talk to anyone on the plane." After a few days in a safe house, Shimei and eight others made a ten-hour journey by car, then crossed the border on foot. She vividly recalled the rain and darkness of the night and the fear of falling behind and getting separated. This penultimate leg is called *zoubian toudu*, which means to "walk around to steal a passage." It is associated with the dark and clandestine, including traveling by night with a flashlight or torch and treading cautiously. Once migrants arrive in South Africa, a final payment is made. Migrants initially stay with family, friends, or in Chinatown, where they begin to find employment, repay debts, and apply for work permits.

Journeying with a snakehead is a game of chance. The snakehead might suddenly demand more money midway, a trip can be forced to detour to avoid interception, and passengers can get stuck in transit. During the height of boat smuggling in the 1990s, the infamous journey of the *Golden Venture* ended with almost three hundred passengers, mostly from Fuzhou, stranded in New York City after the cargo ship, which had sailed from Thailand to Kenya, and then around the Cape of Good Hope, crashed onto the shore of Rockaway Beach in Brooklyn.

Lian Fang was one of many Chinese migrants who accidentally ended up in South Africa on their way to the United States. He managed a shop in a small town between Johannesburg and Durban where the streets are still named after apartheid's architects, and I met him when he came to Jenny's shop in Johannesburg to order stock. Later, on a road trip, I paid him a visit. Lian Fang nonchalantly spoke of his migration journey. He deadpanned, "When you leave China with a snakehead, you have to climb many mountains through Asia. If you don't get eaten by a tiger, you have made it to heaven [*tiantang*]." From a village in Fuzhou, he was determined to reach America—heaven—where it was purportedly easy to make money. Even washing dishes for minimum wage would be an improvement from "doing farm work at home," his state-determined future as a peasant. He paid an extraordinary sum of money to a broker to make a long, dangerous journey that involved hiking through mountains, crossing seas and oceans, and entering the United States from Mexico. Amazingly, Lian Fang embarked on this journey not once but twice, and by his own bad luck, both times ended up stranded midway, in South Africa. Luckily, he had a family network to make something out of his misfortune, including his brother, who operated a shop across the parking lot from where Lian Fang's shop was.

The gendered subjectivities and capacities required of these journeys are apparent in Shimei's fear and Lian Fang's nonchalance. Prospective migrants consider different migratory processes—air or boat travel, international connections, real or fake documents—and the risks, costs, and time involved (Chu 2010). Zones such as the US-Mexican border are gendered necropolitical spaces. Border crossings are dangerous for female migrants, who are vulnerable to sexual harassment and assault by male border agents, handlers, and other travelers (De León 2015; Wright 2011). Criminologists note the vulnerability for female migrants on boats and in safe houses where men and women are trapped in crowded, close quarters for long journeys. Female migrants face the threat of violence from guards, enforcers, and debt collectors and can be coerced into sexual commerce on arrival (Zhang, Chin, and Miller 2007).

Discourses of *toudu* capture a set of attitudes toward risk and fate that is most clearly embodied in the figure of the Fujianese stowaway. Jenny proudly described Fujianese as the most willing to eat bitterness, the most daring, and the least afraid to die. Anthropologist Julie Chu observes of aspiring Fuzhounese villagers, "The costs and benefits did not seem to add up in a rational, calculative model of 'risk'" (2010, 261). Chu explains Fuzhounese worldviews through its variation of mahjong. In the Fuzhounese version, the tiles circulate faster, there are fewer pauses for tactical moves, and the introduction of wild cards makes it possible to immediately win. Navigating an uncertain world, Fujianese migrants aim to "grasp the elusive patterning and flow of life's fortune and, in turn, intuit a way forward in a world of increasing transnational circulation" (Chu 2010, 267). Migrants take risks to change their fates.

Papers, IDs, and Barcodes

Despite the postapartheid nation's inclusive principles, its immigration policy has been exclusionary and territorial, especially toward Black migrant workers from southern Africa whose labor built South Africa's economy. During my fieldwork in 2014, Chinese migrants were impacted by a series of immigration reforms, the first major overhaul of immigration policy since the language of "illegal aliens," "aliens," and "illegals" was codified into law in 1995 (Peberdy 2001). The 2014 reforms tightened immigration restrictions to address global security, international human rights, and clandestine migration. They affected visitors' visas, business visas, and work permits, in addition to amending critical skills and procedures for deportation and asylum.[6] The Department of Home Affairs (DHA) clamped down on "loopholes in legislation," fraudulent documents, and "border jumpers." The reforms fortified border management; changed processes for applying for visitor, work, and business visas; and stopped renewing special permits for Zimbabweans. Anyone without valid papers became an "undesirable person" and was deported. These policies were primarily aimed at curbing southern African migration, which severely impacted Malawian and Zimbabwean workers, but it also adversely affected Chinese traders and workers reliant on work visas, whose status in South Africa became uncertain overnight.

Work permit application procedures were complicated to start. From the thick packet Shimei's family showed me, the requisite paperwork of standardized forms, in English and brimming with legalese, involved even more supporting documents: employer sponsorship on company letterhead, "proof" of an attempt to fill the position with South African job seekers, bank statements, police clearances, medical records, and other identity documents. Migrants hired local Chinese migration brokers and South African immigration lawyers, with the same poor outcome for both. In legal limbo, traders and workers were returning (*huiguo*) to China. When we met in 2020, Mr. Zheng estimated that one hundred thousand migrants, one-third of the migrant population, had left. That same year the Immigration Act of 2002 was revised to grant Chinese business travelers, among other "BRICS business executives," ten-year multiple-entry visas. As Aihwa Ong points out, "nation-states constantly refine immigration laws to attract capital-bearing subjects while limiting the entry of unskilled laborers" (1999, 112).

Chinese migrants talked about their legal status in China and South Africa in strikingly similar ways. In the PRC, individuals become "legal" or "illegal" through forms of state identification. Household registrations (*hukou*) are tied to registration booklets that function as internal passports, resident identity cards (*shenfen*), and governmental dossiers of personal records (*dangan*). These documents are centrally stored and regularly updated with marriage, education, reproduction, employment, and relocation information. In the late 1980s, individuals were, for the first time, required to carry IDs in public, thus making their legal status, household registration, and dossier immediately accessible (Wang 2004). Individuals came to understand themselves through their "file selves," or the accumulation of bureaucratic documents over their lifetimes (Chu 2010).

In South Africa, migrants similarly understood themselves through a personal dossier of passports with identification numbers, work visas, official seals, and stamped dates of entry and exit. These connections were most apparent to me when my interlocutors talked about their legal status—having or not having an ID. A state-issued South African ID, such as an unexpired visa or proof of permanent residence, enabled participation in the formal economy. An ID allowed one to open a bank account, send remittances, register a business, and travel to and from China and South Africa. An ID afforded a degree of daily security. All racialized migrants, documented or undocumented, Chinese or non-Chinese, faced insidious harassment from police and immigration officers. Police set up roadblocks near the China Malls and Cyrildene Chinatown to "randomly" stop vehicles to check IDs. The Johannesburg Metropolitan Police Department, which had no jurisdiction over immigration, nevertheless extorted bribes from migrants lacking English fluency and legal knowledge. On occasion, customs, immigration, and revenue services would raid the China Malls or Chinatown. Most of the time, Chinese without IDs were detained and had to pay thousands of rand to be released. But unlike southern Africans, who were deported and would return to China City a few weeks later, Chinese were never deported.

Legal status is more fluid than I initially understood. As Chu explains the moral orientations of villagers in Fuzhou, legality and illegality are not mutually exclusive, static positions but "distinct phases in a trajectory of becoming" (2010, 93). Legal status is something to work toward. In South Africa, migrants could lose legal status overnight when visas expired. In the other direction, migrants who entered without authorization could attain legal status through a seemingly alchemical process. I never understood how people managed to achieve legal status within the bureaucracy of two states. Mr. Zheng, of course, held the missing piece. His work entailed facilitating entrances into South Africa and making IDs. In 2020, after he retired as Chinatown boss, I finally asked him about how he did his work. Surprisingly forthcoming, he explained how he transitioned people from "illegal" to "legal," a workaround that came straight from the upper echelons of the state: a senior DHA official, an Afrikaner man in Pretoria. As Mr. Zheng explained, in the computerized immigration system, each person is given a barcode, a number attached to the date of first entry "that follows a person for life," like the identification number that links Chinese citizens to their personal records in the national database. This barcode is the singular identifier of a Chinese national's South African file. Mr. Zheng had a DHA insider lifting barcode stickers. Clients would destroy their passports on entering South Africa, thereby erasing the paper trail of exits and entrances, and request a new visa. One trader from Fuqing pointed out the cooperation of the Chinese embassy: "Everyone in this country wants to make a buck. The embassy also wants money in this country. They just close one eye." Mr. Zheng affixed the stolen barcodes to blank passports and brought them to the airport, where an immigration officer retroactively changed the date of entry. Next he took them to Pretoria to run through the DHA's computer system to ensure the document could withstand the highest level of scrutiny. As he explained, only with the barcode would a dossier be complete (*dangan shi wanzhengle*) and provide full legibility as "legal." He took great pride in the rigor of his method and ability to mobilize social connections, albeit these social relations (*guanxi*) were all bought with money. This was not only a lucrative profession but the source of his reputation. Through underground practices, ordinary Chinese migrants circumvented state rules to overcome the limits placed on their mobility and potentiality, whether by traversing borders or, as chapter 7 examines, moving money. Extralegal practices are part of an alternative moral economy of circumventing the state to take control of one's destiny.

Notes on Sojourner Colonialism

The Chinese Century captures the promise of a Sinocentric future, a hetero-patriarchal nationalist vision of familial and national prosperity under the Belt and Road Initiative and the Chinese Dream. For the Chinese women and men I met, Johannesburg was a stop along the way to realizing this elusive promise. Collectively their stories are representative of the large-scale lasting effects of privatization, labor casualization, and rural reforms that drive inequality in China and south–south migrations. The unevenness and speed of China's rise *in* China instills a sense of foreclosure, belatedness, and stasis, temporal conditions created by the state. To fulfill alternative destinies in China, migrants forecast emerging markets and take a detour to South Africa to catch up. For both individual entrepreneurial migrants and Chinese state enterprises, the African continent functions as a frontier for capital accumulation and a spatial fix for resolving market reform's domestic paradoxes. A spatiotemporal analysis of Chinese entrepreneurial migration elucidates a sojourner mobility. These migrants are sojourners, not settlers like Chinese South Africans who have planted roots, and they are not driven by a desire to stay but a reproductive futurism oriented toward a rising China. In South Africa, sojourners experience dislocation between the past and future of China (where the speed of development has left them behind and to where they hope to return) and the present in South Africa (where they do not wish to stay yet often do, indefinitely). Chinese migration to South Africa is an instance of globalization *from below*: below the state, and at the bottom of global orders in which temporary downward mobility toward the Global South might secure more permanent upward mobility in China. Ordinary migrants rely on clandestine channels to circumvent visa regimes rooted in longer histories of anti-Asian laws and racialized xenophobia. They live on the edge of legality, formal economy, and regulatory regimes to maximize profit and geographical flexibility, and they rely on migration facilitators to make themselves both legible and illegible to states. Although dominant discourses envisage them as foot soldiers for Beijing, their aspirations, migration routes, and legal precarity indicate otherwise.

On a world-historical scale, the unevenness of Sino-African engagements stems from the differential incorporation of Africa and China into the capitalist world system and colonial legacies. If the underemployed Chinese semiproletariat can find a spatial fix and become petty entrepreneurs in South Africa, South Africans and southern African migrants cannot (Mbembe 2021, 38–39). China was able to rid itself of Western powers and build a strong state and economy that rivals the West. But decolonization unfolded differently in South Africa and southern Africa, which have been vulnerable to neocolonial predation, structural adjustment, and foreign investment. Herein lies the fundamental unevenness of Sino-African encounters that plays out in the daily exchanges between African and Chinese actors. But Chinese migrants understand this asymmetry through developmental imaginaries that naturalize a global racial hierarchy of people and nations.

The sketch of sojourner colonialism I have offered in this chapter is the first of two parts. Entrepreneurial migration entails making profit and getting those profits back to China, an extralegal economy of extraction. In chapter 7, I return to the other half of the equation: how profit is remitted to China, which lays bare the underdeveloping, colonial effects of entrepreneurial migration, and what makes sojourning *colonial*. Finally, the Chinese sojourner needs to be situated within histories of racial capitalism and settler colonial relations. As racial migrants to a settler colony, Chinese migrants inherit the intermediary position of Asian traders, nonwhite settlers, within South Africa's colonial, apartheid, and postapartheid economies. I now turn to this set of colonial and racial entanglements.

3

Afro-Asian Adjacencies

The invasion of the Asiatics into their business thoroughfares was a serious menace to the future development of the Colony. They had been told that every Asiatic trader in this place employed two or three hands. If these shops belonging to Asiatics were necessary in their midst, then they were shops which white men might have opened, which white men alone could have obtained a living from.

Rand Daily Mail, "Asiatic Traders," 1905a

In the last five years, more than 6,000 Chinese shops have popped up in every dorp [town] of South Africa, effectively forming the country's biggest-ever chain store. And, say retail experts, it amounts to a largely unlawful enterprise that threatens to destroy local commerce and cost the taxman billions. Suddenly there's a Chinese shop (maybe three) in every suburb, village and town in South Africa. Every single one.

Welz and Schoonbee, *Noseweek,* "Howzit China?," 2012

China City is a cosmopolitan place where Afro-Asian worlds, old diasporas, and new migrations collide. Inside the two-story complex are four hundred shops run by Chinese, Indian, and Pakistani migrants who arrived in the early 2000s from Fujian, Guangdong, Gujarat, Punjab, and Karachi, as well as a few Indian South Africans. At China City, Chinese traders and workers outnumber South Asians three to one. The mall's multiracial migrant communities infuse the space with a kaleidoscopic social vitality. Black South African and Nigerian security guards patrol the corridors and joke around with traders and Malawian and Zimbabwean shopworkers, whom they nickname by home country. The wholesale market attracts shopkeepers, entrepreneurs, and street vendors from all over the city and the larger region. On weekends, working-class Afrikaner, Black, Indian, and mixed-race "Coloured" South Africans pack the mall in search of bargains.

Chinese, Indian, and Pakistani traders cordially coexist as neighbors in a cheek-by-jowl cosmopolitanism laced with geopolitical frictions and competition. The marketplace is loosely stratified by ethnicity, nationality, and commodity. Pakistani migrants specialize in cell phone accessories and electronics repair. These are compact operations that require only a few square meters and can be subleased from a Chinese tenant, with a faded yellow-painted line on the floor demarcating shop borders. Over generations, Indian South Africans have imported exquisite fabrics and tailored garments that come from the Oriental Plaza in nearby Fordsburg, the city's premier Indian business district, which was founded during apartheid. At the China Malls, design-a-curtain shops abound, where Indian and Pakistani newcomers employ Malawian tailors to sew custom curtains from Chinese-made fabrics. Chinese traders wholesale polyester-cotton imitations of South Africa's iconic *shweshwe* fabric and "authentic" curios imported from China. There is a minority of African tenant-traders, including Cameroonian, Ethiopian, and Senegalese traders who sell the same mass-produced fabrics and curios, and Egyptian and Somali traders who deal in knockoff luxury fragrances. With the greatest access to supply chains, there is nothing Chinese don't sell: clothing, shoes, headscarves, wigs, birthday party decorations, wedding invitations, furniture, electronics, toys, cosmetics, handbags, and herbal medicines. The China Malls have become a one-stop shop for South Africans and a visible sign of a future made in China.

The revival of the 150-year Chinese presence in South Africa and the global rise of China have reenergized the nineteenth-century "Chinese Question" concerning the so-called yellow peril—the threat Chinese immigrant laborers posed to white settler colonies (M. M. Ngai 2021). Today the Chinese Question is about the dawning of the Chinese Century and the geopolitical and economic uncertainties it poses to the world, and specifically the West. This chapter examines the pervasive anxiety about the ubiquitous Chinese shop and the Chinese trader in South African popular imaginaries. This anxiety is not new. As the epigraphs from the South African press make clear, the Chinese trader of the new millennium resembles the "Asiatic" Indian trader from the turn of the twentieth century. Understanding contemporary Sinophobia, the racialization of the Chinese trader, and the politics of Chinese wholesale malls led me to the archive to excavate longer relational histories of Asian racialization in South Africa, including Chinese and Indian emigrants, laborers, settlers, sojourners, and traders and the spaces where they worked. These figures and spaces have gone by many names: the Indian or Chinese "coolie" laborer on sugar plantations and gold mines; the Indian hawker, peddler, trader, or shopkeeper and the "Asiatic Bazaar" of early Johannesburg; the Indian *dukka* (native trading shop) and Chinese *spaza* shop during apartheid; and the China Malls and Oriental Plaza of today. China City emerges within the convergence of South Africa's mineral revolution and post-Mao China's economic reform. It is also where the pasts, presents, and futures of "Asian capitalism" meet.

In this chapter, I examine the historical *adjacencies* among multiple racial figures that underpin South African views of Chinese migrant traders today. When sifting through articles in the *Rand Daily Mail* (RDM), Johannesburg's English-language newspaper, I noticed that Chinese and Indian people appeared side by side but rarely together. Early twentieth-century stories of unruly Chinamen and Indian shopkeepers populated the edges of the same pages. During apartheid, the names of Chinese and Indian shopkeepers were listed together in reports of "Asiatic traders" in white areas. From leafing through the RDM, the closeness yet separateness between Chinese and Indians provides a glimpse into the logics of categorization, or rather the illogics of the colonial archive and obfuscation of entangled processes (Lowe 2015).[1] These proximities in print illuminate the coeval trajectories of Chinese and Indian migration and racialization that produced them as distinct yet intertwined figures of the *Asiatic* and *coolie*, terms that were made meaningful in relation to the terms *African*, *Black*, *European*, *Native*, and *white*.[2] In this way, Chinese and Indian peoples have been twin figures of

Asian labor and capital and diasporic cotravelers from the arrival of Chinese and Indian laborers to the rise of China and India as global superpowers.

Adjacency is inspired by the Sino-Indian proximities I encountered at China City and in the archive and comparative and relational approaches to colonial racialization. Colonial racialization is specific to how settler colonialism, imperialism, and capitalism are constituted through logics of land and labor. In colonial Alaska, Native peoples were "Asian / Asian-adjacent" to Asian laborers brought to cultivate Indigenous land (Pegues 2021, 10). In North America, an "evolving triangulation" of Native, settler, and alien has been critical to the expansion of white property. Racialization is an expression of settler power and its capacity to racially differentiate (Day 2015, 33). I use adjacency to tease out many kinds of entanglements: social, spatial, temporal, historical, global, and racial. Adjacency builds on Lisa Lowe's (2015) conceptualization of intimacy, a heuristic that draws together processes of slavery, settler colonialism, imperialism, and indenture to illuminate the multitudinous connections and relations among laboring peoples across sites and archives. Adjacency brings into focus colonial and racial entanglements connecting Chinese and Indians and lineages they share as laborers and merchants in South Africa. It names the logics that produce "Chinese" and "Indian" as the same or distinct subgroups constituting "Asian" and attends to the indeterminacy and contingency of racial categorization. Analytically, adjacency names a proximate relation of being side by side but not intersecting. The concept suggests ever-near-parallel tracks of migration and racialization and the gap between them while emphasizing what does not converge or overlap. As a form of sociality, adjacency implies intimacy, friendship, and affiliation with a degree of remove. Adjacency is not quite solidarity.

Through the lens of adjacency, in this chapter, I peel back another set of historical layers and relational entanglements around the Chinese migrant as entrepreneur, worker, and sojourner. The Chinese trader is intelligible through the ex-indentured Indian laborer-cum-settler and Chinese laborer that go back to the earliest period of the white settler colony. In this moment, as before, the Chinese or "Asian" trader is a highly visible, politically contested figure in relation to other racialized Black, Indian, and white subjects. Likewise, the Chinese Question today cannot be understood through histories of Chinese migration, diaspora, and exclusion alone but is enmeshed with the Asiatic Question and the colonial Labor Question and concerning African labor and Indian settlement. These historical racial and colonial entanglements are necessary for grasping how Chinese sojourner colonialism is implicated in settler colonial relations in South Africa today.

This chapter traces another palimpsestic layer of the mining belt mall by situating it within the wider historical and geographic expanse of the Afro-Asian and Indian Ocean worlds. China City's success as a wholesale market is partially owed to the commercial intimacies between Chinese and Indian traders and African consumers under colonialism and apartheid. By taking a centennial view, I show that the Chinese trader is not a new figure of the Chinese-led future but as old as the colony itself. Like the City of Gold, racial figures are composites of colonial racial forms and relations.

I begin this story in the sugarcane and gold fields where Chinese and Indian laborers became conjoined through imperial circuits and colonial categories. Chinese and Indian racialization as "Asiatic" and "coolie" was triangulated with the "Native" laborer. These racial entanglements inform Chinese racialization and Afro-Asian relationalities today. Colonial stereotypes have endured, as has the racial adjacency between Chinese and Indians. Returning to China City, I trace how these historic affinities play out in the everyday interactions between African, Chinese, and South Asian migrants. Inspired by Indian Ocean methodologies, I read the mall as a living archive of mobilities, encounters, memories, and sensoria (Srinivas, Ng'weno, and Jeychandran 2020). The mining belt mall and Cyrildene Chinatown are only the topmost layers of Afro-Asian worlds. The longer perspective illustrates the enduring, malleable, and relational character of Asian racialization as "foreign" capital and labor.

Sugar and Gold

Between 1860 and 1911, over 150,000 Indian indentured laborers from lower castes in Bihar, Madras, and the United Provinces were brought to the sugarcane plantations of the Natal, Britain's "Garden Colony," as a stopgap for a shortage of Zulu labor. They were joined by "passenger Indians," independent immigrants who paid their own way, including Bania and Muslim merchants, financiers, traders, and peasants from coastal Gujarat. In South Africa, the free Indian population became artisans, peasant farmers, and traders supplying "coolie rations" to laborers (Meer 1985, 50; Hart and Padayachee 2013, 687, 701). Indian laborers, who were British imperial citizens, were permitted to renew or remain in South Africa after completing their contracts. For a time they could purchase crown land with the cost of their return passage. Ex-indentured laborers and free traders from Natal migrated to Johannesburg in the Transvaal. By 1905 an "Asiatic invasion" was underway, with Indians outnumbering white people in Natal (M. M. Ngai 2017, 68).[3] After the South

African War (1899–1902) between the Afrikaners and the British, the latter won control of the Transvaal but then faced a postwar labor shortage in the mines. Between 1904 and 1910, sixty-four thousand contract laborers from northern China docked in Durban and journeyed by rail to the Rand, where they joined African laborers. Chinese and Indian laborers and traders arrived at a moment when ideas of race, labor, and citizenship were in flux. In 1910 the Cape, Natal, Orange River, and Transvaal Colonies became the Union of South Africa, the nation-state that unified the Afrikaners and the British in a common project of white supremacy, settler colonialism, and capitalism. In 1911 the importation of Asian labor was abolished across the union. Shortly thereafter, South Africa instituted the Natives Land Act of 1913 to create an industrial reserve of African labor, consequently making labor shortages and the need to import Asian labor obsolete. This transitional moment laid the foundation for colonial racial capitalism in South Africa.

Paralleling Indian migration patterns, independent Chinese migration tracked alongside indenture. Since the 1870s, free Chinese, who became the forebears of South Africa's Chinese diaspora, arrived in South Africa from Canton, the mercantile and emigration hub near the Pearl River delta. Seeking gold, they journeyed to Australia, California, and South Africa. Free Chinese traversed the Indian Ocean and South China Sea on British steamships that also carried Indian laborers; both made their way to South Africa via Mauritius (Yap and Man 1996, 36–37). Limited by anti-Asian legislation, free Chinese, like Indians, also became shopkeepers. In South Africa, the Asian racial form brought together Chinese and Indians as "Asiatics" and "coolies"—two Asian groups, two labor regimes, and two sister colonies—as twin racial figures. Processes of racialization were synchronous, overlapping, differential, and economic. As Renisa Mawani writes of colonial proximities in British Vancouver, racial migrants were "constituted dialectically against one another and in a shifting and unstable racial order" (2009, 5). The imbrication of Asian racialization with the formation of the white settler nation-state is what has made these racial figures, categories, and adjacencies so enduring.

In southern Africa, Asian migrants triangulated Black and white racial classifications into "Europeans, Coolies, and Kafirs," ushering in "a new era of racialization in southern Africa" (Pillay 2017, 34, 23). *Coolie* (*kuli*) was a term for menial Chinese and Indian laborers across Africa and the Americas. The use of the term began with Portuguese travelers passing through ports and waters en route to Asia, and by the eighteenth century, it took on a transcontinental definition referring to Chinese and Indian contract laborers "shipped abroad." In the postabolition era, when Asian labor was in high demand, the term was associated with Asian laborers who systemically replaced enslaved Africans on sugar plantations (Jung 2005, 679; Yun 2007). As Lowe observes, "In the British colonial archive, the use of 'coolie' to refer to Asian labor from China, India, and other parts of the world suggests that, from the British colonial perspective, it was the instrumental use of a particular category of labor, rather than the precise Asian origin of the workers, that was emphasized" (2015, 25). In South Africa, *coolie* functioned as a malleable category of labor *and* race and described people from East Asia, South Asia, the Middle East, and North Africa. As a category of labor, *coolie* operated on a logic of fungible national origins whereby each group could be compared by productive capacities. As a racial category, *coolie* became a term for all Indians, regardless of labor status, class, region, ethnicity, or religion. Its expanded usage effaced the distinction between free and indentured Indians, thus resolving the problem of Indian claims to imperial citizenship as British subjects.[4] In Johannesburg, Indian merchants distanced themselves as "Arabs" but were still reclassified and relocated to the Coolie Location (Datta 2011, 67). Among free and indentured Indians, the term *coolie* dissolved the distinction between them through race.

Through their racial adjacency, Chinese laborers were absorbed into the ever-capacious *coolie* category. In mine records and newspapers, Chinese mine workers appeared as "coolie labor" and "Chinamen," in contradistinction to the "Indian coolie." The interchangeable use of *coolie* and *Asiatic* to describe Chinese and Indians demonstrated the porosity of these categories (Harris 2010, 149; Huynh 2008a). But the referents of these terms were foremostly Indian, which was a matter of population.[5] In one of the few comparative studies of Chinese and Indian indenture in South Africa, Karen Harris notes, "the Asian question became the Indian question" (2010, 156). The approximate interchangeability of Chinese and Indians as "Asiatics" or "coolies" emblematizes their racial adjacency. A feature of Asian racialization, adjacency denotes the ways these terms—*Chinese, Indian, Asiatic*, and *coolie*—function as *near* synonyms.

The Chinese Question was implicitly formed within the more widely discussed Asiatic Question in the pages of the RDM. On the Asiatic Question, Transvaal governor Alfred Milner wishfully hoped that the Indian government would limit the emigration of petty traders "who are out of place here" but encourage "the introduction, under conditions ensuring their ultimate return to their native country, of Indian laborers, whom we greatly need" (quoted in *Rand Daily Mail* 1904a). Indians presented an "Asiatic invasion" the moment they crossed over from unfree to free, laborer to merchant; as a *Transvaal Leader* article from 1906 claimed, "The indentured coolie of to-day is the free man of tomorrow, and the free man becomes the trader" (quoted in M. M. Ngai 2017, 68). As nonwhite settlers and economic competitors, Indian traders stirred "trade jealousy" among white settlers. The status of Indian traders was a flashpoint for the Transvaal's future. As Milner stated, "The problem does not begin and end with a shopkeeper's quadrille, but it is more far-reaching than the questions whether this country shall be governed by Englishmen or Boers, or whether its mines shall be worked by Kaffirs or Chinese" (quoted in *Rand Daily Mail* 1904b). The Asiatic Question and the Chinese Question were enmeshed through concerns about securing labor and in the struggle between the Afrikaners and the British over which white minority would prevail. Chinese and Indian peoples could be combined or distinguished in the service of capital accumulation, white settlement, and imperial expansion.

The Rand was one node within the British Empire and global gold rush of the nineteenth century. American, Australian, and British prospectors, miners, and workers who flocked to the goldfields, including Cantonese in search of the Gam Saan (Gold Mountain; M. M. Ngai 2021). Global regimes of migrant labor were built on the successes and failures of each other and drew on the shared transoceanic infrastructure for transport and finance. The British experience with Chinese and Indian labor on the sugar plantations of Mauritius and the West Indies preceded the use of Indian labor in Natal's sugar estates, which subsequently informed the use of Chinese labor in the mines (Harris 2010, 149). As a testament to their fungibility, Chinese were considered for sugarcane fields and the Indians for gold mines (Yap and Man 1996, 20–21). When making the case for Chinese labor on the Rand, Lord Harris cited "more than 50 years the exportation of Asiatics from East to West." Comparing Chinese and Indian labor, "I do not think you can get a better workman than the Chinese coolie anywhere in the world. But the Indian is very easily managed, very docile, very patient, and very laborious, although, not being a meat-eater, he is not able to put into his work the physical strength of one who is" (quoted in *Rand Daily Mail* 1904e). Colonial administrators wagered that the harsh labor conditions in the mines would be unfit for Indian laborers who were still British subjects. But Chinese laborers were another story. The devastation of treaty port imperialism, the First Sino-Japanese War, natural disaster, and famine left the Qing government unable to refuse. Additionally, the importation of Indian laborers could hasten developments in the Transvaal, where a coalition of Chinese and Indians, led by Leung Quinn and Mohandas Gandhi, were protesting anti-Asian laws. The

Chinese and Indians were differentiated as British and non-British subjects, but both were legally "Asiatic." As Gandhi characterized, they were "strange bedfellows in this struggle" (quoted in Yap and Man 1996, 145).

The importation of Chinese labor took lessons from Natal to safeguard against replicating an invasion of Chinese in the Transvaal. Indian settlement was the "object lesson" of Natal (Harris 2010, 155). Whereas formerly indentured Indian men and women were permitted to remain, the Chinese—all men—were repatriated with no contract extensions. As Karen L. Harris points out, "the indentured Chinese represented a temporary expedient and could never, like the Indians, become ex-indentured and part of South African society as the Indian could" (2010, 154). Furthermore, before the Chinese arrived, Asian exclusion acts were already in effect in all of South Africa's colonies. Although these acts were designed to curtail Indian immigration, Chinese were absorbed into the legislation as "Asiatics." Tu Huynh similarly observes that Chinese laborers, in conceptual and geographical proximity to Natal Indians, were seen as a "commercial parasite that threatened to overrun a society" (2012, 148).

The contemporaneous histories of Chinese and Indian indenture reveal the adjacencies of colonial racialization and interminority relations. Linked through British imperialism, Chinese and Indian migrant laborers and traders traveled together as twin figures of the "Asiatic" and "coolie" over the long twentieth century. Racial categories were shaped through global labor migrations, geographical imaginaries, transcontinental labor regimes, and settler ideologies of nativism, protectionism, and white supremacy. Chinese and Indian peoples were made commensurate as alien labor *and* capital of *almost* fungible national origins while unevenly inhabiting the categories used to describe them. Capital constructed this racial adjacency and mobilized this similitude and difference. The Chinese were proximate to Indians as laborers, distinguished by imperial status, and racialized in contradistinction to African labor. Asian racialization turned on the adjacency between Chinese and Indians and another peripheral relation: the juxtaposition between "coolie" and "Native."

Black and Yellow Perils

When faced with a postwar labor shortage, British administrators and Randlords weighed the Chinese Question of importing Chinese labor against the problem of coercing sufficient Native labor from Portuguese East Africa and from South Africa. Chinese were chosen as a matter of immediacy. As H. J.

and R. E. Simons note, "There was no time to spare . . . they wanted a ready-to-hand proletariat at the lowest possible cost who would restore the mines to full working capacity without delay. . . . They would not wait for taxation and land seizures to turn African peasants into work seekers" (quoted in B. M. Magubane 1979, 79). Between alien and Indigenous labor, transporting a Chinese "ready-to-hand proletariat" overseas was faster than administering mechanisms to create an Indigenous proletariat. As one administrator rationalized, "England's position in South Africa was endangered by the native's unwillingness to work; hence the only alternative was to import Chinese." In the postwar crisis, "the coming danger in South Africa was not the Yellow Peril, but the Black Peril" (*Rand Daily Mail* 1904c). Between the threat of Asians "swamping" the Transvaal and "native indolence," the government passed the Transvaal Labour Importation Ordinance in 1904 to bring Chinese contract laborers to the mines (Kynoch 2005, 534). In 1907, Sir George Farrar addressed a parliament divided over the Chinese Question: "If there was labour in the country, labour indigenous to the country, that labour would be taken and not coolie labour" (quoted in *Rand Daily Mail* 1907c). One proponent of the importation scheme clarified that "it would be foolish to deny the existence of a feeling of repugnance to the whole system. We tolerate the Chinese. We do not like them" (*Rand Daily Mail* 1907b). Crystallizing these dynamics, a cartoon in the *Graphic* depicts white men supervising the arrival of Chinese men at the mining compound while African "strikers" leave.

Following the abolition of slavery in the Americas, the Chinese contract laborer there took a "liminal, ambiguous intermediary position . . . to supplement, replace, and obscure the labor previously performed by slaves, yet to be differentially distinguished from them" (Lowe 2015, 27). Lisa Yun pushes back against linear narratives of enslavement to freedom in which Chinese coolies are ambivalently represented as transitional figures. The transitional paradigm retrenches binaries of slave/free and Black/white and racializes Asians as intermediaries between these terms. Coolie and slave economies were not distinct but "concomitant and coproductive" (2007, 7). Informed by scholarship on indenture in the Americas, I place Asian unfree/bonded labor in South Africa alongside the migrant labor system, the primary engine of colonial racial capitalism in the Transvaal. Linked through British imperialism, these colonial labor systems were coeval. The Chinese supplemented the labor previously performed by Africans while being viewed as distinct. Chinese labor importation was concomitant with the migrant labor system and served as a stopgap before it emerged full-fledged and would make labor shortages obsolete. The importation of Chinese labor

3.1   "Farewell to the Mines: Strikers Leaving Their Quarters." *Graphic*,
July 7, 1907. Courtesy of Museum Africa.

directly undercut African wages and indirectly set the stage for land seizures.
In the Transvaal, heated debates over Chinese labor secured a political win
for the Afrikaner Het Volk party that paved the way for the Natives Land
Act of 1913, which was instrumental in accelerating Indigenous dispossession
and creating a self-reproducing reserve—a "ready-to-hand proletariat"—for
the mines. As Mae M. Ngai bluntly states, "The resolution of the Chinese
Question cleared the way for white South Africans to tackle the underlying
problems of mine labor—the recruitment and retention of African labor and
the employment of unskilled whites in mining—while ensuring that South
Africa would be built as a 'white man's country'" (2021, 267).

The mines entered Africans and Chinese into a zero-sum equation of
racialized labor, pitting them against each other at every turn. Blackness
became the other side of Chinese racialization. The comparisons administrators and Randlords drew between Chinese and African labor set the "model"
Chinese worker against the "indolent" native. They were crudely compared
as units of labor through cost to recruit and maintain, number of months of
employment, weight of gold output, and frequency of "disturbance." Although
the cost of transporting and maintaining a Chinese workforce was double that
of Africans, supporters of the importation scheme praised the efficiency and

productivity of Chinese, who could become "the most efficient unskilled labour force in the world" (*Rand Daily Mail* 1907a). The emphasis on efficiency is part of a larger trope of Asian economic efficiency (Day 2016; Lowe 1996; Lye 2005), and it is specific to the profitability of gold mining. Despite the precious metal's importance, the high production costs associated with low-grade ore and the internationally fixed price of gold made profits marginal (M. M. Ngai 2021; Richardson 1982). Juxtapositions of "Kaffir versus Chinese," "Native versus Chinese supply," and "Yellow versus Black" filled the pages of the RDM. For instance, "The Chinese coolie, hard upon whose introduction the output has steadily increased, has already proved himself to be a very useful worker, and in gaining further experience should surpass his co-labourer, the Kaffir" (*Rand Daily Mail* 1905c). An iconography of juxtaposing "lazy kaffirs" with "industrious Chinese" reinforced this coracialization (Huynh 2008b, 402).

Throughout this story of settler, Native, and migrant, relations of adjacency and antagonism recur. Afro-Asian relations of gold were akin to those of sugar. In Natal, Indian laborers were introduced to weaken the bargaining power of Africans. Africans and Indians were separated and made to fear one another. As Fatima Meer details, Africans and Indians "were at the same time kept within 'viewing' distance of each other, so that they could be constantly reminded of their strange and different ways. There was the use of African whipping boys on the estates, and the sentencing of a transgressing coolie to the kaffir barrack where he could be terrorised and ridiculed as the master intended ... the appointment of an Indian overseer over African mill-hands and the use of African police to suppress Indian strikes" (1985, 54). In the mines, Chinese worked underground while Africans occupied the most poorly paid surface positions; interactions between them were minimal by design. Tensions occasionally erupted into fights, including one involving the deployment of African mine police to quell protesting Chinese mine workers, which set off a larger conflict between African and Chinese laborers (Kynoch 2005, 533).

In addition to the specific context of South Africa, Chinese racialization drew from global anti-Chinese ideology, the product of more than a half century of Chinese and European encounters in the New World (M. M. Ngai 2021, 247). Racial imagery circulated across metropoles and settler colonies through postcards, telegrams, and print media. Despite being touted as model workers, Chinese became notorious for riots, desertion, violence, gambling, opium, and the "unnatural vices" (Huynh 2012; Kynoch 2005). The invading horde materialized in the form of mine workers roaming around the "Cantonese quarter," the area that later became First Chinatown. On occasion, mine workers broke into white homes and farms, stealing money to repay gambling debts. Racial anxieties were contiguous and compounding. The threat Chinese posed to white property and social order amalgamated settler fears of an Asiatic invasion and the "Black Peril" sexual threat of African domestic workers in white homes. Within a few years, the British experiment with Chinese labor ended; Chinese laborers were indispensable to the mining elite but undesirable to white residents. In the metropole, liberal concerns about "Chinese slavery" in the mines divided the parliament during the 1907 election. By 1910 all Chinese had been repatriated, leaving few descendants to carry this history.

The adjacencies among African, Chinese, and Indian laborers—embodiments of the Asiatic Question, the colonial Chinese Question, and the Labor Question—shaped Chinese racialization in the early twentieth century and produced the Asian laborer-turned-trader at their interstices. In South Africa, Asian racialization has oscillated between Chinese and Indian, labor and capital, free and unfree, and migrant and settler. Asian migrants complicated the Black/white relations of settler colonialism in South Africa. Chinese and Indians came to South Africa under both "free" and coerced conditions. Alien labor supplemented Indigenous labor, and settlers were inserted as "middlemen" into the economic structure of colonial racial capitalism. Asian traders economically threatened white settlers, and as such their commercial activities were severely restricted, but they also benefited from colonial land and taxation policies that dispossessed Africans. Asian capital has been continuously imagined as a national threat, anthropomorphized as the Indian trader at the turn of the twentieth century or the Chinese trader who has inherited these racial relations and colonial entanglements in the postapartheid era. Even as South Africa's citizenry has radically changed, the threat of the Asian trader and "economic modalities of Asian racialization" (Day 2016, 6) have persisted.

An Enduring Racial Form

Fighting the Coolie

Before the Chinese trader of the early 2000s, there were the Chinese laborer and the Indian trader at the turn of the twentieth century. Johannesburg's Indian traders were part of a wider Gujarati commercial diaspora in eastern Africa and South Africa and a "bazaar economy," a global circuit of wholesale markets and financial networks parallel to the European world economy (Markovits 2007; Raya 1995). From the 1860s onward, Gujarati merchants seized the opportunity to sell "Oriental goods"—souvenirs, curios, silk, and cotton textiles—to American and British consumers and tourists in Australia, South Africa, and the United States. In colonial South Africa, Indian traders represented an economic threat of outsize proportions. Returning to the RDM quote that opens this chapter, "They had not come in small units; they had not come in such numbers as to seriously menace their commercial development." By Manichaean logic, Indian traders took away commercial and employment opportunities from white men. Every Indian shop was one "which white men might have opened, which white men alone could have obtained a living from." On course to outnumber white people, "alien" Indians threatened settler futures. Toward inciting violence among readers, "Now, were they going to stand by calmly and see the white people gradually elbowed out of the town by Asiatics, who were just as alien to them as any man who came from the South Sea Islands or the North Pole?" One solution, the author of the RDM article suggested, was to "lynch them" (*Rand Daily Mail* 1905a).

Trading licenses, immigration restrictions, consumer boycotts, and forced relocation were deployed to curb "unrestricted Asiatic trading." In the inaugural city plan, the Coolie Location was contiguous with the Kaffir Location near the city center. Following an outbreak of the bubonic plague, Indian traders were scapegoated, and the Coolie Location was razed to the ground. New coolie and Native locations, along with an "Asiatic bazaar" for trading, were proposed on Johannesburg's outskirts. "The advantages of keeping the native quarters completely away from the white population, will be obvious to everyone [*sic*]," the planners stated. The relocation of Indian traders was less obvious. At stake in its creation was "the existence and future of Johannesburg, as a white man's town in a white man's country." Based on fears of competition, contagion, and vice, poor white people and Indians should be kept "completely apart." African and Indian populations would be placed together to create a self-contained market: "In addition to trading in the bazaar itself, the proximity of the Kaffir location will give every opportunity for commercial dealings with the natives" (*Rand Daily Mail* 1904f). Since Johannesburg's inception, city planners had sought a symbiosis between the racialized groups on its peripheries. Afro-Asian proximities were by design.

Throughout the twentieth century, white people continued to call for boycotting Asian traders. A 1913 story in the RDM addressed white consumers:

> Many of you . . . are busy making a coffin for yourselves and your posterity. You deal with the Asiatic because his goods are cheaper than those of the European, and you forget that the Coolie, like the

Kaffir, can live much cheaper than the white man, and can therefore sell cheaper. You forget that the money of this white trader remains here and is brought into circulation; that the white trader lives together with you here, often supporting your church, whilst the money of the Asiatic is sent out of the country. (*Rand Daily Mail* 1913)

The future of the nation hung in the balance: purchasing from the Indian trader amounted to "digging a grave for yourselves and your children" (*Rand Daily Mail* 1913). The overseas circulation of money epitomized the foreignness of capital. The Indian trader, perpetually foreign in their "cheap" way of life, took money out of the pockets of white people and local circulation at a moment when the Transvaal relied on loans from Britain. Throughout eastern Africa and South Africa, Gujarati merchants were accused of accounting in Gujarati script to evade taxes and underreport earnings. Endogamous networks of credit, trade, and overseas remittances connoted economic disloyalty (Aiyar 2015, 11; Oonk 2013, 151–53). During the World War II heyday of black-market profiteering, a stereotype emerged of the cunning Indian shopkeeper profiting off poor African customers and operating outside state control. This lasting perception fueled boycott campaigns led by European colonists to African political leaders after independence (Aiyar 2015, 17–18; Hart and Padayachee 2013, 692–93). During apartheid's early years, the RDM published an editorial titled "The Immigrants Oust Afrikaners: Fighting the 'Coolie,'" which stated,

We have only one means against the Coolie I say with emphasis Coolie, for we on the platteland [veld] do not know the word Indian. . . . To fight the Coolie there is only one method. We can forget repatriation. Fight him through commerce. The Native will pass by a Coolie shop for a European's shop, but, oddly enough, a very great section of our Afrikaans-speaking people in particular will pass by a European's shop to go to a Coolie shop. . . . Do our people not realize that the Coloured is not a danger but rather an asset to harness against the Coolie and the Native? (*Rand Daily Mail* 1956)

Though they were written more than four decades apart, there are striking similarities in these RDM pieces from 1913 and 1956. Over generations, Indian merchants remain perpetually foreign "Coolies." The Afrikaner author of the 1956 article then calls on Coloured Afrikaans speakers to align with white people against Indian and Black South Africans. Recalling the

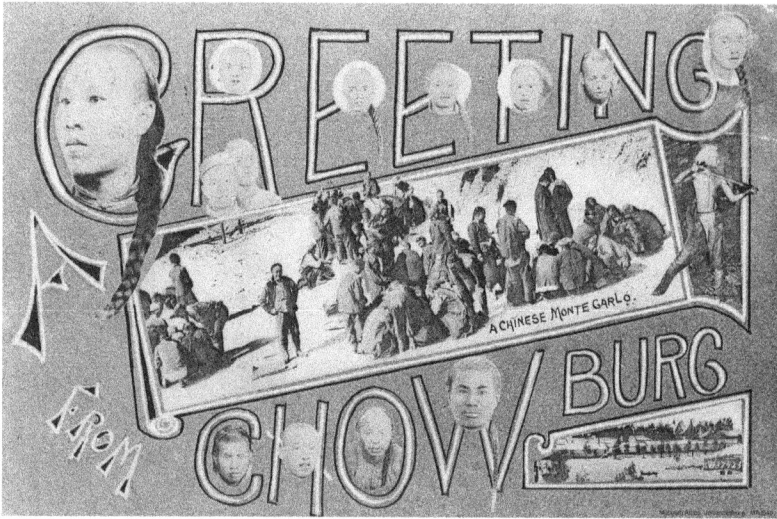

3.2   "Greeting from Chowburg," postcard, ca. 1906. Courtesy of
       Museum Africa.

Asiatic Question from fifty years earlier, if Indian citizens could not be repatriated through state power, they could be boycotted through mass anti-
Asian sentiment.

Like Indian traders, Chinese mine workers were scrutinized for economic deviance. "Both the northern and southern Chinese are inveterate
gamblers," the RDM alerted readers; "a careful lookout will be kept for anything of this sort, and especially that cases of men taking their discharge early,
after remitting large sums, or taking large sums of money with them" (*Rand
Daily Mail* 1904d). Additionally, there was the accusation that "the Chinese
spend little or none of their pay here, but remit their money to China, so that
the community as a whole, and the trading community in particular, derives
no benefit from their presence in the country" (*Rand Daily Mail* 1905b).
The image of the Chinese gambler circulated alongside the Indian trader.
The picture postcard "Greeting from Chowburg," printed in an Orientalist
typeface, features a gambling scene captioned "A Chinese Monte Carlo" in
an allusion to the famous casino by the sea. Chinese underground financial
activities were evidence of their unassimilable foreignness. Whether through
the Chinese mine worker or Indian trader, Asian difference was associated
with black markets, secrecy, hoarding, and tax evasion, unseeable economic
activities that diverted money from the local economy of white settlers. The

sentiment of "boycotting the Coolie"—the unlawful trader, importer, and overseas remitter—has persisted. Through an ingrained similitude, perceptions of Indian traders imprint on the Chinese. The twenty-first-century Chinese migrant trader poses a national economic threat not to a "white man's country" but the postapartheid economy during the "rise of China."

Chinese Unlawfulness

In November 2012 the South African magazine *Noseweek* splashed "Howzit China?" on its cover, posing the Chinese Question with a South African twist. Returning to the epigraph, it opens with a striking familiar alarm of a proliferation of Chinese shops "that threatens to destroy local commerce and cost the taxman billions. . . . Suddenly there's a Chinese shop (maybe three) in every suburb, village and town in South Africa. Every single one" (Welz and Schoonbee 2012). The story deploys recognizable tropes of invasion, competition, and inscrutability. Like the Indian peddler one hundred years ago, the Chinese shopkeeper is a ubiquitous character, a dealer in "fun junk," counterfeits, plastic, and cheap thrills. Alluding to goods dumping, the authors ask, "And what of the mass of nonessential imports flooding the South African market and those of neighbouring states, at the expense of local manufacturers, wholesalers, retailers and our own unemployed workers?" The story taps into fear of exponential growth through chain migration and reproduction. *Noseweek* calculates: "Visualise it: 12,000 couples equals 24,000 young, start-up Chinese shopkeepers who have managed to enter, settle and work in South Africa. . . . That's 240 Boeing-loads of would-be Chinese shopkeepers." It gives one example: "From one pioneer in the 'Chen' family, there are today 172 members of the same family scattered across Lesotho doing various types of trading." Featuring a photograph of a young child, the story fixates on Chinese women's reproductive capacities, noting that "it is common to find a toddler scooting in the aisles while mother minds the till." Through the persistent adjacency between Chinese and Indian, Chinese men and women are arriving in South Africa to "work and settle."

The authors cast the shopkeeper as model minority and cunning criminal: "Most South Africans, perhaps ignorant of the scale of the phenomenon, appear to have accepted them as just the umpteenth bunch of brave, eager immigrants to reach our shores who will further enrich our multicultural, multi-ethnic society." What is so concerning about Chinese migrants, as the article repeatedly states, is their "unlawful" nature. Recalling the Gujarati shopkeeper with illegible books, Chinese shopkeepers operate outside state regulation: "They have the guise of formal traders . . . while deliberately avoiding tax and business registration, as well as the requirements contained in labour legislation. They cannot be romanticised as informal traders simply trying to make a living; they entered the country with the explicit intention of operating under the radar of domestic law. Effectively, they are criminals who cannot even plead ignorance of the law" (Welz and Schoonbee 2012). Chinese traders are simultaneously inscrutable, malevolent, and hardworking. They allegedly dodge the "taxman," undercut local producers, copy branded designs, exploit workers, and cheat customers. Chinese migrants, the article implies, must be subjected to the full force of the law. As Lowe observes, in the United States "the presence of Asia and Asian peoples that currently impinges on the national consciousness sustains the figuration of the Asian immigrant as a transgressive and corrupting 'foreignness' and continues to make 'Asians' an object of the law, the political sphere, as well as national culture" (1996, 18). In my fieldwork, I heard conspiracy theories of "clever Chinese" evading taxes; committing fraud; stuffing cash under mattresses and smuggling it out of the country in shipping containers, suitcases, and red, white, and blue "China bags." As chapter 7 shows, there is truth to these charges of extralegal diversions, but representations of Chinese unlawfulness are based in racial stereotypes. Meanwhile, in the new South Africa, Black African migrants have been the targets of xenophobic violence, stereotyped as criminals, and blamed for soaring unemployment among poor and working-class Black South Africans. The *Noseweek* article speculates that containers containing counterfeit goods are "trucked to Joburg in the middle of the night and offloaded at warehouses run by Nigerians" (Welz and Schoonbee 2012); it amplifies xenophobic, racist stereotypes about Nigerians as scam artists and gangsters and positions African and Chinese migrants akin to the earlier Black and Yellow Perils. Whereas Black foreign nationals have become scapegoats for mass unemployment, Chinese traders are scapegoated for the disappearance of employment altogether after 1994.

Since 2010, the People's Republic of China (PRC) has been South Africa's largest import-export partner. In 2020 South Africa was the second largest African buyer of Chinese manufactured goods, with more imports than exports (China Africa Research Initiative, n.d.). Trade unions remain the most vocal critics of free trade with China and the loss of manufacturing jobs in South Africa.[6] Although economic links with China flourished under President Thabo Mbeki, in 2006 Mbeki addressed the South African Students Congress about the asymmetrical trade relationship. Trade relations were becoming "an unequal relationship, the kind that has developed between African countries as colonies—including this one—and the colonial powers. . . . China cannot just come here and dig for raw materials and sell us manufactured goods" (*Mail and Guardian* 2006). Analysts and pundits raise concerns about trade inequalities and the "flooding" and "swamping" of South African markets with unfairly priced imports. The new "Asiatic invasion" of commodities resuscitates colonial suspicion toward the Indian trader as middleman and profiteer. Whereas the Indian traders' cheap way of life explained their competitive advantage over Europeans, the reorganization of global production and South African industries has given Chinese entrepreneurs an upper hand in low-end markets. Through enduring racial adjacencies, the Asian trader, whether Chinese or Indian, continues to embody a national economic threat of "Asian capitalism."

Fetish and Fakery

Chinese goods are firmly part of the South African cultural milieu, with their own moniker: Fong Kong. Fong Kong has an array of meanings: cheap, low-quality, knockoff, counterfeit, and fake. The Hunger Boyz' breakout *kwaito* hit "Fong Kong" ushered the term into the South African lexicon. In 2010, Senyaka of the Hunger Boyz reflected, "We wrote this song as a protest against what the Chinese were doing to the black man. . . . They would sell you takkies [sneakers] that were like rotting pieces of meat. In two weeks the things would just literally rot on your feet" (quoted in Sosibo 2010). Since then the term has taken off. It is no coincidence that Fong Kong (or Zing Zong in Zimbabwe) sounds like Hong Kong, among the world's leading markets for counterfeit luxury items. Fong Kong is characterized by an excessive and obvious fakeness. But the term applies to all goods at the China Malls, not only counterfeits.

Sentiments about the low value of Chinese goods figured into everyday conversations at the China Malls. As Frank, a longtime employee of Johannesburg's very first China Mall, recounted, "After 1994, Chinese came with cheap, cheap, cheap, very bad stuff. And that's why people said Fong Kong in South Africa. But some Chinese are bringing good-quality stuff. Now they are bringing good stuff because COSATU [the Congress of South African Trade Unions] [is] fighting for those things. Chinese, *even if we are Africans, we are poor*, you cannot just bring something that is not worth it. You need something that is better quality, so Chinese started to change, bringing good things." This narrative understands the boom in Chinese goods as a postapartheid phenomenon. In an oppositional dynamic, pressure from organized labor successfully pushed back on the new Chinese economic presence. In a global hierarchy, low-quality goods have been dumped into African markets, as if African consumers are less deserving of quality goods and consumer protections. At China City, one Zimbabwean shopworker defined it as "fake, it doesn't last long." Roger, a Malawian shopworker who had worked at several big wholesalers at China City, described Fong Kong as "something that is not original, something cheap . . . something that you cannot use for a long time." Pointing out the profitability of selling poorly made goods, he deduced, "Chinese brought those things to Africa so that we can . . . buy and use, buy and use." Fong Kong is difficult to define because it is a conglomeration of abstractions: quality, authenticity, original, real, and fake. It projects fetishized representations of goods back onto their perceived producers: *the Chinese*. Jerry, a Nigerian security guard with experience with Chinese goods, illustrates the chain of associated meanings: "Anything Chinese in Nigeria we call Fong Kong because we believe it's fake. We believe it's *fake* because everything Chinese make, they make it *weak*." The material quality of Chinese goods must be visually and physically inspected. Fong Kong invites a mode of interaction with goods as disingenuous in original-ity or quality and the traders who sell them as suspect, sticking together people, goods, and racial and national "Chineseness."

In "Faking Globalization," Ackbar Abbas argues that the "fake" is a useful "symptom" for understanding global capital. The fake responds to "the pro-cesses of globalization and to the uneven and often unequal relations that globalization has engendered" (2008, 251). Chinese goods and the Chinese traders who sell them are racialized through the fake. In mainstream South African discourses about China, goods and people are depicted as insepa-rable entities: fake, disingenuous, and cheap plastic "imports" that enter the country through unofficial channels. A profile on the China Malls depicts a trader in this way: "She gestures at her stock of 'Proudly South African' caps and scarves: 'I only deal with quality material, this is not fong kong,' she adds with a wide grin, patting the dust off the hats" (Dibetle 2006). Fong Kong marks goods as suspect and is inseparable from the racialization of the inscrutable, duplicitous Chinese. As Mellie, a Chinese South African intermediary for Chinese migrant entrepreneurs, joked, "The South Afri-can Chinese call the Chinese that come from China imports." To ordinary South Africans, Chinese traders represent an influx of goods made in China and are scapegoated for unemployment and deindustrialization after 1994. Asian racial forms have been resiliently adapted to the political and eco-nomic landscape that figures the Asian as an economic threat. No longer the competition the Indian trader presented to white commerce in a white man's country, today's Chinese trader undercuts national industries while being too foreign to assimilate into the multiracial nation.

A longer historical approach to Sinophobia treats the anxiety around the Chinese trader and capital as nothing new but instead a refashioning of white settler anxieties about the Indian trader-settler, Chinese indentured laborer, and Indigenous African laborer. In a dramatic reversal, Chinese laborers once shored up the Labor Question in South Africa's key industry; now Chinese traders have become the face of the new Labor Question of unemployment. While Chinese laborers were previously pitted against African laborers, Chinese traders are pitted against African consumers and workers. The new Chinese Question concerns what "China"—an idea, economic presence, and geopolitical force—bodes for African futures.

Afro-Asian Johannesburg

Lineages

In *Bengali Harlem and the Lost Histories of South Asian America*, Vivek Bald chronicles the lives of Indian traders who traversed imperial circuits and settled in working-class African American, Creole, and Puerto Rican neighborhoods in Harlem and New Orleans during Jim Crow and the cosmopolitan worlds they created despite racial segregation. In Johannesburg, the bazaar and racialization of consumption left an Afro-Asian legacy between Chinese and Indian traders and African consumers. Shopkeepers, including ex-indentured laborers, ran small retail shops or native trading stores (*dukka*) in rural towns and townships. *Dukkawallah* was the moniker for the Gujarati trader in the hinterland who brought cheap commodities to African consumers and exported local goods to Indian markets (Raya 1995, 547–50). In Kenya, Sana Aiyar observes, Indian shops "were spaces of intimacy where aspirations for material accumulation were simultaneously realized and crushed for ordinary Indians and Africans" (2015, 75). In South Africa, markets serving Africans, derogatorily known as the "Kaffir trade," were the backbone of Indian businesses during World War II. Like the proximity between the Coolie Location and the Native Location of early Johannesburg, Indians provided transport and moneylending services to Africans, Afrikaner farmers, and indentured Indians (Hart and Padayachee 2013).[7] Positioned as middlemen within the colonial economy, Asian traders were on the peripheries of a racially stratified economy yet also beneficiaries of it.

Chinese in Johannesburg followed a similar trajectory as Indians in eastern Africa and South Africa. Anti-Asian laws barred independent migrants from owning property and gold mining. Free Chinese became shopkeepers in multiracial areas, including what became First Chinatown; some operated laundries and eating houses for African mine workers (Yap and Man 1996, 200). Multiple generations of Chinese shopkeepers sold low-cost goods to South Africans across the color line. Within apartheid's categories of Black, White, Coloured, and Indian, Chinese were classified as Coloured, a catchall category between Black and White that was further subdivided along ethnic and national lines. Whereas Chinese and Indians were previously nearly interchangeable as "Asiatics," they became categorically distinct under apartheid. Chinese were too small for a Chinese group area but were able to petition to live and work in white areas. Today Chinese migrants run convenience shops reminiscent of the *dukka* known as *spaza* shops, China shops, and five-rand shops, a riff on the American dollar store purportedly started by Taiwanese shopkeepers. These small shops, as the *Noseweek* article decries, exist all over (Welz and Schoonbee 2012). In the remote townships outside Cape Town and Johannesburg that I visited, one family from Fujian runs multiple shops, grocery stores, and shebeens. Pioneering families pick destinations out of atlases, choosing places where there is minimal Chinese competition but that are within driving distance of Johannesburg's China Malls. Among locals, these shops are part of their daily routines—a place to sit between bus transfers, to buy birthday presents, and to play after school. South African–born Chinese children become community darlings, given endearing nicknames like Baby Jet Li and Mama Africa. Despite the thickness of local ties, Chinese traders are not tied to where they trade. After they leave, often Bangladeshi, Indian, or Pakistani migrants take over their vacant shops, inheriting their leases and unsold stock.

Chinese shops exist within Yellow Peril imaginaries and collective memories of struggle. Among older South Africans, the apartheid-era Chinese shop imparts a feeling of solidarity for Chinese newcomers unaware of these histories. In Cape Town, a cab driver from District Six, where Coloured communities were relocated, fondly remembered the Chinese and Indian shops of his youth, which were "very instrumental with assisting with the struggling majority." The driver distinguished Chinese and Japanese as "Blacks of the East" and "whites of the East." Japanese, who were geopolitically favored but largely indistinguishable from Chinese, were treated as "honorary whites" (Park 2009). A Chinese South African community leader who came of age in his family's Cape Town shop explained the reinvention of *spazas* as Chinese migrants arrived during the twilight of apartheid, noting that they "were always predominantly Black-owned little shops, and then Chinese arrived from China in the 1990s and some of them moved into the Black areas to trade. The locals found it fascinating because when the Chinese first arrived . . . they were small shopkeepers in Black areas because that's where they could trade, that's where they could live, they couldn't live in white areas . . . we did that out of necessity . . . it wasn't a choice." Whereas Afro-Asian proximities were previously imposed, now they were by choice. Chinese newcomers became implicated in enduring racial imaginaries and geographies, inheriting the memories of mom-and-pop shops and adjacencies between Chinese and Indian traders. The success of the China Malls is indebted to Afro-Asian commercial connections born from segregation and survival, as well as the vibrant wholesale markets Indian traders established.

Reinventing the Bazaar

The China Malls are places of abundance, repetition, exhibition, and informality. They resemble Yiwu's enormous wholesale markets, where traders from all over the world go to import, including traders at China City. The China Malls are part exhibition, part market, and part shopping mall (Jackson 2012). The same items appear in shop after shop, creating an experience of surplus and sameness. Bartering is part of the shopping experience. Shops exhibit a mix of formal and informal practices. A No Refund, No Exchange sign hangs above the register, which might simply be a drawer. Receipts are often handwritten—on request. Inside each of China City's four hundred shops, narrow aisles burst with stock. Goods densely populate the shelves, and they are unstickered to accommodate quickly changing prices. In the hypercompetitive environment, sheets of newspaper cover back-room windows to thwart nosy competitors. Packaging is of the no-frills variety and free of logos. Goods are often sold out of the cardboard boxes in which they arrived and end up in nondescript plastic bags. These boxes imprinted with Made in China, which mainstream malls would hide in back rooms, clutter the corridors. Shipping containers find new purposes as on-site warehouse storage, making global circuits hypervisible and bringing the port city inland. As the modern shopping mall can be described as an arcade, China City is decisively anti-Benjaminian. There are no stylized glass displays, ambient music, light-filled domes, or spacious atriums signaling luxury. The industrial aesthetic is straightforward: tile floors, gray walls, high ceilings, and fluorescent lighting. The sounds of trolley wheels grating against the ground, the multilingual cacophony of banter and barter, and workers packing orders fill the air. The pleasure of the mall is not the experience of strolling but the magnificence of abundance that spills into its walkways. Conjuring the faraway and exotic, sections are named after Chinese cities. Lunar New Year decorations, paper lanterns, and dragon iconography further conjure "China."

China City also feels like the Oriental Plaza, which, when it opened in 1974, gave Indian traders—who were relocated to Coloured areas such as Fietas and Turffontein under the Group Areas Act—a central place to trade. The plaza's selection of affordable everyday items and rarities brought together a wide cross-section of Johannesburg. The wholesale market was praised as "an oasis where East and West will meet" and "a mecca for bargain hunters, and as Eastern as incense" (*Rand Daily Mail* 1974a). The Oriental Plaza was praised as a uniquely cosmopolitan interracial space, a sensory experience and exotic destination: an open-air market with a minaret, calligraphic signage, novel spices, and imported fabrics. Recalling the bazaar, the Oriental Plaza's dazzling excess was attributed to "the Asian mania for disorder" (*Rand Daily Mail* 1976). The plaza continues to be a popular destination, marketing itself as "Where Africa shops."

With the Oriental Plaza as the anchor, a vibrant Indian and Muslim wholesale market hub took off in Fordsburg and the surrounding mining belt, which paved the way for Chinese wholesalers in the early 2000s. As one Crown Mines–based property broker explained, the Oriental Plaza put Fordsburg on the map. In the 1990s, Muslim entrepreneurs opened several Cash & Carry wholesale clubs in the old Crown Mines area. Much like the China Malls, the Cash & Carry stores sell basic food and household goods to middle-income consumers, small traders, and street vendors from the region. In the late 1990s, a Chinese developer purchased a multistory building near the mining belt on the border of Fordsburg, which catalyzed a flurry of Chinese mall development (Harrison, Moyo, and Yang 2012). The China Malls have profoundly changed the geography of wholesaling and informal economies.

Chinese newcomers have created competition for the Oriental Plaza by undercutting prices and attracting South Asian tenants. Among Indian South African traders and customers, the Oriental Plaza comes to mind when visiting China City. For instance, Ayesha is an independent fashion designer born, raised, and based in Fordsburg. She traces her family history to the early twentieth-century migration of "passenger" Indians to Indonesia, Kurdistan, and Natal. Her late father was a fabric importer, wholesaler, and retailer at the Oriental Plaza, where hundreds of Indian-owned fabric shops used to draw in designers every week. Now, she noted, the Oriental Plaza is mixed with Pakistani wholesalers and tailors and is much quieter. Ayesha recounted, "On a Saturday, the Oriental Plaza would be so packed,

3.3   Conjuring China at China City. Photo by the author.

3.4   Shipping container warehouses at China City. Photo by the author.

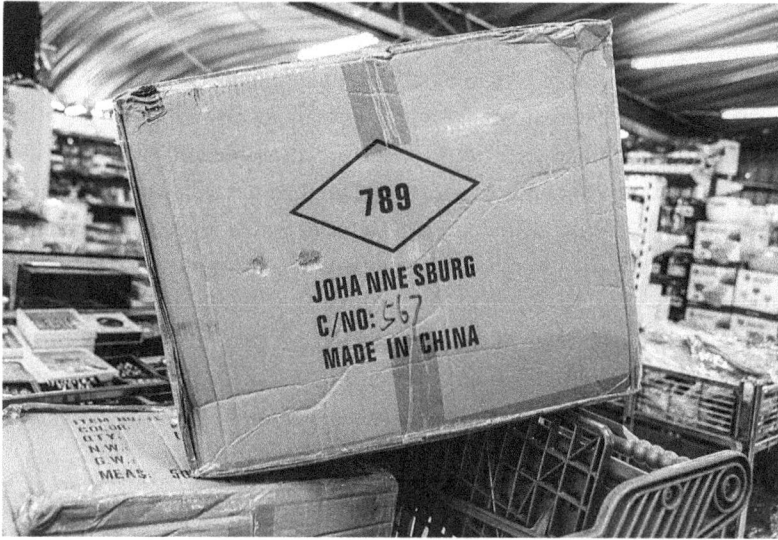

3.5 "Johannesburg, Made in China." © Mark Lewis.
Courtesy of Mark Lewis.

The Oriental Plaza
it's a mecca for bargain hunters, and as Eastern as incense

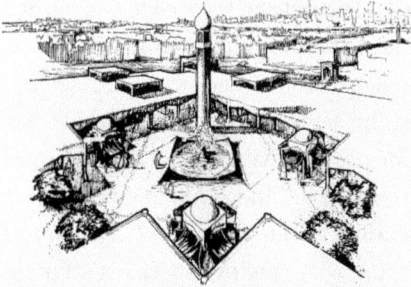

—opens July 3

3.6 "An oasis trading town . . . like stepping into the East." Oriental Plaza
supplement to the *Rand Daily Mail*, July 3, 1974. Courtesy of William
Cullen Library Historical Papers.

everybody would come do their shopping there. They would be buying their spices, their clothing. . . . And now on a Saturday morning, you know everyone is at the China Mall." As an independent designer for Muslim women's apparel and a former designer for South African department stores, Ayesha was intimately familiar with South Africa's relationship with China. At the time, China's share of South Africa's textile imports neared 80 percent (Martin 2008, 353). Ayesha visited apparel factories with a South African delegation in Fujian and sent manufacturing orders to Chinese cut-trim-make factories. After her label went bankrupt, for a long time Ayesha "boycotted" the China Malls because of the impact of imported Chinese clothing on the South African apparel industry, claiming that the malls had "taken the bread out of my pocket." By the time I met her shopping at China City on a busy Saturday, she had resigned herself: "If you can't beat them, join them."

China City—with its migrant communities, multiracial customers, linguistic diversity, spatial density, and culture of bartering—follows the tradition of the bazaar. It is a site of mundane Afro-Asian affinities, tensions, and diasporic worlds that exist side by side. Examples can be found in the biographies of one lone corner of the mall. Born and raised in Durban, which is home to Africa's largest Indian population, Abraham was a longtime tenant of the mall until he emigrated to Canada. Partition and apartheid shaped his family's fate: Abraham's parents fled India for South Africa in 1947, and two years later the Nationalist Party took power. Abraham was born in an Indian township during the early years of apartheid. His father, who was from a business family, was a "dealer of spices." Abraham ran a cell phone accessories shop in Johannesburg's Central Business District and traveled to Guangzhou and Hong Kong to arrange imports. He moved to China City when it opened, preferring the "Asian market" and its "Asian theme," and switched to jewelry and fake designer handbags. Whereas his father sourced from local Indian wholesalers, Abraham bought from Chinese wholesalers who routinely visited him with samples. "The whole world is made in China," Abraham conceded.

Around the corner from Abraham was one of China City's largest wholesalers, an importer from Zhejiang who employed a Pakistani manager to supervise over a dozen Malawian shopworkers. Across from Abraham was a party goods wholesaler from Fujian who was wildly jealous of his Chinese neighbor. Ali's family-run kitchen goods shop was two doors down. Ali left Karachi in 1995 in search of pharmaceutical markets. When choosing between Kenya and South Africa, he perceived South Africa's markets to be more advanced and wanted to see what the new democracy had in store. Whereas the same goods tended to appear at shop after shop,

Ali imported widely from China, Dubai, Indonesia, Korea, Pakistan, and Saudi Arabia in the tradition of the worldly trader.

The corner was lively with laughter, chatter, and the sound of sales announcements and radio hits. The camaraderie between Malawian, South African, and Zimbabwean shopworkers, regardless of the relationships between their employers, was energetic. Interactions between Chinese, Indian, and Pakistani traders and workers were refracted through geopolitics, including border disputes around Kashmir, the PRC's military support for Pakistan, and the legacy of partition. Ali saw the relationships between Indian and Pakistani traders as "very friendly, very brotherly," but Abraham thought otherwise: "They don't get along at China City. The Chinese are their intermediaries." There was an atmosphere of both conviviality and racial antipathy and distrust between the Chinese and South Asian traders and the African workers. Malawian and Zimbabwean workers shared and compared bitter experiences working for Chinese, Indian, and Pakistani employers. A minority of South Asian employers like Abraham and Ali were the exception, as they employed Black South Africans with a living wage. For Abraham, fair compensation was a matter of decency.

Islam is a powerful force in Afro-Asian affinities. At China City, most Indians and Pakistanis are Muslim, highlighting the particularity of these migrant networks. Muslim Malawians prefer to work for Indian and Pakistani traders, who close their shops for Friday prayers, during which all of them—traders and workers, African and South Asian—visit nearby mosques together. At the mall they share a makeshift prayer room in an empty shop and a utility sink for washing. Communal relations extend beyond the mall. Malawian and South Asian traders and workers cluster in Fordsburg and Mayfair—formerly neighborhoods for white mine workers just north of the mining operations and now the epicenter of Johannesburg's Muslim communities, where South African Indian Muslims and Ethiopian, Somali, and South Asian migrants live, work, and worship (Sadouni 2013). Abraham likened Mayfair to "the Casbah in Morocco." Like the mall, the "vibrancy of the area is what makes it tick . . . the different races." China City's tightly networked migrant social communities formed contiguous pockets with occasional mixing. After the mall closed to the public, Malawian and Zimbabwean workers, many of whom were hometown friends, roommates, and relatives, made their way back to Mayfair or Soweto in groups. The Chinese left in carpools for Cyrildene Chinatown or returned to the apartments at the mall. A group of Indian and Pakistani men stuck around for a game of cricket in the parking lot at dusk.

"Afro-Asian gastropoetics" (Goffe 2019) have been central to cross-racial exchanges at the China Malls and Oriental Plaza. Since its opening, the Oriental Plaza's food court offered a rare respite from how segregation was lived: "For this crowd of shoppers who'd broken off their bargain-hunting at Fordsburg's Oriental Plaza to have a bite, eating alongside Blacks was a non-event. . . . [It is] probably Johannesburg's only low-budget multiracial eating place, a venue for people from all sectors of our society" (*Rand Daily Mail* 1976). China City's food court is a semicircle of rusty shipping containers renovated into food stands. Multiracial diners squeeze into tables adorned with the red plastic Coca-Cola tablecloths that are ubiquitous in South Africa, but there are no major food franchises. A Chinese stand serves plates of Westernized Chinese food and off-menu traditional northeastern Chinese fare. Next door is a halal takeout spot serving bunny chow, a curry unique to South Africa that is served in a hollowed-out loaf of white bread. At each mall entrance, an Indian South African franchise peddles savory pies—but not samosas, because that would compete with those offered by the food court tenants. Inside are a handful of Pakistani-run convenience shops. Reminiscent of the *dukka*, they are packed to the brim with cold drinks, samosas, Nestlé ice cream bars, ice cream made in Fordsburg, Simba chips, *chaat* (savory snacks), Chinese dried sour plums, plus necessities like cigarettes and cellular data. There are foodways for all of the mall's communities. Every morning, an elderly Chinese man whistles while pushing a shopping cart bearing breakfast staples. At noon, an Indian restauranteur and a trail of Zimbabwean employees briskly make the rounds with bags of takeout food. Malawian and Zimbabwean workers eat on the literal edges of the mall, purchasing "fat cakes," which Chinese liken to their own version of fried dough, and pap from food stalls outside the gate. When short on time, security guards and shopworkers get eggs, cheese, bread, and Coca-Cola from convenience shops. In the parking lot is a Chinese grocer from whom curious shoppers and Chinese tenants can buy tofu, Chinese vegetables, imported sundries, fireworks, joss paper, and plane tickets to China.

For all of these fluid crossings, there are hard racial, ethnic, national, religious, linguistic, and cultural boundaries. Chinese and Indian communities in eastern Africa and South Africa have upheld norms of endogamy. Among Indians in Kenya, especially concerning food, marriage, and religion, "being 'Indian' revolved around racial distance from Black Africans, social and economic patterns of settlement, and contact with their civilizational homeland of India" (Aiyar 2015, 11). During the era of the Bandung Conference, the height for Afro-Asian solidarity, fraternity, and friendship, interracial relations were undercut by concerns of racial mixing and interracial sexuality. Afro-Indian relationships were limited by "a culturally particularistic and highly gendered postcolonial Indian self, reliant on the twin consciousness of racial superiority (brown over black) and its correlative, sexual purity (fear of miscegenation)" (Burton 2016, 18). Among Chinese migrants, distance from Black Africans *and* South Asians limited interracial sociality. Chinese traders ostracized a Chinese woman who ran a cell phone accessories shop with her Pakistani husband. Many of the mall's amenities and spaces were for Chinese tenants only. I asked Jenny why Indian and Pakistani traders were not allowed to live there. I expected her to express a preference for a Chinese cultural space, but it was because Indians and Pakistanis socialized with Black Africans and might invite them inside. Afro-Asian relations are mediated through gender and sexual politics (Sudhakar and Reddy 2018). Previously, the white mining elite pitted African and Asian laborers against one another. Now relationships among African, Chinese, Indian, and Pakistani peoples are limited by perceived proximities to Blackness. Reframing Sino-African worlds through Afro-Asia and Indian Ocean worlds brings into view contemporary spaces of Chinese migration as threaded through older labor migrations and diasporas. Before the China Malls, there was the Oriental Plaza, the bazaar, and the Coolie Location. In these spaces, Afro-Asian proximities came about more often by design than by choice, and intimacies were fraught. Then and now, adjacencies characterize the limits of interracial social life.

An Afro-Asian Transit

The heralding of the Chinese Century in South Africa is layered with the memory and materiality of Afro-Asian pasts. The multifaceted meanings of Chineseness (racial, ethnic, national, and economic) did not begin with China's rise or the strengthening of diplomatic relationships between the PRC and South Africa in the late 1990s, but the racial triangulations and adjacencies since South Africa's settlement and the mineral revolution. Formed in the interstices of the Asiatic Question, the Chinese Question, and the Labor Question, Chinese racialization was triangulated with African, East Asian, European, and Indian racial identities and the positions of settler, Native, and migrant. Asian racialization was forged through global processes of white supremacy, empire, capitalism, and settler colonialism and rotated on multiple axes of difference. As an analytic, adjacency encapsulates modes of relationality among peoples, histories, categories, and regions to reveal connection and contemporaneity, approximation and contiguity, and discontinuity and incommensurability. Through the collision of world-historical forces, Chinese and Indian peoples have traversed distinct yet parallel pathways in South Africa as racialized migrants, laborers, and merchants. Bearing on Afro-Asian relations today, colonial administrators pitted Chinese and African laborers against one another and kept the two groups separate. Under apartheid, Chinese and South Africans forged relations of interdependency and solidarity through commerce. These historic adjacencies and economic modes of racialization inform racial formations and labor relations in the present. The arrival of the Chinese Century has rekindled fears about the "Asiatic." In eastern Africa and South Africa, Indians are "settled strangers," perpetually seen as foreign exploiters of local economies over generations of settlement (Oonk 2013). Chinese newcomers are inserted into the intermediary position of the exploitative Asian trader and a threat to the settler nation. Chinese migrants inherit the ghostly traces and sticky associations of Chinese and Indian traders, the *dukka*, *spaza*, plaza, and bazaar. In a recursive fashion, what repeats is not always the stereotype but the relation.

A transit marks passing over and passing through. From the British imperial century to the BRICS era, Afro-Asian histories have made a full revolution around China, India, and South Africa. In a dialectical return, the Asian economies that enriched Europe and the United States threaten to displace them as overaccumulation in the North/West shifts to production in the South/East. This transiting from Asia to Euro-America and back to Asia is illustrative of the century-long cyclical movement of capitalism (Arrighi 1994; Frank 1998). But a granular approach reveals how historical transformations of this transit have been starkly uneven. At the mining belt mall, Chinese migrants return to the Rand not as unfree labor but as enterprising sojourners in search of fortune. Chinese traders employ southern African migrants, many of whom come from the same countries that once sent migrants to the mines. Unaware of histories of indenture, Chinese migrants use the language of the "coolie" (*kuli*) to describe "Black labor" (*heigong*). While some patterns have reversed, the afterlife of gold plays out in the racialized labor dynamics at the China Malls.

4

Afterlives of Gold

The essence of modern capitalism is the ruthless transfer of wealth from the colonized to the colonizer, from black to white, from worker to capitalist.

Bernard Makhosezwe Magubane, *The Political Economy of Race and Class in South Africa*, 1979

If we seriously want to enliven, and make useful, and keep useful the concept of racial capitalism, we have to get over thinking that what it's about is white-people capitalism. There *is* white-people capitalism, but that's not all of capitalism. . . . There is a world movement of racial capitalist relations. Those relations do not all emanate from the global North, from the Anglo-European, North American centers of power—economic and military power—and

4.1   "On the Rand: White, Black and Yellow," ca. 1906. Courtesy of
Museum Africa.

> they matter, and they remain racial. If all the white people disappeared and
> capitalism stayed, it would remain racial.
>
> Ruth Wilson Gilmore, in Michael Dawson and Ruth Wilson Gilmore,
> "Racial Capitalism Now," 2022

"On the Rand: White, Black, and Yellow" is one of many picture postcards from
the oft-forgotten history of Chinese indentured labor on the Witwatersrand's
goldfields. The image crystallizes the color line between African and Chinese
laborers and white mine managers and owners. In the era of racist pseudoscience,
the photograph perpetuates the assumed civilizational superiority of Europeans
against the inferiority of African and Chinese mine workers. The African and
Chinese workers, marked by exoticized dress and long braids, symmetrically
surround the mine owner, the dignified white patriarch seated in the center. In
the back row stand African "boss boys" and Chinese mine police, distinguished
by attire, demeanor, and posture from those they oversee. These disciplinary
figures were indispensable to maintaining social order and maximizing
productivity. Without them, the scene is incomplete.

Within a few years of this photograph, Chinese laborers left the Rand. In
1911, one year after the formation of the Union of South Africa, indentured
labor was abolished across the union and the migrant labor system took

off. The large-scale mobilization of labor within South Africa and southern Africa—"South Africa's labour empire" (Crush, Jeeves, and Yudelman 1991)—tethered together capitalism, race, and colonialism. South African scholars named this configuration *migrancy*, which refers not to individual migrants and migration but capital's dependence on migrant labor (Crush, Jeeves, and Yudelman 1991, 4). Migrancy—Black migrancy and mine migrancy, by other names—was crucial to South Africa's racial capitalist development. A century after the photograph, a different configuration of "White, Black, and Yellow" plays out. At the mining belt mall, Chinese capitalists employ "Black labor" (*heigong*), precarious migrants primarily from Malawi and Zimbabwe, countries that previously sent the highest numbers of workers to the mines. Signaling the reconfiguration of race, capitalism, and empire in the Chinese Century, Chinese are recast in the role of capitalists, not workers, while the China Malls lure newly arrived Black nationals with the promise of prosperity. Whiteness is no longer at the center, but it remains an invisible force behind this reconfiguration.

"Just as the 'labour question' was key to European colonial domination and post-independence political struggles," writes Ching Kwan Lee, "it is also the fulcrum of Chinese capitalism in Africa today" (2009, 648). I take this one step further: two registers of Black labor—its historical role in the development of capitalism and as the Chinese category of Black labor (*heigong*)—are key to understanding the colonial and racial valences of Chinese capitalist projects in South Africa. A critical feature of the global history of capitalism and modernity has been the exploitation of "Black labor made mobile." As Cedric Robinson established in *Black Marxism*, from the African continent to the New World, "Black labor was pressed into service" to develop the capitalist world system ([1983] 2000, 120). The category of Blackness and the profit motive were born together on the plantation and in the mine. Not ending with the abolition of slavery, the exploitation of Black labor made mobile continues into the present conditions of low-wage migrant labor. As framed by the epigraphs that open this chapter, I consider racial capitalism beyond the Black-white dynamics and "white-people capitalism" of southern African and North Atlantic histories of slavery, conquest, and plundering that form the basis of racial capitalism scholarship. Toward theorizing from South Africa, I engage with South African thinkers and analytics and center the migrant labor system and its legacies in the making of racial capitalism. At the mining belt mall, Han Chinese racial formulations of Blackness (*hei*) and Black labor (*heigong*) articulate with the role of Black labor in the global history of racial capitalism and the legacy of

Black/mine migrancy in South Africa. Racial capitalism in the Sino-African context attests to the dynamism of racial capitalism to incorporate subjects and regions and remake itself.

This chapter is told from the vantage point of China City's African migrant workers. Across the China Malls, a racial division separates Chinese traders and workers from African workers. African migrant labor was indispensable to gold mining and remains indispensable to low-wage sectors in Johannesburg and in the malls. Although Africans and Chinese are both racialized migrants and legally precarious, Chinese migrant traders exploit African migrant workers, without whom they would not turn a profit on low-end commodities. The hierarchy reflects the different locations that Africans and Chinese occupy in the capitalist world system and is rooted in colonial legacies that are "actively constitutive for capitalist accumulation" in the present (A. Goldstein 2022, 67). In the twenty-first century, a new global color line of Chinese capital and African labor germinates amid the remains of South Africa's empire of labor.

To create a different narrative of the historical present, I dwell in the historical traces of gold not as background but to imagine the unfolding Chinese Century through the afterlives of gold. Decades after the closure of the Rand's mines, the past of gold mining continues in the toxic environment, circular migration from southern African countries to Johannesburg, and the cultural memory of gold mining over generations. Gold's afterlives are at once material and metaphorical, enduring and ephemeral.[1] Engaging ethnographic fieldwork with historical analysis, I read the mall through the mine, drawing parallels between the two to illuminate how the afterlives of gold shape Sino-African labor relations and African labor mobilities, migrant lifeworlds, place-based imaginaries, and political consciousness in the present. Mine migrancy's core features—the circularity of labor migration and the racialized devaluation of migrant labor—resurface at China City. As I detail, southern African migrant communities also remake older forms of circular migration, social reproduction, solidarity, and radical traditions from the mines. These afterlives are uneven and recursive. While recently arrived Chinese unwittingly extend historical processes born on the goldfields, African workers transpose the Black-white color line onto Sino-African dynamics.

As the mining belt mall metaphorizes, Chinese racial formations and racialized modes of accumulation overlay Euro-American ones in the post-apartheid present. Situating Sino-African labor relations in longer histories of gold insists on the dynamic, palimpsestic character of racial capitalism whereby Chinese capitalist projects form only one layer while building on and expanding existing colonial and racial formations. Colonial regimes of Black/mine migrancy are not merely "context" but the material prerequisites, or preconditions, for Chinese capital accumulation in the present. To be clear, the modes of exploitation and scale of accumulation at the China Malls are nowhere near those of the mining industry, nor are Chinese petty capitalists equivalent to white mine owners. There are many white and nonwhite profiteers of African migrant labor, not only Chinese migrants. Bearing these differences in mind, reading the mall through the mine nevertheless illuminates patterns and logics related to Black labor and migrancy to reveal continuities in capitalist relations and inequalities that Chinese migrants inherit and renew.

Race, Capitalism, and Migrancy

Whereas chattel slavery was the engine of racial capitalism in the United States, in South Africa it was the migrant labor system and the mineral revolution, not slavery, that bound race to colonialism and capitalism. Slavery existed on Afrikaner farms and in the British Cape Colony until it was abolished in 1833. But the migrant labor system, a "semi-slave system" in which mining capital secured Black labor at low wages, was larger and longer lasting than slavery in South Africa (Legassick and Hemson 1976, 3). Each year from 1910 to the early 1980s, up to five hundred thousand young men from Angola, Botswana, Lesotho, Malawi, Mozambique, South Africa's Native Reserves, Swaziland, Tanzania, and Zimbabwe sojourned to the City of Gold where they toiled under dangerous conditions and lived in single-sex compounds. Contracted for a fixed period, they cyclically returned home with cash wages to recuperate before returning to the mines. The migrant labor system recruited migrant workers from within South Africa and neighboring territories. While labor recruitment from South Africa's reserves tied the procurement of cheap labor with dispossession of land, recruitment from the region relied on cooperation between colonial administrations in Mozambique, Nyasaland (Malawi), and Northern and Southern Rhodesia (Zimbabwe). These two recruitment mechanisms drew from distinct but overlapping colonial formations, yet the common denominator was the superexploitation of Black labor.

The mineral revolution in diamonds and gold created a political economy of race and cheap labor that depended on the expropriation of land and the division of productive and reproductive labor enshrined in the Native

Reserve system (Saul and Gelb 1981; Worden 1995). Early twentieth-century segregation created a two-tiered economy and distinct settler mode of accumulation (Biermann and Kössler 1980). The 1913 Natives Land Act legally enshrined the land dispossession of frontier wars and annexations from the seventeenth to nineteenth centuries. The act allowed ownership of 93 percent of land for the white settler minority and pushed African inhabitants into the remaining 7 percent, parcels of unproductive land that became the Native Reserves (Beinart and Delius 2014, 669). As Bernard Magubane observes, "the process resembles the American solution to the 'Indian problem' in the nineteenth century—the herding of an indigenous population into tiny pockets of rural obscurity, in areas which had been systematically underdeveloped by the development of the capitalist industry and agriculture elsewhere" (1979, 90). Along with the forced removals, taxation forced Africans into wage labor for the mines, towns, white farms, and urban industries. Toward a comparative analysis of colonial racial capitalism, the superexploitation of Black labor and Native dispossession played out through different logics of land and labor in both North America and South Africa. In the New World, European settlers seized land and extracted labor from Indigenous people and enslaved Africans. But in South Africa, Indigenous Africans racialized as "African," "Black," and "Native" provided both land and labor: "Africans were progressively dispossessed of their best lands and incorporated as instruments of labor for the settlers" (B. Magubane 1979, 17). In South Africa, Robin D. G. Kelley notes, "the complete elimination of the native was hardly the objective. Yes, the expropriation of the native from the land was a fundamental objective, but so was proletarianization. They wanted the land *and* the labor, but not the *people*" (2017, 269, emphasis in the original). The rural reserves functioned as reservoirs of African labor and the site of social reproduction that made the mines not only profitable but viable.

The mines relied on an industrial labor reserve that oscillated between two modes of production: the "precapitalist" subsistence economy of the rural reserves and the capitalist urban wage economy (Wolpe 1972). Social reproduction linked these two spheres. The term *social reproductive labor* describes the naturalized, gendered familial and communitarian labor that maintains and reproduces human labor power and life itself, every day and across generations. The labor required to produce commodities and people are part of the systemic totality of capitalism (Bhattacharya 2017; S. Ferguson 2016). As Magubane explains, "The reserves fulfill the functions that capitalism prefers not to assume—those of social security for the migrant workers." Accordingly, "the typical income of an African miner is made up of what his employer pays him as a single man and what his wife ekes out from the subsistence sector" (1979, 96). Since the costs of social reproduction were borne by rural households, mines and factories could pay wages below the cost of reproduction, turning the displaced costs of social reproduction into absolute surplus value. It was important that a semiproletariat was created and maintained but never fully proletarianized. In a delicate balance, the colonial regime sought to immiserate the reserves just enough to coerce Africans into wage labor, but not to the point of destroying structures for social reproduction that made the whole system possible.

The recruitment of "foreign" migrant workers ran parallel to recruitment from the reserves and linked multiple colonial projects in southern Africa. Migrant miners were recruited through the coordinated efforts of the South African state, the Chamber of Mines, the Witwatersrand Native Labour Association (WNLA), and British, German, and Portuguese colonies in East Africa and southern Africa. During the 1960s and 1970s, foreign workers made up over 70 percent of mine workers (W. G. James 1992, 36). The migrant labor system reproduced its workforce by "turning the labour tap on in some regions and off in others," effectively creating a "buyer's market" that kept wages low (W. G. James 1992, 59, 45). It was not only the mines that relied on southern African workers, but regions that relied on the mines. As Wilmot James notes, "For reasons rooted in their colonial past, many societies of southern Africa were firmly locked into the migrant labour system: kin networks, social systems and entire regions had become dependent on mine wages earned in South Africa" (1992, 36). At the peak of migrant labor flows in the early 1970s, the migrant labor system ended abruptly as colonial rule fell throughout southern Africa. In 1974, President Hastings Banda of newly independent Malawi ended recruitment after a plane carrying migrant workers crashed. Anticolonial struggles in Mozambique presented another imminent threat. Confronted with the loss of half its Black workforce, the mines pivoted to recruiting Black South Africans and Zimbabweans until independent Zimbabwe recalled mine workers and banned recruitment in 1981 (Crush and Tevera 2010; F. Wilson 2001). By the early 1980s, unrest over apartheid reached new heights, while gold levels sharply declined. Increased African labor organization and the closure of major mines in the 1980s was the death knell for the migrant labor system.

The impact of the migrant labor system cannot be overstated. Unparalleled in scale and duration, no other urban industry in the world maintained such a large proportion of migrant labor and over such a length of time (F. Wilson 2001). The system's dual economy of industrial capitalist center and rural reserve entrenched racial and colonial geographies and became the basis for self-governing ethnic "homelands" (Bantustans) during apartheid. It engendered a carceral regime of passes and compounds that regulated, contained, and captured flows of Black labor. As an adaptable model, the migrant labor system was exported to agriculture, manufacturing, and domestic work. Through its vast intercolonial recruitment networks, the migrant labor system united southern Africa under one system of capitalist development (Capps 2016). Decades after the end of the migrant labor system, migrancy remains a feature of South Africa's economy. Migration to urban industrial centers had become a defining characteristic of regional mobilities within southern Africa (Niemann 2003, 125). It is this legacy of generations of southern African migrants who labor in South Africa's key industries and service economies that appears at the China City mall. The southern African precariat allows Chinese entrepreneurs to earn livelihoods wholesaling low-end imported commodities within hypercompetitive market conditions. The imbrication of Chinese capitalist activities with the aftereffects of mine migrancy and the devaluation of Black labor and life makes these activities not generically exploitative but racial capitalist and imbricated in colonial pasts and presents.

Journeying to the City of Gold

Dino, an employee of four years at a children's clothing shop at China City, told me, "I never planned where I would live." Dino is from Blantyre, the commercial center of Malawi. He explained, "Many people from my country are coming here, they are working, [and then they] come back home." After high school Dino decided to "go and try my luck here." Like many shopworkers, he has worked at several China Malls—and only China Malls. "Here if you don't have the *paper*"—a catchall term that workers use for visitor visas, work permits, and asylum documents—"you can still work for the Chinese." He added, "China City is the place where Malawians work." Dino's story is common among generations of migrant workers. Malawi was the second-largest source of migrant mine workers to the Rand, sending 120,000 miners and providing one-third of all miners in the early 1970s (F. Wilson 2001, 109). Throughout southern Africa, gold's legacy of circular migration to Johannesburg continues at the China Malls.

Across the malls, most shopworkers are from Malawi and Zimbabwe, southern African countries that are part of South Africa's empire of labor. Although southern Africans have long moved throughout the region prior to the creation of colonial borders, the migrant labor system irreversibly changed regional mobilities (Mlambo 2010, 52). For generations of southern Africans, the Rand became integral to social, cultural, and economic life. Despite the low wages and dangerous conditions, circular migration continued over generations across kin networks and regions. In popular Malawian imaginaries of South Africa going back to the late nineteenth century, Johannesburg is a place of production, consumption, and modernity (Msika 2017). Venturing to the city to work has long been part of "being a man" and a sign of male maturation (Moodie and Ndatshe 1994, 14). In Zimbabwe, to journey to Egoli (Johannesburg) or "go kuWenela" (with the WNLA to the South African mines) were masculine rites of passage. Men could work in the mines to raise cash for colonial taxes and bridewealth to support and start their own families (Mlambo 2010, 68–69). Men could earn more as part-time miners than year-round farmers (F. Wilson 1972, 131).

After the end of the migrant labor system, circularity still defines labor migrations. Southern African migrants make up most of the Black labor force in low-wage sectors. Workers typically stay for longer periods in cities, but they do not settle there, instead sending wages and goods to their rural households (Crush and James 1995). As the region's biggest economy, Johannesburg remains a destination for migration, "a place that people continue to migrate to in search of gold, and for a better life than the one left behind" (Asmal 2015, 8). While the composition of migrant communities varies across malls, at China City, most workers are from Malawi and Zimbabwe; the workers are embedded in regional gendered migrations of men to the mines, and the corollary, women to labor in homes as domestic workers. Many workers at China City, both men and women, have adult children, aunts, uncles, siblings, and partners working at different shops or malls. Or they are on their own, for male workers "soldiering alone," a mark of masculinity. Malawian workers, mostly young men from Blantyre, Lilongwe, and Machinga, come from farming families. Their earnings supplement rural incomes and go toward starting a business or attending university or vocational school after returning home.

Grant worked for two Chinese employers over nine years in Johannesburg. In Lilongwe, Grant struggled to find enough work repairing cars and electronics. As the oldest son, he assumed the breadwinner role when his father died. When Grant came to Johannesburg, he stayed in Mayfair, near the China City mall—a neighborhood originally built for white mine workers that is now a cosmopolitan Muslim migrant area. Grant's friends were already working for Chinese employers and helped him find his first job selling suitcases and hats at China City. After his longtime employers announced that they would cut his pay because of more competitive market conditions and poor sales, he took a well-paying warehouse job with a different wholesaler and participated in a rotating savings club (*stokvel*) with fellow employees. With a favorable exchange rate between the South African rand and the Malawian kwacha, his wages, however small, went to fertilizer, seeds, and properties, which have greatly expanded and diversified his family's income and holdings.

Zimbabwean workers from Bulawayo, Harare, and Plum Tree make up the other majority group of China City's African workforce. In Zimbabwe, political violence, land reform, urban "cleanup" campaigns, hyperinflation, and the collapse of public services in the 1990s and early 2000s propelled an exodus to Botswana, South Africa, and the United Kingdom. Zimbabweans now account for the largest group of foreign nationals in Johannesburg. Whereas single men traditionally migrated to work on farms and mines, the economic crisis has feminized migration (Crush and Tevera 2010; Makina 2010; Potts 2010). At China City, Zimbabwean women outnumbered men, and they described the hardship of arduous workdays, long train commutes, and the additional labor of caring for the children they brought with them.

In her early thirties, Anita used to sew garments for South African department stores in Zimbabwe. She and her sister left home in 2010 to support their younger brother; another brother worked as a miner in Zimbabwe. The sisters went first to Botswana where Anita was a domestic worker. After running into trouble with immigration authorities, they went to Johannesburg, where they worked at three different China Malls and lived together in Soweto. On average, the remittances from one person working in South Africa supports five people in Zimbabwe (Crush and Tevera 2010, 3). With the high cost of consumer goods in Zimbabwe, Anita sent blankets and a television back. But, she said ashamedly, she never sent "even a dime home." Despite the low pay and tiring days, Anita commented, "Us, Black people, foreigners, we are surviving because of Dragon Plaza, China City. I'm getting fed because of China City. I'm getting shelter because of China City. If there is no China City, I don't think I'm going to survive . . . we are earning a living, we are surviving."

As the stories of Dino, Grant, and Anita suggest, the China Malls are havens for people on the margins. While African migrants do not have papers to seek employment in formal labor markets, Chinese traders pay subminimum wages under the table to minimize costs. Were it not for the China Malls, my African interlocutors' options would be limited to piecework as gardeners, construction workers, or domestic workers, common occupations among their friends and relatives. At the malls, jobs are filled through word of mouth. Through friends and family already working at the malls, most shopworkers find work immediately after arriving in Johannesburg. Some workers even learned about opportunities at the China Malls before leaving home. Like the mines, the malls were a destination for prospective migrants. All along the old mining belt, they have become a niche employment sector among young men and women from Angola, Malawi, Mozambique, Zimbabwe, and farther afield. Shopworkers move from one Chinese (or South Asian) trader or mining belt mall to the next but remain firmly within the migrant networks of these malls. One worker, who has worked at two China City shops over his five years in Johannesburg, unwaveringly stated, "I come to work for Chinese only." In my years of coming and going, I was struck by how many workers stayed put at China City, even if they changed employers. Before leaving Johannesburg in 2020, one Malawian worker, believing we would meet again in a few years, parted with, "I'll be here, just maybe change my shop." Like Chinese traders, African workers are sojourners who stay until they have earned enough to return home. In the meantime, they visit home every few years, which often coincides with the Chinese New Year season when the traders return home. African and Chinese mobilities and economic dependencies are intertwined, and China City is a site of their world making. Residual mine worker cultures make up the mall's social fabric.

China City's African Lifeworlds

Migrant networks create a kaleidoscopic social vitality unique to the China Malls. In 2014, my first summer at China City, I spent most afternoons with Julian, Marcus, Peter, Roger, and Ziggy—the "Malawi Boys," as security guards called Malawian workers suspected to be up to no good. Mostly in their early twenties, all five lived together in Mayfair, sharing one of three bedrooms in a flat of fifteen Malawian men. Of the five of them, all except for Roger worked at three adjacent shops in the bustling outdoor vending area by the loading zone: Marcus sold sneakers, Ziggy and Julian LED lighting, and Peter furniture. Roger used to work at one of China City's busiest wholesalers until he was fired; he now worked at a mall up the road and would come by his old stomping grounds during deliveries. Most days we passed the hours sitting on a variety of makeshift chairs: metal trolleys, cracking plastic chairs stacked together, and stools expertly fashioned out of rolled-up cardboard and tape.

Emblematic of the ethos of sharing, the friends wore sneakers from Marcus's shop and swapped clothes they bought from the mall: knockoff L.A. Lakers and NYC snap-back caps, and shirts emblazoned with Cash Money Life. For these young men, masculinity trafficked in the cultural cache of American hip-hop and resistant Black masculinity (Anderson 2009). In between serving customers and trips to the warehouse, they passed time with a cheap MP3 player, playing an eclectic mix from Bob Marley to Rick Ross to dancehall. Eva, one of two Chinese workers at the lights shop, would often express her exasperation in Chinese: "So noisy!" While the Chinese workers at these three shops shared lunch and conversed with each other, Julius, Marcus, Peter, and Ziggy took full advantage of the open-air environment and passed cigarettes back and forth. Coworkers and roommates, their daily routines were synchronized, from arriving and leaving work together on foot to meals. Once the Chinese workers finished lunch, one person would walk across the gate to the stalls selling pap, and another would get water for washing hands.

This corner of China City was a microcosm of migrant cultures in the mines. Through the recruitment of families and friends from the same hometown, the mines formed an "occupational life-world" (Moodie and Ndatshe 1994, 18) of male camaraderie and migrant cultures (Breckenridge 1998). Brothers, uncles, and other male relatives, regardless of which compound they resided in, gathered to smoke, drink, play, and relax. Like the ways "the home world integrated into the world of work" in the gold mines (Moodie and Ndatshe 1994, 21), family and hometown networks converged to create pockets of community throughout the mall. Marcus had already been friends with Julian and Roger in Malawi. The oldest son of a Christian pastor and a devout Rastafarian, he dreamed of returning home to make art. He displayed his paintings at the shoe shop for extra income, proudly stating, "I don't steal, I make art." When I met him, he had been in Johannesburg for eight months. His sisters were working in Durban and Pretoria as live-in domestic workers. Marcus's "brother" from home helped him find a room and his job, and later he referred Julian and Peter to the lighting shop. At seventeen years old, Ziggy was the youngest and newest member of the group. His uncle, who worked at Mr. Zheng's wholesale shop, helped him find the job at the lighting shop. From the beginning, Ziggy was looking to steal. After Roger lost his job repairing computers in Malawi, a former classmate called him up with a job at his shop at China City.

That summer, Marcus's boss gave him one week's notice that he was closing the location and gave him the option to work for his brother at a new

Chinese wholesale mall down the street. On his last day, Eva hired him at the lighting shop, allowing him to stay at China City with his friends. Eventually Marcus, who claimed to never steal but also never sold a painting, was fired for stealing and went to work for a Nigerian phone repairman inside the mall. Peter, who constantly bickered with his supervisor, was relocated to a sister shop across the way from Marcus's new spot. Ziggy, "having nothing to gain from this shit," quit and found work at another China Mall. Several months later, he returned to the lighting shop, this time at night. The most agile in the group, Ziggy made an opening in the roof and robbed the shop clean—a feat that won the admiration of shopworkers and security guards. During the nationwide xenophobic violence in 2015, Roger, at his mother's urging, took the "free bus" for repatriating Malawian citizens. The others joked that Roger was "weak."

The sociality of the mall is punctuated with constant arrivals and departures through hiring, firing, and deportations. Social collectives are constantly forming, dispersing, and reforming through hometown networks. At the same time, many people—from shopworkers to taxi drivers and contingent laborers—remained at the mall for years. It could be an anchor for precarious communities. Just as Chinese migrants draw on family networks, provincial associations, and underground economies, African workers rely on informal sectors, ephemeral social formations, and "people as infrastructure" to survive (Simone 2004). Johannesburg's transnational migrants expansively define kinship, brotherhood, and association and form communities through hometown associations, mutual aid, and burial societies (Feldman-Savelsberg and Ndonko 2010; Landau and Freemantle 2010). With no official papers to gain them access to banking, undocumented workers form informal rotating credit associations (*stokvel*) for sharing money, which have been a survival tactic for the "unbanked" (D. James 2014; Verhoef 2001). As Marcus explained to me, each month they paid a fixed amount into a pool, and each took their turn taking the pot to send home. Once the money arrived, they entrusted family members to keep the money for them. This way, "when the day comes for me to go back to our place," Marcus explained, "I have something." This method depended on the full participation of all members; if someone lost their job or was arrested, all pulled together to help that person find work again. When it came time to send money home, they relied on a trusted "brother" or broker. As the China Malls are hot spots for informal economies, transporters for money and goods and mobile money service providers regularly appeared at China City. In my ten years visiting China City, there has been a

Zimbabwean driver parked in the same spot who delivers orders to China Malls and Zimbabwe-bound buses departing from town. In a gesture akin to the practices of burial societies for fallen mine workers, after a Malawian worker died from malaria, Malawian and Zimbabwean workers contributed to a fund to repatriate his body for burial.

Within the migrant labor system, subsistence economies and migrant households ensured social reproduction when wages were otherwise insufficient. Likewise, collective economic practices and mutual aid sustained workers who earned low wages, even allowing for money to be remitted home. Solidarity was not narrowly based in ethnic identity or hometown but was strategic, for navigating the day-to-day. In the past, the mines had divided their workers by ethnicity, language, and region, but Marcus's group at the mall brought together the Chewa and Yao ethnicities and Christian and Muslim religions. Whereas reproductive labor was often women's work, among my interlocutors these labors are distributed within their households, such as the men in Marcus's group or between Anita and her sister. Conviviality and solidarity flourish under conditions of precarity and vulnerability (Nyamnjoh 2017). For Marcus, "When a friend is in trouble, you help him or help her. It's like monkey business, you scratch my back today and I'll scratch yours tomorrow." Likewise, Roger poignantly articulated, "Friendship means the one who can stand by you when millions are against you." Such expressions of brotherhood, solidarity, alliance, mutual aid, and friendship impart the China Mall with its unique social vitality.

Papers, Police, and Precarity

In search of better futures for themselves and their families, China City's African workforce experiences a double exploitation as surplus labor and an illegalized population under South Africa's immigration laws. With the arrival of refugees and economic migrants at its borders, the postapartheid state has, through these laws, instituted new forms of exclusion, and the exclusion of Black Africans has been the signature of the postapartheid reimagining of citizenship and nonracial democracy. Xenophobic sentiment and vigilante violence against Black foreign nationals from southern Africa have marked the postapartheid period and erupted in nationwide crises in 2008 and 2015. Frustrated with the stasis in political and economic transformation, poor Black South Africans in townships see Malawians, Mozambicans, Somalians, and Zimbabweans as competing for scarce jobs and social resources. Although often understood as a post-1994 phenomenon, xenophobia goes back to colonialism and migrant labor for the mines (Hassim, Kupe, and Worby 2008). Caroline Kihato emphasizes that xenophobia was born in the gold-fields: "Blacks were temporary sojourners to the city of gold. And although they toiled in its mines, industries, and streets, they had no rights to live in it or make decisions about its future" (2013, 5).

Like the lives of Chinese migrants, the transnational lives of China City's African workforce have been circumscribed by borders, xenophobia, and papers—legal documents such as visitor visas, work permits, and asylum applications pasted into dog-eared passports. Under strict immigration re-strictions, southern African migrant workers often migrate through clan-destine channels. My Malawian and Zimbabwean interlocutors recounted taking multiday bus journeys to get to Johannesburg: passing through Mozambique, crossing the border at Beitbridge, and then walking through forests and game reserves. Many have become accustomed to making the harrowing journey. Upon arriving in Johannesburg, southern African mi-grants apply for short-term visitor visas and asylum, or "free papers." Until it was shuttered, migrant workers applied at the refugee reception center in Crown Mines. Once papers expire, migrants live with the constant reality of police harassment, arrest, and deportation. With xenophobia pervasive in employment practices, Chinese traders are among the few who will employ southern African migrants without papers.

During my fieldwork, South Africa's 2014 Immigration Act went into effect. Criticized for being racist, xenophobic, and draconian, the new act intensified border management and the deportation of "undesirable per-sons" with "fraudulent or no documents at all." It expanded the surveil-lance of racialized bodies, which has always been a feature of urban life in Johannesburg. Police stake out areas with high concentrations of migrants and detain them based on a general profile and language. Greedy police threaten detention and deportation, and then exchange cash for leniency (Landau 2009, 204). Migrants are "mobile ATMs" for police (Templeton and Maphumulo 2005). With a police station down the road, China City workers risk twice-daily encounters with police demanding to see passports, a practice reminiscent of pass laws that policed Black urban mobilities until the 1980s. Workers also encounter thieves on Sundays when they take home their pay, incidents recalling the Rand gangs that robbed mine workers (Van Onselen [1982] 2001). Marcus described his daily commute: "I'm just passing, and you're in the jungle. You bump into the lion and you run. You escape yourself. Then you're going home." Precarity is self-compounding: undocu-mented migrants have few employment options, and they risk losing their pay going to and from work. Chinese migrants also struggle with legal status, xenophobic sentiment, and routine police harassment, but they are rarely detained or violently targeted. Unlike southern Africans, Chinese are not perceived as competitors for jobs. Chinese migrants are foremostly figures of foreign capital, not foreign labor. The legacies of the migrant labor system and specific racial contours of xenophobia shape power relations between African and Chinese migrants in the present.

Chinese traders employ a contingent labor force exclusively of migrants without papers. Unlike South Africans, migrants without papers are not entitled to a minimum wage, safe working conditions, or medical leave. They have no right to collectively organize, claim unfair dismissal, or demand severance pay.[2] Labor relations at the mall reflect the widespread casualization of labor in China, including pervasive subcontracting, the exploitation of domestic migrant labor, and the evasion of labor laws (Friedman and Kuruvilla 2015). African workers are critical of how traders take advantage of their vulnerability. Sebastian, a Malawian worker who had been deported several times and came back to China City every time, understood the preference for migrants without papers. White employers paid higher wages but only hired Malawians with papers. Chinese employers seized on the reality of Malawian "suffering."

Capital requires the constant production of a surplus population, and racialized groups without citizenship have historically constituted surplus populations (R. A. Ferguson 2004). The continuous economic migration of southern Africans to Johannesburg creates a reserve army for Chinese capital. Chinese traders extract racialized use value from precarious migrants, while actively maintaining conditions of precarity. South Africa's visa regime is infamous for being "punitive financially" (Crush and Tevera 2010, 21). Updating papers takes money and time. Workers already struggle with affording taxi fare and are rarely granted a single day off each month, making it impossible to queue up in long lines at immigration centers in Johannesburg or, even farther away, Pretoria. Nor does paying an expediter who works at the Department of Home Affairs guarantee papers. Dino explained the predicament: "You start working, you working every day, seven days a week. You don't even have time to go to Home Affairs and straighten your passport. And the Chinese doesn't give you a chance to straighten your passport, so we have no choice. If they catch me, what they do? I give them fifty rand, they will leave me, I go back to work. That is how we survive." Grant similarly expressed, "It takes a long time to make some papers; that means you can lose [your] job when you go [to] that side and when you come back you can't find [a] job. That's the problem, we are scared." The problem is not only Chinese employers but the visa regime: "The South African government is too hard on us," Grant explained. Employment practices, informal but normalized across shops, make regularizing legal status impossible. Workers remain dependent on traders for steady employment. When immigration officers turn up, security guards relay an alert, shops shutter, and workers flee. On one such occasion, Marcus recounted telling his boss, "My passport is bad. I am running. I will come back in thirty minutes. I'll be working here. They say, 'It's cool. You have to go, go fast!'" Chinese traders are complicit with these tenuous conditions. It is in their best interest for African workers to remain paperless but not be detained.

Differently positioned as racialized foreigners, African and Chinese migrants are tightly bound in an uneven interdependency. African workers depend on employment with informal Chinese traders; traders wholesaling cheap commodities rely on migrant labor. The mall mirrors the mine: "Migrant workers therefore used employment in South Africa as a means to advance their family or individual goals, just as the mine owners were using the workers to produce gold from ore that, without access to cheap labor, would not have constituted a profitable resource" (Niemann 2003, 128). My African and Chinese interlocutors understood their interdependent relationships, albeit in different terms. One trader characterized the relationship as *duili xianghu yikao*, meaning opposed (*duili*), mutual (*xianghu*), and dependent (*yikao*)—ironically, a Maoist phrase for class struggle.[3] Security guards are uniquely insightful by virtue of their jobs. As Jerry, a loquacious guard from Nigeria, explained, "Most of us are foreigners, and we need to survive, and we don't have the card [permit] to work in a good place." He added, "We have to consider [traders] too are taking a risk" by employing undocumented workers, yet "we have to take whatever they give us." In this economy of sojourners, differential precarities connect Africans and Chinese laterally, on the margins of formal economic life and the South African state, and hierarchically across race and class.

The Color Bar, Then and Now

Evolving in step with the migrant labor system was the legal apparatus of the "color bar" that divided Black and white labor. African workers took the most dangerous and poorly paid jobs and were barred from advancing into semiskilled or skilled jobs reserved for unionized white workers.[4] China City has its own informal color bar: a Sino-African color line. A racial hierarchy organizes the mall: at the very top is the mall developer, an entrepreneur with start-up capital from a state-owned enterprise; next are the Chinese managers, college-educated urbanites; then comes Jan, the head of security, a white Afrikaner; then Black South African and Nigerian security guards; and, at the very bottom, Black South African and southern African custodial workers and contingent laborers who maintain the mall daily. Within each shop, the Sino-African color line manifests as a set of unspoken rules about wages, jobs, and authority, which I learned in my role as a "Chinese worker." Chinese traders, the bosses (*laoban*), run the business; Chinese workers handle money and closely monitor several African shopworkers, who perform the near entirety of the physical labor. Whereas the color bar legally served white capital and protected the white worker, the Sino-African color line informally serves Chinese traders and Chinese workers. Chinese workers are afforded privileges and protections over Black workers, and they are hired into longer-term positions and paid monthly; African workers turn over quickly and are paid weekly, one-fifth of what Chinese workers earn and below minimum wage. Even though class separates Chinese traders from Chinese workers, the workers identify with their employers, a coethnic alignment reinforced by their entrepreneurial aspiration to become a boss, which impedes solidarity with African workers. Turnover among African workers is high. Most last only a few months before moving on to the next Chinese employer. Except for long-term shopworkers who hold their positions for years at the same shops, African workers do not advance in responsibilities or pay. As Jerry bluntly explained, this is because "the Chinese will never allow the Black man to rule their shop."

At China City, Black (*hei*) is written into the very lexicon of employment. Among themselves, Chinese traders and workers use the terms *heigong*, *heipo*, *heiren*, and *heigui*—and only these terms—to describe African workers, which is common across Sino-African contexts (Driessen 2019; Sheridan 2023). Blackness defines labor identities in a totalizing way. Men are called *heigong*, meaning black (*hei*) worker (*gong*); women are called *heipo* (black woman, *po* being a feminine suffix). In China, *heigong* refers to undocumented workers, and specifically the precarious rural migrant workers who are "illegal" residents in the cities where they work. At the mall, *heigong* only applies to African workers and never to Chinese workers; the latter are also liminal legal subjects, but they are racially unmarked as *yuangong* (employee). Racial terms such as *heigong* change usage and meaning as they circulate in new places and acquire new layers of meaning.

In South Africa, *heigong* layers racial difference onto legal status. Yet the term continues to confer precarity and the lowest position within a labor hierarchy, which is newly occupied by undocumented African workers who are racialized as Black and its manifold meanings. In modern Chinese discourses, the color black (*hei*) has been associated with negative qualities associated with the dark, immoral, illegal, and undocumented. Initially, Blackness was an "internal" concept to China. Only recently did Black become a racial category linked to Africa and Africans. Although China did not have an extensive history with slavery, the concept of Blackness became associated with slavery through the premodern figure of the dark-skinned *kunlun* slave and maritime encounters between enslaved Africans and the Chinese (Dikötter [1992] 2015; Snow 1988; Wyatt 2010).[5] Until the 1920s, Africans were categorized as the "black slave race" (Dikötter [1992] 2015, 93). In the early twentieth century, Chinese intellectuals be-came aware of South Africa through the South African War and accounts of harsh treatment from repatriated Chinese mine workers. They reinter-preted early Chinese accounts of Africa through Euro-American racialist discourse and missionaries (Karl 2002, 121-22). Resonating with Western discourses of Africa, they saw Africa as "the last truly unhistorical space of the modern world, an unhistorical space peopled, moreover, entirely by 'slaves'" (Karl 2002, 121). The binary of historical/ahistorical space and peo-ple/slave became foundational to modern Chinese ideas of race, ethnicity, and nation (Karl 2002, 122). In the Han Chinese imaginary, Blackness has always signified enslavement (Shih 2013, 157). There will always be a degree of incommensurability around racial meanings. But at China City, Black-ness (*hei*) resolutely signifies racial Blackness at the bottom of modernity's global racial hierarchy.

Capitalism produces fetishized representations of capital and labor, such as the Jewish capitalist, the Asian laborer, and the Black laborer (Day 2016; White 2020). In South Africa, anti-Blackness and racial capitalism produce the African worker as "labour-in-itself: a brute biological force in need of mastery" (White 2020, 33). In the mines, pejorative names de-humanized African workers as animalistic labor power to be disciplined. At the mall, African workers are called "black devil" (*heigui*), a derogatory term for Black people (*heiren*) that is akin to the English N-word and con-notes evil and subhuman status. The frequent slippages between *heigui* and *heigong* or *heiren* to describe African workers uphold the idea of Africa and Africans outside of history, modernity, and humanity. When these terms are treated interchangeably, associations between Blackness (*hei*), slavery, illegality, precarity, migrancy, and the demonic crystallize to reinforce the disposability and exploitability of African migrant labor. Resonating with

Euro-American racial formations, Chinese traders' reliance on and devaluation of African migrant labor is the hallmark of Chinese racial capitalism.

African shopworkers perform the necessary duties of attending to customers, cleaning, and physically moving huge amounts of goods from container to warehouse to shelf by hand and trolley. This division of labor mirrors the historical gendering of the mining and domestic labor sectors. Clothing shops require the feminized work and emotional labor of cleaning, ironing, mending garments, attending to customers, and sometimes watching traders' young children. By contrast, electronics, furniture, and commodity shops require assembly of goods and heavy lifting associated with masculine brawn, recalling how African men have been commodified for their "strong, energetic, and powerful bodies" (Morrell 1998, 616). Marcus described his work at the shoe store as menial, "just cutting boxes," while other jobs were about "power, size." Reduced to bodily capacities and dehumanized and disciplined as instruments, workers, as Marcus characterized, are "treated like a wheelbarrow or trolley, just to handle things." As before, African workers embody "labour-in-itself."

Eva, who supervised Julius, Marcus, and Ziggy at the lighting shop, was a low-wage service worker in Guangdong. She explained the role African workers fill: "Because a lot of Malawi people come and look for these jobs and their salary is very low, Chinese will use them. Before Zimbabwe or Mozambique would steal, so they moved to Malawi, but now Malawi likes to steal. But you need to recruit a Black person [*heiren*] to perform coolie labor [*zuo kuli*], to move something heavy. You can't recruit white people because they are not strong, and lazy, and they like to drink." Under the color bar, African mine workers were relegated to a narrow skill band of menial work and "were often seen by white workers and management as an undifferentiated mass who held the same inferior status" (W. G. James 1992, 80). African workers, grouped together as *heiren*, are nationally differentiated, stereotyped, and contrasted with inept white workers. African labor is fungible insofar as workers are interchangeable with workers from the same or different countries. Ruth Wilson Gilmore expands on Karl Marx to point out that capital "pivots" labor power supply and demand and shifts to a new "reserve army of labor" to accumulate (2007, 71). A key feature of the migrant labor system is its geographic flexibility. The selective hiring that Eva described resembled the controlled sourcing of mine workers to depress wages.[6] Eva invoked two related meanings of *kuli*: the Chinese coolie and the bitter physical work associated with this figure. With a twist, *kuli* detaches from Chinese indentured labor on the

4.2   A worker pushes a trolley at Dragon City. © Mark Lewis.
        Courtesy of Mark Lewis.

Rand, a story unknown to most Chinese migrants, to define African labor as menial and exploitable.

My African interlocutors articulated their working conditions through an analysis of racial capitalism. From the day we met, Roger shared an incisive critique of the color line. Pointing out inequalities with respect to race, wages, and skill, Chinese workers actually "learn the job from us, but the salaries [are] different. They are paid more because of different races." He forcefully explicated: "These people, they are tyrants, Chinese. But especially those Chinese [who] work for other Chinese [bosses] to rule these Black people. . . . [The bosses] just take [the workers] from the village, while they don't know anything, you understand. They don't know anything; they don't know about life. What they know is only farm stuff. So, when [the bosses] come and give them an order to rule other people, [the workers] take those things for granted." Although the Chinese workers came from similar humble village backgrounds, they made a point of exercising their newfound authority. The Black/white dynamics of the color bar transpose onto Sino-African relations. African workers call Chinese traders "boss," a homophone of *baas*, the paternalistic Afrikaner superior who demanded deference (Swart 2001). The figure of the Chinese boss grafts over the white *baas*. Roger expresses the militant masculinity of mine workers: "When they say jump, they want us to say, 'How high?'" But, he adds, "my knees are not made for bowing or kneeling."

A collective consciousness around mining and slavery imprints on how workers experience labor. Traders make minute demands, picking at details such as how to pack stock into boxes while counting out loud and how to fold and tape boxes. They punitively dock wages for damaging low-quality goods or being late to work. When their bosses were not looking, workers mimed cracking a whip. A common grievance was shouting as a mode of communication, which Marcus described as "very bad, like slave masters, of course." Marcus's boss said little, only "open," "close," "go throw this in the dustbin," "go buy me food," and, on payday, "money." With little linguistic common ground, ad hoc communication between Chinese traders and managers and African workers recalls Fanakalo, "the industrial lingua franca of southern Africa" (Van Onselen [1982] 2001, 248). A hybrid of Afrikaans, English, and Zulu, it was born out of "necessity between various groups of people—white and black—who shared no base-line language" (W. G. James 1992, 75). A command language, Fanakalo reduced Africans to being the recipients of instructions.

Wages are the most vital part of the traders' bottom line and the most embattled aspect of the color line. In 2014, I spent much of my first summer at China City at Brother Wang's party goods shop. Brother Wang was my downstairs neighbor in Chinatown. In a particularly lively exchange, Sebastian, a Malawian who had been with Brother Wang for six years and came back each time after he was deported to Malawi, opined, "Chinese are always thinking about money, dreaming about money." A Zimbabwean worker, who was wearing a red shirt reading An Injury to One Is An Injury to All, quipped, "The big problem with Chinese is they take Black people and give them no money." Purity, who recently arrived from Malawi, responded, "We drive their business; they use our power." Within earshot but unable to decipher the conversation, Brother Wang shouted "Quickly!" to break it up. Every Sunday payday was confrontational. One by one, Brother Wang called up Anita, Purity, and Sebastian to collect their pay in cash, and each time they demanded more. "Talk too much, take off," Brother Wang explained, to which Sebastian replied, "If we get docked, we will talk more."

Workers viewed me as someone who might expose their working conditions or help advocate for better pay with their bosses. Nana, one of the mall's few South African workers, remained salaried at only ZAR300 (US$25) per week for several years. She sold drinks and snacks near the busiest entrance to China City and easily took in ZAR10,000 on a busy Saturday. With four cameras focused on the counter and a computerized inventory, she could never take so much as a drink costing twenty rand or she would face accusations of "eating their money." "They drink our blood," she charged. Security guards were aware of the problem with wages. This was especially true of subcontracted, undocumented Nigerian guards who were ineligible to be properly credentialed as security guards and were paid less than their credentialed South African colleagues. Jerry and his Nigerian colleagues supplemented their China City earnings as nightclub bouncers. He reflected, "When you appreciate somebody, you give people what it's worth. You don't enslave people." He acknowledged that labor at China City was not "forced labor," yet "you know they don't have a choice, but that doesn't mean that you should enslave them." Invocations of power, blood, greed, and slavery are established tropes for describing colonial labor exploitation (Pierre 2013).

Among shopworkers and security guards, the polemical use of the word *slavery* enables a materialist critique of exploitation and unfreedom. Although slavery was more limited in South Africa than in the United States, the term is still used to denote exploitative relations.[7] Comparing the rhetorical usage of slavery with African discourses of *shibalo* in colonial Mozambique is instructive. While *shibalo* refers to a specific system of forced contract labor, including mine labor, Mozambicans used the term to describe a variety of situations of poorly remunerated, coerced, and enslaved labor. Rather than taking the broad usage of the term as imprecise, social historian Jeanne Marie Penvenne recasts it as Mozambicans' "sense of history and their awareness of the system's broader implications" (1995, 4). Like *shibalo*, when used rhetorically, *slavery* is part of a critical consciousness forged within the Black Radical Tradition, which Robinson defines as "an accretion, over generations, of collective intelligence gathered from struggle" ([1983] 2000, xxx). As Roger astutely remarked, "Under slavery the master fed you; now they give you just enough to buy food." Rather than boosting wages so African mine workers could buy their own food, mine owners provided food as wages in kind, not only as a strategy to pay workers less but, above all, to ensure that the men had enough energy underground (F. Wilson 1972, 57). In 1942, the newly formed African Mine Workers' Union stated, "The African miner is a slave, herded in a compound, under the control of his master. . . . He is compelled to eat the food that will turn him into an instrument for the production or profit for his employer. . . . This is not the life of a free human being. This is the modern counterpart of the old slave compounds" (quoted in Crush 1994, 303). Encapsulating a Marxist critique of social reproduction and the limits of wage exploitation, Roger poignantly stated:

> My belly is full, but I am hungry. You know, they just give us the money to buy some food and work for them, to have some energy to work for these Chinese. . . . At least you know what you earn, you cannot die. But you cannot get what you need because every person needs a better life. . . . I have problems at home. I have to sort out the problems. . . . But if I want food just for now to have energy to work again, it's proper. But I also need the future.

The striking resonances between these statements gesture toward a shared historical consciousness. From Roger's view, Chinese employers pay enough to ensure basic day-to-day but not long-term survival—full, but still hungry. While Chinese traders understand their daily work as being for the future of their families back home, African workers are reduced to living labor without dependents to support or dreams to fulfill. Despite these criticisms, China City is still regarded as a place for survival. Marcus rationalized, "Half a loaf of bread is better than no bread." He optimistically remarked about China City, "This place is like a stage. No matter how much they are paying a week, we don't care. We on the stage . . . I know one day that I'm going to make it."

At the mine and the mall, labor conditions are shaped by cost-and-profit structures. When the international price of gold was fixed, mine owners absorbed increases in capital-intensive production costs by lowering wage rates of politically powerless African miners (W. G. James 1992). In the cutthroat environment of the China Malls, wholesaling low-end imported goods only becomes profitable at scale. Traders rely on low-wage labor to literally move—unbox, assemble, sort, and pack—large volumes of goods from container to warehouse to customers. When workers demanded more than the average ZAR300 per week, Jerry explained, "If the bosses pay more than three hundred or something, they already think that they are paying them so much money. Because the bottom is so low, they think, too much money!" While the price of cheap imported commodities is not fixed like gold, maintaining a low floor is integral to turning a profit.

Whereas the color bar enshrined job, skill, and wages into law, the standard weekly salary at the China Malls is dictated by the informal rules of the local labor market. Without the ability to collectively organize to demand better working conditions or wages, workers use what their peers doing comparable work earn to demand more pay. Traders gossip about others who stray from the norms, accusing them of breaking norms (*tai lipu*). When I asked Eva the harm in paying workers more, she explained, "This is the market price, you give every Black person this much money" unless the shop is especially busy and the work extra arduous. She continued, "If you give five hundred and I give three hundred fifty, your worker will talk to my worker." The worker will leave to look for a job paying ZAR500, and "you have ruined this market."

Just as African workers are not homogeneous in their experiences and views, neither are Chinese traders. My boss, Xiao Li, was in the minority at China City. From a middle-class background, she had worked for a multinational company in Shanghai after college. She wanted to pay her employees, three Zimbabwean women with children, more than ZAR400, but that was already on the high end. She admitted to me in private, "They need to have a livelihood [*shenghuo*], too." When her employees asked for raises, she did not grant them out of fear that other traders would confront her or talk about her behind her back. It was in her best interest to not rock the boat, even as she recognized the hardship of scraping by. The actions of the most sympathetic are constrained by powerful social norms and "market forces." While wages and working conditions are difficult to effect, workers improvise freedom to survive. The dynamics between Chinese capital and African labor seem generally adversarial, but this is not the whole story. As chapters 5 and 6 will illustrate, Sino-African relations are more nuanced in their interdependencies, intimacies, and proximities.

Contesting the Color Line

At China City, workers' petty resistances subvert Chinese exploitation of Black labor, recuperate their humanity, and ensure survival. An archetypal weapon of the weak, stealing is a quotidian form of resistance against the color line. Shopworkers schooled me in their ingenious ways: finding a locksmith to duplicate a key, carrying out merchandise in empty boxes and asking custodians to safeguard them, and selling directly to customers and pocketing the money. With ample markets for stolen goods, stealing is a way to make ends meet. It is also payback for exploitation in the tradition of banditry, "a cry for vengeance on the rich and the oppressors . . . a righting of individual wrongs" (Hobsbawm 1959, 5). Widely practiced, stealing is why workers change jobs from shop to shop or mall to mall. Even though

Marcus was morally opposed to stealing, he stated matter-of-factly, "You find a job, show them your ID, work, steal, and go." Roger lucidly explained why workers steal:

> As a person, as a human being, I need shelter, I need clothes, I need some basic human needs. . . . The money we earn there is not good enough to have basic needs. That's why some other people steal from them [Chinese], they break [into] their shop . . . they take the money, not because they are thieves, or whatever they can think of, but poverty force[s] them to do so. . . . They are working to eradicate their poverty. But they don't gain. . . . They don't have any choice other than to steal.

Stealing is necessary for survival, and it is tinted with resentment and vengeance. It is an immediate form of redressive action and economic redistribution when organized resistance is difficult. But stealing calcifies Chinese stereotypes of Black criminality and intensifies surveillance.

Space, race, and power converge to socially produce geographies of domination and subaltern geographies, one based in surveillance and the other in freedom. Out of fear that workers would steal when opportunity struck, Chinese traders monitored them intensely. They installed security cameras, checked workers for merchandise when exiting, and relied on the security apparatus on their side: camouflage-clad security guards, armed response vehicles, cameras, infrared sensors, control rooms, and watchtowers. At one especially busy mall, shopworkers wore jerseys with ID numbers like criminals or fungible units of labor power. Just as Chinese conversed in Mandarin and local dialects to make public conversations private, traders tried to prevent African workers from speaking in "Black languages" (*heihua*) and would shout "Quickly!" and "No talking!" to stop conversation. Traders were afraid of employees conspiring with each other or with security guards, contingent workers, or, in the worst case, outside syndicates.

While security guards were foremost concerned with protecting the property of Chinese tenants, they often condoned petty theft among the African workers. Mine managers, for all their formal authority, routinely accommodated the informal rules and moral economy of mine workers to maintain production—a "precarious equilibrium at best" (Moodie and Ndatshe 1994, 75). Jan, the head of security at China City, was a brash, chain-smoking Afrikaner who made his career in the military fighting liberation movements and the private security industry. Given his background, his sympathy with the workers surprised me. "They don't have work permits; they don't have asylum," Jan explained; an employee "must still be able to send money to his family wherever they come from, and that's why these inside jobs take place, because they don't earn such a big salary and that's a way for them to survive." He related a recent incident: "I asked him, Why do you bite the hand that feeds you? He was sick and he asked the shop owner to give him money for the doctor. The shop owner refused to give him money, and he was pissed off. 'You are either going to give me the money or I'll take it.' And, unfortunately for him, he was caught." Jerry also saw stealing as the predictable outcome of low wages: "That's why the Malawians and the Zimbabweans steal. Even we don't have a problem with that. We keep telling them if they can do it and get away with it, it's fine. But your boss, if you get caught, we club you, you lose." Not all shopworkers were willing to take this chance, nor were all security guards sympathetic. Instead of handling incidents with police, workers caught stealing were beaten behind closed doors and blacklisted from entering or working at the mall.

Cardinal forms of discipline from the mines resurface at the mall. Guards take the role of "boss boys," the Mozambican foremen retained by white overseers to maximize productivity by doling out beatings. Boss boys were part of the everyday violence among men in the mines (Breckenridge 1998, 673). Beating workers remains a valorized performance of masculinity. A few mall guards took pleasure beating the men caught stealing, bragging that they "broke every bone in his body." The mall subcontracts four Nigerian guards, referred to as "muscle," for this purpose. The guards, who lack the official accreditation of their South African counterparts, operate outside in zones of exception. As Jan explained, "With the Nigerians, they're more my muscle to ensure that if there's a situation, it's handled there and then." As Baba, a guard from Lagos esteemed for his quiet reserve and keen eye, explained, "Before, [South African] security cannot touch any shopworker here, but when we [the Nigerian guards] come here . . . we start to beat. When they scared, we talk to them . . . when they see the face, they know this one is serious. Because anywhere you want to work, you have to put a scare there." Workers most feared beatings from specific guards; they paid attention to differences in uniform, rank, and reputations. Throughout southern Africa, a colonial hierarchy of white men and Black "boys" underpinned social relations of labor. The diminutive term *boy* reflected the inferior status of Black migrant men absorbed into the wage economy (Morrell 1998, 630). Until the 1970s, all Black men who worked for whites in South Africa were called "boys," with such names as "home boy," "machine boy," police boy," and "boss boy" (Moodie and Ndatshe 1994, 19). Boss boys were often the personal retainers of white superiors (Moodie and Ndatshe 1994, 61). Jan paraded his "Nigerian boys," who then kept "Malawian boys" such as Marcus, Roger, and Ziggy in line. Security guards were enforcers of law and order; they disciplined African labor in the service of Chinese capital accumulation and protection of property. At the same time, their capacity for solidarity and leniency created opportunities for freedom.

Within the mine existed subaltern spaces, the "spaces in which black workers carve out hidden domains of social intercourse, experience, and activity which are beyond the powers and comprehension of white compound architects and managers" (Crush 1994, 319). At the mall, workers reminisced about feeling "free" back home, free in a world without constant monitoring. They forged a subaltern geography within the labyrinth that is China City: six blocks, two levels, shops inside and outside, warehouses, parking lots, and container yards. Hometown friends and relatives often helped one another get jobs at nearby shops. Social life clustered in corridors. A trip from A block to C block became a longer excursion by zigzagging through B block to talk—minor acts that "create a certain play in the machine" (Certeau 1984, 30) and happen in the "pores of the working day" (Marx 1976, 534). Traders could not control workers wandering beyond their shops. In the mines, resistance was grounded in densely networked migrant cultures and hometown solidarities of work teams and compounds (Moodie and Ndatshe 1994). Work stoppages, "go-slows," and absenteeism were everyday forms of resistance to workplace control. African workers refused the drudgery and racial degradation of labor and demanded the right to pleasure. In colonial South Africa, Zine Magubane writes, "The only space of freedom for blacks was in the avoidance of work" (2004, 162). At the China Mall, freedom from work happens in being on the clock but out of sight, stealing back time and slowing down work, and refusing to be merely living labor.

Social life unfolded in hidden spaces and in plain sight, and it transformed the space of work into more than it was supposed to be. Secluded rooftops, bathrooms, freight elevators, loading zones, and recycling areas become unmonitored spaces for friendship, joy, and affiliation. A sunny back stairway with a utility sink was where workers, security guards, and custodians congregated over cigarettes and food. At lunchtime, food stalls and convenience stores became places to congregate. A makeshift prayer area in an empty shop transformed a sleepy corner into a cosmopolitan space where South Asian and African Muslims could gather across race, ethnicity, class, and nationality. Every morning and afternoon, the parking lot came alive as

4.3   Resting in the stairwell's shadows.
        Photo by the author.

workers arrived or left the mall together. Workers resisted drudgery through friendships and romance, observable through elaborate handshakes, nicknames, affectionate glances, hand-holding, break-time visits, and etchings on the walls. When working every day, dating at the mall was practical. Although guards and workers were forbidden from fraternizing (considered dangerous grounds for conspiring to steal), one guard, a queer Black South African woman, alluded to fraternizing taking place. She snickered, "We [guards] are here enjoying China City every day." I bonded with the few female guards over the nuisance of flirtatious, sometimes harassing male security guards and traders. We regularly gossiped about happenings beneath the surface. When I asked another guard about how she spotted forbidden intimacies, she lightheartedly answered, "You can see it in their movements; it is more than friendship." In yet another way the mall resembled the mine,

4.4 Warehouse intimacies. Photo by the author.

surveillance and control were never total. These spaces for social vitality exemplify what AbdouMaliq Simone calls "the surrounds"—"those spaces beyond capture, not immune to it, not free of it, but rather as something aside from it, as loci of continuous rebellion. This is rebellion that might not always look like rebellion" (2022, 24).

Racial Capitalism in the Chinese Century

Since the mineral revolution, migrancy and the color bar have underwritten South Africa's capitalist development. These two intertwined features resurface at Chinese wholesale malls along the mining belt where consumptive economies are layered on top of extractive ones. China City is not only implicated in but made possible by the afterlives of gold. The landscape serves as a constant reminder of the great mineral wealth that was unearthed through the labor of southern African migrants. The capitalist activities of Chinese petty entrepreneurs are enmeshed with the material and immaterial afterlives of gold mining. Reading the mall through the mine produces an understanding of Chinese capital not simply as generically nonracial global capital or a nationally bound, ethnically specific variety of capital ("capitalism with Chinese characteristics") but as global racial capital in a world made by colonialism.

All capitalism is racial capitalism, as Ruth Wilson Gilmore insists, but its configurations are highly specific products of how capitalism, race, and other salient categories of difference (gender, ethnicity, nation, caste, sexuality) have been constituted in space and time. In this case, Chinese capitalist projects function through logics, imaginaries, and practices that draw from Chinese racial discourses to retrench racial inequalities made through South Africa's political economy of cheap labor, settler colonialism, and the ongoing regional empire of labor. Migrant labor at the China Malls is the product of the protracted life of gold mining. Southern Africans are categorized as "Black labor" (*heigong*), a term with layered racial and non-racial meanings in China and South Africa, that imbues Chinese capitalist activities with an anti-Black character. In the political economy of China City, the profitability of cheap commodities depends on the cheap labor and rightlessness of a surplus population of undocumented southern African migrants. Through colonial taxation and land expropriation, the migrant labor system enshrined conditions for a self-reproducing labor reserve. Similarly, the reproduction of migrant workers' precarity is built into the structure of work. The exploitation of migrant labor is by no means particular to Chinese migrants but endemic to the City of Gold.

As the China Malls are sustained by generations of circular migration, the place-based memory of mine migrancy transposes dynamics, affects, and struggles from the demolished mines onto the new malls. The afterlife of gold manifests unevenly in the African and Chinese imaginaries. Chinese traders and workers do not know the history of Chinese indenture where they stand, instead deploying the term *kuli* to devalue Black labor as menial and fungible. The invocation of *kuli* indexes the radical repositioning of China in the twenty-first century. For African shopworkers within two generations of mine migrancy, the afterlives of gold remain alive in family histories of going to Johannesburg, hometown-based migrant cultures, and political consciousness. The former migrant mine worker's struggle for dignity and a better life is ever present in the spaces the shopworkers inhabit and the borders they traverse.

The critical features of the Black/white division of labor of the color bar and its figures—the migrant worker, *baas*, boss boy, and police—persist, albeit in different embodiments. Regardless of the identity of the capitalists, the color bar, one of the most elementary relations of labor and race in South Africa, remakes itself in new guises. Blurring temporal distinctions between "old" and "new," the dialectics of race and capitalism continuously transform themselves while absorbing Chinese difference into what has been the primary domain of whiteness. Returning to the postcard "On the Rand: White, Black, and Yellow," a new global color line of Chinese capital and African labor has taken hold. Whiteness is not absent but exerts itself in the legacies of colonial mine migrancy and capitalist social relations that Chinese traders enter. The incorporation of Chinese sojourners signals a reconfiguration of racial capitalism. Beyond Black and white, racial capitalism reproduces itself through new racial embodiments and modes of extraction while also reinvigorating radical traditions and visions of freedom.

PART II

Racial Formations

5

Criminal Obsessions and Racial Fictions

Contrary to the experience of crime, which disrupts meaning and disorders the world, the talk of crime symbolically reorders it by trying to reestablish a static picture of the world. This symbolic reordering is expressed in very simplistic terms, relying on the creation of clear-cut oppositional categories. . . . Narratives of crime elaborate prejudices and try to eliminate ambiguities.

Teresa Caldeira, *City of Walls*, 2000

You know when one fish is rotten in the pond, all the fish are rotten. And when a Black person, a Malawian person, steal from the Chinese, they say all of them are thieves.

Marcus, interview at China City, 2014

The end of the month is a dangerous time. It is when South Africans collect salaries and grants, shops are flush with cash, and the China Malls are congested. The final days of May 2015 were punctuated with multiple high-profile robberies and murders of several Chinese entrepreneurs, a string of disconnected events that became connected through their retelling. Near China City, a Taiwanese man was mistaken for a trader and critically injured in a robbery on Highway M2, a main thoroughfare that links several mining belt malls and Cyrildene Chinatown. It's a stretch where state and metropolitan police set up road blockades to extort bribes from cash-carrying traders, and organized syndicates and petty thieves wait for an opportune smash-and-grab or carjacking. Shortly after, a trader leaving China City was held up at a traffic light and lost several million rand in cash. Mall security discovered text messages incriminating a shopworker, a Malawian male employee of nine years, who purportedly tipped off a syndicate. In the final days of May, four men, masked and armed, robbed a Chinese trader on Highway M2. The footage, which was captured by a dashboard camera, went viral on WeChat. One savvy importer got rich off the overnight surge in demand for dashboard cameras. The same week, a China City resident was found murdered in her shop. The alleged assailants were two Malawian workers, one relatively new and another an employee of six years. As I will recount, this grim story took on a life of its own. At the heart of Chinese paranoia about armed robberies is the perceived betrayal by African employees, especially ones of many years. But from the vantage point of employees, robberies can deliver redress and retribution.

That same month, over one hundred miles from Johannesburg, two serious events unfolded in Newcastle, an industrial district in KwaZulu-Natal where mainland Chinese have replaced Taiwanese as major investors in the clothing and textile industry. On payday, a Fujianese factory owner and his Chinese bodyguard were robbed and shot in the truck. Shortly after that, a second Fujianese factory owner was fatally shot by an employee, marking the tenth Chinese national killed in South Africa since January of that year. My Fujianese interlocutors followed these stories as closely as those that had happened nearby. Hometown connections and social media closed the distance between places. Local Chinese media outlet *Nanfei 365* reported the second death as an "employee robbery and murder [*yuangong qiangjie yuhai*] (*Nanfei 365*, 2015b). When it was time to collect weekly cash wages, the employee, a Black South African man who had been working at the factory for a year, stormed in with outside men. They took the money and shot the factory owner. The story intersperses details of what transpired with images from the crime scene and photos of the assailants. Whether the assailants were "employees" or "gangsters" was unclear because of the interchangeable use of terms throughout the piece—a common conflation that reveals how Chinese migrants racialize African workers as Black and represent them as always already criminal. As Marcus's observation at the beginning of this chapter indicates, African workers were fully cognizant of this blanket racialization. Like so many crime stories that flooded WeChat, the story has a pedagogical function of warning employers to avoid paying in cash and be suspicious of African employees. The author contextualizes the robbery-murder within the factory's location in a "Black area" with abundant cheap labor and ongoing tensions between Chinese factory owners, South African workers, and labor unions. In recent years, the story reports, labor disputes over the national minimum wage had led to an increase in robberies of Chinese. In the tale of the factory owner's untimely end, the labor conflict—the contradiction (*maodun*) between employers and employees—had "become a problem that cannot be ignored." Violent robberies of Chinese employers by African employees are flashpoints of race and class and central to transnational processes of racialization in which Blackness comes to signify criminality.

Crime is a catchall analytical category that I use to understand how African and Chinese actors make sense of different forms of social action: petty theft, armed robberies, and employee murder, each involving varying degrees of violence and premeditation, with property as the common denominator. My Chinese interlocutors saw these on a spectrum, with a fine line dividing them. Theft, robberies, and killings were the only matter my Chinese interlocutors insisted that I write about in this book. But my African interlocutors saw things quite differently. In South Africa, crime has long functioned as an informal, private, extralegal means for redress and justice (Comaroff and Comaroff 2016; Diphoorn 2015). One person's definition of crime can be another's justice. Taking an anthropological approach to crime, I am concerned less with actual acts, facts, and statistics than everyday narratives of crime and safety and the social truths "crime" produces. As Teresa Caldeira (2000) has theorized, "talk of crime" instills fear, organizes daily life, and naturalizes racial fictions. Narratives of crime reorder a world disrupted by violence, while perpetuating a representational violence of their own (Caldeira 2000, 34). To make sense of their world, Chinese migrants see themselves as victims of crime, a vulnerable racial, ethnic, and national minority in a Black majority country at the mercy of African employees. The general Chinese view of Sino-African relations is the direct inversion of how African workers see the relationship. The power relations between capital/labor, boss/worker, and Chinese/Black are flipped. The relational construction of Chinese victimhood and Black criminality is a pillar of contemporary Chinese racial formations in China and South Africa. As I explore in this chapter, crime—talk of crime, fear of crime, racial profiling, and surveillance—is the stuff of Sino-African encounters and Chinese racial formations.

Narratives of crime are critical to understanding the racial distrust and affective texture of Sino-African encounters. The first part of this chapter uses crime to tease out negotiations between Chinese capital and African labor. African migrant workers, part of longer histories of regional migration and radical traditions, take what's owed to them by stealing, minor acts of resistance and survival that heighten Chinese distrust of African workers. An antagonistic struggle between capital and labor does not sufficiently explain the fraught dependencies between Chinese traders, Chinese workers, and African workers who depend on one another to get by in vastly uneven ways. Crime uniquely reveals the mixture of trust, betrayal, anxiety, fear, suspicion, antipathy, anger, and revenge swirling beneath the surface of everyday interactions. Crime shines a light on the structure of feeling in Sino-African dynamics in both directions: Chinese paranoia about African betrayal and a diffuse, atmospheric anxiety about Blackness, and African resentments of Chinese exploitation and displays of racial paternalism.

In a variation of palimpsestic reading, I contextualize Sino-African relations through another historical frame of reference: the Afrikaner farm at the turn of the twentieth century. Chinese traders' fear of betrayal and sense of racial injury resemble the racial paternalism between the white *baas* and Black tenant worker and white paranoia about farm murders today—yet another way the Black/white dynamics of South African settler colonialism and racial capitalism are recast in the Chinese Century. Reading the mining belt mall through the farm (what may seem an unusual pairing at first) illuminates how African workers associate Chinese migrants with the racial positionality of whiteness and its signature practices of surveillance and paternalism. This is not to say that Chinese are white in the way that white is a socially constructed identity. Whiteness marks a racial position of power. As Zine Magubane writes of colonial South Africa, "Indigenous people took the prerogative to decide for themselves what constituted the boundaries of whiteness at any given moment" (2004, 139). Whiteness and white supremacy do not need white bodies to be present.

Crime also offers a privileged site at which to examine Chinese racial formations and the relational construction of Blackness and Chineseness. Criminality is a key trope of Blackness in Chinese racial imaginaries. Building on chapter 4's examination of the resignification of Black labor, this chapter delves into Black's (*hei*) racial associations with illegality through the sticky figure of the "triple illegal" (*sanfei*) African migrant in Chinese cities. Circulating across China and South Africa, racial stereotypes and images of crime and disorder entrench stereotypes of Africa and Africans as dangerous. Building on scholarship on white possession, I argue that Chinese racial identity is based in proprietary relations that poses Black criminality as a threat to Chinese safety and property. In what follows, I begin with the transnational making of racial Blackness (*hei*) between China and South Africa. I then return to stories about crime and the affective states, stereotypes, and identifications that crime talk organizes. Finally, I explore quotidian processes of racialization, including the racial subjectification of African workers as Black (*hei*) and racial education of Chinese newcomers. The stories I feature were deeply affecting and shaped my relationships to people and place. They were the hardest to write, but critical in illuminating the everyday complexities of race.

Blackness across Johannesburg and Guangzhou

As Stuart Hall has theorized, race is a "floating signifier," a discursive construct within a cultural system and signifying field. The meaning of race is unfixed; there is no final, transhistorical meaning, no essential truth. Race undergoes continual resignification, shedding old meanings and picking up new ones, "made to mean something different in different cultures, in different historical formations at different moments of time" ([1997] 2021, 362). *Hei*, which translates to the color black and the racial category Black, is one such floating signifier. *Hei* signifies a bundle of associations of the sinister, dark, hidden, shadowy, and illegal (Sautman 1994). Its genealogy begins with the "black devil" (*heigui*) and quasi-bestial "Black person" (*heiren*) in ancient literature and is closely related to the premodern dark-skinned person, or *kunlun*. Derived from the Kunlun Mountains, the term was initially a neutral descriptor for the geographic otherness and darker complexions of Chinese or Malay peoples living on China's frontier. Following centuries of Chinese encounters with "dark-skinned foreigners" from Southeast Asia and East Africa, the term acquired a pejorative meaning in the thirteenth century (Wyatt 2010, 19-20). The opposite of the venerated jade-white skin of ancient China, the color black has negative class associations with sun-darkened complexions and manual labor. As a modifier, *hei* turns Africa (Feizhou) into Black Africa (Hei Feizhou) to emphasize the darkness associated with the continent. As Sino-African ties ramped up in the early 2000s, state media outlet Xinhua prohibited the usage of the name Hei Feizhou (Hood 2013, 290). *Hei* turns worker (*gong*) into black worker (*heigong*), a term that confers illegalized status on Chinese rural migrants in China and racially marks African migrant workers in South Africa. *Hei* was part of the everyday lexicon among my Chinese interlocutors. Its usage in African contexts is situational and often connotes a threat to security (Sheridan 2023). To describe Black Africans and South Africans, Chinese migrants use "Black people" (*heiren*) and the derogatory "black devil" (*heigui*) in racial ways.

Premodern and modern ideas about Blackness (*hei*)—as savage, beast, barbarian, devil, and slave—continue to shape Chinese racial discourses today. My Chinese interlocutors often described an African worker as a "black devil" (*heigui*). When I asked them why they used *heigui*, some explained that African workers lacked humanity, reason, soul, or consciousness (*renxing*). A modestly successful trader from Fujian casually opined that Black Africans were brutish animals (*chusheng*). Demonizing and animalizing the other are key logics within contemporary Han Chinese racial thought (K.-H. Chen 2010).[1] But not all my interlocutors used the pejorative *heigui*. Younger Chinese migrants with higher education levels favored the more politically correct, neutral term *heiren*. Lisa, a recent high school graduate from Jiangmen whose parents are rural migrants in China, worked for a Fujianese trader who used *heigui* gratuitously. Lisa refrained from using the term. *Heiren* referred to the living and *heigui* the dead; the difference was a recognition of humanity. Joyce, born in 1976 in Guanxi Province, had been wholesaling in South Africa for a decade. Although Joyce's relationship with her longtime Zimbabwean female employee was better than most, racist stereotypes were latent. When I interviewed her, she compared herself to the uncouth, overtly racist Fujianese traders around her: "*Heigui* doesn't sound good. Many bosses at the shops really like saying 'heigui heigui,' but you are in a Black country [*heiren de guojia*], and you should not disrespect them. Black people will sometimes steal stuff, but there's no way to change that . . . you cannot change this habit. [You] don't have to yell. A lot of bosses act like they are savages [*chusheng*] because armed robberies and stealing are often committed by Black people. . . . It's the same everywhere. They do that in China too." Joyce's comment, "They do that in China too," connects discourses of Black criminality in South Africa and China. Who "they" are is indeterminate, referring to African foreign nationals and Chinese rural migrants who occupy a similar place in Chinese imaginaries of urban space, danger, and disorder. Racial categories, imaginaries, vernaculars, and ideas are transnationally constructed. In colonial South Africa, the circulation of images of Africans between colony and metropole produced Blackness as trope and metaphor (Z. Magubane 2004). Chinese crime discourses in South Africa combine two racial fictions: the criminalization of African migrants in China and the attribution of crime in postapartheid South Africa to the end of white minority rule. Ideas of Black criminality shuttle back and forth between China and South Africa through depictions of the city, whether Guangzhou or Johannesburg, as dangerous. Most Chinese migrants brought up crime and public safety in Johannesburg. The same phrases always came up in conversation: Johannesburg is a city of disorder (*Yuebao hen luan*); Johannesburg is not safe (*Yuebao bu anquan*); public security is poor (*zhi'ian bu hao*); and armed robbery (*qiangjie*) is frequent. Crime proxies for race and links racial imaginaries between China and South Africa.

Since the early 2000s, African migrants, many of whom are Nigerian, have sought entrepreneurial opportunity in southern coastal cities—most famously Guangzhou, also known as Chocolate City and Little Africa. African migrants in Chinese cities are pejoratively called "triple illegal" (*sanfei*), which refers to a trifecta of undocumented entry, employment, and residency. The floating population of Chinese rural migrants and *sanfei* foreigners have been criminalized and scapegoated for increases in urban crime and disorder (*luan*; Lan 2017; L. Zhang 2001). As Lisa Marie Cacho reminds us, criminalization has two meanings: being stereotyped as criminal and being prevented from being law abiding. To be criminalized in the first sense is to be misrecognized or incorrectly profiled. In the second sense, criminalization is a relationship to the law in which visa regimes, borders, bureaucratic documents, and state categories illegalize people and livelihoods (Cacho 2012, 4). While *sanfei* refers to all "illegalized foreigners," African migrants, who are also sometimes referred to as "triple illegal Black people" (*sanfei heiren*), are paradigmatic of this criminalized population. Depicted as vectors of disease and scorned for romantic partnerships with Chinese women, African migrants occupy an outsize place in Chinese collective imaginations. Online there is a plethora of articles, blog posts, and comments about African immigration. Commentators express a variety of ideologies. Proponents of multiculturalism seek to integrate African migrants through immigration and naturalization in the image of a "global family" (Amar 2021). Symptomatic of the global rise of right-wing nationalism, vitriolic anti-African sentiment demands the expulsion of African migrants. In between these poles is the veiled racism and xenophobia of allowing "legal" foreigners only (*Zhihu* 2021).

The presence of African migrant communities reflects China's changing place in the world. China is no longer an isolated country but an alternative migration destination to Europe and the United States. As an example of criminalized representations, a blogger writes,

> Since the founding of New China, under the improvement by the government, the domestic development has taken on a new look. At least the living standards of the people now appearing have been infinitely close to those of Western countries. In addition, our country has always been the safest country in the world, so it has attracted many foreigners. In this environment, many foreigners began to come to China for development, especially Black people in Africa, which have become an epidemic in China, especially in Guangzhou, the streets are full of Black people. Among these Black people, some people are even triple illegal Black people [*sanfei heiren*]. (*Sohu* 2019, my translation)

The author lauds domestic policies that elevated Chinese cities to Western standards of development, but development brought migration. African migration is framed as the unintended consequence of China's catching up to the West. As African migrants seek entrepreneurial opportunities in China, they threaten the timeless public safety of the city and achievements of market reform. To draw a contrast, in South Africa, Chinese migrants often enter, reside, and work without papers, but their legal statuses and informal activities are never compared to *sanfei* foreigners. *Sanfei* discourse sticks together illegality, criminality, and Blackness (Ahmed 2004). Racialized as Black, African foreigners, regardless of "legal" or "illegal" status under a restrictive visa regime, are central to Chinese imaginaries of public safety, order, and development in China and South Africa. In South Africa, Chinese migrants treat Black South Africans and African migrants as protocriminals and disorderly presences.

The Specter of Crime

Crime, policing, and securitization have made up the bedrock of social organization during apartheid and the postapartheid era. During apartheid, policing was directed at enforcing racial separation and suppressing political resistance. Pass laws policed the mobility of Black South Africans. Criminality equaled the transgression of racial boundaries. Blackness bore, and still bears, the mark of criminality (Bremner 2004; Comaroff and Comaroff

2016). The end of apartheid dissolved rigid racial boundaries, and in doing so, unleashed anxieties about race, space, crime, and the future of democracy. For white South Africans, the figure of the criminal replaced that of the Native as a container for terror (Bremner 2004). Like many cities in the Global South undergoing political transitions, spectacular wealth is contiguous with immense poverty. In South Africa, the tumult of political transition, unemployment, and income inequality has driven the increase in vehicle theft, burglary, robbery, assault, and murder. In the 1990s, Johannesburg was named one of the world's most dangerous cities—a reputation that is hard to displace. The privatization of policing and securitization has been the hallmark of contemporary South Africa; the nation boasts the largest private security industry in the world. In some places, security personnel outnumber police officers seven to one (Diphoorn 2015). Johannesburg is an anxious city of fortified enclosures, defensive urbanism, and gated communities insulated by electric fences, barbed wire, and boundary walls (Bremner 2004, 2010; Caldeira 2000; Falkof and van Staden 2020; Murray 2020). Regardless of the reality of rising or falling crime rates and the specific places where different kinds of crime take place, the entire city is imagined as a scene of crime and defined by an "ontological insecurity" (Murray 2020).[2] Martin Murray observes that after 1994, a "scattered assortment of island-like enclosures has been laid on top of an already distorted urban landscape divided along racial lines" (2011, 3). Three decades after democracy, crime still functions as a placeholder for a range of concerns about class, mobility, gender, race, and status—essentially, "the whole edifice of postapartheid South Africa"—among whites and upwardly mobile nonwhite residents (Falkof and van Staden 2020, 9).

Like China City, Cyrildene Chinatown is a mixed space of legal, illegal, and extralegal practices and overlapping state and nonstate sovereignties. Residents constantly speak of crime and poor public safety. The flashing lights of armed response patrol cars, orange uniforms, and elevated posts for observance remind residents of constant surveillance. To Chinese residents, private security is an assuring sign of protection. But to African employees and visitors, it is a terrorizing sign of brute force. Homes, shops, restaurants, and businesses are outfitted with razor wire, wire netting, and bars on windows and enclosed by spiked palisade fences and boundary walls. Unlike the nearby affluent suburb, with sleek electric fences, stylized gates, and pristine high walls, Cyrildene Chinatown's fences and bars are rusty and reinforced with cheap and unsightly razor wire. Within this fragmented city of enclosures, Chinese migrants densely reside and work in enclaves to insulate

5.1   China City's securitized flats. Photo by the author.

themselves from the unknown danger of Black bodies, especially Black men who are seen as the primary perpetrators of armed robberies. China City is one such securitized enclave, an all-inclusive compound with an apartment complex, grocery store, and banking amenities—all of which minimize the need to leave the premises. As Hannah Appel observes in her ethnography of multinational oil corporations in Equatorial Guinea, compound housing is the practice of lived separation, white fear, and frontier making. Domestic arrangements mirror the ways in which multinationals insulate themselves while extracting profit from foreign locales (2019, 103).

Fear of crime is a potent force that imprints on experiences of place and directs the most banal aspects of everyday life. I became accustomed to the defensive habits, routes, and rhythms for moving through Johannesburg: avoiding the inner city, traveling by car, being vigilant around strangers, returning home before nightfall, and bulletproofing vehicles. Migrants learn

5.2   A biometric fingerprint reader controls entry
       into China City's flats. Photo by the author.

to be fearful when it comes to proximity with Black bodies. Lisa explained that while walking in Chinatown, "I will be very vigilant, I will definitely keep my distance . . . at least one meter away. . . . This is a street and you will often hear about robberies. I will protect myself. If I see a Black person, I will go around [the long way] and not let them come too close." When I asked Sarah, the former teacher from Hubei, about her strongest memory in South Africa, she recounted, "When I was working for someone else, a Black person [*heiren*] came to knock on our [car] window. It looked like he had a gun." Although nothing transpired, "I'm scared because I always hear of Chinese dying." Sarah's paranoia was informed by her husband Joe's frightful experience of being robbed at home in Chinatown. Both women were outwardly respectful of Black customers and employees, but fear of crime remained a powerful part of their daily lives in Johannesburg.

5.3 China City's security headquarters. Photo by the author.

Armed robberies (*qiangjie*) are not everyday occurrences, but talk of them is constant. Often armed robberies are "inside jobs" when shopworkers and occasionally security guards sell information to outside gangs. They are possible through detailed inside information: the timing and amount of cash transfers, the coverage of security cameras, license plates, home addresses, and driving routes. The targets are typically not random: traders, the bosses who take home the money, are targeted for inside jobs, not Chinese workers. One Fujianese manager, whose absentee boss made her vulnerable to being mistaken as the shop owner, expressed reassurance that she would not be targeted. Anyone watching the shop or consulting with shopworkers would learn that she was not the one taking the money home. "People are always saying Black people are stupid [*sa*]," she said. "They are not stupid, not even one bit." To prevent inside jobs from occurring, traders guard information

5.4　A BMW is parked behind walls, gates, and razor wire in Cyrildene Chinatown. Photo by the author.

about cash sales and plans. They display monetary amounts on calculators and speak in Mandarin or regional tongues. When shopworkers learned to speak a few Mandarin phrases, traders found this amusing. Numeracy, however, was alarming. Questions about containers, sales, money, dates, and times were off-limits between African workers and Chinese.

My African interlocutors understood crime as petty theft, which was necessary to supplement low wages and which security guards often permitted. My Chinese interlocutors, however, imagined crime as a continuum from both small theft (*xiaotou*) to conspiratorial inside jobs. Fear of crime blurred the line between all kinds of violent and nonviolent action to people and property. Armed robbery was conjured as a combination of the ubiquitous impersonal nonviolence of stealing goods and the selective personal violence of armed robbery and murder. Crime talk melded the ubiquity, gravity, and proximate danger between these two categorically distinct kinds of action and made them commensurable. To traders, minor transgressions predicted something much graver down the line. As Baba, a Nigerian security guard who took me on his patrols, imparted, "The people you know well will be the ones who rob you."

5.5 A sign advertising Bad Boyz Hillbrow, Cyrildene Chinatown's security firm. Photo by the author.

Unsettled Scores

In May 2015, I had returned to China City for one month when the mall was shaken by the death of a resident. One morning, a woman named Ling Jie (Sister Ling) was found dead in her shop. Originally from Zhejiang, she had been trading in Johannesburg for over a decade. In the early morning, a customer alerted security guards about the shop, its door ajar and the lights off. Inside, security discovered her body rolled up in a bolt of fabric and the register empty. The cause of death was strangulation. The assailants were two Malawian workers, an employee of a few months and another of six years. The story was striking in more ways than one: a premeditated murder rather than an opportunistic robbery, the impassioned act of strangulation, and the ceremonious wrapping of her body in the very commodity she imported and the employees handled. In the weeks to come, the Chinese Consulate General teamed up with Malawian authorities to issue an arrest warrant for the suspects. Ling Jie's husband, who was in Zhejiang, flew back for the funeral, which was held on a Saturday morning near Cyrildene Chinatown so her friends and family could attend before opening their shops. For weeks a feeling of alarm lingered in the air. Eventually her relatives took over the shop and business resumed. The flat she shared with her husband, now tainted with superstition, remained empty. Months later, when I was looking for a flat at the mall, her unit remained empty. It was not offered, nor did I ask about its availability.

The story took on a life of its own as my interlocutors spun their own versions. I have reservations about writing about Ling Jie's death. She is someone I encountered only in passing, not as a person but as an event. I risk committing a second order of violence and fueling the libidinal economy that surrounds stories of death (Hartman 2008b). But I present the basic elements of this story because of what discrepant narratives reveal about the meanings of violence and the affective states and racial fictions such an event cultivates. The story commanded tremendous power not because of its sensationalism and exceptionality but because it represented the extreme actualization of the quotidian tensions of race and labor. Crime narratives are not only about the specific incident but also the social context (Caldeira 2000). Writing about the colonial archive, Ann Laura Stoler sifts through the disjointed reconstructions of the murder of a planter family in the Dutch East Indies. Colonial agents struggled to comprehend the murder as personal or political, an isolated act of revenge or a warning of collective action to come. In the colonial economy of knowledge, what is said, by whom and to whom, repeated, left unspoken, and becomes credible evidence can reveal the most intricate workings of colonial violence and relations. Stoler writes, "Framings make sense of events, but what constituted 'context' varied by observer. . . . Different perspectives yield different stories and causal arguments. In so doing they redefine the very breadth of 'context' and the parameters of the 'event'" (2008, 191). Rumors offer plausible explanations, predictions, and social and political commentary (Stoler 2008, 231). Like everyone, I was caught up in the rumor mill of the mall. My African and Chinese interlocutors had different framings of Ling Jie's death, its causes, and contexts that retrofit the Sino-African dynamics at China City in a frame of colonial violence.

Among Chinese traders, Ling Jie's death ossified stereotypes about Black criminality. Many Chinese traders see themselves as benevolent employers. For a long-term employee to kill Ling Jie after six years—steady employment he should have been grateful for—attested to the lack of moral character, ruthlessness, and "savagery" of Africans. Old Cheng, a gossiper known to embellish, returned to the scene of the crime with the lucidity of a firsthand witness. As he speculated, Ling Jie opened an hour earlier than most traders when the mall was empty. Because the light switch was in the back of the shop, she was easily ambushed in the quiet, dark room. Traders try to rationalize the unfathomable to make it seem avoidable. Old Cheng's version was pedagogical: don't open early or alone, don't keep the light switch in the back, and be hypervigilant around African workers. I heard whispers that Ling Jie was an unfeminine tomboy and too harsh toward her employees, reasserting gender norms in the search for explanation. Most unsettling, however, was the characterization of the event as a revenge killing (*chousha*). As much as traders tried to isolate specific circumstances or character faults, what was discomfiting—even unspeakable—was its ordinariness. Even Jan, the bristly Afrikaner head of security, understood the root cause of the murder as employing "foreigners" over "local South African boys" under exploitative conditions. Chinese traders, when confronted with the extreme consequences of the labor regime in which they participated, recognized that they could meet a similar fate.

Although the historical contexts are quite different, the affective economies and relations of power of the plantation offer an interpretive frame for this event. In the United States, enslaved people's uprisings were imminent. The master's "existence was always haunted by the specter of extermination" (Mbembe 2017, 19). Quotidian acts of resistance were tinged with insurgency as "being found with a pen or pencil is almost as bad as having murdered your master" (Hartman 1997, 63). On the plantations of Sumatra, Dutch colonists feared slaughter and sabotage, a scale of terror that never bore out (Stoler 2008, 226). Race inhabits the imagination as a sign of neurosis and generator of fear and terror (Mbembe 2017, 32). Among Chinese traders, armed robberies captivate imaginations and amplify visceral fears and paranoia of racial straw men. The events of May ricocheted across China City. After a major incident occurs, Marcus told me, the mall goes on "maximum security." Traders acted extra defensively about their surroundings and interactions with shopworkers. They confiscated phones, barred the entrance of workers and friends from other shops, and safeguarded objects that doubled as weapons. Fear of crime is racialized and gendered. Chinese women expressed caution when going to secluded warehouse or upstairs storage spaces with African male workers alone. These measures were not new, however; traders only talked about them more.

Among China City's underpaid and overworked Malawian and Zimbabwean workers, excitement was palpable. I heard it in the uptick in Marcus's pitch when he asked me, grinning widely, "Did you hear? Did you hear?"

after the news of the murder broke. The violence, as egregious as it was, was the tip of an iceberg of fomenting resentment and part of a longer history of retribution among Black workers in South Africa. In the mines, violence had been inseparable from work underground. To maximize production, Black workers routinely received beatings from Black "boss boys" and white superiors akin to the mall's private security. Occasionally, Black migrant mine workers returned violence in kind. They did not see themselves as merely victims of white violence but "relished the capacity for exuberant retaliation" (Breckenridge 1998, 692). Migrant workers brought their own conceptions of and strategies for justice to the mines and fought back, more often individually than collectively. In the tunnels underneath it, underground violence haunts the mining belt mall. Older meanings of violence and justice resurface in the consciousness of workers and my own interpretive frame. Analyzing one mine worker's account of retaliation, Keith Breckenridge keenly observes, "It was no accident . . . to use *ijombolo*—the drill stick—to *work* on his adversary" (1998, 692, emphasis in the original). At the mall, it was likewise no coincidence that Ling Jie's body was wrapped in the very fabric workers handled day in and day out for months and even years. Violent crime, when performed with such symbolism, is profoundly political. As was evident in the shopworkers' quiet rejoicing, the event signaled that some traders had gone too far in the pursuit of profit. It was the feeling, as Roger expressed in an unrelated conversation, that Chinese "have to share what they have . . . they [are] overdoing it." By sharing the vantage point of African workers, I do not insinuate that Ling Jie was to blame. Instead I try to understand the meaning of violence when formal legal redress is not possible, and I question what constitutes a crime and to whom.

The tragedy resembles an older South African story of white paranoia and Black retaliation, one that unfolded in the hinterlands far from the City of Gold. In *Midlands*, a book I by chance read around the time of Ling Jie's death, journalist Jonny Steinberg chronicles the murder of a white Afrikaner farmer in KwaZulu-Natal in the nascent days of democracy. Steinberg's inquiry goes beyond the murder to explore the motivations and meanings of crime within a rapidly changing terrain of race and class. Alongside the migrant labor system for urban industries, a colonial land tenancy system for farms played an important role in the development of South Africa's political economy. As Steinberg explains, among generations of poor Black tenants and workers on Afrikaner farms, "Stealing from a white land-owner is often a form of punishment, a signal sent across the racial frontier that the white boss has gone too far." Stealing and graver acts are not arbitrary but rooted in an unspoken set of rules that "Black peasants have made for white people." As Steinberg learned, "There are rules for those white farmers who defend their property too harshly, and for those who are not vigilant enough. There are rules for farmers who sink below a commonly held threshold of human decency, and there are rules for those who are considered kind . . . white farmers have absolutely no idea that those rules exist" (2002, 51). When white farmers found their fences torn down, their cattle dead, or their fields in flames, they were at a loss for explanation, but Black tenants knew why.

Since the early 2000s, Afrikaner farmers have decried farm murders as "white genocide," a reactionary response to redistributive land policies after the end of apartheid. Crime mobilizes identifications, solidarities, and antipathy in response to violation (Comaroff and Comaroff 2016). By a similar logic of racial injury, Chinese traders also understand themselves as a racial, ethnic, and national minority group. Like the aggrieved minority of white farmers, Chinese traders see themselves as a minority in a Black majority country and targeted for robbery. The pervasive sense of collective injury and vulnerability can create a unity among Chinese migrants while diminishing social differences and competitive tensions. The culture of fear and obsessions with crime, always coded as Black, are central to the formation of a victimized Chinese identity. My interlocutors described their experience in South Africa in terms of being fearful (*kepa*) and experiencing terror (*kongbu*) all around them. Revenge killing and armed robbery are how traders register a conflict between capital and labor insofar it is between traders and workers, but the relations of power are inverted. In this parable of Chinese bosses and African workers, Chinese become innocent victims while minimizing their role in exploitative regimes that sow retribution.

Armed robbery is indisputably a terrifying experience that can shatter a person or community's sense of safety. It is also fundamentally about property. Chinese racial identity is grounded in a logic of possession and relationship to property that racialize Chinese as victims of Black criminality. I extend George Lipsitz's, Aileen Moreton-Robinson's, and Alyosha Goldstein's theorizations of white possession to comprehend how Chineseness functions as possession. In the United States, whiteness is a form of property, a set of privileges with a "cash value" for the accumulation of capital and generational upward mobility. As property, whiteness must be invested in and safeguarded from others through exclusionary measures. Whiteness is a possessive logic not limited to phenotype or identity. It extends to everyone under white supremacy (Lipsitz [1998] 2006, viii). Under the proprietary relations of slavery and settler colonialism, whiteness is defined by a capacity to possess and make claims to land and people. Whiteness disavows white racial violence and expropriation to claim victimization by racial others (A. Goldstein 2014, 1078). Considering this inversion, Moreton-Robinson notes that "white colonial paranoia is inextricably tied to an anxiety about being dispossessed by racial others" (2015, xxiii). As these scholars theorize, white possession reproduces itself through practices of gatekeeping and disavowal, discourses of security, and affective states of injury and paranoia.

Chinese possession names Chineseness as property, a set of social and economic privileges that Chinese must continuously defend and reproduce. A sense of racial injury glues the diasporic community together, diffusing differences and animosities for the greater good of public safety and property. Chinese possession manifests in watching each other's shops, hiring private security guards to police communal spaces, and creating gated communities. The China Mall, after all, was born from a collective urgency to get off the street and trade in an enclosed, securitized space, even if trading in one central space made business more competitive. Chinese traders similarly build an identity around a shared disavowal of labor exploitation and sense of victimhood. Akin to white disavowal of racial violence, Yinghong Chen keenly observes, "Chinese are racially supersensitive and superinsensitive at the same time. The paradox continues a history with China as a victim of foreign racism while denying its own racism" (2011, 575). In Sino-African contexts, Chineseness is akin to whiteness, not as identity but as possessive logic and unmarked dominant racial position.

As Zine Magubane and Jemima Pierre have theorized whiteness and Blackness in colonial South Africa and postcolonial Ghana, whiteness is a racial position. Whiteness refers to social relations, positions of power, and ideology, not phenotype (Z. Magubane 2004, 150). Whiteness indexes economic and political superiority, status, and power within a global order. It is a sign of cruelty, greed, and terror (Pierre 2012, 86). Some of my African interlocutors aligned Chinese traders with the privileged position of whiteness, using the same tropes of greed and excess used to describe white people, or sometimes they simply saw Chinese as white. For instance, Anita classified me as white, explaining that the world was divided into two races, Black and white, with no distinct place for Asian or yellow. I was white because of the power of my Americanness and "white English," not "Black English." Chinese were white because they were "rich" and "everywhere" in Africa. Treating whiteness as a social relation, I read the dynamics of China City through labor management and paternalistic racism on the white-owned mine and farm. African workers addressed their Chinese employers as "boss," a close homophone of *baas*, the Afrikaner boss. *Baasskap*, "unalloyed white supremacy" in Afrikaans, was the prevalent model of farm and family governance on white settler farms throughout southern Africa (Jaffe 2017, 46). The institution revolved around the Afrikaner *baas*, the racially superior white patriarch and landlord who bestowed benevolence and violence on Black tenants forced off their land (Swart 2001; Sylvain 2001). On farms, Black tenants quietly fought back, which made the relationship between Black tenants and white farmers one of distrust: "The white landlord who looked his tenant in the eyes saw a person with many conflicting identities and desires. Behind their landlords' backs, black tenants have always fought a scrappy, mischievous, ever-silent battle" (Steinberg 2002, 64). Echoing Baba's warning about one's inner circle, a white farmer told Steinberg, "You cannot trust the people who live here. Take your eye off them and they will rob you blind" (2002, 72). Likewise, through the specter of the inside job and revenge killing, paranoia creeps into everyday interactions between traders and shopworkers. The longer the tenure of the workers, the more knowledgeable and critical they are to daily shop functions, and the more resentful, and closer to information, they become. The hallmarks of paternalism, distrust and paranoia, coalesce with attachments, dependencies, and intimacies that are strengthened and strained over time. My experience working at a shop was a study in the anxieties of betrayal, distrust, and dependencies that restage the quintessentially South African pastoral melodrama.

Chinese Racial Paternalism

Almost every day, Jenny and I sat behind the counter of her party goods shop. The enclosed area was less than one square meter, just enough room for two plastic stools, and contained locked drawers where she kept warehouse keys, cash, business documents, and the security camera monitor. Work usually felt lighthearted, with joking around and laughter, but beneath the surface was distrust. I had two roles: the first was to help her run the register; the second was to prevent the four employees and customers from stealing, a role I was reluctant to fulfill. Jenny required that I keep an eye on the camera monitor, and for a period, record the time stamp whenever African shopworkers exited or entered, so if an incident occurred, she could check the video footage. The first time Jenny left me in the shop alone with Alice, one of two longtime employees, she called the landline twice within minutes of leaving to remind me to pay attention (*zhuyi*). It was a test to check if I was sitting by the monitor. I was being monitored for monitoring. To keep my job, and hence my access, I went along with it. And so, I occasionally glanced at the cameras, feigned interest by asking how to rewind, and nodded along when Jenny reminded me to pay attention. Usually traders seemed uneasy when I conversed with shopworkers, afraid of what employees would say about them. To protect workers, I interviewed them on the phone or in secluded areas before or after work. Jenny would periodically leave with one or two shopworkers to visit the warehouse. In those moments, I could have conversations with other workers. The employees understood that I had to perfunctorily perform a supervisory role. Spending countless hours beside Jenny also gave me perspective on the Chinese side of the color line.

Like most shops at China City, at Jenny's there was a two-tiered hierarchy of shopworkers: a rotating cast of casual workers referred to as "Black labor" (*heigong*) who turned over every few weeks to months, and two longtime employees, Alice and Julius, whom she called *lao heipo* and *lao heigong, lao* meaning "old" to designate seniority. Jenny paid the casual workers the same measly entry-level weekly wages as most traders, but paid Alice and Julius a monthly salary of triple that amount. Jenny only hired workers who were introduced by security guards or friends of workers. Even when she needed to hire, when people came by to ask for work, she would respond "No job" without looking up. Jenny was exceptionally cautious and became ever more so after narrowly dodging an armed robbery. Several years back, she and her cousin were turning over a container every two weeks. Their success did not go unnoticed. The two women were trailed home and dodged bullets in their front yard, a close call that prompted Jenny to move into China City's flats. Jenny started new employees at a low base wage, from where they could move up if they "worked nicely." Going to the warehouse to retrieve stock was an initiation and a test. She would shout at new workers "Make boxes nicely!" and instruct them how to count as they packed. She accused them of sleeping on the job and had allegedly once thrown a pair of scissors at someone but missed. It was hard to reconcile this version of her with the kindness and vulnerability she showed to me, but the stark difference was the point. Jenny valued obedience, capability, smartness, and physical strength. She poorly tolerated idleness and lack of initiative. Having seen many workers through the years, Jenny needed only a week to assess which track they would be on. These practices of hiring, training, and tracking were the norm across the mall.

Julius was from Malawi and was Jenny's employee for seven years. She regarded him as one in the family (*ziji de jiaren*) and believed he would work for her until the day she would close the shop and return to Fujian. As a reward for his loyalty, she planned to give him enough money to buy a house in Malawi and start his own business, a common goal among Malawian workers. Julius earned her trust through gestures of protection. She spoke fondly of a time he defended her from a threatening customer, or when he warned her about taking a route home after sunset. Alice, from Zimbabwe, was nearing five years' time with Jenny. Before working at China City, like many migrant women in Johannesburg, she sold sweets at a street stall with two young children by her side. Alice sought independence from an abusive ex-husband. Jenny admired Alice, but rarely showed it. She privately praised Alice for her quickness—"As quick as a Chinese person!"—and business savvy. Jenny planned to take Alice to visit her hometown and introduce her to import-export opportunities. But in the beginning, she would push her thumb into Alice's forehead while calling her stupid. "You can die with those words when you think about them," Alice told me. In such moments of cruelty, I thought about the abuse Alice weathered from her ex-husband and now Jenny. On the farm, the *baas* provided housing, employment, land access, and education for Black tenants. Like the *baas*, Jenny felt a paternalist sense of responsibility for Alice's and Julius's futures. She would reward them with opportunities for entrepreneurial endeavors, a benevolent gift with which to uplift themselves. But Jenny was also scornful and guarded, afraid they could plot against her. Trust between traders and workers was undermined by the fear of betrayal.

In their seven years together, Julius stole five times, usually something small, and sometimes with Alice. Every time, Jenny fired Julius but then rehired him because he was indispensable. On the same day the Fujianese factory owner in Newcastle was killed, Jenny caught Alice and Julius stealing goods worth less than a hundred rand (about eight US dollars) on camera. They carried out a bag of goods to a would-be customer for cash and pocketed the sale for themselves, a popular side-hustle strategy. Jenny called security and made Alice and Julius rewatch the camera footage while berating them like children. Jenny used a moralizing, condescending tone—"How could you do me like that?"—and scolded Alice for setting a bad example for her children. Jenny wanted them to apologize, but Alice and Julius held their heads high. "Their skin is so thick," she said derisively. Security guards tried to de-escalate, but it was clear that their outward allegiances were with Jenny, the tenant. Traders from down the hall arrived to investigate. "All Black people are like this," Jenny said, nearly spitting her anger. The other Chinese traders nodded in concurrence. So debasing was the confrontation that a customer, a Black South African woman, asked her why she had to humiliate Alice and Julius in public. At the time, I had only been working for Jenny for a few weeks. I meekly stood in the cramped booth, unsure of what I could say, and sympathetically made eye contact with Alice and Julius.

"Jenny don't trust" was one of the first things Alice told me. On the heels of Ling Jie's death and the slew of robberies that month, Jenny was on high alert. The previous week she had demanded that Julius bring her the papers he had stapled when he returned the stapler she kept behind the counter. Julius was dumbfounded by this request and her insistence. Over the past months, Jenny had claimed to smell alcohol on Julius, a colonial stereotype of African workers and an indicator of erratic behavior. In the heat of that moment of theft, Jenny wanted to fire both but could not run the shop without one of them. Alice stayed on, but Julius was fired. Although I never asked Jenny, gender likely played a deciding role. Alice posed less of a physical threat than Julius. She might be more predictable, compliant, and with children to support, could not lose her job. Jenny did not report the incident to the police, which could initiate deportation for Julius. Instead, the security guards escorted him out and likely beat him behind closed doors. Later the guards urged me to talk to Jenny about hiring Julius back, as she had in the past. Julius struggled to find work and returned to China City several times, but this time Jenny could not be persuaded.

Alice and Julius's minor infraction is a prism refracting paternalist relations and Chinese ideologies of global racial hierarchy. From Jenny's perspective, the incident was not about the small amount of money but about trust and character. Returning to that day, Jenny, furious, referred to Julius as a brute (*chusheng*). The derogatory term animalizes Black people. It implies backwardness, savagery, and the fundamental lack of feeling, emotion, and sentiment (*renqing*) that makes one human. After a few hours had passed, Jenny more calmly explained that trust was reciprocal in "taking heart and giving heart." Making broad generalizations about moral character, as she saw it, Chinese reciprocated their treatment: "I am bad to you; you are bad to me." In contrast, Africans did not: "I am good to you; you are *still* bad to me." Jenny believed that no matter how much salary she paid or how she treated Alice as an employee, Alice would steal from her, as if the propensity to steal were an essential, immutable trait. "To hit her, to yell at her, or to treat her well" was inconsequential because there was no "heart to heart" connection between them. In Chinese epistemologies of the human, "heart" (*xin*) unifies the sensory, emotional, and rational; it means "heart-mind," a sign of the human capacity for ethical relation (Eng, Ruskola, and Shen 2011). In Sino-African contexts, Di Wu theorizes "emotional proximity," which is achieved through shared knowledge that resides in the heart (2021,

208). From Jenny's perspective, Alice lacked the human capacity for ethical relation and shared understanding, which returns to the modern Chinese idea that Africans are outside humanity and history (Karl 2002). Racist stereotypes about Africans are steeped in ideologies of race, development, and the human. Chinese migrants transpose meritocratic ideals and progress narratives of China's modernization onto South Africa. Recall that Jenny, like many of my interlocutors, believed that China had lifted itself out of foreign domination and poverty because of Chinese people's capacity to "eat bitterness" and work hard. Chinese faulted Africans with a lack of initiative to overcome colonialism and subsequently naturalized capacities for development (Ferreira da Silva 2015). When workers stole, Chinese traders interpreted these acts of resistance and survival as a moral failing to bootstrap oneself up the global racial hierarchy.

Since the incident, Jenny's surveillance of Alice reached unbearable levels. On multiple occasions she accused Alice of stealing, and each time, the camera footage turned up nothing. Alice confronted Jenny: "How can we work together like this when you do not trust me? It is obvious you do not want me anymore." Jenny retorted, "I have lots of ladies who can work for me, and how can I trust you after I opened my heart to you and you do me like that?" Jenny characterized Alice as replaceable, adding "I gave you so many chances." Even though Alice would have difficulty finding a job that would pay her as much, her dissatisfaction reached a breaking point. She confided that she was too tired to continue and planned to leave. When Jenny went back home to China for several weeks, Alice discussed her exit strategy with me every day. What hurt Alice most was the characterization of her labor as fungible. "Do you think she will miss me?" Alice asked. "She says she has lots of ladies who will work for her . . . she needs my power, not my brain." I left Johannesburg for a month and thought I would never see Alice again, but she never hatched her plan to depart. She took an unannounced break and stayed with family in Limpopo. Jenny phoned Alice every day, demonstrating that she indeed needed her. Alice took this gesture as "love" and told me she had "forgiven" Jenny.

Several months later, during my last month at the shop, Alice's migraines required medical treatment. Jenny admitted that, over time, she had developed feeling (*ganqing*) toward Alice. In the interim, Alice lined up a new job. A regular customer noticed Alice's efficiency and offered her a better-paying job at a grocery chain. She left unannounced after Christmas, this time for good. When I returned to Johannesburg the following year, Jenny hardly mentioned Alice's absence. When I asked about her, she dismissively replied,

"Don't worry about *heipo*," reducing Alice to a generic Black female worker. However stoic Jenny appeared, I sensed that she felt a loss when Alice, like Julius, left. In the way Jenny and Alice relied on each other, Chinese traders and African workers are bound in unequal material dependencies and sentimental bonds. As much as Chinese traders acted as if African employees were expendable, there were attachments and appreciations that were kept private.

The fraught intimacies, approximations of kinship, and affective intensities of Sino-African relations are central to how relations of capital and labor play out, as arguments that feminist scholars of capitalism have made (Appel 2019; Bear et al. 2015; Gibson-Graham [1996] 2006; Wilson 2004; Rofel and Yanagisako 2019). Sentiments are not extraneous to capitalism. They are human capacities that constitute social actors and incite and constrain processes of production (Yanagisako 2002). The relationship between Chinese traders and African workers is not simply oppositional but bound up with sentiments and dependencies that are unevenly felt. Sino-African power relations are complex in the subtleties of subjugation and retribution, oscillating between exploitation and affection. They are thoroughly racialized and gendered in expectations of docility and displays of emotion. The intimate familiarity traders and shopworkers cultivate over time can become potentially dangerous. The relationship between Chinese bosses and African workers uncannily mirrors the historic drama of trust, betrayal, and exploitation between the white *baas* and the Black tenant. Chinese racial paternalism is based in ideas of Chinese developmental superiority and African inferiority. As Chinese traders see it, African workers should be grateful for the low wages they receive, which in turn fuels resentment, stealing, and retribution on the part of the workers. Chinese traders invert the power relationship with African shopworkers, imagining themselves as vulnerable minorities and victims of violence rather than recognizing their positions of power over African migrants. Sentiments, attachments, and intimacies can function as tools of subjugation. The specter of crime curtails possibilities for trust and connection and drives the relational construction of Blackness and Chineseness. Within Chinese collective imaginations, the criminal is always already—and can only be—Black.

Criminal Doubles

At China City, shopworkers from Malawi, especially from the southern area Machinga, gained a reputation for petty theft and inside jobs. Before them it had been Mozambicans, whom traders had fully stopped employing by the time I arrived. The Malawian shopworker was a figure of notoriety. Security guards, who had nicknames for the mall's many workers and tenants, masculinized and belittled them through the moniker "Malawi boys." I interviewed Baba, the Nigerian security guard, several months after Ling Jie's murder. Baba encapsulated the reputation of Malawian shopworkers: "Malawi boys, the shopworkers, if they work for you, even twenty years . . . you sleep one second . . . maybe it is one thousand [rand], they are watching you every day [for] five years, six years. . . . One day they will take the one thousand and they don't care . . . they will kill for one thousand." "Malawi boys" referenced more than a propensity to steal but also shrewd opportunism, unpredictability, and capricious loyalties. Among themselves, Malawian workers boasted about their ability to harness occult medicine (*muti*) to cause goods to disappear or to clean out a shop in two minutes. But the stereotype was born from being forced to steal. As Roger remarked, "They [workers] take the money, not because they are thieves, or whatever they [Chinese] can think of, but poverty force[s] them to do so. . . . They are working to eradicate their poverty. But they don't gain. . . . They don't have any choice other than to steal." Roger highlights the double meaning of criminalization: being stereotyped as criminal and structures such as labor exploitation that illegalize livelihoods. All kinds of crime were collapsed in the "Malawi boys," a screen for paranoid fantasies and the focus of surveillance.

At the China Malls, surveillance is implemented by a robust apparatus of multiple groups of security guards, each with different powers and uniforms, security cameras, watchtowers, and informants like the street vendors ("robot boys") who call in tips of suspicious activity outside the mall's borders. The disciplinary gaze is decentralized and multiple, a panoptic power in which employees are aware of always being watched. Surveillance draws on racial imaginaries and has racializing effects in differentiating bodies and cohering racial populations. As Simone Browne defines it, racializing surveillance "signals those moments when enactments of surveillance reify boundaries, borders, and bodies along racial lines, and where the outcome is often discriminatory treatment of those who are negatively racialized by such surveillance" (2015, 16). African workers were keenly aware of being stereotyped and surveilled. "You know when one fish is rotten in the pond, all the fish are rotten. And when a Black person, a Malawian person, steal from the Chinese, they say all of them are thieves," said Marcus. It did not matter to Chinese traders or workers how shopworkers acted as individuals; they were all "Malawi boys." Similarly, Anita, who worked for several Chinese employers, stated, "If they see a Black person, they just think, this one [is] stealing, even if we don't steal." As other shopworkers articulated, stealing was because of low wages. "They need us," Anita explained, and "they know these people will steal from them because they are not giving us enough money." As she saw it, when her boss installed security cameras all over the shop, the primary purpose was to monitor workers, not customers. Anita said to me, "I'm telling you, the cameras, they put them there for us, for workers, so they can see . . . they don't really trust us." Anita, Marcus, and others felt the surveilling gaze of Chinese traders and workers and the security apparatus that prioritized Chinese safety and property. Anita insisted that Chinese were white. Whiteness was not a matter of skin but of social relation and gaze.

In *Black Skin, White Masks*, Frantz Fanon theorizes the racial primal scene whereby the Black subject is interpellated. The subject becomes Black under the white gaze. Fanon posits, "For not only must the black man be black; he must be black in relation to the white man" ([1952] 2008, 90). In the Sino-African encounter, African workers come to see themselves as Black under a Chinese gaze. Racial subjection happens through surveillance and speech. The utterance of the epithet *heigui* functions like Fanon's hailing, "Look, a Negro!" When traders referred to African workers through these terms, workers recognized themselves—even across a language barrier. With a dejected tone, Marcus told me, "But there are some other ways that we can know what these people are talking . . . they look at you and they continue to talk . . . you can know by body language. But we don't care, we just work. It's better that we don't know what they are talking about . . . it wouldn't be good." Each utterance of *heigui* interpellates African subjects into Chinese racial discourses that discount Black subjectivity and positions them within a racial hierarchy. African workers also turn the terms of racial subjection on their heads. In 2013, I met a Mozambican candy vendor at another China Mall. He was acquainted with everyone and cheerfully greeted Chinese traders as "brother" and "friend." An older Chinese woman, visibly irritated and nervous, complained about him to me in Mandarin. Surprising us both, he exclaimed, "But I'm a good *heigui*!" He flipped the script to disarm himself. Chinese denigrations of Blackness are not uncontested or lost on African subjects.

The Malawian shopworker is the hypervisible criminal, and the Chinese worker its disavowed double. Alice surprised me when she matter-of-factly stated, "Black people steal small but Chinese people steal big." I was taken by surprise when Jenny mentioned that "one must pay the most attention to your own Chinese," using the phrase "hands and feet clean or unclean" to describe Chinese workers. If African workers steal a bag or box of goods from the shelf or warehouse, Chinese workers, who have far more access to information and keys, dip into the cash drawer or go for the entire warehouse. In one memorable tale, a Chinese worker, whose boss sponsored their work visa and provided a room in their China City apartment, cleaned out the warehouse, took the money from the apartment, and sold the boss's car before fleeing to China. When Chinese workers stole on any scale, their actions were never attributed to identity. Instead of the response "All the fish are rotten," they were individual outliers of "bad heart" or "low quality." When Chinese traders talked about betrayals by Chinese workers, they did so in hushed conversations. Chinese workers who stole brought shame to naive employers and sullied the integrity of Chinese. Instead, Malawian workers dominated everyday crime talk. Crime narratives help us symbolically make sense of the world; they do not accurately depict it. Simplified stereotypes and rigid categories help classify the world into good and evil. Although experiences of crime are complex, "a few essentialized images . . . eliminate the ambiguities and categorical mixtures of everyday life" (Caldeira 2000, 33). This was the case with how Chinese workers talked about crime in Chinese/Black, good/evil, and victim/criminal binaries.

Jenny watched Alice's every move but rarely any of mine. Alice commented on the difference: "Because we're Black and you're Chinese." The modes of surveillance between African and Chinese workers are different. Chinese workers watch their African counterparts, following them with their eyes or on the camera monitor. With few cameras on them, Chinese workers are held accountable for the money count at the end of the day and are monitored off the clock for their trustworthiness as individuals—a diffuse, continuous mode of surveillance through gossip and social media. Irreputable spouses or social company, gambling habits, romantic infidelity, and sexual liaisons are all indicators of the trustworthiness of Chinese workers. For Chinese workers who live with their bosses, social monitoring (as well as the gendered labor of cleaning and cooking) continues at home. Chinese workers are bound to their bosses through feelings of trust, obligation, dependence, and a binding investment in Chineseness and the protection of property.

Everyday practices at work calcify the hierarchy between Chinese traders, Chinese workers, and African workers. Chinese workers are charged with being an entrusted set of eyes for traders and accordingly are positioned not as workers but as surrogate bosses. Chinese workers identify more with the traders, whom they hope to become one day, than the African workers they monitor. Under the legal apparatus and social norms of the color bar, white mine workers aligned themselves with white management and oversaw Black mine workers. Whereas Black workers were systemically beaten, white workers were "unbeatable." Chinese workers also make this racial and class alignment to become exempt from the harshest forms of surveillance. To summarize, crime produces racial difference by differentially criminalizing Blackness and Chineseness. In Chinese imaginaries, African workers embody an abstract threat of criminality and subsume anxieties about Chinese workers' potential to steal and betray. Racial fictions are reproduced through surveillance practices that reify race through who watches and is watched.

Surveillance, Skin, and Camera

Understanding the pervasiveness of anti-Blackness requires understanding the tacit knowledge, affective economies, embodied dispositions, and learned behaviors that produce racial difference and racism. Quotidian practices of surveillance produce a specific habitus, ways of seeing, and visual genres and signs. Surveillance is mediated through deliberately placed cameras, phone screens, recorded footage, and photographs. These technologies and ephemera capture and function as visual evidence of the "truth" of criminality. Building on Fanon's idea of epidermalization and Paul Gilroy's "epidermal thinking," Browne theorizes surveillance as a historically specific way of reading the surface of the racial body, and increasingly through biometric and digital technologies (2015, 91). Nicole Fleetwood sees the visual as "how we come to know what we know, particularly about the black body and the meanings that get attached to and circulate around it" (2011, 6). Chinese traders and workers in the China Malls developed ways of looking and profiling. The purpose of the racial profile, a set of visual signs, is "to educate the eye and to generate proper recognition of the de facto criminal" and "to see in racial others the unseen truth of criminality" (Nguyen 2014, 800). I learned that watching multiple camera feeds and synthesizing a real-time snapshot is a way of seeing that is cultivated. Recorded footage of stealing and robberies regularly appears in social media feeds. Traders saved their ephemeral surveillance footage, especially moments of "being caught in the act." They watched these video clips repeatedly and showed them to others to elicit sympathy, horror, or a laugh. Spurred by the events of May 2015, Jenny demanded that Lois, a new employee from Zimbabwe with a shy demeanor, take off his hoodie and stand against the wall for a photo. In case he stole, she would give the photo to authorities and circulate it on social media. Disturbed by the insinuation, Lois quietly protested but had no choice but to comply with the preemptive mugshot.

Race and the "unseen truth of criminality" are seen and felt on the surface. Race making is affective, visceral, epidermal, and ordinary. Blackness is not only a floating signifier within a cultural system of signs but, as Fleetwood (2011) theorizes, also affective. Blackness circulates and sticks to bodies and signs to produce the Black body as an object of fear (Ahmed 2004). When I sat next to Jenny at the counter, I noticed how she would perk up when African visitors came in with an empty backpack, loose hoodie, or billowing dress but how she paid little attention to others. This discernment seemed arbitrary to me but was intuitive to her. In an interview, Jenny described how her instincts developed:

> You just encounter many incidents over time. You just know when people come, and I tend to be more watchful. This is a very backward, disorderly country [*luan guojia*]. If you are not careful, you can run into trouble. Whoever comes in—anyone, Black women workers [*heipo*], Black male workers [*heigong*], black devils [*heigui*]—I will look at their appearance, [listen to] what they say. If they are speaking in a Black language [*heihua*] with our workers, I can tell if they are bad or good. For the most part, I can guess. . . . You have to be very careful. You aren't doing business; you won't feel these suspicions. But we are in the store every day doing business and are scared . . . many Black people [*heiren*] are bad.

In Jenny's explanation of racial profiling, racial knowledge is intuitive, a feeling developed through repetition and time and based in fear. Racial common sense is an embodied disposition and judgment, being able to "guess" whether visitors are "bad or good," while reinforcing negative stereotypes of criminality. Since I was not a trader, I would not "feel these suspicions." Jenny's statement encapsulates Kuan-Hsing Chen's observations about Han Chinese racism. Racism works through a binary self/other logic that becomes "instinctual" through the accumulation of experiences encountering unfamiliar others (2010, 261–62). Racial ways of seeing become engrained to the point of feeling instinctual. Chinese racial thought draws on racial ideas in China and consolidates them through daily encounters and habits.

Practices and ideas become "a general, transposable disposition" that conditions instincts to the point they feel natural and far exceed the contexts in which they are learned (Bourdieu 1984, 170).

Racism is not a "natural" fixed state, nor are racial ideas static. Racism must be continuously remade through the enforcement of norms and boundaries. To give an example of how racial ideas and racism are learned, I turn to sisters Xiao Li and Eve. When I wasn't working for Jenny most days of the week, I worked at Xiao Li's clothing shop. Back in Hunan, Xiao Li and Eve were educated city dwellers. Xiao Li had worked at a corporate office, and Eve had been a teacher. They saw themselves as modern, cosmopolitan, and open-minded. When Xiao Li arrived, she learned the mall's social norms from her neighbors, traders who had been around much longer. When her younger sister Eve arrived, Xiao Li instructed her on how to comport herself in public. On Eve's first outing to a shopping mall, Xiao Li instructed her to be watchful of Black people and keep her belongings close to her. Eve thought this was excessive until someone tried to pickpocket her phone. Xiao Li and Eve used to look down on traders who yelled at their workers. Initially, Eve tried to be friendly toward the three Zimbabwean women who worked at the shop. Once, when Eve was bent over to share her food, her neighbor walked in and ridiculed her for her subordinate posture and generosity. Over a few months of tense exchanges with customers and employees, Eve toughened up. She became more vigilant in public. Admitting a change in attitudes, she stopped being kind to Zimbabwean workers because she felt they did not reciprocate it.

Racist attitudes and behaviors are learned and socially reinforced. As Wu found in his ethnography of Chinese migration to Zambia, younger, open-minded Chinese migrants learn to become suspicious of Africans from older migrants and through their role as supervisors (2021, 148). For newcomers like Xiao Li and Eve, inclusion into the community hinged on learning racist attitudes and practicing distance, vigilance, distrust, and skepticism. In my experience as an outsider, traders attempted to teach me derogatory terms as part of my orientation. Chinese acquaintances routinely made racist comments in front of me under the assumption that I shared similar views as a Chinese American. Traders rarely left their shop unattended with African employees. During my first summer at the mall, traders asked me to watch their shop while they left, even though I knew nothing about their business. Despite the competitive environment, Chinese could come together under the auspices of security and property. Anti-Blackness and Chinese possession worked together.

Chinese Possession and Black Criminality

I never planned to write about crime. But I became fascinated with the work crime does, the obsessions it cultivates, and actions it authorizes. Among Chinese migrants, crime is a superconductor for ideas about race, morality, development, progress, and the human. Just as ideas of race were produced in the traffic between metropole and colony, Chineseness, whiteness, and Blackness (*hei*) are transnationally constructed and build on one another as they circulate across China and South Africa. Crime discourses consolidate associations between illegality and Blackness through the *sanfei* foreigner. Chinese fears of crime are also formed within the settler colonial relations of South Africa, running in parallel to white fears of Black crime and histories of dispossession, paternalism, and retribution. To zoom out, Chinese racial formations are important for taking stock of the globality of race in the twenty-first century, and specifically the ways Chinese meanings of Blackness (*hei*) fit into global articulations of anti-Blackness that devalue and disregard Black life. As global China becomes increasingly present in Africa, the Caribbean, and Latin America, locations with specific racial histories and epistemologies, attention to how anti-Blackness mutates is necessary. White supremacy, whiteness, and "white-people capitalism" do not need white bodies for their modes of racial power and possessive logics to be reproduced.

Racial formations of Sino-African worlds are multilayered and triangulated. Chinese perceptions of Africa and Africans are shaped by Euro-American racial discourses—especially US racial stereotypes and Chinese modern racial thought. African perceptions of Chinese vis-à-vis whiteness as a signifier of social privileges and economic power were forged within colonial histories. But Chinese are not white; they have been and still are oppressed by white supremacy. Their consolidation as "the Chinese," whether by whites or Africans, is proof of their racial otherness. And yet, Chineseness may become increasingly, and uncomfortably, associated with the racial power, status, and privileges of whiteness on local and global scales. Chinese racial formations are increasingly salient in and beyond China and the silos of area studies. As my ethnographic approach to racial formation tracks, Chinese racial knowledge is produced through the cross-pollination of imaginaries and ideas, everyday practices, and contact zones where sticky notions of difference congeal. Proximate dangers of closeness and conspiracy coexist with fears of racial contagion and interracial intimacies to illuminate how race, gender, and sexuality work in concert.

6

The Erotic Life of Chinese Racism

Racism transforms an already porous periphery into an absolute, thereby making it necessary to deny all kinds of crossing. . . . Racism can also be described as the emotional lifeblood of race; it is the "feeling" that articulates and keeps the flawed logic of race in its place.

Sharon Patricia Holland, *The Erotic Life of Racism,* 2012

To study the intimate is not to turn away from structures of dominance but to relocate their conditions of possibility and relations and forces of production.

Ann Laura Stoler, "Intimidations of Empire," 2006

Published in 2014, Howard French's *China's Second Continent* enjoyed commercial success and acclaim among Western readers and much debate among China-Africa scholars on the question of empire. In the book's first pages, French introduces Hao, a memorable character who embodies the twenty-first-century Chinese successor of the ugly American. After his business fails in Henan, Hao goes to Dubai, and then Mozambique, where land is rumored to be cheap and abundant. In his worldview, the hyperfertile land has become weedy since the Portuguese left and is destined to be transformed by Chinese agricultural industriousness. Emblematic of chain migration, Hao plans to bring out more family members to expand his "clan" and hopes his sons will have "a lot of offspring with local girls" as a strategy for land acquisition. Hao explains to French, "The mothers are Mozambican, but the land will be within our family" (2014, 21). Yet Hao disdains local women, saying, "The women here are too black. Actually they are different colors, different shades of black, but to us they are all dark" (2014, 36). French ends the chapter on a sensational note, with Hao talking about sex: "With Chinese women you have to caress her first, get her in the mood, you know; produce water. . . . The ones here are not like that. You just make love to them straight away" (2014, 40). In French's tale of the Chinese farmer's rapacious desire for women and land, familiar colonial tropes of race, sex, and settlement are central to casting Chinese migrants as neocolonial pioneers, both the new Americans and the new Portuguese.

Narratives of neocolonialism are shaped by representations of globalization as rape in which the China-Africa story becomes the China-*in*-Africa story (Gibson-Graham [1996] 2006; Sylvanus 2013).[1] In this geopolitical imaginary, global China invades the passive local body of Africa, whether through the penetration of Chinese traders and goods into African markets, the erection of mega-infrastructures across the continent, or the extraction of oil and minerals from feminized land. The rape script is not exclusive to Western critics; it also animates Kenyan artist Michael Soi's *China Loves Africa*, a series of satiric paintings depicting "a type of economic re-colonisation." While China-Africa relations are rhetorically framed as friendship, Soi has called China Africa's "sugar daddy" (Remi 2014). A counterpoint to benign friendship, Soi's series revolves around sexual scenes laden with asymmetrical power relations. His works are crudely on the nose and traffic in racist caricatures and heteropatriarchal imagery. A commentary on resource extraction, *China Loves Africa 66* shows a Chinese man pushing an African woman sitting in a wheelbarrow as if she is raw material. The woman-as-nation figure waves a Chinese flag while concerned citizens curiously look on from the sidelines. Another, *China Loves Africa 15*, takes place in a strip club. Chinese businessmen salaciously gawk at a faceless dancer's body while African male servers offer them bottles of

Tusker, Kenya's iconic national beer. In Soi's eroticized scenes, feminized commodities and sexual labor denote the exploitative character of China-Africa engagements and the emasculation of postcolonial African nations. In *China Loves Africa 68*, a Chinese man fondles a bikini-clad African woman and consumes a continent-shaped chocolate ice cream bar. Meanwhile, two men clad in underwear styled from the European Union and US flags passively watch from the side; the flowers they offer are no match for Chinese soft power, signaling a reversal of the emasculation of Asian men. Sex allegorizes economic and geopolitical relations as coercion. Chinese state capital is commonly perceived as "unnatural" (C. K. Lee 2017, 1). In Soi's work, China's "love" for Africa is perverse and rapacious and its economic and diplomatic practices nonnormative.

Gender, race, and sexuality are important to representations of Chinese neocolonialism in Africa and everyday Sino-African encounters.[2] Twenty-first-century capital flows between China and South Africa have engendered new encounters, desires, and anxieties. In the ever-expanding frontiers of capital, capital forces movement and transgression, and in the process unmoors norms of race, gender, class, and sexuality in the process. As Roderick Ferguson writes, capital "calls for subjects who must transgress the material and ideological boundaries of community, family, and nation." As such, "the production of labor, ultimately, throws the normative boundaries of race, gender, class, and sexuality into confusion," leading to new social formations (2004, 17–18). "China-Africa" represents not only an economic and geopolitical formation but also a project of normalization that produces and regulates racial, gender, and sexual difference in the service of transnational capital accumulation. This chapter approaches Han Chinese racial discourses and specifically anti-Black racism through intimacies, proximities, gender, and sexuality. Turning to the body and encounter, I rescale Sino-African engagements from macrofigures, countries, and continents to social partitions, racial boundaries, and bodily comportments. Interracial intimacies of sex, kinship, affiliation, and bodily closeness illuminate the most granular workings of power. As feminist scholars have theorized, everyday encounters are contact zones, sites of "co-presence, interaction, interlocking understandings and practices, and often within radically asymmetrical relations of power" (Pratt 1991, 8). In the quotidian spaces of the intimate, the microphysics of power, moral management of selves, and gendered and sexual contours of racial and imperial formations can be discerned (Doyle 2020; Z. Magubane 2004; Mawani 2009; McClintock 1995; Stoler 1995, 2006). Global China is not only a politics of geopolitical and economic influence.

There is a specific biopolitics of race, gender, and sexuality and knowledge about race that governs everyday interactions and resonates with European imperial cultures and colonial formations in southern Africa.

In the era of China's ascendance, global white supremacy incorporates Chinese subjects into local projects of anti-Blackness, which cannot be understood without the intersections of race, gender, sexuality, and nation. Like crime, interracial intimacy is a thematic and analytic prism for transnational processes of racialization and Chinese anti-Blackness. Everyday racism upholds the fiction of race such as the boundaries of racial Blackness and Chineseness. If race is about manufacturing social homogeneities, racism maintains those homogeneities by "militarizing their borders, patrolling their places of possible transgression" (Goldberg 2009, 5). Whether subtle or blatant, Chinese anti-Black racism is exaggerated when refracted through gender, sexuality, and the body. In *The Erotic Life of Racism*, Sharon Holland examines race and racism through the quotidian and the intimate. Racism is the "emotional lifeblood of race; it is the 'feeling' that articulates and keeps the flawed logic of race in its place" (2012, 6). Following Holland, our understanding of Chinese racism is incomplete without its psychic and erotic dimensions. The taboo of interracial intimacies exposes the limits of Sino-African relations, the Chinese-only logic of endogamy of anti-Black racism and Chinese possession, and the contours of Han Chinese racial nationalism. This Han racial nationalism imagines a nation of ethnic majority Han descendants of the Yellow Emperor sharing one skin color, language, and cultural heritage. It plays out through sexual and reproductive politics centered on the Chinese woman and African man, the woman-as-nation and the "triple illegal" (*sanfei*) foreigner. Like discourses of Blackness (*hei*), heteropatriarchy and racial nationalism circulate between China and South Africa. Chinese migrants replicate nationalist politics of purity and endogamy, making the politics of sex a politics of Chineseness.

In addition to mapping out regimes of difference in the Chinese Century, this chapter examines sojourner colonialism and racial capitalism in a biopolitical register. It examines the production of difference and the everyday boundary making that maintain racial nationalist fantasies and the conditions for the accumulation of capital. At the China City mall, concerns about sex and bodies take shape within the complicated terrain of ambivalent attachments, asymmetric dependencies, bitter resentments, and racial distrust. Boundary making upholds the rigid hierarchy of Chinese traders, Chinese workers, and African workers. Collective life is reduced to the relations necessary to reproduce capitalism and happens through technologies of partition, which, as Ruth Wilson Gilmore posits, act "to control who can relate and under what terms" (quoted in Melamed 2015, 78). Elaborating on this idea, Jodi Melamed adds, "Manufacturing densely connected social separateness" is racial capitalism's hallmark, as "capital partitions, divides, and separates groups between political geographies *and* is the dominant relation to flow between and bind them" (2015, 81, emphasis in the original). At China City, social life is partitioned into dense nodes of close quarters and insular separateness. Capitalist relations, racialization, and Han Chinese racial nationalism play out through everyday intimacies and proximities of skin.

To contextualize kinship and sex at China City, I begin by giving an overview of the sea change in gender, sexuality, desire, intimacy, and love in post-Mao China. I then explore two kinds of interrelated intimacies at China City: interracial intimacies that draw on anxieties about miscegenation and stereotypes of Black male sexuality, and the quotidian intimacies of inbuilt contact between African and Chinese bodies—exchanging money between hands, sharing toilets, and bumping against each other in narrow aisles and cramped warehouses. My examples draw from an ephemeral archive of accidental moments, casual remarks, unverifiable gossip, and commonsensical practices that offer glimmers of racialization processes (Manalansan 2014; Muñoz 1996). These uneasy intimacies and deliberate nonintimacies reveal the gendered and sexual contours of contemporary Han Chinese racial nationalism, anti-Black racism, and global China that open up a more robust understanding of global racial formations beyond the West.

Making Households, Remaking Kinship

From different provinces and different rural, urban, generational, class, and education backgrounds, the Chinese migrant community in South Africa represents a microcosm of Chinese society, including changing ideas about gender, sexuality, and kinship. In tandem with the rise of the globalizing market economy of the 1990s, China's sexual revolution has changed meanings of sex, love, and desire. The sexual revolution saw the emergence of gay and lesbian identities, the medicalization of male sexuality, pornography, sexual education, red light districts, and sexually transmitted disease and HIV/AIDS (E. Y. Zhang 2011). The nature of sexuality and love metamorphized from sentimental, romantic love (*qing'ai*) to sexual love (*xing'ai*) as the individual pursuit of personal passions, financial profit, sexual pleasure, and individual happiness have replaced collective struggle (Rofel 2007). As Everett Zhang remarks, "the most profound effects of China's sexual revolution are seen within the domestic realm and in responses to the tension that obtains between the normative modes of sexuality encompassed within traditional family structures and sexual desires authorized by an emerging individualistic ethos" (2011, 126). The nuclear family and marriage have been destabilized and restabilized. Two neologisms for the term *mistress*, "second wife" (*ernai*) and "little third" (*xiaosan*), index the rise in divorce and extramarital affairs. Since the phasing out of the One-Child Policy in 2015, families are allowed to expand for the first time since the 1970s. The good life fantasy of the family has been recharged under President Xi Jinping, whose leadership is modeled as a paternalistic love for his family and nation, and his signature domestic initiative is the Chinese Dream. Chinese citizens are encouraged to cultivate their capacities for heteroromantic, sacrificial, and family-focused love. But self-sacrificing love is self-defeating, especially among rural migrant workers who wear themselves out for their families (C. Y. Zhang 2022). In Johannesburg, gender and sexual norms are further destabilized. Chinese migrants' anxieties about casual sex, marital infidelity, and commercial sex are further complicated by the possibility of interracial intimacies. Anxieties about sex are wrapped up within changing sexual and family formations and ideals of cultural citizenship and identity. In postsocialist China, sex "is a critical site where the normalizations of cultural citizenship are being reformulated" (Rofel 2007, 95). Between China and South Africa, upholding heteronormative, endogamous sexual norms confers being "truly Chinese."

At China City, traditional family life and sexual mores carry over to Johannesburg as migrants build business and social networks around kin relations (*qinqi*) and an ethos of sacrificial love. Chinese traders are part of family businesses, family firms or "kinship enterprises" that marry entrepreneurial endeavors with familial and relational bonds, while reconfiguring kinship in the process (Rofel and Yanagisako 2019).[3] As Aihwa Ong writes about transnational Chinese capitalist practices in the 1990s, logics of flexibility "are produced within particular structures of meaning about family, gender, nationality, class mobility, and social power" (1999, 6). Living at Mr. Zheng's house gave me a close-up view of the flexibility demanded of transnational family enterprises and the blurring of boundaries between shop and home and productive and reproductive labor. His relatives and close hometown friends ran several businesses at China City and in Cyrildene Chinatown. They lived in his large two-story house or his father-in-law's house next door. Mr. Zheng provided the shop and start-up capital to create a symbiotic network of businesses and economy of scale. A hierarchy of gender, seniority, responsibilities, and profit sharing organized social re-lations. In the carpool from Mr. Zheng's house to China City, his relatives sat near the front of the fourteen-seat minibus while young women workers piled in the back. Between shop and home, everything was integrated. At home, relatives went over the books and prepared meals to eat together at work. They took turns making one-month trips to China to visit children and import goods through a family-run export business. The house dynamic changed seasonally. When Mr. Zheng's wife and son were in Johannesburg, the house was reenergized around the family unit. I joined the three of them for dinner at home and in Chinatown with family and hometown friends where business was a conversation staple. For the rest of the year, he lived like a bachelor and stayed out late at the KTV Bar with friends (and, poten-tially, girlfriends). Mr. Zheng's relatives' entrepreneurial opportunities and my participant observation were made possible through our relationship to him and his entrepreneurial network.

The most successful businesses at China City are family firms like Mr. Zheng's, with spouses, siblings, in-laws, and cousins with households and companies in both countries. The involvement of relatives made possi-ble the demanding nature of running a shop seven days a week and making trips to import stock and visit children. Given birth restrictions in China, many children were born in South Africa and raised in China. For most, South Africa is only a temporary home to earn money for a stable future for themselves, their families, and their children in China. Some traders came to South Africa with their spouses or waited for them to join them later on. A few were divorced, which perhaps made it easier to leave. Among the earliest wave of mainland migrants in the 1990s, a handful of Chinese women mar-ried white South African men for permanent residence. Many single men and women in their twenties find Chinese spouses in South Africa; others return to their hometown to search in a wider pool. Relationships and family circumstances play a large part in when and where migrants will settle. Being far away from home and running a shop on one's own is a lonely, tiresome affair. The topic of much gossip, men and women with families in China found new romantic-cum-business partners, maintaining secret relation-ships and binational households across the world.

Entrepreneurial Partnerships

By the time I left Johannesburg in 2015, it was more common to hear about Chinese leaving than arriving. In early 2020, I met Ren Jie (Sister Ren) who recently came to Johannesburg. A few months prior, she heard about the job from the shop owner, a hometown acquaintance from Fuqing. The owner was looking for someone to run her shop while she visited her family over the Spring Festival. Ren Jie had a daughter attending Xiamen University, a four-year-old daughter living with an aunt, and no husband tying her down, so she jumped at the opportunity to earn more money abroad. She flew to South Africa on a tourist visa, procured a fake ID, and took over the shop. Like most Chinese workers, Ren Jie planned to open a shop of her own. On one of my lunchtime visits, Cai Jie (Sister Cai), a woman with salt-and-pepper hair who sold purses down the hall, came by to see Ren Jie.

"I want to be a little third (*xiaosan*)," Cai Jie said, laughing.

"When I was young, my mother told me to find a guy who is tall and handsome. Now I don't care if he's ugly," Ren Jie joked, "as long as he is reliable."

"Looks don't matter in the dark." The two middle-aged women burst into laughter. Cai Jie then turned to me and said in English, "Only this one—money," rubbing her fingers together as if counting bills. After Cai Jie left, Ren Jie told me about her friend's financial troubles. She sold bags during the daytime and waited tables in Chinatown in the evening to pay off gambling debts.

I bonded with many of my single female interlocutors over being women on our own without the conveniences and protections of couples and families. Older women like Jenny and Ren Jie treated me like a younger sister as much as a researcher. They sought to teach me behavioral norms about gender for my own protection. In this case, Ren Jie unpacked the interaction to me, explaining how people find each other and make a household (*zuo jiating*). It was very difficult for someone like her to be alone in a new country. Like Jenny when she first arrived, Ren Jie was a single wageworker with no immediate family, precarious legal status, and two children to support in Fuqing. Ren Jie, who planned to open her own shop, sought a Chinese man, a more established trader, to help her. Whereas Americans seek equality between spouses, she explained, Chinese men are responsible for raising wives (*yan laopo*). With this patriarchal responsibility, male bosses are supposed to materially support female workers; together they can pool their money and energy to open a business. Such arrangements are commonplace at China City, with the ubiquity of husband-and-wife-owned shops, and in China, where migrant workers often work as couples in which the wife is the "junior worker." Women's underpaid productive labor and unpaid reproductive labor makes men's productive labor, and thus the couple's work, possible (C. Y. Zhang 2022, 114). Although Ren Jie was a relatively new face at the mall, she had maturity on her side and cheerfully boasted about having several suitors waiting in the wings. Ren Jie, who had married, divorced, and raised two children, set herself apart from inexperienced young women who sought approval from men. Men viewed young women as a dime a dozen and would spit them out (*sui zhua, sui fan*).

The first time I heard the term *xiaosan* was from Xiao Yu, one of Mr. Zheng's distant relatives. Xiao Yu and her husband ran one of Mr. Zheng's family businesses at China City, a clothing store, and lived next door in Chinatown. Across the mall corridor, Xiao Yu's younger brother managed another business. At both shops, rows of photos of children back in Fuqing adorned the walls. Xiao Yu started every day at the crack of dawn preparing breakfast and lunch for the whole household at these two shops. Frequently homesick, she would show me photos of the four-story home in Fuqing that she and her husband built from the ground up with their earnings. Like many new multistory houses in Fuzhou, it sat empty. She and her husband alternated making visits home during the Spring Festival and the summer break. In one of our earlier meetings, Xiao Yu played for me "Xiaosan," a 2012 pop song about an affair, insisting that it would further my research. The melancholic lyrics go, "Finally you became someone else's little third / I also know that it is not because of love." Both her younger brother and brother-in-law had taken up Chinese girlfriends in Johannesburg while leaving their wives and sons in the dark in Fuqing. These infidelities were the source of heated quarrels. After a big argument, her brother-in-law even moved out of Mr. Zheng's house and into China City's flats with his girlfriend. When Xiao Yu's younger brother became involved with his co-worker Faye, Xiao Yu meddled.

Faye was a recent high school graduate from Jiangmen. Before moving to Johannesburg, she and her ex-boyfriend had run a grocery store in Durban. Faye and her new boyfriend, who was working as a barber in Chinatown, were scouting for shops for rent to open a business together when she met Xiao Yu's brother. Faye's reputation with men preceded her, but it didn't deter me from spending time with her. On one of our Friday evenings out, over a carafe of rosé and pasta, Faye coyly inquired if I was romantically involved with Mr. Zheng, a question that shocked and embarrassed me. From her point of view, it was unusual that an ordinary young woman would have access to such an important businessman. This was not the first time young Chinese women would question me about my relationship with the powerful Chinese men who gatekept my fieldwork. Xiao Yu fixated on her brother's affairs and viewed Faye as a threat to her family. Xiao Yu asked me questions about Faye and enlisted her employee, a close friend of Faye's whom I often sat next to in the minibus, to inform her about any romantic happenings. Eventually Faye was fired. Within a few years, she returned to Jiangmen.

Like Faye, female shop assistants at the mall were typically born in the 1980s or 1990s and from smaller cities in Fujian or Guangdong. They embodied the cosmopolitanism, entrepreneurialism, and open-mindedness of the postreform generation of hopeful young women recruited for their docility and productive potential. They were easy to pick out with their sequined jeans, mesh tops, platform shoes, lightened hair, and clear plastic purses. Unable to drive, in the mornings they stood on the corners in Chinatown waiting for rides to various China Malls. In the late afternoon after work, they walked arm in arm around Chinatown. With limited options for employment back home, instead of moving to a bigger city like Guangzhou, they planned to work abroad after graduating from high school, and often at the urging of their parents. With few preexisting contacts in Johannesburg, they relied on each other for friendship and support while seeking partners, whether other single wageworkers to pool savings together, or more established traders who were sometimes married. How long they stayed in South Africa depended on whether they found someone, managed to start a business, and what their visa status was. On Friday nights, I hopped in the backseat of their boyfriends' cars and joined their trips to the "white" shopping mall near Chinatown. With my American English and consumer knowledge, I accompanied them to restaurants, clothing stores, and makeup counters.

Anxieties about sexual morality played out through the "Chinese girls," who were infantilized as girls (*nuhaizi*), classed as "working girls" (*dagongmei*), or feminized as "beautiful girls" (*meinu*). It was young women, not men, who were scrutinized in relationships between bosses and workers. In China it is socially and culturally acceptable, even understood as natural, for men to engage in extramarital affairs, but it is not for Chinese women, who are dubbed promiscuous (Frazier and Zhang 2014, 243). Unmarried young women wageworkers are subjected to paternalistic protection, romantic desire, and sexual scrutiny. In Johannesburg, "bad girls" like Faye were desired, then villainized, and then fired. With migration debts to pay off, some women worked at shops during the day and moonlighted as sex workers in Chinatown's underground sexual economy. These sex workers would meet Chinese and/or South African clients at karaoke bars, restaurants, salons, massage parlors, and casinos. Sex work was taboo and a spectral presence surrounding young single Chinese women, including myself; my frequent mixing with Black African, Chinese, and South Asian men was suspect. In Chinatown, when I was waiting for a ride at night, a man rolled down his window to ask about a massage. I became acutely aware of the Chinese girl's symbolic importance to upholding the racial boundaries of Chineseness. In China and Johannesburg, Chinese kinship relations and sexual norms are already in flux; race and interracial intimacies add another layer of complication.

Policing Interracial Intimacies

When I first arrived at China City, I was immediately drawn to Jerry, a security guard known for his playful banter with Chinese traders and his mimicry of Mandarin—his special brand of "Fong Kong" Chinese. Since first encountering Chinese shopkeepers back home in Nigeria, his dream was to "build a family with a Chinese." In my presence, the other guards joked with him about what languages his children would speak, and if they would appear Chinese from the waist up and Black from the waist down. Jerry pined after Ellie, Mr. Zheng's niece who ran two stores—one that sold women's fast fashion apparel and the other shoes and bags—with seed money from him. She had the glamorous aura of a pop star with sleek shoulder-length hair, sunglasses, platform shoes, and a white Mercedes-Benz. Ellie was in a long-term romantic and business partnership with a Taiwanese entrepreneur ten years her senior. The couple constantly bickered and weathered much gossip from African and Chinese observers alike because of his age and plain appearance. On several occasions Jerry asked me what Ellie saw in him. During his rounds, he would make extra passes by Ellie's shop to peer in and wave. She was friendly, but complained to me, in English, "Too much black." These kinds of unevenly reciprocated affections are emblematic of how Sino-African relations are asymmetric and replete with racial anxieties and distancing devices. At China City, interracial sex is freighted with the weight of historical miscegenation anxieties in China and South Africa.

Since the 1980s, heteropatriarchal nationalist anxieties about African men, Chinese women, and mixed-race children have garnered renewed attention in China. The 1980s were a pivotal decade with the opening of markets, economic modernization, and mainstreaming of racial ideology into popular discourse. Amid the rising tide of ethnonationalism, Han Chinese identity unified people against ethnic minorities and racial "foreigners" in China. Throughout the 1980s Chinese universities were in upheaval over the presence of African students. Official Mao-era discourses of solidarity with African peoples never fully translated to ordinary people. The protests represented the backlash against state-based Afro-Asian solidarity and generous scholarships awarded to African students (Y. Cheng 2011).

Gender and sexuality are essential to understanding this story of anti-Black sentiment. Chinese students boycotted class and passed out Protect Our Women leaflets on campus after African male students entered women's dormitories. Accusations of African students with HIV/AIDS drove class boycotts. In 1986 a Chinese student association sent all African embassies in Beijing a letter stating that Chinese would not "allow any Negro to hang about our universities to annoy Chinese girls and to introduce on our academic grounds manner[s] acquired by life in tropical forests" (Y. Cheng 2011, 564). In 1988, protests at Nanjing University warranted the emergency evacuation of African students. A protester told the press, "'When I look at their black faces, I feel uncomfortable. When I see them with our women, my heart boils." Another student stated, "If a girl goes with a black man, Chinese will want to beat either him or her, and they will curse the girl forever" (Sautman 1994, 425). Chinese women are represented as virtuous girls in need of Chinese men's protection from African men, and with unruly desires in need of discipline.

Contemporary anxieties about interracial intimacies draw from gendered, racialized, and sexualized figures and tropes from the campus protests and HIV/AIDS public health discourses. Medical anthropologist Johanna Hood (2013) documents the ways in which scientific public health discourses about HIV/AIDS (*aizibing*) represented African bodies as vectors of disease and pathologized Black sexuality, subsequently creating lasting racial, gender, and sexual stereotypes of "Africans." Public health campaigns targeted Chinese women's reproductive health and their role as mothers and reproducers for the nation.[4] Popular Chinese media depicted Black male bodies as anatomically different and contaminating of Chinese women (Pfafman, Carpenter, and Tang 2015). As part of the discourse of *sanfei* in China, the Black African foreigner is stereotyped as hypersexual and a criminal threat to the individual and national body. Symbolically important to racial nationalism, Chinese women's bodies must be protected from Black masculine sexuality to reproduce future generations of Han Chinese.

Anxieties of interracial sex in Johannesburg resonate with concurrent discourses about Sino-African intermarriage and mixed-race children in China. In the 1980s and 1990s, friendship between ordinary Chinese and all foreigners was discouraged. Marriages of Chinese women to foreigners only became acceptable in the 2000s and followed a global racial hierarchy of white at the top and African and South Asian at the bottom (S. Lan 2017, 146–47). In the 2000s, the revival of Chinese development in African countries coincided with African migration to Chinese cities—notably, Nigerian migrants in Guangzhou. As business partnerships and marriages have increased in China, racial nationalist sentiments have seen a resurgence. Han Chinese racial nationalism is based in an imagined national community modeled after the endogamous family. African migrants are seen as "biologically unrelated to the national-reproductive community" and excluded from the national body (K. Huang 2020). Mixed migrant couples struggle to stay together and gain state recognition for their unions and families while facing hostility from their families and society. The stakes are high. Chinese relatives with coveted party memberships risk being thrown out. Mixed-race children encounter similar difficulties as their parents regarding government registration, visas, and hostility and prejudice (Adebayo and Omololu 2020; S. Lan 2017; Marsh 2014). The challenges interracial couples and families face is a product of the immigration system and "the state's unwillingness to incorporate a foreign population into its national imaginary" (S. Lan 2017, 162).

Making clear the heteropatriarchy of Han racial nationalism, Chinese women face double sexual standards. The mothers of mixed-race children are held to a double standard compared to Chinese men who seek out non-Chinese women. In 2009 netizens ridiculed Lou Jing, a television show contestant of Chinese and African American heritage, and her Chinese mother. As one netizen pointed out, "If it were an affair between a Chinese man and a black woman, then there would be applause instead of criticism" (quoted in Frazier and Zhang 2014, 243). In 2020, when a new permanent residency policy was floated, netizens posited that the policy would increase the sexual freedom of Chinese men in their relationships with Chinese and non-Chinese women and expel non-Chinese men who "seize" Chinese women and have mixed-race children (K. Huang 2020). The backlash against Chinese women is a product of the "scarcity" of single Chinese women, an unintended consequence of the One-Child Policy that privileged male children to carry the family line. Chinese women who partner with African men unfairly bear the resentment of decades of national family planning policies (Pfafman, Carpenter, and Tang 2015).

Han Chinese racial nationalism, anti-Blackness, and heteropatriarchy play out in online discussions about interracial relationships and mixed-race children. One netizen articulates a Sinocentric global racial hierarchy and eugenicist ideology: "African blacks are an inferior race. Children of Chinese and African blacks should be regarded as mixed but inferior race. If we take no action, this kind of race will blacken China. This has nothing to do with racial discrimination, but simply a matter of eugenics. We should admit that the white is a superior race, the same as us. The children of whites and Chinese are accordingly relatively superior" (quoted in Y. Cheng 2011, 567). Like the one-drop rule, the ideology of antimiscegenation holds that whiteness adds value while Blackness pollutes. A new "kind of race" threatens to "blacken" the national body and set back development. The comment reflects the repopularization of eugenics since the 1990s and older notions of civilizational superiority of yellow and white over Black from early twentieth-century Chinese racial thought. Another netizen focused on Chinese in the Global South: "It's okay if you want to marry, just don't leave your children/descendants in China. I don't want future Chinese people to be like those half-black half-yellow people in Latin American countries, with lowered intelligence, having lost the purity of their blood, with only a name to claim" (quoted in Pfafman, Carpenter, and Tang 2015, 544). Across these comments, mixing with whites, "the same as us," is acceptable, but not with racial others. Mixed-race Chinese do not belong in the future of China, whether within the People's Republic of China (PRC) or in the diaspora, and should be exiled to "less-developed" countries. These virulent expressions of nationalism and racism are instructive in grasping developmental, racial, eugenicist, and heteropatriarchal thinking. The endogamous nuclear family is a pillar of Han Chinese racial nationalism within and beyond the PRC. Yet Chinese are not monolithic in their views. There are netizens who embrace an increasingly global and multiracial society (Frazier and Zhang 2014). Although Chinese women are burdened with reproducing "Chineseness" and in need of protection from Black male sexuality, at China City the Chinese men are also subject to intense scrutiny and chastised for desiring Black femininity.

China City after Dark

For several months I experienced China City after hours. I lived on the fifth floor of the mall's on-site apartments for Chinese tenants, a newly constructed, unmarked brick building hidden around the back of the mall. The security control room for the entire mall was located on the ground floor, which made clear the unified project of securing property and domestic life. In addition to the guards in the control room, a turnstile entrance connected to a fingerprint reader controlled who could enter and exit. Only Chinese lived there, and guests were only Chinese. These were the "Chinese flats," the name security guards used. When the flats were first available, they were marketed as housing for Chinese workers, like worker dormitories in China. In industrial areas and export process zones in China, rural migrant workers live on factory premises, an amenity for a transient population without residential status to access social provisions. Worker dorms play an important role in the social reproduction of a migrant labor force. For bosses, the dorms also allow employers to surveil and extract longer, more flexible hours from workers (P. Ngai 2007). In Johannesburg, the mall flats were a convenient arrangement for single workers without reliable transportation or housing options outside Chinatown, and for bosses with large wholesale operations who required employees to be available for early openings, late closings, and receiving shipping containers at irregular hours. Workers called this arrangement "eating and living with the boss." Once traders became targeted for robberies, bosses started to move in, too. The flats were a mixed social space: families, young and old trader couples, grandparents, toddlers, bosses, workers, and friends. People socialized along hometown affiliations and replicated routines from their lives in China. In the early evening, I would write my field notes to the aroma of dinner down the hall and the sound of household gatherings. From my room on the top floor, I watched people leisurely stroll around the vast parking lot after dinner. On Fridays, there were evening outings to shopping malls, Chinatown restaurants, and casinos. In the parking lot, there were barbeques and games of badminton. Mirroring the competitive environment of the mall, residents were lively and open or insular and guarded.

At the flats I met Zheng Yongrui, who had the unfortunate situation of living in the only flat on the ground floor, directly in front of the main entrance through which over one hundred residents passed. Back in Wenzhou, a city in Zhejiang known for its entrepreneurial spirit, he made his living as a loan shark; it was a decade-long career until he was forced to stop. In his late thirties and unmarried, he came to South Africa to start over and settle down, working at his brother and sister-in-law's menswear shop and sharing their two-bedroom flat at China City. Sporting Nike sneakers, designer shirts, and a one-carat diamond earring, he styled himself as a *shuaige*, or a cool, handsome, fashionable young man, the counterpart of the pretty Chinese *meinu*. While he bragged about having many girlfriends in China, in the one year he had been in South Africa he had remained single. "All of these working girls [*dagongmei*] want to be some boss's little third [*xiaosan*]," he griped. When my Chinese acquaintances saw me talking to him, I received an outpouring of warnings. People treated him as a liar and scam artist. They doubted his immigration status, his claim to be the owner's brother, and where he really came from.

Eventually I learned the reason for his scarlet letter. Zheng Yongrui allegedly brought a Black South African woman home to the flat, which spiraled into a reputation of sleeping with African women and inappropriately flirting with or touching African female workers, an utmost violation of the unspoken rules of race where it mattered most in the public space of work. People spread rumors that she was a dealer at the casino he frequented, a serious girlfriend, and HIV-positive. The story took on a life of its own. There supposedly was even an eyewitness who saw them go into the flat. In the weeks to come, residents, outraged that he had violated the informal rules of racial separation, complained to management, but management could not intervene in residents' private lives. The flats are a Chinese-only space. The first time I entered the flats as a visitor was to retrieve something for my boss Jenny. Despite the security measures, Jenny casually told me to ask any person to scan me in because I was Chinese. The only non-Chinese people with access were custodians. Even security guards, entrusted with securing the building, rarely went behind the turnstile. I witnessed new residents, not knowing the rules yet, scolded for bringing African employees to help them move in. With paranoia about theft through inside jobs, traders did not want shopworkers to know where they lived. As a property manager told me, although some Indian and Pakistani traders were interested in living on-site, when they inquired, there were never any rooms available. China City was strictly for the Chinese majority. The concern, Jenny explained, was South Asians' perceived proximity to Blackness—their friends and guests might be African; the specter of criminality was the reason for keeping the flats a Chinese-only space.

Among hundreds of Chinese tenants at the mall, Zheng Yongrui was the mall's only known transgressor of sexual taboos. Chinese gossiped openly about him and his family with the aim of ostracizing him. Gossip is a practice for evaluating the morality of people and actions (Van Vleet 2003). Gossip enforces racial, gender, and sexual boundaries through shame. Although Chinese women are held to a double standard, the prohibition on interracial relationships applies to both women and men. What happened this single time mattered because, as Sara Ahmed remarks, "borders need to be threatened in order to be maintained, or even to appear *as* borders, and part of the process of 'maintenance-through-transgression' is the appearance of border objects. . . . It does not make borders (out of nothing), but responds to their making, through a reconfirmation of their necessity" (2015, 87, emphasis in the original). In this case, the latent anxiety surrounding Chineseness surfaced once the racial order of things was disrupted. At China City, interracial intimacies threatened the boundaries of Blackness and Chineseness and labor hierarchies. Anxieties about racial homogeneity were inextricably bound up with obsessions over purity, contagion, borders, sexuality, and reproduction. Anxieties about sex slid into contagion, and Chinese migrants took great lengths to maintain physical and symbolic distance from African bodies in quotidian situations.

Porosity and Pollution

In 2016 a Chinese laundry detergent company made international headlines. Amid increasing African migration to Guangzhou and Yiwu, the commercial for Qiaobi detergent retold a familiar colonial story of race, lust, and danger. The ad depicts an urban apartment with sunlit white walls, pink and purple boxes of detergent on the shelves, and gleaming new appliances. A light-skinned Chinese woman throws her clothes into the washing machine to an upbeat tune when suddenly a Black African man, a laborer with a paint bucket in hand, appears at the door. On his face, streaks of white paint form a generic tribal marking to indicate the traditional, primitive, and uncivilized. Signaling contagion and danger, his white shirt is smeared with blood-like red paint. He flirtatiously winks at the woman and whistles, and she beckons him to come closer. As their faces close in on a kiss, in a twist, she pops a mint-green detergent tablet into his mouth and shoves him into the top-loading washing machine. After the wash cycle is complete, she opens the lid. To her delight, a young Chinese man with skin as light as hers emerges from the machine.

The commercial powerfully evokes colonial tropes of civilization, modernity, cleanliness, domesticity, and sexual threat, recalling the symbolism of soap in colonial southern Africa (Burke 1996).[5] Like laundry detergent, soap was important among Victorian middle-class consumers, as it "purifie[d] and preserve[d] the white male body from contamination in the threshold zone of empire" (McClintock 1995, 32). The intimacies of difference are intelligible within Western constructions of whiteness, colonialism, imperialism, sexuality, and gender. In the image of the dangerous *sanfei* foreigner, the African man intrudes in this scene of urban middle-class domestic modernity. His mouth is unhygienic and his body dirty. In contrast, the young, single Chinese woman is the embodiment of modernity. Her body and domestic space need protection from the encroaching, hypersexualized African man. The detergent transforms him into a suitable object of desire—from African to Chinese—while implying a linear narrative of progress and development. Even as white bodies are absent in the commercial, whiteness is ever-present through its proxies of light skin and cleanliness. At play are core tenets of Chinese racial discourses based in color consciousness between Black and white, the dark-skinned agricultural laborer and the fair-skinned elite. Mobilizing these racial meanings, the commercial celebrates whiteness as cleanliness, affluence, and urban modernity while representing the Black body as dirty, uncivilized, and dangerous.

Unsurprisingly, the commercial let loose international ire with coverage on the BBC and CNN and in the *New York Times*, *New Yorker*, *Shanghaiist*, and *South China Morning Post*. The *Huffington Post* declared it "the most racist advert ever" (quoted in Horowitz 2016). Chinese racism had arrived on the global stage. This remark was an instance of American media singling out Chinese racism, a racist response to a racist ad that suggests that Chinese racism is worse than its American counterpart. An Australian news site asked, "Is this the most racist commercial ever made?" and pointed out that the commercial was a copy of an Italian laundry detergent ad, implying that Chinese were being held to a double standard (news.com.au 2016). Indeed, Qiaobi's ad closely copies the setting, music, and plot of a 2007 Colereria Italiana commercial for a color-safe detergent powder. But in the Italian version, a white man goes into the machine and a Black man emerges. The tagline is "Coloured is better." Naming unoriginality suggests that Chinese racism is a belated copy of Western racism. By this logic, China is following in the footsteps of the West, from repeating racist tropes to imperial adventures in Africa. Chinese discourses of hygiene traffic in established racial and sexual stereotypes of Black bodies as dirty, subsequently remaking globally circulating Western and Chinese racial ideas, old and new.

The Qiaobi commercial also taps into prohibitions of intimate life and racial hygiene that have been central to regimes of racial separation in South Africa. The development of urban segregation at the turn of the twentieth century can be traced to the "sanitation syndrome" and "medical menace" targeting Africans and Indian immigrants in Natal and the Transvaal. Disease acted as a social metaphor to justify spatial separation (Swanson 1977). Anxieties about racial contagion in South Africa have been closely related to white anxieties about Black sexuality and white domesticity. The "Black Peril" panic fixated on Black domestic workers in Johannesburg's suburban homes, painting the African "houseboy" as a threat to the white "mistress" (Keegan 2001; Van Onselen [1982] 2001). Race insidiously reached into every corner of everyday life under apartheid. South Africans lived under total social and residential segregation with separate amenities. Interracial intimacies were outlawed under the Prohibition of Mixed Marriages and Immorality Act until 1985. And yet, race was never absolute. As rigid as racial categories were, there has always been mixing, porosity, and ambiguity, which is evident in the vast category "Coloured." In practice, apartheid officials imprecisely relied on appearance, markers of social status, and "common sense" for racially classifying individuals (Posel 2001).

Contemporary Chinese representations of Black bodies as dirty contain echoes of the pseudoscientific racial discourses of Chinese intellectuals at the turn of the twentieth century. These modern racial thinkers, influenced by Western racial ideas, constructed Black and white foreigners as barbarians and devils. This difference was imagined as debris on the skin. "The white ones are cold and dull as the ashes of frogs, the black ones are ugly and dirty as coal," one nineteenth-century intellectual wrote (quoted in Dikötter [1992] 2015, 26). Racial matter was represented as ashen skin that sheds from frogs or the dirty dust that rubs off of coal. The racist beliefs of the dirtiness of Black bodies, and particularly skin, is closely linked to antimiscegenation ideologies and colonial racial hygiene. For instance, in 2011 a netizen commented: "Black people always make me feel like they haven't fully washed themselves, I can't accept/handle someone who is dark all over their body." Another person commented, "Those who are too dark I truly am unable to accept. Just looking at them I lose all sexual desire! Turn the lights off and it's okay" (quoted in Pfafman, Carpenter, and Tang 2015, 549). Discourses of hygiene are intertwined with race, sexuality, and skin. At China City, where Chinese and Africans work in close quarters, racial hygiene was practiced by fortifying bodily boundaries.

Epidermal Encounters

When I wasn't working at Jenny's party goods shop, I worked at Xiao Li's fast fashion shop. Xiao Li and her husband jumped at the chance to open a second shop when a small shop in a prime location became available to rent. Already busy with the main shop and raising a toddler, Xiao Li asked her younger sister Eve, at the time a teacher in Hunan, to work full-time for a few months. Eve epitomized the modern woman of the Qiaobi commercial— educated, attractive, cosmopolitan, and independent. She was quiet, private, and stylish but not flashy. With Xiao Li's mother-in-law helping with child care, the house was full. Instead Eve moved into the mall flats, where we bonded as outliers. We went on evening strolls in the parking lot and on many outings. Eve wanted me to take her to places where other Chinese did not go, places that were hip but in gentrified, predominantly white, securitized parts of the city. Over cigarettes (a secret she kept from her older sister) I listened to her talk about London fashion and reminisce about the independent films she used to watch in China. Eve's other friend at the mall flats was a woman in her early twenties who grew up in Germany, where her parents were traders. Conscious of appearance and skin tone, Eve was quick to point out that her milky complexion was lighter than Xiao Li's. Thirty years old and single, Eve was considered a "leftover woman." She had few prospects in Johannesburg. Believing the Chinese men to be beneath her class, education, and *suzhi* level, Eve sought a professional white or Chinese South African. She agonized about a missed connection with a stranger, a white guy she locked eyes with at a stoplight in Xiao Li's car. Once, in a huff, she let it slip, "I would rather die alone than be with a Black man."

In 2016, I introduced Eve to Matthew, a filmmaker visiting from London. The three of us waited for an Uber ride in the mall parking lot. Matthew and I gave Samuel, a Black South African security guard, a high five. Handshakes were an everyday occurrence; African shopworkers and security guards choreographed elaborate ones with each other. When Samuel reached his hand out to shake hers, she reluctantly extended her hand and nervously smiled. Immediately after letting go, she wiped her hand on her white lacey dress. There was more to the visceral response than the hierarchy between a tenant and security guard might suggest. Matthew teased Eve about her reaction. Suddenly embarrassed in front of us, a white British artist and a Chinese American academic, she admitted her racial prejudice, believing he was dirty. This kind of racism was opposed to the progressive, educated, worldly person she strove to be.

The quick wipe of the hand was an instance of disgust, what happens when bodies come into "sensuous proximity" with objects and suddenly "'recoil' from their proximity, as a proximity that is felt as nakedness or as an exposure on the skin surface" (Ahmed 2015, 83, 95). The affective politics of such proximities are based on managing the distance between Black and Chinese bodies and containing the unseeable forms of "race" that materialize on the surface of skin. Even in situations such as a platonic handshake, proximate encounters are entangled with anxieties around interracial intimacy. As skin is the racialized epidermis, fear of skin contact plays out in mundane moments, reproducing relations of separation and anxieties about race, sexuality, and gender. These modes of racial separation are insidious. Chinese imagine racial contagion and seek to fortify bodily boundaries in quotidian situations. In fleeting encounters, relations of power and anti-Blackness become apparent. The minor details of bodies and routines were heightened in the earliest days of the COVID-19 pandemic when I was in Johannesburg. Traders cautiously returned from Lunar New Year trips home and self-isolated, masked, and socially distanced to protect themselves from relatives, neighbors, and friends. My interlocutors talked about airflow, cramped spaces, windows, viral particles, and sanitation. The spread of the virus through touch and air exaggerated the patterns of distance and separation that I had previously noticed regarding microscopic toxins and racial germs.

Conjuring Contagion

Jenny's single room on the fifth floor of China City's flats had a large window that overlooked the shipping container warehouses and skyline. I admired the creativity of Jenny's utilitarian and thrifty sensibilities. There was a large window facing the parking lot and shipping container warehouses. The windowsill was lined with dried orange peels for steeping and an aloe plant for its therapeutic gel. A magenta plastic clothes hanger propped the window open all day, through which gusts of wind would blow dust into the flat. Adjacent to the window was a washing machine; on the opposite wall, far away from the dirt, several pairs of handwashed underwear dried on a rail. Her apartment, like her shop, was cluttered, but there was an order to it all. When we opened in the morning, I would fill the kettle from the sink in the back of the shop. Jenny insisted that I fully open the tap for several minutes to flush out any toxins that might have collected in the pipes overnight, which I found wasteful considering the severe drought in parts of the country. Beneath the enclosed counter were rolls of toilet paper, mugs, utensils, bowls, and a sponge. Even though there was already a sponge by the sink, Jenny was adamant that I use the sponge under the counter. Once she corrected me, explaining the sponge by the sink was for African workers. This minor detail revealed a biopolitical project.

I moved out of Chinatown and into China City's flats, where I was Jenny's next-door neighbor. I spent a lot of time with her outside work. In the months leading up to her trip to China, I accompanied her to buy South African specialties like biltong and rooibos tea to gift to friends and family. But I was perplexed by many of the goods she stocked up on: dried foodstuffs easily found in China, name-brand infant formula, and an array of vitamins and supplements. When I asked her why she was hauling these heavy products home, she explained that they were of dubious quality in China. Food safety has been a major issue there, with high-profile incidents of food contamination over the past two decades. The uncurbed prevalence of poisonous fake food—from milk powder and soy sauce to beef—had led ordinary citizens to distrust regulatory bodies and food safety. Since the poisonous industrial chemical melamine was discovered in infant formula in

2008, imported formula had become a precious commodity (Y. Yan 2012). Jenny was not alone in her thinking. I asked one woman when she and her husband were planning on sending their one-year-old son to Fuqing. She matter-of-factly responded, "When he doesn't need milk anymore." The clarity of her pragmatism unsettled my assumptions about family life.

These banal practices and routines were both familiar and strange to me. Growing up in a Chinese immigrant household, I recalled the peculiar ways my mother separated dirty clothing and ritualistically boiled "tainted" dishes. When accompanying Jenny, I remembered the many shopping trips my parents took in preparation for their biannual trips to visit relatives in their hometown, Hangzhou. They stuffed their suitcases to the brim with vitamins, supplements, face cream, and locally grown ginseng. They returned with suitcases full of DVDs, books, and tins of tea. Although much time had passed, I was attuned to these idiosyncratic habits of bodily comportment, health, and hygiene. But in South Africa, these practices took on different meanings; pollutants included racial matter.

Fears of environmental toxins in China follow traders to South Africa and converge with discourses on contagion, hygiene, and disease. As I realized, there was a connection between how traders thought about pollutants and race that were mediated through the body and its boundaries. A healthy Chinese body is impermeable to contagion, a capacious category that encompasses both the imagined racial contagion of African bodies and environmental pollutants. Chinese try to fortify bodily boundaries and contain racial difference by avoiding physical contact, whether avoiding skin-to-skin touch or the residue of bodily fluids. These understated mundane practices are crucial to the ideological reproduction of race and class relations that demand the reproduction of clear lines of separation in all aspects of shop and home life, including the most banal facets that seem unrelated to race. Shaped by their experiences with pollution in China, my interlocutors were preoccupied with the porosity of the body and ever-present pollutants—particulate matter in the air, industrial waste in the water, toxic chemicals in food, and aerosolized virus particles. In Chinese cities, the air pollution crisis has made breathing political. Ordinary citizens attempt to protect their airways and bodies from harmful particulate matter with masks and home filtration devices (Kohrman 2021; Zee 2022). While China's rapid industrialization brings hazardous air and water pollution, South Africa brings reprieve. Chinese migrants repeatedly raised South Africa's air quality in our casual conversations. The mild weather and fresh air were South Africa's most redeeming feature, as if making up for the migrants' sense of dislocation and fear of crime. Transnational imaginaries of environment, health, and body link Africa and China, between which migrants shuttle back and forth. From food to air, real and imagined contagions in China continue to influence how migrants conduct their lives in South Africa from the routinized practice of running the tap to decisions over children's future.

The conceptualization of epidemics in premodern and modern Chinese medical thought sheds light on the racialization of contagion and how pollutants become metonyms for race. Before the imperial era, Chinese medical literature represented epidemics as the result of cosmological and meteorological constellations. Like the Greek *miasma*, medical explanations of disease believed epidemics were caused by geographical or seasonal "polluted vapor ascending from the earth" that spread and flowed, often through water, and adhered to the body. Offering another explanation, folk medicine conceived of epidemics as demonological possession. Demons (*gui*) emerged from corpses to infect those nearby, while seasonal demons (*yigui*) invaded the air (Volkmar 2000). The demon (*gui*) as vector of disease is important. Chinese traders and workers at China City frequently referred to African men as "black devil" (*heigui*), a term that links contagion, evil, and the Black body. More recently, the Black body has been imagined as a viral vector. The derogatory term has also been important to the representation of HIV/AIDS as an epidemic of Black African origins (Hood 2013). In the early days of COVID-19, while the Western world manufactured conspiracies of wet markets and lab leaks to blame China for the virus, Chinese scapegoated another racial other. In April 2020, about a thousand kilometers from Wuhan, African migrants in Guangzhou were blamed for new "imported" cases. African nationals were violently evicted from apartments and hotels and targeted for passport seizures, deportation threats, testing, and quarantine (Castillo and Amoah 2020).

Race, disease, and pollutants align under the capacious concept of contagion. Like the microscopic toxins that are too small to see but nevertheless flow through pipes, "racial germs" are transmitted through a sponge, an object that mediates contact—however many degrees separated—between utensils, saliva, and mouths. These objects and particles, real and imagined, animate social action (M. Y. Chen 2012). The unseeable matter of racial difference emblematizes the rescaling of racial politics. At the turn of the twenty-first century, nanotechnology has partially replaced the role of anthropological pseudoscience in making race a property of the human body. Under the so-called new racism, genomic technologies rebiologize race, scaling it down from the epidermal to molecular (Gilroy 2000). In Chinese discourses of racial contagion, race is imagined on multiple scales from the body politic to the molecular, invisible but materially real like toxins. Conceived as ever present in the environment and transmissible, racial contagion can be contained through practices of distancing and quarantine. The simple act of keeping two sponges is as built into daily habits as wearing a face mask in a smoggy city or during the pandemic. The banality points to the taken-for-granted labor of maintaining racial boundaries and containing racial difference. Racialization does not only manifest in macrolabor relations and racial stereotypes but also in embodied habits.

Pollution Behaviors

Dirt is not only a stereotype associated with African bodies; it also socially and symbolically orders the separation of African and Chinese bodies. In *Purity and Danger*, Mary Douglas ([1966] 2003) conceptualizes dirt and pollution behaviors as ways to eliminate dirt and positively organize the environment. Eliminating "dirt," in whatever form it takes, is a project of social order. The individual body is a scaled-down version of the social body and the structure of ideas. "The mistake is to treat bodily margins in isolation from all other margins," Douglas writes ([1966] 2003, 150). Pollution behaviors focus on the body's surfaces and orifices. As practices, pollution behaviors anticipate pollution and defilement. Similarly, Chinese migrants invent a host of pollution beliefs and behaviors that reflect the all-encompassing ways that maintaining a racial order through separation governs the conduct of everyday life.

Within the range of public intimacies at the mall, ordinary objects become imbued with the sacredness of boundary objects. Anita, a Zimbabwean shopworker who had worked at several Chinese shops, a Chinese restaurant in Johannesburg, and as a domestic worker in Botswana, was highly cognizant of these boundaries. With a tone of humiliation, she conveyed, "I'm willing to trust Chinese, but they don't trust us . . . some of the bosses, you can't even touch his cup." Douglas explains the politics of touch in the caste system, writing, "When a man uses an object it becomes part of him, participates in him" ([1966] 2003, 156). In South Africa, ideas about "black germs" reinforced apartheid policies in everyday life. Domestic workers lived in "back rooms" away from the main house, used special outdoor toilets, kept separate plates, and were prohibited from sitting on furniture (Ginsburg 2011, 146). Whites sought to physically distance themselves from Black bodies in arbitrary ways that reflected the anxious condition of reliance on Black labor in all areas of life. "House rules were a response to the visceral uneasiness many whites felt around Africans," Rebecca Ginsburg writes. "Whites were uneasy about the prospect of whites and Africans coming together over things in intimate and uncontrolled ways" (2011, 146). Nicky Falkof notes the ironies and histories behind these rules: "Black workers could clean a white family's bath and make their beds but the entry of a black body into a family's swimming pool would in many cases have been experienced as a pollutant, a breach of a potent taboo based on a long-standing discourse of sanitation, separation and purity that legitimated the segregation of colonial cities" (2016, 632). The paradox of domestic labor applied at Mr. Zheng's house, which employed a Black South African woman as a longtime domestic worker. She lived in the intact apartheid era back room and cleaned when the Chinese residents were at China Malls. Similar rules of separation applied to the usage of shared kitchens and bathrooms (M. Huang 2020). At the mall, Zimbabwean workers like Anita, who had previously cleaned houses and served food, were predisposed to the racial dimensions of their Chinese employers' unspoken shop rules.

Cups and sponges are objects that directly or indirectly touch mouths. The mouth is an eroticized edge of the body and site of ingestion with different social and cultural histories (Tompkins 2012). In Chinese views of the body, the mouth mediates the interior body and the social world, dynamically connecting the individual body and the body politic. Eating (*chi*) is where the natural body meets the social body (Yue 1999). On one occasion, Da Jie, a trader in her fifties from Dongbei, called me over because a nearby shopworker had a pair of scissors in his mouth. A former nurse in China, she was cautious about health and hygiene and often wore a face mask in the car. In this moment, she seemed repulsed by his saliva and something else. On the heels of the murder of a China City resident, she seemed distraught over what he was doing with the sharp object. But perhaps she also found troubling the work tool doubling as a toy and "the promiscuous orality of the experience," Nayan Shah writes of white fixation on Chinese men sharing opium pipes (2001, 95). Yet regardless of how wary Chinese migrants can be about racial proximities, racial matter, and ingestion, they nevertheless frequent Chinatown's restaurants and China City's eateries, places characterized as "dirty" that employ African workers in both the front and back. Pollution behaviors are as arbitrary as the social construction of race itself: handling and cooking food is acceptable, but sharing a sponge is not. Reproducing everyday racial hierarchies of Black and Chinese difference vis-à-vis the cleanliness of whiteness engenders ritualized pollution behaviors. Far from trivial, these routines and habits insert physical distance between bodies in arbitrary but symbolic ways. Filters, whether physical barriers like air filters or social norms, facilitate inclusion and exclusion. As Matthew Kohrman writes, filters "are all about binaries, keeping a category in or out. But they are also binary busters. They never work 100 percent of the time, after all, and before long, they start to get gummed up and fail to keep tidy divisions" (2021, 166). The same is true with the regulation of racial, gender, and sexual difference at China City. Racial categories are porous and malleable. And yet, returning to Holland, "Racism transforms an already porous periphery into an absolute, thereby making it necessary to deny all kinds of crossing" (2012, 6).

The Biopolitics of Global China

In chapter 5 and this chapter, I moved from the political economy of the mining belt to the security control room and gated apartment complex. These stories of infidelity, betrayal, alliance, and encounter explore Chinese sojourner colonialism and racial capitalism through the microlevel, quotidian, affective, and biopolitical, without which our understanding of them would be incomplete. Intimacies and proximities are crucial to the ideological and day-to-day reproduction of hierarchical relations of Chinese capital and African labor and the reproductive futurity of entrepreneurial migration. Across these forms of intimacy and separation, African and Chinese subjects conduct their daily lives, comport their bodies, and discipline their desires in ways that uphold the racial and class hierarchy. In Johannesburg, Chinese migrants experiment with forming new households and business, domestic, and romantic partnerships that are intertwined with the building blocks of entrepreneurial migration: the accumulation of capital, the prosperity of the family, and the reproductive futurity of the child. In the process, they stretch norms of gender, sexuality, and kinship and test the boundaries of racial and national belonging. Within these destabilizations, one ideal—endogamy—becomes the criterion for proper Chineseness. Practices of endogamy are the product of ideologies of racial purity, racial nationalism, and anti-Blackness in China. Endogamy maintains the social privileges of Chineseness for Chinese, safeguarding Chineseness as property through exclusion. Endogamy applies to more than intimate and domestic life and, as chapter 7 details, to underground economies.

As the politics of racialized gender and sexuality play out on the body, anxieties about racial separateness encompass interracial intimacies and banal forms of bodily contact. Chinese migrants adhere to a host of pollution beliefs and behaviors that reflect the insidious ways the social relations of racial capitalism and anti-Blackness govern the conduct of daily life. At stake in maintaining physical and social distance between bodies is the racial and class hierarchy of Chinese bosses, Chinese workers, and African workers. But as the histories of interracial intimacies in apartheid South Africa show, color lines have never been rigid but are porous, fragile, and subject to transgression. Physical proximities, quotidian encounters, intimate familiarities, and mundane ways of comporting the body reproduce racial orders but also threaten to upend them. Something as simple as separate sponges— minor details and banal practices that seem almost inconsequential—reify "Black" and "Chinese" as distinct and opposing racial identities. Anxieties about racial mixing and social punishment of transgression attest to the work that goes into naturalizing racial fictions.

The Chinese Century, like the imperial cultures of the American and British centuries, transforms more than an international order. The emerging Sinocentric world is a moment of remaking race, gender, and sexuality through Chinese racial genealogies. As a global system, anti-Blackness is expanded by Chinese racial formations and racial nationalism through discourses that take root in new global locations. Blackness is transnationally produced through the circulation of figures of race and gender, such as the African migrant in China, the single Chinese woman, the mixed-race child, and the nuclear family. These figures and stereotypes, while they resonate with US and Western versions, are not copies but adapt premodern and modern Chinese racial thought in the service of racial nationalism and capitalism. The micropractices from the mall signal a changing global order of Blackness, Chineseness, and whiteness and their meanings. Modern Chinese racial discourses have always been global in the way they reference China's place in the world. In the early twentieth century, Chinese intellectuals envisioned a global racial order of white/West, Chinese/China, and Black/Africa in terms of civilizational superiority (Karl 2002). In the 1960s, Mao Zedong envisioned an antiracist, anti-imperialist socialist internationalism of Chinese, Africans, and African Americans against the West. Since the 1980s a resurgence of Han Chinese racial nationalism has been underway, in part as backlash to the transracial solidarities of the Mao era. Today a different Chinese racial imaginary is taking hold, global in scale but not antiracist or anti-imperialist. Ethnoracial chauvinism takes new meaning in the twenty-first century when the Middle Kingdom resumes its rightful place at the center of the world, which is no longer the sole provenance of the West. In the minds of Chinese netizens and my Chinese interlocutors in South Africa, Chinese/China and white/West are on similar footing while Blackness/Africa remains at the bottom. Whiteness remains valorized as the aspirational ideal that many Chinese migrants aim to surpass. Global white supremacy and anti-Blackness stays intact as Chinese move from the global periphery to center and are incorporated into its machinery.

PART III

Frictions and Futures

7

Follow the Surplus

An understanding of the situation must begin with an enquiry into the degree of exploitation of African resources and labour, and then must proceed to follow the surplus to its destination outside of Africa—into the bank accounts of the capitalists.

Walter Rodney, *How Europe Underdeveloped Africa*, (1972) 1981

During my first visit to Sandton, Johannesburg's financial district in the northern suburbs, the Sino Steel Plaza building caught my eye: seventeen stories of blue glass windows with bold red characters reaching toward the sky. Next to it was the China Construction Bank and a Rock & Roll McDonald's, its iconic golden arches in the shadow of global China. The year 2000 was a watershed moment. Beijing hosted the inaugural Forum on China and Africa Cooperation (FOCAC).

That same year the Beijing-based Bank of China and the China Construction Bank, two of six Chinese state-owned banks, opened their first South African branches in Sandton. Johannesburg has long functioned as a continental gateway from colonial outpost to present-day "world-class city." From the beginning, Chinese banks recognized Sandton as the "advance base for [the] development of the African market," as the China Construction Bank (n.d.) explained. In 2007 the Industrial and Commercial Bank of China acquired a 20 percent share of the Standard Bank of South Africa, which began as a subsidiary of the British overseas Standard Bank and operates in twenty African countries. These banks have facilitated tremendous growth in trade, investment, and the internationalization of the yuan.

The presence of the People's Republic of China (PRC) across the continent of Africa is reflected at O. R. Tambo International Airport. In 2015, when Johannesburg hosted FOCAC, Bank of China displays welcomed international travelers from the arrival gate to the baggage claim area. Splayed along a long walkway was an outline of Africa and mainland China, connected by a red ribbon representing the New Silk Road. In this twenty-first-century mapping, the continent, presented as a mosaic of people, animals, and urban development, lags behind China's roads and skyscrapers. Europe, North America, and the rest of the world do not even appear. Every February the international terminal is decorated with red lanterns and glittering displays of luxury goods for Chinese tourists traveling over Chinese New Year. Since the early 2000s, the Chinese travel market—an estimated one hundred thousand globe-trotting business elites and urban middle-class families—has been one of South African tourism's most lucrative, fastest-growing markets. International travelers are greeted by advertisements for global wallets, collaborations between China Union Pay and Standard Bank to make the conversion of foreign currencies simple and instantaneous. Sino-African worlds comprise infrastructures for the transnational flow of people, goods, and capital. As the map visualizes, infrastructures are as important as the places they connect.

Seen from the financial district and airport, money and people seem to have never moved between these two countries with such ease. But the China City mall tracks a different set of twenty-first-century mobilities. Ordinary migrants are worlds apart from celebrated investors, state officials, and big-spending tourists. In China they occupy vastly different social locations; in Johannesburg they rarely cross paths. My interlocutors identified as "normal businesspeople." They knew they were not the intended users of Chinese banks in Sandton, of China Union Pay cards, or of foreign exchange

7.1   Bank of China display at O. R. Tambo International Airport. Photo
       by the author.

apps. As capital-intensive, state-driven projects proliferate, transnational mobilities of capital proceed along two mostly parallel tracks: one along official Beijing–Sandton channels and another underground. The world of Chinese migrant entrepreneurs forms a parallel shadow economy that blurs the boundaries between the formal and informal, the licit and illicit, and the legal and illegal.[1] In this chapter, I give an account of the extralegal activities of Chinese sojourners and their *underdeveloping* effects. While Chinese traders provide low-cost goods and employment opportunities, the cumulative extraction of value from southern and South Africans as laborers and consumers exacerbates uneven geographies of accumulation and development initially established by Euro-American colonial racial capitalism.

Development is at the heart of debates over the politics of Chinese capitalist projects in Africa, from the Belt and Road Initiative to Chinese traders as agents of development (Mohan and Tan-Mullins 2009; Nyíri 2006). Development is shaped by colonialism and imperialism that developed Europe and the United States through the plundering of Africa, the Americas, and Asia. The racial grammar of twentieth-century development discourses divides the world into the economically, scientifically, and technologically developed white West and its racial others. Poverty is naturalized as incapacity for development (Ferreira da Silva 2015, 36). Whereas East Asian development has been celebrated, even model-minoritized, developmental discourse about Africa traffics in racial vernaculars of corruption and governance (Pierre 2020). But in the twenty-first century, the racial grammar of developmentalism is changing (Koshy et al. 2022) As Mao Zedong represented the PRC as the leader of the Third World, the PRC aims to lead the Global South through trade, infrastructure, and investment, most visibly under Xi Jinping's Belt and Road Initiative and BRICS. Against the self-representations of the PRC, the practices of ordinary migrant traders retrench global inequalities.

Researchers have diligently tracked investments, trade, debt, and demographics between African countries and China. But as Ching Kwan Lee observes, discussions of China in Africa "misconstrue Chinese capital as a quantifiable thing rather than a set of contested processes" (2017, 3). Through ethnography, I capture the heterogeneity of Chinese capitalist projects, or what gets blackboxed as "Chinese capital." Anthropologists study capitalism through its quotidian practices, contested processes, and social relations of accumulation, production, and circulation, making abstractions concrete and material. "Flows" are always made through frictions, channels, and "channel-making activities" (Tsing 2005). The economic growth dubbed "Africa Rising" is the product of extraction, exploitation, and financialization. Writing about the immense inequalities that neoliberal globalization has created in southern Africa, James Ferguson points out that the global does not flow but "hops" between points, "efficiently connecting the enclaved points in the network while excluding (with equal efficiency) the spaces that lie between the points" (2006, 47). Hannah Appel details enclaving processes in Equatorial Guinea whereby capital circulates among multinational corporations and expatriate communities "from the airport to the rig" (2019, 61).

These contemporary observations from Africa reiterate points that Marxist Pan-Africanist visionary Walter Rodney made about flows and channels decades earlier in *How Europe Underdeveloped Africa*. The very purpose of colonialism was the "consistent expatriation of surplus produced by African labour out of African resources" (Rodney [1972] 1981, 149). Indeed, capital flowed from colony to metropole and back in the form of reinvestment but the "net flow was from colony to metropole" (Rodney [1972] 1981, 212). Imperial banks, including the Standard Bank of South Africa Limited, transferred surplus to London money markets where value further accrued. Trading companies introduced "several straws for the sucking out of surplus" (Rodney [1972] 1981, 159). In tandem with overseas banks, shipping companies, roads, railways, and ports provided the infrastructure connecting mine and plantation to metropole. Rodney's critique was grounded in the historical specificities of European colonialism but is germane to Sino-African contexts.

Taking up Rodney's call to "follow the surplus," I am concerned with how money flows through frictions, hops, channels, and straws and to what effects. Making and sending profits to China both happen in the liminal zone of (il)legality. My interlocutors embraced quasi-legal practices. They migrated through clandestine channels and later achieved legal residency status, registered companies with the South African Revenue Services but underreported turnover, and used Chinese underground banks and South African banks. The trade-off for economic profit is legal vulnerability. Traders described their economic practices as "straight" (*zhenggui*), meaning compliant with official norms and laws, or "going underground" (*zou dixia*) through unofficial, informal, or extralegal channels. Going straight or underground exists on a spectrum ranging from widely accepted illegal activities to criminal acts. The distinction is between violating the law (*fanfa*) and committing a crime (*fanzui*)—unlawfulness and criminality, each with different moral meanings. Legality and legitimacy are not one in the same, nor are *illegal* and *legal* coherent classifications. Legality is produced within the porous boundaries between markets, states, moral economies, and the law. My purpose is not to expose extralegal practices to expose the "truth" as an investigative journalist might. Rather, I am interested in what these practices mean to their ordinary practitioners and the political effects of these practices.

This chapter approaches racial capitalism—and questions of development, colonialism, and imperialism nested within it—by following the money. After all, profit—which is made through the exploitation of a southern African precariat and the postapartheid Black consumer class—gets stuck if there is no way to convert South African hard currency into yuan in China. I link the transnational mobilities of migrants with money, of capital and capitalists, and economies and the people in them. As chapter 2 detailed, entrepreneurial migration is a future-oriented, China-centered project of sojourner colonialism. Movements of migrants and money share a transnational infrastructure and set of moral dispositions. The end goal for traders is to make money (*zhengqian*) for their futures in China, which means getting money out of South Africa is of utmost importance. My interlocutors embraced flexibility in every sense, keeping a foot in China and South Africa—family ties, bank accounts, business registrations, homes, visas, and passports—and an eye on up-and-coming destinations. But flows are rarely smooth. Like visa regimes, foreign exchange laws regulate and restrict movement of profit. Extending my discussion of migration brokers, visas, and passports, money moves through the cash economies, regulatory loopholes, and intermediaries who animate monetary mobilities across legal and illegal domains and borders. Race and the legacies of apartheid appear throughout this story of money, and in unexpected ways. The expatriation of surplus—how money moves, and its underdeveloping impact—is what makes sojourning colonial.

"A Lot of Cash Is Going Around"

The shipping container or suitcase full of cash is a trope associated with Chinese traders and exemplifies popular imaginings about illicit global money flows. Another anthropologist in Johannesburg shared with me a conspiracy theory from a Zimbabwean production manager, who speculated that Chinese traders import containers of fabric or pencils, something cheap and unsuspecting, and return containers full of US dollars back to China. According to this factory manager, Chinese had depleted the dollar supply in Zimbabwe and there were no longer denominations above twenty dollars in circulation. Grant, a longtime Malawian worker at China City, was certain that his boss took a suitcase of cash back to Shanghai in three-month cycles, bringing profits back and importing more goods. Linked to the suitcase of cash is the belief that the China Malls only benefited Chinese and not Africans. Grant said, "They just make money, and that money is not used in this country, our country . . . they just take the money and go to their country." These were, after all, "China Malls, not Africa Malls," Grant pointed out. Embedded within these cash stories are critiques of capital outflow and lack of economic reinvestment. These critiques are informed by African workers' experience with labor exploitation and remittance of wages for their own futures back home.

Cyrildene Chinatown and the China Malls are places that run nearly entirely on cash. Chinatown contains a tightly networked, insular economy of landlords, grocers, restaurants, sidewalk vendors, hotels, taxi drivers, and salons. At the China Malls, salaries and rent are paid in cash each month. Cars, property, and even international airline tickets are purchased in cash. On any given day, an extraordinary amount of cash is in circulation. Large wholesalers turn over cash on the order of ZAR100,000 per day. Anthropologists of money have theorized money as simultaneously a social relation, material reality, and symbolic system (Maurer 2012). Cash builds and maintains social relationships and obligations. Exchanging cash necessitates and builds trust along ethnic lines. Strangers become bound through monetary relations, especially where there is no paper trail. Materially, cash is an unruly medium of exchange and accumulation. It physically degrades, is prone to theft, and as national currency, can depreciate in value in relation to another nation's currency. Bills need to be checked for authenticity, straightened, sorted, and bagged (Maurer 2012). Cash physically builds up in neat stacks and messy piles under literal and figurative mattresses: in safes and vaults, beneath floorboards, and in locked drawers. The day-to-day amassing of banknotes presents a physical problem of weight and volume. I learned to appreciate the materiality of cash and the feeling it instills; I admired how artfully traders counted bills, which I was never able to master despite my best efforts. The whirring sound of Mr. Zheng's cash-counting machine delighted my ears. To pay rent, I visited Cyrildene Chinatown's only ATM at the far end of the street. The absence of ATMs attested to the self-replenishing circuit of this cash economy. I internalized the paranoia of carrying cash, irrationally looking over my shoulder for the few blocks I walked. Once I started working, I felt the responsibility of getting the count right. I learned firsthand that bills pile up quickly and that moving money from a shop to a bank account in China requires an infrastructure more complicated than a suitcase or foreign exchange app.

Traders translated currency as swiftly as apps but in analog fashion. In everyday small talk, the daily exchange rate between the South African rand and the US dollar, down to two decimals, came up as commonly as the weather. The rand's value was converted into the dollar, the measure of global value, then converted to yuan, its final currency form. The exchange rate took on a life of its own. It determined the real value of wages or profits and when to transfer money to China. Among China City's entrepreneurs, the use of cash ran counter to the increasing use of digital, mobile, biometric, and/or electronic payment technologies toward cashless economies in African countries (Breckenridge 2010; Kendall et al. 2012). In China, digital money has made cash nearly obsolete. Most payments are made through QR codes and mobile payment platforms. But among my interlocutors, cash was king. Cash "rac[es] from pocket to pocket without the logistical drag of conversion, storage, restriction, accounting, and dematerialization" (Appadurai 2000, 634). For entrepreneurial migrants between national currencies, banking systems, and regulatory regimes, banknotes represent money that is not behind red tape, ready to be converted and remitted to China, where it will go toward school fees and houses.

The problem with cash, however, is that it makes traders, or anyone who looks like one, vulnerable to robberies. All Chinese bodies—marked on the surface by race, clothing, accents, and sensibilities—become "ATMs," as many of my interlocutors characterized them. For safety, cash is transported in discreet and not-so-discreet gift bags, shoeboxes, cardboard boxes, plastic bags, socks, and armored vehicles. Chinese women outwardly signaled

7.2   Clear pink purses. Photo by the author.

their empty-handedness by carrying clear plastic purses. Jan, a white Afri-kaner and China City's head of security, viewed cash use and informal business practices as the main reason for armed robberies. He estimated that 80 percent of Chinese traders do not use banks and have "wads of money" hidden away at home: "Your older generation still believes, pop it in a mattress, pop it in a box underneath the register." As Jan saw it, Chinese were being held up at their shops, at traffic lights, and at home because they dealt in cash and cut corners to enhance profits: "It's cash money. Nothing is registered. They don't have records of what money is coming in or what's going out, so it's a lucrative business, it's a cash-flow business. Cash comes in, nobody knows, and it gets packed away, and yeah, that's the reason they've been targeted . . . the situation is a lot of cash is going around."

Holding on to cash has connotations with the "Asiatic" practice of hoarding. Traders conduct their businesses in secrecy, evoking "Yellow Peril" tropes of the Asian horde and hoarder (Lye 2005). Karl Marx depicts the "naïve form of hoarding" of holding onto gold and silver as expressions of wealth, attributing this practice to "Asiatics" from India and China. Hoarding is not rational but comes from "the passionate desire, to hold fast the product of the first metamorphosis" of commodity into money (1976, 227–28).[2] Hoarding continues to be seen as backward and parasitic to national economies. Taking money out of circulation affects national monetary supply and velocity of circulation. In defense of hoarding, Gustav Peebles writes, "Hoarding is far from barbarically stupid if one does *not* trust the surrounding social institutions where one might otherwise 'save' one's economic value. . . . [P]eople who are accused of hoarding are merely people who have not yet bought into the social institutions that would allow them to circulate their money" (2008, 253, emphasis in the original). Jan also recognized that "maybe [the Chinese traders] don't have enough faith" in South African banks. Indeed, the traders do not trust local institutions, which operate in English and require institutional compliance from beginning to end. Crucially, import and sales taxes cut into razor-thin profit margins. Stories abounded about millions lost to asset seizures and accounts frozen due to "suspicious activity," which have become measures against money laundering, corruption, and terrorism in South Africa. As Marieke De Goede finds, after 9/11, cash is related to "wider societal anxieties about the untraceable, undocumented, and uprooted in globalized societies." Movements of money need "cohesive accounts with clear origins, histories, destinations, and trajectories" (De Goede 2012, 98, 103).[3]

Chinese traders resisted banking for numerous reasons. Ideologically, they did not feel compelled to pay into South Africa's tax base, the kind of economic reinvestment and civic participation expected of them. The state colonizes the future by guarding the collective hoarding of money. But from the perspective of hoarders, "is it merely money directed toward a different future, a future that does not mesh with the state's . . . planned vision of the future?" (Peebles 2008, 253). My interlocutors located their futures in their children, families, and houses in China. A Chinese blogger (Shen 2011) explained the imperative of flouting tax laws and using underground banks. The purpose of most petty traders is to maximize profit and send profit back to China, not to stay for the long term and reinvest locally. Moreover, Chinese traders often do not need local banks. In South Africa, migrants reinvented alternative Chinese financial systems—the underground bank (*dixia qianzhuang*) and informal credit associations (*biaohui*)—to transfer foreign currency and obtain credit.[4] Since the late 1970s, petty entrepreneurs in China have turned to what Kellee Tsai (2002) calls "back-alley banking," a network of rotating credit associations, private money houses, pawnshops, and neighborhood loan sharks. Because private entrepreneurs fall outside the developmental priorities of Chinese state banks, alternative institutions are necessary. Private financial institutions are forbidden in China but are locally condoned and popular.[5] Like clandestine migration, back-alley banking allows ordinary people to "transcend limitations defined by the central state and create possibilities for economic survival, if not wealth, from the raw materials of day-to-day existence" (Tsai 2002, 247).

Where there is informality, there is an attempt to eliminate, contain, regulate, or incorporate it. South African banks have attempted to capture various segments of Chinese markets by devoting special divisions to work with large corporate Chinese accounts and partnering with the China Malls to reach small-scale traders. The pseudonymous NCB, one of South Africa's major banks, has been successful working with these two very different Chinese constituencies. Not the only major bank to do so, it opened a location on the old mining belt, staffed it with Chinese and Taiwanese South Africans, and partnered with China City. The advantage is more than language. As one China City manager put it, "We can understand each other." From the vantage point of the South African state and banks, the incorporation of Chinese into formal banking is part of a larger project of "banking the unbanked" or "formalizing the informal." Keith Breckenridge notes in the South African context, this is "one of the most important but imponderable characteristics of money in Africa: the idea that unbanked people have . . . 'lots of cash' that might be available to capitalize banking lending" (2010, 655). Banking unbanked Chinese traders is part of the state's aim of capturing informal economic activity. Bringing in cash circulating outside the banking system stabilizes the national money supply and facilitates financial surveillance and taxation. Even as banking has become more accessible, migrant entrepreneurs do not always operate in the official realm (*zhenggui*), going underground (*dixia*) instead.

On the Edge of the Law

It is often assumed that an absence of the state allows informal markets to flourish, as if "the state" is a coherent entity that acts in uniform top-down ways. The state is often present in informal spaces and produces informality not through deregulation or a lack of regulation, but the uneven regulation of *disregulation*. State actors act arbitrarily when they reach beyond their authority and redefine legality by irregularly applying rules and laws to different categories of people (D. M. Goldstein 2016, 7–8). In the case of back-alley banking in China, state employees are responsible for implementing central policy through the day-to-day work of collecting fees, issuing licenses, and enforcing regulations (Tsai 2002, 17). The same goes for customs, immigration, tax officials, and police officers in South

Africa who bend the law for personal gain, which creates an adversarial relationship between the South African state and Chinese nationals. In a cat-and-mouse game, traders find ways to outsmart the law, state actors catch on, and traders reinvent workarounds. The dynamic is made possible through a two-way informality of traders' innovations and the state's irregular enforcement. Legal and illegal practices do not exist in discrete domains but are interrelated in "webs of illegality" (D. M. Goldstein 2016). Impressionable state actors and institutional middlemen such as South African accountants, bankers, and shipping agents continuously shift the edge of the law.

Dion, a white South African, is one of a few accountants who work with Chinese traders. Eighty percent of his clientele comes from a few China Malls. He was eager to speak to me, pen in hand to take copious notes, but apprehensive about being recorded. In our conversation, Dion lamented how only a minority of clients provided detailed bank statements, which were usually from personal not business accounts. He suspected most clients kept millions at home and never fully reported their remittances. A financial magician, Dion transformed numbers scrawled on a piece of paper into glossy, spiral-bound financial reports for revenue services. His work entailed overlooking discrepancies and breaches while maintaining the ethical and legal norms of his profession. Akin to Mr. Zheng's work of making an immigration dossier complete, Dion turned informal, patchy records into a "cohesive account" (De Goede 2012). Accountants make illegible activities legible to the state while operating on the edge of the law.

Clarence worked as an accountant at the Crown Mines NCB branch. Born in Taiwan in 1989, Clarence came to South Africa as a child. His parents were shopkeepers in Bloemfontein, and many relatives were wholesalers at the China Malls. This common background is as important as language. Financially advising Chinese clients was a delicate matter of allowing clients to make their own choices while absolving himself and the bank from any illegal entanglements. As Clarence explained to me,

> To be honest, from a banking perspective, we explain the risk involved and the legal everything . . . what [clients] can do legally and so that they listen to our advice a lot and actually it's actually the customer's choice . . . however, if you exceed it, that is your risk and we don't accept any of the risk involved in this. We usually only do the legal stuff in the bank, so whatever illegal, we try not to get into too many details, because in a way we don't want to expose too much

of the banking side to that illegal part. So everything we do is under ethics . . . we let the customers decide.

In between the bank, the state, and traders, Clarence facilitated flows between official and unofficial economies. Walking a tightrope, Clarence's role was to encourage clients to withhold details while advising them so that clients, not the bank, would absorb legal consequences, a move to maximize profits and redistribute liability.

Mellie, a second-generation Chinese South African woman, had a unique vantage point working for Chinese and South African shipping companies as a clearing agent. Clearing agents help importers pay tariffs and duties and enter goods into a computerized system to calculate taxes. They collaborate with entry clerks, some of whom are former customs officers, to lowball the value of imports, hide counterfeit goods, and bribe customs officers, a practice of "technical smuggling" (Hearn 2016, 84). "Money talks in this country," Mellie said. She left the business because clearing agents were "killing the economy." To clear her conscience, she testified for the state against her former employers. Compared to Dion's and Clarence's situations, where withholding was encouraged, Mellie needed to know more, not less, to effectively cover for clients. Traders were inventing new ways to outsmart state actors. Mellie comically recounted when Chinese importers used Black South African names "because obviously they think the Blacks would get privileges and the customs officials are Black and they won't hit on their own kind." Shipping agents devised new ways to get around increased port surveillance. To crack down on smuggling, ports increased the usage of an X-ray scanner from a few hours a day to twenty-four hours. Mellie would stay overnight and patiently wait for the shift change, when containers could pass through unstaffed scanners. Between South African bureaucracy and the informalities of profit maximization, an insular network of accountants, bankers, and shipping agents helps traders find, maneuver, and make loopholes and cracks in the porous regulatory apparatus. Whether white, Chinese, or Taiwanese South Africans, their identities were important to facilitating "understanding" and maintaining "trust."

In Chinatown and the China Malls, a liminal zone emerges in between public/private space and state/nonstate actors whereby private security carries out the work of day-to-day policing. This is not particular to Chinese migrants but exemplifies "twilight policing" in South Africa, an overlapping sovereignty that is neither public nor private that emerged alongside the transformation of governance and security after 1994 (Diphoorn 2015).

The overlapping sovereignties of private security guards; community leaders; metropolitan and state police; and immigration, revenue, and customs agents in Chinatown and the China Malls protect private property and shield informal businesses and undocumented migrants from state surveillance. Cyrildene Chinatown has a South African Police Service branch, but Chinatown residents pay for an armed response team to keep the police at bay. Mr. Zheng's Chinatown office managed security guards; monitored surveillance cameras; and responded to bar fights, squabbles between neighbors, disputes over money, and domestic violence house calls. At the China Malls, management adjudicates conflicts "in-house" to avoid bringing police onto the premises. China City employs dozens of South African guards and contracts with an armed response company and Nigerian guards who provide "muscle." These security forces act as a protective first line of defense alerting residents and tenants when state officials arrive, and they intervene in encounters between migrants and the state. Through webs of state and nonstate actors, these overlapping sovereignties work to maximize profit by minimizing state regulation.

The domains of transnational migration and capital flows are connected through the logic of entrepreneurial migration: of maximizing and expatriating profits to China where they will be reinvested. These domains may seem discrete, but they are connected through the moral economy that treats extralegality as a legitimate means to actualize potential. Going around physical borders is connected to moving money underground through a shared network of people. In addition to his work as a migration broker, Mr. Zheng was in the business of foreign exchange. During our interview, I frequently had to pause the tape recorder not because he wanted to go off the record, but because we were interrupted by a noisy cash transaction. Channels for various mobilities converged in a handful of people because of the political knowledge, social ties, and cash flows required. These intermediaries facilitate the movement of people and money not only across national borders, but also across (il)legal, (in)formal, and (un)official domains to make movements and subjects legible to states. While individual migrants and intermediaries strive to transcend the limitations imposed by states, their everyday activities exacerbate existing uneven geographies of accumulation and development. In the era of neoliberal capitalism, the "new imperialism" has unfolded as molecular movements of capital across racial hierarchies of global space. These molecular flows happen through processes of accumulation that build on ongoing colonial relations and racialized dispossession (A. Goldstein 2022; Harvey 2003). The outflow of profit made from African workers and consumers to China is routed through the concentration of poverty, unemployment, and lack of financial services wrought by apartheid.

Foreign Capital Flows through the Township

Cash is the nimble medium that enables a host of flexible practices that make trading profitable because it is untraceable. Cash requires no receipts to account for where it came from or is going. Even as states determine the value of cash, it disregards the boundaries of states, economies, and the law—up to a point. But the rubber hits the road with remittances (*huikuan*) of unaccounted money. I wondered how South African bills made their way to China, where they would be used—in other words, the material processes of exit and entrance, transformation, and conversion across currency that such a flow entailed. The legal option is through South Africa's Singular Discretionary Allowance, which allows ID holders (citizens and permanent residents) to send ZAR1 million per year abroad tax-free through approved foreign exchange providers. This option is only available to traders who conduct their businesses "straight" from start to finish. Clarence explained the prevalence of underground banking: "Everyone has been cutting corners like that, and then if you've been cutting corners, then you can't send money back." Chinese foreign exchange firms and underground banks filled in the gap.

Allegedly, between 2000 and 2010 the South African Reserve Bank seized billions of rand from twenty-some small Chinese foreign exchange firms. Before Mellie worked in shipping and at the China Malls, she worked for one of these firms until it was shut down. These were the halcyon years of wholesaling during which the demand for a money market emerged. For three years, Mellie and her clients would "monitor the market" every half hour to see if it was "moving up or down." It was a lucrative business: her firm was moving out US$500,000 per day and making a few cents on the dollar. *How* the money moved stunned me. Mellie did the hard, messy work of scouting ID holders in townships where poor Black South Africans would trade usage of their discretionary allowances for a few hundred rand in cash. In other words, South Africans sold their annual allotments to Chinese clients. Mellie put her body on the line. She showed me bite marks on her shoulder from being attacked on the job and recounted attempted carjackings. "It's a hard job, the worst job," she said; a "rotten business." The conversion of bills to foreign currency happened through official channels. Through a handful of willing notaries, Mellie made certified copies of the

IDs. She took the cash to a legitimate foreign exchange company, which transported it to the Reserve Bank, where the cash would be cleared with the ID and finally transferred to a Chinese bank account as yuan. These were fraudulent operations, but, as Mellie described, they were "legit companies" using the "loophole system, which was not right . . . it was following the rules where the loopholes were."[6]

These defunct Chinese foreign exchange companies lay bare how abstracted, deterritorialized "global capital" moves through particular actors, locales, and material processes in messy, embodied, and territorialized ways. Capitalism relies on difference and its constant reproduction. In this case, the illegal flow of money across national borders and currencies was legally routed through poor South African communities, citizenship papers, legitimate foreign exchange companies and notaries, and the racialized economic inequality underlying it all. As Appel (2019) reminds us, race is central to practices of extraction and enclaving. For global capitalism to continue to expand, Achille Mbembe posits, it needs "massive *racial subsidies*" to extract value from or "to produce, order, segment, and racialize surplus or superfluous populations to strategic effect" (2021, 32, emphasis in the original). Along these lines, Grace Kyungwon Hong argues that the speculative economies of late capitalism have expanded the category of surplus to "existentially surplus." As finance has overtaken production, surplus populations now include nonlaboring subjects "that are surplus not to production but to speculation and *circulation*" (2012, 92, emphasis in the original). In this case, circulation doubly refers to the creation of value and the movement of money. It was the acute localization of surplus populations in townships that enabled the making of legal loopholes, viability of illicit money markets, and ultimately the mobility of profits would otherwise be stuck in South Africa and fully taxed. The people recruited to activate these mobilities were primarily poor Black township residents historically shut out of the formal economy and financial institutions, as well as those disproportionately represented among the unemployed. In the years Mellie was scouting, the unemployment rate had reached 30 percent. Under what Deborah James (2014) terms "credit apartheid," predatory informal moneylenders (*mashonisa*), community banks, and savings clubs (*stokvel*) filled in the absence of financial institutions serving poor Black South Africans.

There is another history of Black township and Chinese encounters that lingers on the edge of Mellie's story. It is not insignificant that a Chinese South African was the interlocutor. Mellie knew the ins and outs of regulatory systems, Chinese business norms, and townships. In Durban her family operated a butchery that served Black South Africans. Fahfee (or fafi) is an illegal century-old Chinese-run lottery played among Black South Africans in urban townships and rural towns (Birberick 2018; Krige 2011). In her memoir, Ufrieda Ho (2011) pays tribute to her father, the "fahfee man," and remembers accompanying him to the township to collect betting slips and distribute wins. Her father's secret occupation was a lifeline when Chinese were excluded from employment opportunities during apartheid. To Ho, fahfee exemplified the interdependency between Chinese and Black South Africans on the margins of formal economic life:

> Fahfee needed two groups on the edge of society, separate but bound together, to connect momentarily in the collusion of circumventing the ways of the economic mainstream. The end goal for both groups was to walk away with a few extra rand in their pockets even if it meant they were taking from each other. Theirs was a pact forged from their mutual conspiracy against the apartheid system. The machina [fahfee man] and the poor black man of the townships were pushed toward the periphery; neither was part of what whirled in the tight inner circle: white wealth. (2011, 133)

Returning to Mellie's account of the foreign exchange company, the dynamics of capitalism, race, and the law have changed since Ho's childhood. But perhaps the image of the Chinese outsider arriving in the township with cash lingers, a presence that connects older diasporic communities (such as Ho's father's) with new migrants from Guangdong who continue the game (such as my downstairs neighbor). In the case of migrant traders, Chinese capital, not part of the Beijing–Sandton channels, detours through the township, a place that financial institutions had long abandoned. The "free flow" of global capital south and east moves through formal and informal channels made by sedimentations of racial disenfranchisement and impoverishment. To invoke Jodi A. Byrd and colleagues, these are "imperial accumulations of racial capitalism," forms of "predatory accumulation through the deeper temporalizations of colonization, settlement, and racialization" (Byrd et al. 2018, 1).

Going Underground

On the ground level at China City, in the middle of a busy corridor, inconspicuously wedged between two shops, there was a shop fitted with bulletproof glass. With only a number imprinted on the glass, there was no

7.3   An underground bank. Photo by the author.

signage. Known through word of mouth, the shop was an open secret among
the Chinese traders who used its services before it closed. Unassuming, it
hardly invited a second look. Its facade was simple and functional: three
panels of glossy, semiopaque, tinted glass that spanned the entire width
of the shop exterior. Both a window and a mirror, it reflected the viewer's
image on the dark surface and deflected what lay behind. On the outside,
a set of surveillance cameras panned the vicinity from above. An intercom
dangled from the door. A face-level camera was mounted above it. Inside was
a door connected to a biometric fingerprint reader, its luminous green light
shining in the darkness. On the white walls hung three framed photographs
of the owner posing with African National Congress officials. Shrouded in
secrecy, the dark window was a looking glass cordoning off a parallel economic world, a literal and figurative interface between official and shadow
economies. In an accidental discovery, I learned by chance from a security
guard that this used to be the "cash room," or what traders called the underground bank (*dixia qianzhuang*).

   In the eighteenth century, "native banks" (*qianzhuang*) were the preferred
method among merchants to transfer money across regions. In the postreform era, small family-run underground banks are convenient providers

of remittance services (Zhao 2012). Underground banks were scattered throughout Cyrildene Chinatown and the China Malls under the camouflage of storefronts, restaurants, and travel agencies. At this cash room, the man in the photographs was the operator. The cash room was for Chinese only, but not even all Chinese knew about it. People would discreetly bring hundreds of thousands of cash to the spot and stand in front of the face-level camera, ring the intercom, and enter through the fingerprint reader–controlled doors. Within a few days, the equivalent amount, minus a fee, would be wired to a bank account in China. Every day, an armored car made a cash collection. The operation was preemptively shut down because the Reserve Bank was watching it. "Too much cash in and out," a Chinese manager told me.

The underground bank does not try to be wholly invisible; it hides in plain sight. As Achille Mbembe and Sarah Nuttall observe about Johannesburg's orders of visibility, "Beneath the visible landscape and the surface of the metropolis, its objects and social relations, are concealed or embedded other orders of visibility, other scripts that are not reducible to the built form, the house facade" (2008, 22). Surfaces are subject to different kinds of looking. To this point, Anne Anlin Cheng posits, "Sometimes it is not a question of what the visible hides but how it is that we have failed to see certain things on its surface" (2009, 101). Chinese migrants were accustomed to decoding the real and fake. The underground bank is an example of "hanging out a sheep's head to sell dog meat" (*gua yang tou, mai gou rou*), a proverb my interlocutors used to describe false appearances.

Among the many arrangements NCB struck with China City's management, NCB opened its own underground bank–style cash room. The entirety of its planning, construction, and obsolescence proceeded during my fieldwork. The NCB cash room was in a corner of a gated upper-level parking lot, an area Chinese called "the back," which was neither out of sight nor cordoned off. At the edge of the parking lot, the cash room was built with bricks matching the exterior of the mall and the wall, seamlessly blending in. Simulating its illegal counterpart, it had two sets of doors with the tinted bulletproof glass, surveillance cameras, and a keypad for access. Without any markings, it, too, was hidden in plain sight. During its brief existence, all tenants—this time not only Chinese but also Indian and Pakistani traders—could enter with a PIN to make cash deposits. Chinese traders feared being followed on the way to the more widely known cash room. Management added a steel gate and stationed an armed guard next to it, which only attracted more attention. Finally, the receptacle was moved inside the management office in the care of a Chinese manager whom traders trusted with seeing their cash.

The NCB cash room failed for several reasons. Recalling Tsing's "economy of appearances," the surface and architecture of the underground bank is vital to its very ability to operate (2000, 118). While the underground bank went unnoticed in a busy ground-level corridor, the secluded cash room announced itself. The NCB cash room failed the moment it became accessible to all traders—that is, it was no longer a secret among Chinese. Secrecy is a "boundary mechanism" that separates insiders from outsiders (Verdery 2014, 92). Matthias Borgers aptly notes that "underground bankers will have to look more like ordinary bankers and vice versa" (quoted in De Goede 2012, 107). In late capitalist hyperreality, the economy of appearances is one of surfaces without depth, signs without referents, copies without originals. The two cash rooms exemplify Jean Baudrillard's idea of operational negativity in which "everything is metamorphosed into its inverse in order to be perpetuated in its purged form." In a recursive fashion, "It is always a question of proving the real by the imaginary . . . proving the law by transgression . . . theatre by anti-theatre . . . art by anti-art . . . etc." (Baudrillard 1983, 37, 36)—or in this case, bank by antibank.

Globalization has spurred the twinning of financial institutions: the licit, official, and legitimate, and globalization's dark side, its "mirror image" that spans everything from informal and underground economies to illicit criminal economies. On the informal money transfer system of *hawala*, Robert Cox remarks, "the same characteristics that [*hawala*] is vilified for, such as speed, trust, paperlessness, global reach, and fluidity, are precisely those attributes that globalizing investment banking aspires to" (quoted in De Goede 2012, 102). At China City, these twin forms revealed the inseparability of formality from informality: the unofficial economy mimicked the workings of the official economy and produced a fringe market; the official economy mimicked the unofficial to capture its own previously excluded market. It is not only the underground economy that relies on secrecy; the official economy, despite its proclamations of transparency, traffics in similar secretive forms. The underground bank tells a story of the heterogeneity of "global capitalism" and Chinese capitalist projects in Africa. This tale of two cash rooms is not a celebration of the informal. The underground bank shows how capital makes an exit and leaps across borders. The illegal foreign exchange company and the underground bank illustrate that Chinese capital disjointedly moves across enclaves on the fringes of regulatory regimes, while its global mobility is contingent on localized racial inequality, laying bare the racial of global racial capitalism. In the case of the foreign exchange company, the legacy of financial disenfranchisement was crucial to remitting profits for prosperous futures in China. With the underground bank, as with the mall's flats, a logic of endogamy gatekept who was included or excluded. Chinese identity is the precondition for trust, the social glue that coheres underground economies for capital to "hop."

Flows and Leaks

Underground banks are in the business of flow. Underground bank operators perform an important conversion of currency and legality. They need solvency in China *and* South Africa to withstand fluctuations in solvency and monetary value on both ends and to be able to regulate the speed and direction of circulation. Mr. Lai, the mining belt mall developer, community leader, and real estate king from chapter 1, is one of many underground bankers. In Johannesburg, Mr. Lai funnels individual remittances through his registered businesses, which move millions through importing and rent collection. His registered companies provide the institutional vehicle and legal cover for traders small enough to fly under the radar. Regulating the speed, volume, and timing of cash flows and monitoring fluctuations in foreign exchange rates between the yuan, rand, and dollar is tricky business. Ultimately, he explained, "You want to make it work, but it's controlled by the market."

Mr. Lai asserted that, for petty traders, every cent counts. Working around taxes and sending money through the underground bank was the only viable way to do business: "The problem is tax evasion (*toushui, loushui*), or if you want to make it sound better, avoiding taxes (*bishui*)." In South Africa, he explained, taxes are very high and rules and regulations unclear, subsequently creating the conditions for widespread tax evasion. Invoking tropes of weak African states, he remarked, "Africa is very chaotic (*luan*) . . . the government has many loopholes (*loudong*)." This description of tax evasion evokes the watery language of flows. Taxes are diverted (*tou*) or leak (*lou*) through holes (*dong*). Mr. Lai's description of Africa is reminiscent of Peter Hudson's "rogue bankers," the private American bankers in the Caribbean and Central America of the early twentieth century who sought out lax regulatory environments and operated "in the seams between legal jurisdictions, in the regulatory black holes beyond the reach of sovereign nations" (2017, 12).[7] As Hudson's work illuminates, extralegal modalities have been indispensable to imperial accumulation and finance capitalism.

To be clear, Chinese traders are not exceptional as bad financial actors to be singled out; many migrant, diasporic, and expatriate communities in South Africa send unauthorized remittances. Multinational corporations are masterful loophole artists in their use of tax havens and offshore accounts. Chinese actors are not special in this regard. The South African state and international tax system is designed with secrecy and loopholes to enable illicit flows (Moore, Prichard, and Fjeldstad 2018).[8] But individual remittances, however small or ordinary an economic activity, add up to mirror an older colonial pattern. Remittances equal the expatriation of surplus that enriched Europe and underdeveloped Africa. Foreign exchange was a tool for accumulation. Commercial banks worked with metropolitan governments and currency boards to adjust the balance of money that stayed as local African currency against the money remitted to Britain, where it would be backed by sterling reserves and further accrue (Rodney [1972] 1981, 171). Martin Legassick and David Hemson pinpoint the role of American and British investment in South Africa's racial capitalist development: "Foreign capital resisted any but the minimum inroads into its profits by diversion of the surplus to the formation of local capital" (1976, 5). As Rodney has shown, European settlers in Africa remitted their profits to their mother countries for safe keeping. In aggregate, "That sum, like all other remittances by colonial banks, represented the exploitation of African land resources and labor" ([1972] 1981, 164). Chinese migrant entrepreneurs are not European settlers or colonial trading companies. Most are legally precarious in South Africa and on the social margins of postreform China. But the logic of entrepreneurial migration—of making money and getting money out, with minimal diversion of surplus for local capital—holds. The significance sticks, recalling Grant's criticism that his Chinese employers "just make money and that money is not used in this country, our country . . . they just take the money and go to their country."

The frictional movement of money across borders is key to understanding the politics of Chinese capitalist projects in Africa, which layer onto colonial racial capitalist histories of foreign investment and extraction. As Sharad Chari points out, "enclaved extractive capital remains at the heart of the perils and promises of China's and India's forays into varied African contexts" and "we do not yet have a vocabulary for Asian corporate-imperial power in Africa" (2015, 97). In her work on Chinese investment in Vietnam, Kimberly Kay Hoang shows how the protectionist postcolonial state attracts foreign investment for nationalized industries, but shuts down tax coercion, avoidance, and evasion to retain state control (2022, 152). In the age of China's engagements with the Global South, there is a fine line between the developmental benefits of Chinese investment, such as increasing the tax base, and extraction through private profiteering (Hearn 2016, 22). As the Tax Justice Network of Africa (n.d.) insists, "curbing leakages" and stopping illicit financial flows are key social and economic justice issues. To Mellie, cutting corners was "killing our country."

Sojourner Colonialism's Economies

For Chinese sojourners, entrepreneurial migration is foremost an accumulation strategy. South Africa is a detour on the way to realizing the deferred prosperity and promise of the Chinese Century. Chinese migrant traders aim to maximize profits in a hypercompetitive market environment and expatriate profits to China with the minimal drag of taxes and financial surveillance of states. They operate on the fringes of the formal economy, compounding forms of precarity and marginalization they face in the quest for profits. Chinese capitalist projects are heterogeneously constituted across geopolitical alignments and institutional arrangements. Separate from the Beijing–Sandton circuits of diplomacy and finance, Johannesburg's Cyrildene Chinatown is connected to Fujian and Guangdong through nonlinear itineraries. Ordinary migrants move straight, underground, and around regulatory regimes through channels, corridors, and loopholes. These webs of illegality are maintained by a shadow network of community leaders, businessmen, and state actors who link human and monetary mobilities. Even the distinctions *from above* and *from below* do not quite capture the dynamism of economic life.

Chinese sojourners squeeze profits from racialized surplus populations who provide labor *and* loopholes. Race determined who could participate in underground economies and how money moved across economic enclaves. These racial entanglements of Chinese capitalist projects disabuse dominant understandings of "Asian capitalism" as another form of nonracial global flows. Additionally, Chinese unlawfulness is in stark contrast to Black criminality. Recalling the vilification of Chinese traders in *Noseweek* (Welz and Schoonbee 2012), South Africans perceive Chinese unauthorized migration and tax evasion as the threat of "China." But among Chinese migrants, extralegal practices are not illegitimate; they are a means to an end to support their families in China, a country that is developing *too fast*. In contrast, African workers who steal to reclaim some of the profit they generate are stereotyped as criminal. Like Chinese traders, African workers bend the law to survive and better their economic prospects back home. But Chinese extralegality and Black criminality are categorically different within the moral economy of Chinese sojourner colonialism. Chinese rule breaking is the standard, not the exception, in the service of Chinese, not African, economic futures.

The politics of Chinese capitalist projects in South Africa need to be situated within global structures of capitalist imperialism and racial capitalism, which name complementary dynamics: capital accumulates across spatial asymmetries and makes uneven geographies; capitalism functions through racial difference and entrenches racial inequality. These structures overlap through the intimate connections between capitalism, white supremacy, and colonialism. In the spirit of Rodney's anticapitalist, anti-imperialist critique, we might understand Sino-African relations as part of a changing international division of labor—of Chinese capital and African labor, Chinese manufactured goods and African oil and minerals—and the dialectic of Chinese development and African underdevelopment as a capitalist imperialist relation. Chinese migrants are in South Africa because of long-accruing asymmetries of development across Africa, Asia, and Euro-America and the dialectics of development and underdevelopment within postreform China. Ultimately, the profiteering of Chinese sojourners, even if they are peripheral actors, calcifies uneven geographies of accumulation put in place by Euro-American colonial racial capitalism and retrenched by the "ungrounded empire" of flexible Chinese transnational capitalist practices (Ong and Nonini 1997). The extractive practices of Chinese migrants constitute sojourner colonialism and forecast twenty-first-century geographies of accumulation and a new racial grammar of development.

Epilogue

China has, for now, become a far more prominent actor than others in the future-making of Africa, to the point where Africa is now not only a planetary question, but also and more specifically a Chinese Question.

Achille Mbembe, *Out of the Dark Night*, 2021

Located outside the Johannesburg city limits, Modderfontein is an old dynamite town with a history of British and German industry. In the first few years of the twentieth century, twenty miles further east, Chinese laborers lived and worked at the New Modderfontein Gold Mine (Kynoch 2005). Until the 1990s Modderfontein's flagship factory—the African Explosives and Chemical Industries (AECI), part of the Anglo American and De Beers corporations—produced nitroglycerine for the diamond and gold mining industries (Innes

E.1   A rendering of Modderfontein New City. Source: https://www.theguardian
       .com/cities/2019/oct/24/failure-chinese-developer-manhattan-in-africa
       -johannesburg-modderfontein.

1984). As a historic buffer zone for blasts, the area was not developed for human
inhabitants. In 2012 Modderfontein Reserve opened, a pristine 265-hectare
private open space for wildlife conservation. The riverine and grassland
sequester Johannesburg's carbon and provide a lush escape for the city's
denizens (Modderfontein Reserve, n.d.). The following year, the Shanghai-
based developer Zendai Group revealed its ambitious ZAR84 billion (US$6
billion) megaproject, Modderfontein New City (*Nanfei mu de fang xincheng*). The
developer bought sixteen hundred hectares of land from AECI and sought to
transform the poisonous tabula rasa into "the Manhattan of Africa" (Reboredo
2021). At the launch, Zendai's chairperson remarked, "We did not realise that
there was such a vast tract of [undeveloped] land within Johannesburg. This land
has been asleep for over 100 years, but today it is awakened and will become a
future city" (quoted in Greve 2014). Mired in bureaucratic challenges, New City
never got off the ground. The land was sold to a South African developer and
turned into a gated community. Within a few years, New City was declared a
"quiet failure" (Brill and Reboredo 2019; Hogg 2019; Reboredo 2021; Van Mead
2019). It exists in the "would have been" future past.

But New City is not a failure. Its legacy is the spectacular vision of the
Sino-African futures it conjured, a dramatic remaking of the City of Gold
in the Chinese Century. Zendai, in collaboration with London-based

consultants, envisioned New City as a paradigmatic global city. Connected to Johannesburg and the airport by light rail, New City would contain an industrial zone, a finance and trade center, an education and training center, residences, shopping malls, hotels, sports arenas, and an "African cultural theme park." In the computer-generated rendering, New City is all simulation and surface: cerulean swimming pools, glass-encased buildings, and reflective rooftops. The dome-shaped buildings are reminiscent of the tailings that dot Johannesburg's landscape and pay tribute to the city's storied past. Johannesburg's iconic skyline is out of focus in the background of the hazy blue and violet sky. The city's modern skyscrapers pale in comparison to the geometrically striking edifices that conjure techno-Orientalist images of Asian futurity. The old mining city is merely a distant past of Chinese urban futures. New City makes a nod to environmental sustainability and its surroundings. On the ground level, palm-tree-lined pedestrian walkways connect vast green spaces. Huts with thatched roofs invoke a generic Africanness and enhance the naturalistic landscape design. Laboring and consuming bodies are rendered too small to decipher racial, gender, class, and national markers, but it is easy to guess who these low-wage workers would be. In Chinese and Southeast Asian cities, temporary migrant workers have built the spectacular skylines symbolizing Asian ascendance (Bahng 2018; C. Y. Zhang 2022). In the rendering, the only bodies in focus, oddly enough, are white. White faces are projected onto the rooftops, holographic projections coming from nowhere. Western whiteness is a sign of cosmopolitan cool, an aspirational ideal to surpass, and an outsize ghostly trace. The specter of whiteness conjures the white foreigner or "white ghost" (*baigui*) of China's past, a distant relative of the "black devil" (*heigui*). Even in this idealized rendition of Sino-African futures, there is no real time "after whiteness."

Within city limits, another story about the city's mining past and Chinese future splashed headlines. In 2019, a few miles south of the China City mall, Beautiful City, a Chinese-owned blanket factory in Village Deep, was jointly raided by the Department of Home Affairs, the Department of Labour, and the Hawks, a special South African police division for economic and organized crime. At the scene seven Chinese nationals, allegedly with falsified IDs, were arrested for trafficking "illegal immigrants" and employing child labor. Only one of the 150 African employees was South African; the rest were foreign nationals, primarily Malawians, including over thirty children. The trial, which has been prolonged by the COVID-19 pandemic, has become one of the highest-profile stories about Chinese entrepreneurs in South Africa (Maeko 2019). Although Malawian workers are often depicted as taking jobs from Black South Africans, the moral outrage against Chinese nationals trafficking children won out over xenophobia.

Village Deep is named after the Village Deep Gold Mine, where Chinese laborers also toiled underground, lived in segregated compounds, and protested their working conditions. Forced to work through the Chinese New Year, Chinese laborers smashed windows and hurled debris at police (Kynoch 2003, 327). From the British Imperial Century to the American and Chinese Centuries, a dramatic reversal is happening. Instead of journeying to work in mines, factories, and white homes, Malawian and Zimbabwean men and women seek to improve their livelihoods at the China Malls. This generation of migrant workers labors for Chinese traders instead of the white boss. In the 1970s, South African scholars and antiapartheid activists devised the term *racial capitalism* for this interlocking system of migrancy and capitalist exploitation. Racial capitalism keeps churning by incorporating new places and actors, a recursive dynamic that reconstitutes older patterns of exploitation and reenergizes radical traditions in equal measure.

Told from the City of Gold, Sino-African presents and futures are threaded with multiple geological and social pasts. In addition to the legacies of mine migrancy, Chinese capital germinates in the toxic wasteland of the mineral revolution. Chinese investors have bought up derelict shopping malls, burned-down wholesale centers, and tracts of mining-impacted land. In the detritus, they have built water parks, warehouses, factories, and wholesale malls. While many have rote self-Orientalizing names like China City, Dragon City, and Oriental City, others—Beautiful City, New City, New Feeling, and Galaxy Mall—allude to the humanist and planetary aspirations of the Chinese Century. But Chinese entrepreneurs cannot transcend the trace of the "Asiatic." Chinese commodities are still derided as "Fong Kong." Traders are viewed as perpetually foreign, "the Chinese." The factory scandal of Beautiful City is the other side of New City. These projects represent two different visions of the Chinese Century: the promise of a Chinese-led capitalist future and the uncertainty the Asian superpower presents to the region's most precarious. China City is a harbinger of reconfigurations of colonial racial capitalism and imperialism yet to come.

Chinese transformations of the City of Gold are multiple and patchy, disjointedly radiating outward from First Chinatown in the city center to the malls along the central mining belt, Cyrildene Chinatown in the east, Chinese banks in the northern suburbs, and the failed New City project outside the city. Sino-African worlds are not monolithic; they are variously composed of Chinese state capital, large-scale investment, state officials, and business travelers, as well as an underground economy of migrant entrepreneurs on the peripheries of legality. Ethnography allows for a depiction of these kaleidoscopic worlds, social relations, historical traces, and lateral modes of power. Ethnography brings into view the everyday workings of capitalism and race and the tense and tender ties of Sino-African encounters: racial distrust, ambivalent attachments, paternalistic care, and anxieties about racial mixing, betrayal, and revenge. I have resisted telling tidy stories about my interlocutors, some of whom may elicit conflicting emotional responses across chapters. Readers may sympathize with the gendered vulnerabilities Jenny faced but later bristle at her treatment of Alice and Julius. Marcus and Roger are organic intellectuals whose critical analysis of their situations as racial capitalism informed my critique. But their tacit condoning of retribution is discomfiting. In fieldwork and writing, I struggled to square the worldviews and experiences of my African and Chinese interlocutors. These emotionally charged, politically complicated relations are too multivalent to be reduced to oppressors/oppressed, capital/labor, racializing/racialized, and Chinese/Black. I deliberately maintained tensions across chapters to convey the indeterminacies and ambivalences of Sino-African relations, which is why these lateral modes of power are so difficult to pinpoint.

Contemplating racial capitalism, colonialism, and anti-Black racism in a Sino-African context is challenging because of the dramatic role reversals in a relatively compressed period and multiple directionalities of racialization and racism. In South Africa, Chinese migrants represent the global stature of the People's Republic of China (PRC) but are socioeconomically marginal in China. They are legally precarious in South Africa and yet engage in extralegal practices for profit. Traders are forced to cut corners in a race to the bottom and make their transnational endeavors worthwhile. In a loop, Chinese sojourners become the unlawful Chinese of the past and end up reinforcing stereotypes of Asian traders. I needed a way to name the complex social location of Chinese migrants while not losing sight of China's subjugation to Western racism and imperialism. Triangulation, the palimpsest, and adjacency have offered analytical strategies forward. Triangulation problematizes the binaries of West/rest and oppressor/oppressed. Chinese anti-Black racism is intertwined with global structures of white supremacy and signals a regime of racial power that the terms of whiteness and white supremacy may no longer be adequate to encapsulate. Adjacency names the incommensurable gap of analyzing multiple histories, genealogies, and concepts. It underscores the tension of difference in sameness in the sense that Chinese sojourners are not the Chinese state or mining houses, and Chinese imperial forms are not the same as British imperialism.

This book seeks to understand what is new or not new about the Chinese Century as capitalism shifts east and south and the geopolitical alliances, racial projects, political imaginaries, and global futures it engenders. It does so from South Africa, which is not only a significant world-historical place where the Chinese Century unfolds, but a site of rich intellectual and liberatory traditions and generative analytics for theory-making. Inspired by the gold reef beneath the mall, the palimpsest is the central metaphor and analytic for thinking interimperially about the PRC. Instead of debating whether the new Chinese presence is a neocolonial one, the palimpsest situates the globally expansive imperial vision of the Chinese Century and the extractive and exploitative practices of Chinese sojourners within a settler society with active colonial legacies while questioning categorical distinctions between old and new. The Chinese Century is not a new epoch of hegemony, hence signaling rupture, but recursively builds on its Euro-American predecessors to expand and fortify it. The palimpsest offers a way to read the historical present, or what Lynn M. Thomas calls "layered history, one stacked with sedimented meanings and compounded politics" in which "older meanings and politics [remain] through newer layers" (2020, 235). At times the connection I draw is causal. The legacies of gold materially manifest in the generations of migrant workers at China City or the redevelopment of the old mining belt. Other times I overlay one historical moment onto another as an interpretive method for what the present might mean, as I do with the Black/white dynamics of racial paternalism that color Sino-African labor relations or resonances around race, gender, and sexuality between British and Chinese imperial cultures. Within the palimpsest, there is no omniscient vantage point, only partial interpretations situated within vertical and horizontal coordinates, including my own.

Chinese migrant entrepreneurs, though unaware of what precedes them, are interpellated into enduring racial relations and categories while refashioning older racial discourses with contemporary articulations of Chineseness and Blackness (*hei*). The same is not true for African migrant workers whose migrations and political consciousness are informed by generations of labor and struggle. Finally, the palimpsest offers a reframing of African and Chinese agency within broader structures. Against reductive assumptions of one-way domination, Chinese migrants and capital are not the only agential parts of this world-making equation. Chinese newcomers reap the benefits of consumer markets, circular migrations, and racialized surplus populations created by settler colonialism, imperialism, and apartheid. They perpetuate inequality but did not create their structural conditions. In this way, colonial legacies from one long century become the inheritances of the next. From the perspective of southern Africans, Chinese occupy a similar position of power of the white boss and patriarch. African migrants read Chinese newcomers through the recent past while trying to make something for themselves in a changing world.

As the twenty-first century proceeds, colonial racial capitalism re-makes itself in an emerging Sinocentric order, but not in readily recognizable ways. The Chinese Century requires different methodological tools, epistemological reorientations, and critical engagements across fields and disciplines. In transnational and translingual contexts, "race" is not the same thing across Chinese and Western epistemologies. Chinese racial meanings have been formed through "internal" ideas of color, civilization, and class and global encounters with Euro-American modernity, resulting in a Sino-centric global racial hierarchy of Chinese/China, white/West, and Black/Africa. China's place in the world has radically changed, and with it, meanings of Chineseness, whiteness, and Blackness. There is no direct translation of race, but nonequivalence does not preclude analysis of racialization and racial subordination. An ethnographic approach to racial formation tracks how racial lexicons transnationally circulate, pick up new meanings, and become mobilized in distinct ways in the service of capital accumulation. As these processes play out in South Africa, Chineseness is cohered through a logic of possession against a devalued and criminalized Blackness, as well as the invisible referent of aspirational whiteness. Informed by heteropatriarchal nationalism, the Chinese Century is a geopolitical and biopolitical racial world-making project. Chinese capitalist projects in Africa entail a distinct politics of gender, race, sexuality, and class. Hierarchies of desire and racial boundaries play out in the Chinese couple, family, and child and the dyad of the African man and Chinese woman. Operating through multiple histories and scales, racial formations and racism cannot be understood without their nationalist and colonial imbrications, nor quotidian, psychic, and erotic dimensions.

I have focused on Chinese anti-Black racism, even though it is only one part of racialization in Sino-African contexts. Chinese anti-Black racism is an emerging phenomenon we do not know enough about, and it is too often downplayed or taken as self-evident in the study of Africa and China. Anti-Blackness is a core feature and condition of Chinese capitalist projects in Africa, from Chinese imaginaries of Africa as out of time, the devaluation of Black labor, the criminalization of Blackness, and the racial dimension of remittance economies. Contending with Chinese racial ideologies and epistemologies is vital to understanding the persistence and specificity of global anti-Blackness and racial formations in postcolonial Africa today (Pierre 2013). The anti-Black sentiments in this book were difficult for me to witness, document, and write, and were likely difficult for you, the reader, to digest. I run the risk of committing an order of epistemic violence in reproducing racist remarks and derogatory terms, which did not happen in the distant past but in real time. I did not find them in an archive at safe remove but was embedded in the stories, exchanges, and moments. There is no getting past complicity, but I offer this account of Chinese anti-Black racism so we can understand and dismantle it.

To close on global histories and futures, China City is the antithesis of Walter Benjamin's arcades, the epitome of nineteenth-century modernity. The mining belt mall, like the megaproject New City, symbolizes a twenty-first-century modernity not centered in New York City or Paris, but Johannesburg and the Global South. The mall's subaltern geographies suggest that the Chinese Century need not be a totalizing project of global hegemony. It is an unfinished, open-ended vision with room for egalitarian relationships, minor cosmopolitanisms, and residual solidarities. Perhaps another Chinese Century—one that does not fortify colonial legacies but belongs to the global majority—is possible. Like New City, megavisions are not too big to fail. In their detritus, emancipatory possibilities can bloom.

Introduction

1 In 2020, Chinese exports to South Africa totaled US$15,243 million; Chinese imports from South Africa totaled US$9,794 million. For comparison, US exports to South Africa totaled US$4,455 million; US imports from South Africa totaled US$11,440 million (China Africa Research Initiative, n.d.).

2 Many thanks to Siân Butcher for the sharp phrase "mining belt mall."

3 While scholars agree that race, capitalism, and colonialism are inextricably related, there is dissensus about their causal relationship. For Cedric Robinson ([1983] 2000), racialism, a form of racialization, already existed within European feudal society to differentiate ethnicized laboring peoples. In Gerald Horne's (2020) account of the long sixteenth century, religious difference in late feudal Europe mutated into racial difference to fuel New World enslavement, white supremacy, and settler colonialism. In these historical accounts, something like race existed in Europe *before* the transition to capitalism and was refined through colonial encounters with new racial others. Hosea Jaffe argues that race emerged *after* capitalism, which successively gave rise to Europe, European civilization, European man, and race: "Before the slave-trade in Africa there was neither a Europe nor a European. . . . Colonialism, especially in Africa, created the concept and ideology of race. Before capitalist-colonialism there were no races" (2017, 46).

4   The Chinese Century is about the PRC and the United States: China's "soft" economic influence is compared with American "hard" military power, the Beijing Consensus with the Washington Consensus, and Chinese authoritarianism with American democracy. In one of the first usages of the term, Ted Fishman (2004) begins his *New York Times* article "The Chinese Century" with "China used to be far away, the country at the bottom of the world," and notes that the PRC and the United States have traded places: "So perhaps we will be as Europe is to us today, and China will be our America."

5   In 2011, then secretary of state Hillary Clinton sought to "pivot" from the imperial theater in the Middle East to the Asia-Pacific region, calling for "America's Pacific Century." The "Asia-Pacific represents such a real 21st-century opportunity for us," Clinton wrote. Meanwhile, "Africa holds enormous untapped potential for economic and political development in the years ahead" (Clinton 2011).

6   In a key essay on Sino-African racialization, Barry Sautman and Yan Hairong (2016) argue that Chinese migrants do not have the structural power to enact racism, even if their actions may seem racist, and call for a retooling of understandings of race in a south–south context.

7   There is much scholarship that debunks myths about debt diplomacy, labor regimes, and government corruption related to Chinese aid and investment in Africa. The PRC is one of many countries with political and economic dealings in Africa, but the only one singled out as neocolonial. As Ching Kwan Lee (2017) points out, there is no Chinese military presence, trading company monopolies, or foreign direct rule—the hallmarks of European colonialism—and thus neocolonialism is more rhetorically inciting than empirically accurate. Daniel Vukovich (2019) similarly argues that the historical conditions for the old modern empires—specifically, slavery and colonialism from the eighteenth to twentieth centuries—are not available for a burgeoning Chinese empire in a postcolonial world. For Vukovich, exploitation in China-Africa contexts is capitalism, not colonialism.

8   *Chinese capitalism* is a term associated with the advent of capitalism in postsocialist China and the successes of overseas Chinese entrepreneurs in East Asia, Southeast Asia, and beyond. *Chinese characteristics* refers to Confucian values, family structures, education, and social (*guanxi*) networks. This paradigm problematically produces a singular transnational ethnic Chinese identity aligned with global capitalism and erases differences of class, gender, and nation. As Arif Dirlik points out, the essentialist discourse of Chinese capitalism "is quite reminiscent of earlier Orientalist conceptualizations of China and Asia that denied history to the peoples of Asia, substituting for historical temporalities and spatiali-

ties dehistoricized and desocialized cultural characteristics" (1997, 322). Ching Kwan Lee (2017) asserts the need to analyze specific varieties of capital, not varieties of capitalism. Capitalism is too transnational and heterogeneous to be defined by a single logic and methodological nationalism. It is more productive to examine varieties of capital that enter national economies (such as state capital or global private capital), each with its own logic of accumulation, regime of labor, and management ethos. While Lee's formulation is helpful, in the present book *Chinese capital* is shorthand for the small-scale private capital of Chinese migrant entrepreneurs, which is distinct from Chinese state capital.

9   China City is a multilingual space in which Afrikaans, English, Gujarati, Mandarin, Ndebele, Urdu, and Zulu are spoken, as well as regional dialects from Fuzhou, Jiangmen, Nanjing, and beyond. In South Africa, a country with eleven official languages, language marks African foreign nationals as targets for xenophobia. Conversing in English is the common denominator, but doing so is not neutral. Although I did my fieldwork and interviews in English without a translator, when it came time to transcribe, I enlisted my retired mother to double-check my translation. It is always awkward to hear one's own voice on tape, but even more so in one's second tongue. I made a self-deprecating comment about how distorted my voice and pronunciation must sound in the recording, and my mother reassured me, "Don't worry, it's our [my parents'] fault." Asian American ethnographers working on Asia and Asian diasporas do not fit the role of "native anthropologist," but this inside/outside positionality can be beneficial.

Chapter 1. Palimpsest City

1   Race and consumption have been inextricably linked in South Africa. As Deborah Posel writes, "The making of the racial order was, in part, a way of regulating people's aspirations, interests and powers as consumers. The desire and power to consume was racialized, at the same time as it was fundamental in the very making of race" (2010, 160).

2   While the term "Coloured" was introduced by apartheid's racial terminology, it has persisted as an identity category capturing mixed-race subjectivity, especially in the Cape. Like any racial identity, the term is not without complexity and contest.

3   I thank Christopher J. Lee for this observation.

4   In the 1960s and 1970s, the PRC formed relationships with decolonizing and newly independent African countries during the Cold War and focused on developmental projects. Apartheid South Africa, which allied with Taiwan, was excluded from this project. Under the One China policy, the ROC had relationships but the PRC did not (Hart 2002). This

changed when South Africa changed its recognition from the ROC to the PRC in 1998.

Chapter 2. Sojourner Colonialism

Parts of this chapter were previously published as Mingwei Huang (2022b), "Global South Frontiers: Chinese Worldmaking and Racial Imaginaries of Johannesburg," in *New World Orderings: China and the Global South*, ed. Lisa Rofel and Carlos Rojas (Durham, NC: Duke University Press), 169–86.

1   Sana Aiyar offers a useful case study of Asian settler difference in colonial East Africa. Kenya was initially to become the "America of the Hindu" for Indian emigrants. But as Europeans arrived in larger numbers, Kenya became a "white man's country." Aiyar frames Indian settlers as entrepreneurs invested in the colonial project and "intermediary capitalists" in the hierarchy of European, Indian, and Native (2015, 24). In postcolonial East Africa, Arab and Asian settlers are "nonindigenous immigrants." Mahmood Mamdani writes, "You didn't have to be white to be a settler" (2001, 657).

2   My thanks to Iyko Day for this framing of an unsettler sojourner colonialism.

3   Biao Xiang points out a "last bus" mentality: "It was feared that if one missed the bus now, one would miss out on everything. . . . [I]f one does not grab the 'first barrel of gold' at this critical moment, there would be no chance to catch up later. The gate to wealth accumulation and economic security was getting narrower day by day" (2014, 191).

4   During the 1990s, mass layoffs of state workers from state-owned enterprises and work units created multiple forms of unemployment, including *tingxin liuzhi*. Working overseas was seen as an alternative opportunity for laid-off workers and the state (Hurst and O'Brien 2002; C. K. Lee 2007; Solinger 2002).

5   The Chinese community, including Chinese South Africans, is estimated at three hundred thousand, but this figure has a margin of error of one hundred thousand. Official migration figures are difficult to measure with certainty because of undocumented migrants. During the late 1990s and early 2000s, an estimated thirty to fifty Chinese nationals arrived daily in South Africa through the land borders of Lesotho and Mozambique (Park 2009, 160; Yap and Man 1996, 180).

6   As the DHA saw it, "Loopholes in legislation were making it possible for some to undermine immigration laws, thus preventing orderly migration, with a potential to fuel extortion, abuse and exploitation of

migrants, especially of those with fraudulent or no documents at all"
(Apleni 2015).

Chapter 3. Afro-Asian Adjacencies

A different version of this chapter appeared as Mingwei Huang (2022a),
"Afro-Asian Adjacencies in South Africa's Long Twentieth Century,"
Verge: Studies in Global Asias 8 (1): 167–94.

1   The imperatives and organization of the colonial archive was classifica-
    tion and collection, not connection or convergence. As Lisa Lowe writes,
    "Reading the archive, one notes explicit descriptions and enumerations,
    as well as the rhetorical peculiarities of the documents, the places where
    particular figures, tropes, or circumlocutions are repeated to cover gaps
    or tensions; these rhetorical ellipses point to illogic in the archive, as
    well" (2015, 35).

2   Chinese and Indian migration, diaspora, and racialization have been
    siloed within the geographic and historiographical boundaries of Afro-
    Asian, China-Africa, and Indian Ocean studies. In South Africa and
    beyond, Chinese and Indian indenture has been rarely examined com-
    paratively (Lai 2004; Harris 2010), and their racialization even less. On
    this sparse topic, Lisa Yun observes for Cuba that "the contrasts between
    the Chinese and Indian coolie trades arise partly due to the demarcations
    of empire, labor economy, and local developments in emigration. While
    the British dominated the Indian coolie trade, the British, Americans,
    French, Spanish, Portuguese, and Dutch led in the Chinese coolie trade.
    Different imperial agendas, systems of migration, and of course, cultural
    and local politics, created distinct coolie systems" (2007, 8).

3   By the 1890s in Natal, there were 142,000 Indians to 137,000 Europeans
    and 540,000 Indigenous Africans (Zulus); see Hart and Padayachee 2013,
    708n12.

4   Mohandas Gandhi protested the extension of the status of coolie from
    laborers to all Indians: "I was hence known as a 'coolie barrister.' The
    merchants were known as 'coolie merchants.' The original meaning of the
    word 'coolie' was thus forgotten, and it became a common appellation
    for all Indians" (quoted in Boer 2016, 31). Lord Harris, British adminis-
    trator of Bombay, also saw such a distinction: "the Indian trader—who
    is of an entirely different caste from the coolie" (quoted in *Rand Daily
    Mail* 1904e). On the stakes of terminology, Pradip Datta asserts, the use
    of coolies "normalised the possibility of legislative reclassification of
    non-indentured Indians by which their 'imperial subject' status would
    be taken away. . . . 'Coolie' removed the possibility that Indians might
    attain 'freedom'" (2011, 67).

5   By the end of the nineteenth century, Indians outnumbered Chinese by ten to one in South Africa's early colonies. In the Boer South African Republic (later the Transvaal), there were ten thousand Indians to every thousand Chinese. In the Cape Colony in 1904, there were eighty-five hundred Indians to every thirteen hundred Chinese (Harris 2010, 151).

6   In 2005, at the twentieth anniversary of the founding of COSATU at the ABSA Stadium in Durban, COSATU came under fire when the T-shirts for the event bore Made in China labels, in spite of the organization's vocal support for the Proudly South African Campaign and the South African Clothing and Textile Workers Union (SACTWU). The crowd began throwing the shirts onto the field, which security guards collected and handed back to the leadership. In response, COSATU's general secretary, Zwelinzima Vavi, formally apologized: "The SACTWU . . . are the ones who are directly affected by the dumping of cheap products in our country and we apologise to them and our comrades elsewhere in the country" (quoted in Majova 2005).

7   In East Africa, the stereotype of the Asian trader as a cheater comes from how Asian middlemen were positioned in the colonial economy. At the *dukka*, Africans exchanged their agricultural products for currency to pay to the colonial state. Indian traders benefited from colonial taxation and land policies; they cheated their African customers by cutting corners (Aiyar 2015, 10). The trope of the cheating *dukkawallah* has fueled African populism "as Indians were the most visible and immediate obstacle to [African] economic aspirations" (Aiyar 2015, 18).

Chapter 4. Afterlives of Gold

An earlier version of this chapter appeared as Mingwei Huang (2021), "The Chinese Century and the City of Gold: Refashioning Race and Capitalism," *Public Culture* 33 (2): 193–217. Portions are also expanded in Mingwei Huang (2024), "The Globality of Antiblackness," *Made in China Journal*, January 10, 2024, https://madeinchinajournal.com/2024/01/10/the-globality-of-antiblackness/.

1   I am inspired by Black feminist theorizations of the afterlife of slavery to name the ongoing unfolding of slavery (Hartman 2008a, b; Sharpe 2016). Saidiya Hartman notes that "black lives are still imperiled and devalued by a racial calculus and a political arithmetic that were entrenched centuries ago" (2008a, 6).

2   After 1994, under the Basic Conditions of Employment Act, the new Constitution of the Republic of South Africa, the Employment Equity

Act, and the Labor Relations Act, South Africans are entitled to basic rights such as minimum wage, rest days, overtime pay, leave for illness and family responsibilities, the right to collectively organize, and safe working conditions. South Africans can make claims to the Commission for Conciliation, Mediation and Arbitration, a tribunal for redressing unfair dismissal and discrimination. The conditions African migrants experience are not exclusive to the China Malls, and poor Black South Africans often work without these protections.

3   Many thanks to Miya Qiong Xie for this point.

4   The color bar began with the Mines and Works Act of 1911 and was only abolished in 1987 in response to labor militancy and the need to fill skilled positions with Black labor. Throughout the twentieth century, the legal apparatus of the color bar worked in tandem with the migrant labor system and pass laws to regulate extraction from and the mobilities of Black laboring bodies (Crush, Jeeves, and Yudelman 1991, 7–9).

5   In premodern times, *kunlun*, named after the Kunlun Mountains on the western edge of China, referred to dark complexioned Chinese, Khmers, and Malays. The term designated the geographic otherness of frontier peoples and signified dark-skinned individuals within and beyond China's borders. By the time Chinese encountered African peoples in the tenth century, the term for *kunlun* and the "*kunlun* slave" were widely in use. African peoples were incorporated into this term and its associations of magic, bestiality, and slavery. Premodern and early modern Sino-African encounters occurred through the Chinese institution of slavery in Canton (Guangzhou); maritime encounters between Chinese crews, servants, and concubines and enslaved Africans aboard European ships; and Ming admiral Zheng He's voyages to East Africa. These early encounters were sporadic, but literary depictions of "foreign slaves," "devil slaves," and "*kunlun* slaves" from Africa were lasting (Dikötter [1992] 2015; Karl 2002; Shih 2013; Snow 1988; Wyatt 2010).

6   Through this tactic of controlled recruitment, the real value of wages stayed the same from 1897 to 1970 (Crush, Jeeves, and Yudelman 1991, 3).

7   When my interlocutors invoked slavery, they might have been referencing multiple histories of slavery in Africa, including in the Cape Colony, the Lake Malawi Corridor, Nigeria, and Mozambique, or in the United States. Moreover, the imagery of slavery in North America was crucial to African images of Blackness and the cross-national imagining of an essential Black subject in colonial South Africa (Z. Magubane 2004, 191). While the referent is not specific, slavery is capaciously employed to denote a variety of exploitative relations.

Chapter 5. Criminal Obsessions and Racial Fictions

1   Writing about contemporary Han racism, Kuan-Hsing Chen points out three key logics in the Han imaginary from Qing dynasty literature: "to demonize the Other . . . in which the self is human while the Other is not," "to animalize the Other," and "to differentiate outsiders through even finer distinctions, thereby producing additional sets of hierarchies." As such, "there are beings who can physically pass as human but who cannot be qualified as having fully achieved humanity" (2010, 260–61).

2   I am more interested in perceptions and narratives of crime than actual crime rates. According to the City of Johannesburg (2019), between 2005 and 2015, murder, assault, and aggravated assault rates went down, except in the case of robbery, which is driven by income inequality, unemployment, and rapid urbanization. Despite lower crime rates, perceptions of crime have worsened among residents. Crime statistics are famously unreliable. As Martin Murray points out, residents often fail to report crime to police because of lack of faith in resolution; there are also many fraudulent reports of stolen goods to cash in on insurance benefits. Finally, police precincts and private security companies often manipulate reports and data to take credit for reducing crime (2020, 5).

Chapter 6. The Erotic Life of Chinese Racism

1   As Nina Sylvanus observes, "Macrolevel analysis . . . tends to overlook the more intimate encounters—real or imagined—between 'China' and 'Africa.' Numerous edited volumes and monographs tend to represent this trade as an invasion of a foreign economic structure into the passive body of Africa" (2013, 67).

2   Scholarship on Africa and China through the lens of gender and sexuality is sparse, primarily locating gender in the experiences of African and Chinese women (traders, migrants, and workers). A few studies have examined the intersections of race, gender, sexuality, and nationality through Chinese-African relationships (Frazier and Zhang 2014; K. Huang 2020; S. Lan 2017; Marsh 2014). At other times scholars engage with gender through the gendered experiences of women and the gendered positionality of researchers. A result of the masculinist disciplinary approaches to the study of globalization and economy, China-Africa scholarship is prone to replicating scripts of global forces and local victims, hard and soft power, masculine sovereignty and feminine integrity.

3   Sylvia Yanagisako defines kinship enterprises as "a project whose goals and strategies are constantly being reassessed and reformulated by people who construe themselves to be connected by enduring bonds of relatedness and whose relations are shaped by a dense assemblage of beliefs,

sentiments, and commitments attached to these bonds" (Yanagisako 2019, 231).

4   Public health discourses depicted HIV/AIDS as a "foreign disease" related to Open Up and Reform and the popularization of homosexuality. The common usage of the term *yuanshi*—a word that means "origin," "ancient," and "primitive"—to describe HIV/AIDS associates the virus with Africa, a place that is commonly understood as primitive and one and the same with Blackness. Johanna Hood notes that this usage suggests HIV transmissions happen through the kinds of relationships Africans are stereotyped to have (2013, 292–95).

5   In colonial southern Africa, soap, deodorant, skin lighteners, toothpaste, perfumes, and cosmetics were integral to producing "modern" African bodies. Postcolonial notions of hygiene still traffic in colonial tropes of whiteness, light skin, and cleanliness (Burke 1996). The Qiaobi laundry detergent ad is not an aberration. The most popular Chinese toothpaste brand continues to feature a racist minstrelsy image from the Jim Crow South on the tube and uses "Black people" (*heiren*) in the Chinese brand name, even as its parent company Colgate has changed its English name from Darkie to Darlie (Y. Cheng 2011, 575).

Chapter 7. Follow the Surplus

1   Anthropologists have broken down categories of legality and formality. Janet Roitman highlights how, in Cameroon and Chad, people distinguished between the illegal and illicit, categories formed within self-understanding of ethical practice and orientations toward the state. Illegal activities can be licit, "being on the margins, but in the norm." Legal and licit "are expressions of truth about state power, or the relationships through which one governs both populations and the economy" (2005, 21). Daniel Goldstein observes that in Bolivian street economies, "something can be seen as licit or 'legitimate' even though it might technically be illegal, while other things—taxes, for example—can seem illegitimate to local people even if they are formally licit" (2016, 23). On the other hand, as Hannah Appel elucidates, morally questionable legal practices such as corporate tax havens and labor subcontracting must be made licit through liberal instruments and social difference: "Contracts and corporate enclaves, offshore rigs and economic theory are the assemblages of liberalism and racialized labor, expertise and technology, gender and spatialized domesticity, which seem to make an industry operating on the edge of legitimacy and legality formally legitimate, legal, and productive of extraordinary profit" (2019, 21).

2   This characterization of hoarding as "Asiatic" appeared in Karl Marx's writings during the Opium Wars. In an essay from 1853, Marx asserts

that hoarding was proof that the "Celestial Empire" was "the very opposite of Europe" (Avineri 1968, 62; Lye 2005).

3   Following the 9/11 attacks, the media falsely reported that the hijackers
moved US dollars through *hawala*, an informal money transfer system
popular among Muslim migrants. Informal remittances have been the tar-
get of what Marieke De Goede (2012) names the "post-9/11 finance-security
assemblage." Transparency and traceability have become the modus ope-
randi of liberal democracies, and opacity has become a sign of criminality. In South Africa, Know-Your-Customer regulations, part of the global
financial surveillance regime, have made it difficult to open nonresident
bank accounts and have expanded the monitoring of tax payments.

4   In Johannesburg, the association (*hui*) is a popular way to extend credit.
In its most rudimentary form, members contribute to and take turns
taking from a collective pot. As it is often practiced in Fujian and Johannesburg, members can also bid by interest rate (*biaohui*); the highest
bidder takes the pot (Tsai 2000, 2002).

5   Informal finance accounted for a quarter of financial transactions in the
private sector, and in aggregate, has been a major part of China's "economic miracle." Informal finance "is like the unattractive grease in the
wheels of the transitional economy—necessary for movement, but no
one really wants to call attention to it" (Tsai 2002, 3).

6   Since hearing this story, I have looked through South African government and state archives and called financial journalists, but I never found
anything to corroborate Mellie's account. I made it a point to never speak
with Chinese or South African state officials, which could expose my
interlocutors to state scrutiny. I only have Mellie's word and the general
plausibility of this event.

7   Part of my motivation to detail tax evasion is to correct representations
of African states. As Jemima Pierre points out, too often racialized tropes
about corrupt, failed, or weak African states are repeated as fact, while
documented illicit practices of capital flight by global northern corporations are glossed (2020, 92). While there is widespread corruption in
South Africa, there are multiple state and nonstate actors of many racial
and class backgrounds who enable corruption.

8   Tax losses and "revenue leakages" have benefited multinational corporations and wealthy individuals while deepening existing inequality
(Moore, Prichard, and Fjeldstad 2018, 39). Although they are difficult to
quantify, capital flight and offshoring, labeled "base erosion and profit
shifting," amount to 1 percent of global gross domestic product and are
estimated as higher in poorer countries. Tax losses in sub-Saharan Africa are estimated as equivalent to 50 percent of national health budgets
(Moore, Prichard, and Fjeldstad 2018, 64–65).

REFERENCES

Abbas, Ackbar. 2008. "Faking Globalization." In *Other Cities, Other Worlds: Urban Imaginaries in a Globalizing Age*, edited by Andreas Huyssen, 243–64. Durham, NC: Duke University Press.

Accone, Darryl. 2006. "'Ghost People': Localising the Chinese Self in an African Context." *Asian Studies Review* 30 (3): 257–72.

Adebayo, Kudus Oluwatoyin, and Femi O. Omololu. 2020. "'Everywhere Is Home': The Paradox of 'Homing' and Child Upbringing among Nigerian-Chinese Families in Guangzhou City." *International Sociology* 35 (3): 241–59.

Ahmed, Sara. 2004. "Affective Economies." *Social Text* 22 (2): 117–39.

Ahmed, Sara. 2015. *The Cultural Politics of Emotion*. 2nd ed. New York: Routledge.

Aiyar, Sana. 2015. *Kenyans in India: The Politics of Diaspora*. Cambridge, MA: Harvard University Press.

Alexander, Neville. (1983) 1985. "Nation and Ethnicity in South Africa." In *Sow the Wind: Contemporary Speeches*. Johannesburg: Skotaville Publishers. Manuscript.

Amar, Paul. 2021. "Insurgent African Intimacies in Pandemic Times: Deimperial Queer Logics of China's New Global Family in *Wolf Warrior 2*." *Feminist Studies* 47 (2): 419–48.

Anagnost, Ann. 2004. "The Corporeal Politics of Quality (*Suzhi*)." *Public Culture* 16 (2): 189–208.

Anderson, Mark David. 2009. *Black and Indigenous: Garifuna Activism and Consumer Culture in Honduras*. Minneapolis: University of Minnesota Press.

Apleni, Mkuseli. 2015. "Overview of the New Immigration Laws and Regulations and Their Implications, by Home Affairs Director-General Mkuseli Apleni." Republic of South Africa, Department of Home Affairs, April 24, 2015. http://www.dha.gov.za/index.php/statements-speeches/600-overview-of-the-new-immigration-laws-andregulations-and-their-implications-by-home-affairs-director-general-mkuseli-apleni.

Appadurai, Arjun. 2000. "Spectral Housing and Urban Cleansing: Notes on Millennial Mumbai." *Public Culture* 12 (3): 627–51.

Appel, Hannah. 2019. *The Licit Life of Capitalism: US Oil in Equatorial Guinea*. Durham, NC: Duke University Press.

Arrighi, Giovanni. 1994. *The Long Twentieth Century: Money, Power, and the Origins of Our Times*. London: Verso.

Arrighi, Giovanni. 2007. *Adam Smith in Beijing: Lineages of the Twenty-First Century*. London: Verso.

Asmal, Zahira. 2015. "Arrival City." In *Movement Johannesburg*, edited by Zahira Asmal and Guy Trangoš, 8–15. Cape Town, South Africa: The City.

Avineri, Schlomo. 1968. *Karl Marx on Colonialism and Modernization*. Garden City, NY: Doubleday.

Bahng, Aimee. 2018. *Migrant Futures: Decolonizing Speculation in Financial Times*. Durham, NC: Duke University Press.

Bald, Vivek. 2013. *Bengali Harlem and the Lost Histories of South Asian America*. Cambridge, MA: Harvard University Press.

Baudrillard, Jean. 1983. *Simulations*. Translated by Paul Foss, Paul Patton, and Philip Beitchman. New York: Semiotext(e).

Bear, Laura, Karen Ho, Anna Lowenhaupt Tsing, and Sylvia Yanagisako. 2015. "Gens: A Feminist Manifesto for the Study of Capitalism." Society for Cultural Anthropology, March 30, 2015. https://culanth.org/fieldsights/652-gens-a-feminist-manifesto-for-the-study-of-capitalism.

Beinart, William, and Peter Delius. 2014. "The Historical Context and Legacy of the Natives Land Act of 1913." *Journal of Southern African Studies* 40 (4): 667-88.

Beliso-De Jesús, Aisha M., and Jemima Pierre. 2019. "Anthropology of White Supremacy." *American Anthropologist* 122 (1): 65–75.

Bench Marks Foundation. 2024. "Survival Mining in South Africa: Behind the Dominant Narrative." January 2024. https://www.bench-marks.org.za/wp-content/uploads/2024/02/Survival-mining-26Jan24.pdf.

Bendor Properties. 1972. Advertisement. *Rand Daily Mail*. May 17, 1972.

Bendor Properties. 1979. Advertisement. *Rand Daily Mail*. October 16, 1979.

Berry, Chris. 2018. "*Wolf Warrior 2*: Imagining the Chinese Century." *Film Quarterly* 72 (2): 38–44.

Berry, Maya J., Claudia Chávez Argüelles, Shanya Cordis, Sarah Ihmoud, and Elizabeth Velásquez Estrada. 2017. "Toward a Fugitive Anthropology: Gender, Race, and Violence in the Field." *Cultural Anthropology* 32 (4): 537–65.

Bhattacharya, Tithi. 2017. "Introduction: Mapping Social Reproduction Theory." In *Social Reproduction Theory: Remapping Class, Recentering Oppression*, edited by Tithi Bhattacharya, 1–20. London: Pluto.

Biermann, Werner, and Reinhart Kössler. 1980. "The Settler Mode of Production: The Rhodesian Case." *Review of African Political Economy* 7 (18): 106–16.

Birberick, Brittany. 2018. "Playing Fafi in Johannesburg." *Anthropology News*, July 11, 2018. https://americanethnologist.org/online-content/essays/playing-fafi-in-johannesburg/.

Bledsoe, Adam, and Willie Jamaal Wright. 2019. "The Anti-Blackness of Global Capital." *Environment and Planning D: Society and Space* 37 (1): 8–26.

Boer, Nienke. 2016. "Settlers and Laborers: The Afterlife of Indenture in Early South African Indian Writing." *Research in African Literatures* 47 (4): 21–35.

Bourdieu, Pierre. 1984. *Distinction: A Social Critique of the Judgements of Taste.* Translated by Richard Nice. Cambridge, MA: Harvard University Press.

Braudel, Fernand. 2009. "History and the Social Sciences: The Longue Durée." Translated by Immanuel Wallerstein. *Review* 32 (2): 171–203.

Breckenridge, Keith. 1998. "The Allure of Violence: Men, Race, and Masculinity on the South African Goldmines, 1900–1950." *Journal of Southern African Studies* 24 (4): 669–93.

Breckenridge, Keith. 2010. "The World's First Biometric Money: Ghana's E-Zwich and the Contemporary Influence of South African Biometrics." *Africa* 80 (4): 642–62.

Bremner, Lindsay. 2004. "Bounded Spaces: Demographic Anxieties in Post-apartheid Johannesburg." *Social Identities* 10 (4): 455–68.

Bremner, Lindsay. 2010. *Writing the City into Being: Essays on Johannesburg, 1998–2008.* Johannesburg: Fourth Wall Books.

Brill, Frances, and Ricardo Reboredo. 2019. "Failed Fantasies in a South African Context: The Case of Modderfontein, Johannesburg." *Urban Forum* 30 (2): 171–89.

Browne, Simone. 2015. *Dark Matters: On the Surveillance of Blackness.* Durham, NC: Duke University Press.

Burden-Stelly, Charisse, Peter James Hudson, and Jemima Pierre. 2020. "Racial Capitalism, Black Liberation, and South Africa." *Black Agenda Report*, December 16, 2020. https://www.blackagendareport.com/racial-capitalism-black-liberation-and-south-africa.

Burke, Timothy. 1996. *Lifebuoy Men, Lux Women: Commodification, Consumption, and Cleanliness in Modern Zimbabwe.* Durham, NC: Duke University Press.

Burton, Antoinette. 2016. *Africa in the Indian Imagination: Race and the Politics of Postcolonial Citation.* Durham, NC: Duke University Press.

Butcher, Siân. 2018. "Making and Governing Unstable Territory: Corporate, State and Public Encounters in Johannesburg's Mining Land, 1909–2013." *Journal of Development Studies* 5 (12): 2186–209.

Byler, Darren. 2022. *Terror Capitalism: Uyghur Dispossession and Masculinity in a Chinese City*. Durham, NC: Duke University Press.

Byrd, Jodi A. 2011. *The Transit of Empire: Indigenous Critiques of Colonialism*. Minneapolis: University of Minnesota Press.

Byrd, Jodi A., Alyosha Goldstein, Jodi Melamed, and Chandan Reddy. 2018. "Predatory Value: Economies of Dispossession and Disturbed Relationalities." *Social Text* 36 (2): 1–18.

Cacho, Lisa Marie. 2012. *Social Death: Racialized Rightlessness and the Criminalization of the Unprotected*. New York: New York University Press.

Caldeira, Teresa P. R. 2000. *City of Walls: Crime, Segregation, and Citizenship in São Paulo*. Berkeley: University of California Press.

Capps, Gavin. 2015. "Labour in the Time of Platinum." *Review of African Political Economy* 42 (146): 497–507.

Capps, Gavin. 2016. "Tribal-Landed Property: The Value of the Chieftaincy in Contemporary Africa." *Journal of Agrarian Change* 16 (3): 452–77.

Castillo, Roberto. 2020. "'Race' and 'Racism' in Contemporary Africa-China Relations Research: Approaches, Controversies and Reflections." *Inter-Asia Cultural Studies* 21 (3): 310–36.

Castillo, Roberto, and Padmore Adusei Amoah. 2020. "Africans in Post-COVID-19 Pandemic China: Is There a Future for China's 'New Minority'?." *Asian Ethnicity* 21 (4): 560–65.

Certeau, Michel de. 1984. *The Practice of Everyday Life*. Translated by Steven F. Rendall. Berkeley: University of California Press.

Chai, Winberg, and May-lee Chai. 2013. "The Meaning of Xi Jinping's Chinese Dream." *American Journal of Chinese Studies* 20 (2): 95–97.

Chari, Sharad. 2015. "African Extraction, Indian Ocean Critique." *South Atlantic Quarterly* 114 (1): 83–100.

Chari, Sharad. 2021. "'Interlocking Transactions': Micro-foundations for 'Racial Capitalism.'" In *Ethnographies of Power: Working Radical Concepts with Gillian Hart*, edited by Sharad Chari, Mark Hunter, and Melanie Samson, 49–75. Johannesburg: Wits University Press.

Chen, Kuan-Hsing. 2010. *Asia as Method: Toward Deimperialization*. Durham, NC: Duke University Press.

Chen, Mel Y. 2012. *Animacies: Biopolitics, Racial Mattering, and Queer Affect*. Durham, NC: Duke University Press.

Cheng, Anne Anlin. 2009. "Skins, Tattoos, and Susceptibility." *Representations* 108 (1): 98–119.

Cheng, Yinghong. 2011. "From Campus Racism to Cyber Racism: Discourse of Race and Chinese Nationalism." *China Quarterly* 207: 561–79.

China Africa Research Initiative. n.d. "Data: China-Africa Trade." Accessed January 23, 2024. http://www.sais-cari.org/data-china-africa-trade.

China Construction Bank. n.d. "About Us (Johannesburg Branch)." Accessed February 2, 2024. http://za.ccb.com/johannesburg/en/about/110934.html.

Chu, Julie Y. 2010. *Cosmologies of Credit: Transnational Mobility and the Politics of Destination in China*. Durham, NC: Duke University Press.

City of Johannesburg. 2019. *The State of Crime and Safety in the City of Johannesburg*. Johannesburg: City of Johannesburg, June 2019. https://www.joburg .org.za/documents_/Documents/Statistical%20Briefs/Crime%20and%20 safety%20city%20of%20Joburg.pdf.

Clinton, Hillary. 2011. "America's Pacific Century." *Foreign Policy*, October 11, 2011. http://foreignpolicy.com/2011/10/11/americas-pacific-century.

Comaroff, Jean, and John L. Comaroff. 2016. *The Truth about Crime: Sovereignty, Knowledge, Social Order*. Chicago: University of Chicago Press.

Congress of South African Trade Unions. 2006. "China-Africa Trade Agreements." Press release, November 7, 2006. https://web.archive.org/web /20150322073052/http://www.cosatu.org.za/show.php?ID=1096.

Costa Vargas, João H., and Moon-Kie Jung. 2021. "Introduction: Antiblackness of the Social and the Human." In *Antiblackness*, edited by Moon-Kie Jung and João H. Costa Vargas, 1–14. Durham, NC: Duke University Press.

Crush, Jonathan. 1994. "Scripting the Compound: Power and Space in the South African Mining Industry." *Environment and Planning D: Society and Space* 12 (3): 301–24.

Crush, Jonathan, Alan Jeeves, and David Yudelman. 1991. *South Africa's Labor Empire: A History of Black Migrancy to the Gold Mines*. Boulder, CO: Westview.

Crush, Jonathan, and Wilmot Godfrey James. 1995. *Crossing Boundaries: Mine Migrancy in a Democratic South Africa*. South Africa: Institute for Democracy in South Africa.

Crush, Jonathan, and Daniel Tevera. 2010. "Exiting Zimbabwe." In *Zimbabwe's Exodus: Crisis, Migration, Survival*, edited by Jonathan Crush and Daniel Tevera, 1–51. Kingston, ON: Southern African Migration Programme.

Czeglédy, André P. 2003. "Villas of the Highveld: A Cultural Perspective on Johannesburg and Its 'Northern Suburbs.'" In *Emerging Johannesburg: Perspectives on the Postapartheid City*, edited by Richard Tomlinson, Robert A. Beauregard, Lindsay Bremner, and Xolela Mangcu, 21–42. New York: Routledge.

Datta, Pradip Kumar. 2011. "The Interlocking Worlds of the Anglo-Boer War in South Africa and India." In *South Africa and India: Shaping the Global South*, edited by Isabel Hofmeyr and Michelle Williams, 56–81. Johannesburg: Wits University Press.

Dawson, Michael, and Ruth Wilson Gilmore. 2022. "Racial Capitalism Now: A Conversation with Michael Dawson and Ruth Wilson Gilmore." Facilitated by Brian Jordan Jefferson and Jodi Melamed. In *Colonial Racial Capitalism*, edited by Susan Koshy, Lisa Marie Cacho, Jodi A. Byrd, and Brian Jordan Jefferson, 311–32. Durham, NC: Duke University Press.

Day, Iyko. 2015. "Being or Nothingness: Indigeneity, Antiblackness, and Settler Colonial Critique." *Critical Ethnic Studies* 1 (2): 102–21.

Day, Iyko. 2016. *Alien Capital: Asian Racialization and the Logic of Settler Colonial Capitalism*. Durham, NC: Duke University Press.

De Goede, Marieke. 2012. *Speculative Security: The Politics of Pursuing Terrorist Monies*. Minneapolis: University of Minnesota Press.

De León, Jason. 2015. *The Land of Open Graves: Living and Dying on the Migrant Trail*. Berkeley: University of California Press.

De Vries, Fred. 2008. "Megamalls, Generic City." In *Johannesburg: The Elusive Metropolis*, edited by Achille Mbembe and Sarah Nuttall, 297–306. Durham, NC: Duke University Press.

Dibetle, Monako. 2006. "Redbooks, Proudly SA Caps . . . All Made in China." *Mail and Guardian*, June 23, 2006. https://mg.co.za/article/2006-06-23-redbooks-proudly-sa-caps-all-made-in-china.

Dikotter, Frank. (1992) 2015. *The Discourse of Race in Modern China*. 2nd ed. Oxford: Oxford University Press.

Dillon, Sarah. 2005. "Reinscribing De Quincey's Palimpsest: The Significance of the Palimpsest in Contemporary Literary and Cultural Studies." *Textual Practice* 19 (3): 243–63.

Diphoorn, Tessa G. 2015. *Twilight Policing: Private Security and Violence in Urban South Africa*. Berkeley: University of California Press.

Dirlik, Arif. 1997. "Critical Reflections on 'Chinese Capitalism' as Paradigm." *Identities: Global Studies in Culture and Power* 3 (3): 303–30.

Dittgen, Romain. 2014. "South Africa: Joburg's China Malls Phenomenon." ThinkAfricaPress, August 1, 2014. https://allafrica.com/stories/201408042903.html.

Douglas, Mary. (1966) 2003. *Purity and Danger: An Analysis of Pollution and Taboo*. London: Routledge.

Doyle, Laura. 2020. *Inter-imperiality: Vying Empires, Gendered Labor, and the Literary Arts of Alliance*. Durham, NC: Duke University Press.

Draper, Susana. 2012. *Afterlives of Confinement: Spatial Transitions in Postdictatorship Latin America*. Pittsburgh: University of Pittsburgh Press.

Driessen, Miriam. 2019. *Tales of Hope, Tastes of Bitterness: Chinese Road Builders in Ethiopia*. Hong Kong: Hong Kong University Press.

Driscoll, Mark W. 2020. *The Whites Are Enemies of Heaven: Climate Caucasianism and Asian Ecological Protection*. Durham, NC: Duke University Press.

Du Plessis, A. J. 1997. "South Africa: Rainbow Nation of Mineral Wealth." *Engineering and Mining Journal*, May: 16A–16F.

Eng, David L., Teemu Ruskola, and Shuang Shen. 2011. "Introduction: China and the Human." In "China and the Human, Part I: Cosmologies of the Human," edited by Teemu Ruskola, Shuang Shen, David L. Eng, Teemu Ruskola, and Shuang Shen, special issue, *Social Text* 29 (4): 1–27.

Falkof, Nicky. 2016. "Out the Back: Race and Reinvention in Johannesburg's Garden Cottages." *International Journal of Cultural Studies* 19 (6): 627–42.

Falkof, Nicky, and Cobus van Staden. 2020. "Introduction: Traversing the Anxious Metropolis." In *Anxious Joburg: The Inner Lives of a Global City*, edited by Nicky Falkof and Cobus van Staden, 1–18. Johannesburg: Wits University Press.

Fanon, Frantz. (1952) 2008. *Black Skin, White Masks*. Translated by Richard Philcox. Reprint, New York: Grove Press.

Feldman-Savelsberg, Pamela, and Tiokou Ndonko. 2010. "Urbanites and Urban Villagers: Comparing 'Home' among Elite and Non-elite Bamiléké Women's Hometown Associations." *Africa: The Journal of the International African Institute* 80 (3): 371–96.

Fennell, Vera Leigh. 2013. "Race: China's Question and Problem." *Review of Black Political Economy* 40 (3): 245–75.

Ferguson, James. 2006. *Global Shadows: Africa in the Neoliberal World Order*. Durham, NC: Duke University Press.

Ferguson, Roderick A. 2004. *Aberrations in Black: Toward a Queer of Color Critique*. Minneapolis: University of Minnesota Press.

Ferguson, Susan. 2016. "Intersectionality and Social-Reproduction Feminisms: Toward an Integrative Ontology." *Historical Materialism* 24 (2): 38–60.

Ferreira Da Silva, Denise. 1998. "Facts of Blackness: Brazil Is Not (Quite) the United States . . . and Racial Politics in Brazil?" *Social Identities* 4 (2): 201–34.

Ferreira Da Silva, Denise. 2015. "Globality." *Critical Ethnic Studies* 1 (1): 33–38.

Fishman, Ted. 2004. "The Chinese Century." *New York Times*, July 4, 2004. https://www.nytimes.com/2004/07/04/magazine/the-chinese-century.html.

Fleetwood, Nicole R. 2011. *Troubling Vision: Performance, Visuality, and Blackness*. Chicago: University of Chicago Press.

Franceschini, Ivan, and Nicholas Loubere. 2022. *Global China as Method*. Cambridge: Cambridge University Press.

Frank, Andre Gunder. 1998. *ReOrient: Global Economy in the Asian Age*. Berkeley: University of California Press.

Frazier, Robeson Taj, and Lin Zhang. 2014. "Ethnic Identity and Racial Contestation in Cyberspace: Deconstructing the Chineseness of Lou Jing." *China Information* 28 (2): 237–58.

French, Howard W. 2014. *China's Second Continent: How a Million Migrants Are Building a New Empire in Africa*. New York: Alfred A. Knopf.

Friedman, Eli, and Sarosh Kuruvilla. 2015. "Experimentation and Decentralization in China's Labor Relations." *Human Relations* 68 (2): 181–95.

Fujikane, Candace. 2008. "Introduction: Asian Settler Colonialism in the U.S. Colony of Hawai'i." In *Asian Settler Colonialism: From Local Governance to the Habits of Everyday Life in Hawai'i*, edited by Candace Fujikane and Jonathan Y. Okamura, 1–42. Honolulu: University of Hawai'i Press.

Gao, Weinong. 2017. "New Chinese Migrants in Latin America: Trends and Patterns of Adaptation." In *Contemporary Chinese Diasporas*, edited by Min Zhou, 333–48. Singapore: Palgrave.

Gibson-Graham, J. K. (1996) 2006. *The End of Capitalism (As We Knew It): A Feminist Critique of Political Economy*, with a new introduction. Minneapolis: University of Minnesota Press.

Gilmore, Ruth Wilson. 2007. *Golden Gulag: Prisons, Surplus, Crisis, and Opposition in Globalizing California*. Berkeley: University of California Press.

Gilroy, Paul. 2000. *Against Race: Imagining Political Culture beyond the Color Line*. Cambridge, MA: Harvard University Press.

Ginsburg, Rebecca. 2011. *At Home with Apartheid: The Hidden Landscapes of Domestic Service in Johannesburg*. Charlottesville: University of Virginia Press.

Go, Julian. 2021. "Three Tensions in the Theory of Racial Capitalism." *Sociological Theory* 39 (1): 38–47.

Goffe, Tao Leigh. 2019. "Sugarwork: The Gastropoetics of Afro-Asia after the Plantation." *Asian Diasporic Visual Cultures and the Americas* 5 (1–2): 31–56.

Goldberg, David Theo. 2009. *The Threat of Race: Reflections on Racial Neoliberalism*. Malden, MA: Wiley-Blackwell.

Goldstein, Alyosha. 2014. "Possessive Investment: Indian Removals and the Affective Entitlements of Whiteness." *American Quarterly* 66 (4): 1077–84.

Goldstein, Alyosha. 2022. "'In the Constant Flux of Its Incessant Renewal': The Social Reproduction of Racial Capitalism and Settler Colonial Entitlement." In *Colonial Racial Capitalism*, edited by Susan Koshy, Lisa Marie Cacho, Jodi A. Byrd, and Brian Jordan Jefferson, 60–87. Durham, NC: Duke University Press.

Goldstein, Daniel M. 2016. *Owners of the Sidewalk: Security and Survival in the Informal City*. Durham, NC: Duke University Press.

Greve, Natalie. 2014. "Chinese Outline Plans for Mammoth R84bn Modderfontein 'City.'" *Creamer Media's Engineering News*. April 9, 2014. https://www.engineeringnews.co.za/article/chinese-outline-plans-for-mammoth-r84bn-modderfontein-city-2014-04-09.

Günel, Gökçe, Saiba Varma, and Chika Watanabe. 2020. "A Manifesto for Patchwork Ethnography." Society for Cultural Anthropology, June 9, 2020. https://culanth.org/fieldsights/a-manifesto-for-patchwork-ethnography.

Hall, Stuart. (1997) 2021. *Selected Writings on Race and Difference*. Durham, NC: Duke University Press.

Hao Wang Guan Cha 好望观察. 2019. "*Feizhou nuwang: Wo yu Feizhou bude bu shuo de gushi* " 非洲女王：我与非洲不得不说的故事 [Queen of Africa: Stories of Africa and me]. Weixin 微信 [WeChat], September 10, 2019. https://mp.weixin.qq.com/s?__biz=Mzg2ODE4MTY4OQ==&mid=2247485954&idx=1&sn=4a8fbcbd868a7839490962c006b7d2f6&chksm=ceb179d4f9c6foc23436f5b6e36d589afoce37aa4576da0df4ddd647bbfbab197d5ed93953b4&scene=21#wechat_redirect.

Harris, Karen L. 2010. "Sugar and Gold Indentured Indian and Chinese Labour in South Africa." *Journal of Social Science* 25 (1–3): 147–58.

Harris, Karen L. 2017. "BEE-ing Chinese in South Africa: A Legal Historic Perspective." *Fundamina* 23 (2): 1–20.

Harrison, Phillip, Khangelani Moyo, and Yan Yang. 2012. "Strategy and Tactics: Chinese Immigrants and Diasporic Spaces in Johannesburg, South Africa." *Journal of Southern African Studies* 38 (4): 899–925.

Harrison, Philip, and Tanya Zack. 2012. "The Power of Mining: The Fall of Gold and Rise of Johannesburg." *Journal of Contemporary African Studies* 30 (4): 551–70.

Hart, Gillian. 2002. *Disabling Globalization: Places of Power in Post-apartheid South Africa.* Berkeley: University of California Press.

Hart, Keith, and Vishnu Padayachee. 2013. "A History of South African Capitalism in National and Global Perspective." *Transformation: Critical Perspectives on Southern Africa* 81 (1): 55–85.

Hartman, Saidiya V. 1997. *Scenes of Subjection: Terror, Slavery, and Self-Making in Nineteenth-Century America.* Oxford: Oxford University Press.

Hartman, Saidiya. 2008a. *Lose Your Mother: A Journey along the Atlantic Slave Route.* London: Macmillan.

Hartman, Saidiya. 2008b. "Venus in Two Acts." *Small Axe* 12 (2): 1–14.

Harvey, David. 2003. *The New Imperialism.* New York: Oxford University Press.

Hassim, Shireen, Tawana Kupe, and Eric Worby. 2008. "Introduction." In *Go Home or Die Here: Violence, Xenophobia and the Reinvention of Difference in South Africa,* edited by Shireen Hassim, Tawana Kupe, and Eric Worby, 1–25. Johannesburg: Wits University Press.

Haugen, Heidi Østbø, and Jørgen Carling. 2008. "On the Edge of the Diaspora: The Surge of Baihuo Businesses in an African City." *Ethnic and Racial Studies* 28 (4): 639–62.

Hearn, Adrian H. 2016. *Diaspora and Trust: Cuba, Mexico, and the Rise of China.* Durham, NC: Duke University Press.

Hecht, Gabrielle. 2023. *Residual Governance: How South Africa Foretells Planetary Futures.* Durham, NC: Duke University Press.

Hirono, Miwa, and Shogo Suzuki. 2014. "Why Do We Need 'Myth-Busting' in the Study of Sino–African Relations?" *Journal of Contemporary China* 23 (87): 443–61.

Ho, Karen. 2005. "Situating Global Capitalisms: A View from Wall Street Investment Banks." *Cultural Anthropology* 20 (1): 68–96.

Ho, Ufrieda. 2011. *Paper Sons and Daughters: Growing Up Chinese in South Africa.* Athens: Ohio University Press.

Ho, Ufrieda. 2013. "The Arch Angle on Booming Chinatown." *Mail and Guardian,* July 12, 2013. https://mg.co.za/article/2013-07-12-the-arch-angle-on-booming-chinatown.

Ho, Ufrieda. 2022. "SA Chinese Communities Elated after Winning Hate Speech Case." *Daily Maverick,* July 29, 2022. https://www.dailymaverick.co.za/article/2022-07-29-sa-chinese-communities-elated-after-winning-hate-speech-case.

Hoang, Kimberly Kay. 2015. *Dealing in Desire: Asian Ascendancy, Western Decline, and the Hidden Currencies of Global Sex Work.* Berkeley: University of California Press.

Hoang, Kimberly Kay. 2022. "In Search of the Next El Dorado: Mining for Capital in a Frontier Market with Colonial Legacies." In *Colonial Racial Capitalism,* edited by Susan Koshy, Lisa Marie Cacho, Jodi A. Byrd, and Brian Jordan Jefferson, 131–58. Durham, NC: Duke University Press.

Hobsbawm, Eric. 1959. *Social Bandits and Primitive Rebels: Studies in Archaic Forms of Social Movement in the 19th and 20th Centuries.* Glencoe, IL: Free Press.

Hogg, Alec. 2019. "No More Manhattan for Modderfontein: Chinese Megacity a Non-starter." BizNews, March 19, 2019. https://www.biznews.com/thought -leaders/2019/03/07/manhattan-modderfontein-chinese-megacity-non-starter.

Holland, Sharon Patricia. 2012. *The Erotic Life of Racism.* Durham, NC: Duke University Press.

Hong, Grace Kyungwon. 2006. *The Ruptures of American Capital: Women of Color Feminism and the Culture of Immigrant Labor.* Minneapolis: University of Minnesota Press.

Hong, Grace Kyungwon. 2012. "Existentially Surplus: Women of Color Feminism and the New Crises of Capitalism." GLQ 18 (1): 87–106.

Hood, Johanna. 2013. "Distancing Disease in the Un-Black Han Chinese Politic: Othering Difference in China's HIV/AIDS Media." *Modern China* 39 (3): 280–318.

Horne, Gerald. 2020. *The Dawning of the Apocalypse: The Roots of Slavery, White Supremacy, Settler Colonialism, and Capitalism in the Long Sixteenth Century.* New York: Monthly Review Press.

Horowitz, Josh. 2016. "The Full Apology from the Chinese Company behind the Racist Laundry Detergent Ad." Quartz, May 30, 2016. https://qz.com /695240/the-full-apology-from-the-chinesecompany-behind-the-racist -laundry-detergent-ad.

Huang, Echo. 2018. "'A Torture for the Eyes': Chinese Moviegoers Think Black Panther Is Just Too Black." Quartz, March 12, 2018. https://qz.com /1226449/a-torture-for-the-eyes-chinese-moviegoers-think-black-panther -is-too-black.

Huang, Kun. 2020. "'Anti-Blackness' in Chinese Racial-Nationalism: Sex/Gender, Reproduction, and Metaphors of Pathology." Translated by Roy Chan and Shui-yin Sharon Yam. *Positions*, June 29, 2020. http://positionspolitics .org/kun-huang-anti-blackness-in-chinese-racial-nationalism-sex-gender -reproduction-and-metaphors-of-pathology.

Huang, Mingwei. 2016. "Vulnerable Observers: Notes on Fieldwork and Rape." *Chronicle of Higher Education*, October 12, 2016. http://www.chronicle.com /article/Vulnerable-ObserversNotes-on/238042.

Huang, Mingwei. 2020. "The Chinatown Back Room: The Afterlife of Apartheid Architectures." In *Anxious Joburg: The Inner Lives of a Global South*

City, edited by Nicky Falkof and Cobus van Staden, 152–75. Johannesburg: Wits University Press.

Huang, Mingwei. 2021. "The Chinese Century and the City of Gold: Refashioning Race and Capitalism." *Public Culture* 33 (2): 193–217.

Huang, Mingwei. 2022a. "Afro-Asian Adjacencies in South Africa's Long Twentieth Century." *Verge: Studies in Global Asias* 8 (1): 167–94.

Huang, Mingwei. 2022b. "Global South Frontiers: Chinese Worldmaking and Racial Imaginaries of Johannesburg." In *New World Orderings: China and the Global South*, edited by Lisa Rofel and Carlos Rojas, 169–86. Durham, NC: Duke University Press.

Huang, Mingwei. 2024. "The Globality of Antiblackness." *Made in China Journal*, January 10. https://madeinchinajournal.com/2024/01/10/the-globality-of-antiblackness/.

Huang, Mingwei, Vivian Lu, Susan MacDougall, and Megan Steffen. 2019. "Disciplinary Violence." *Anthropology News*, May 10, 2019. https://anthrosource.onlinelibrary.wiley.com/doi/abs/10.1111/AN.861.

Hudson, Peter James. 2017. *Bankers and Empire: How Wall Street Colonized the Caribbean*. Chicago: University of Chicago Press.

Hudson, Peter James. 2018. "Racial Capitalism and the Dark Proletariat." *Boston Review*, February 20, 2018. https://bostonreview.net/forum_response/peter-james-hudson-racial-capitalism-and/.

Hurst, William, and Kevin J. O'Brien. 2002. "China's Contentious Pensioners." *China Quarterly* 170: 345–60.

Huynh, Tu T. 2008a. "From Demand for Asiatic Labor to Importation of Indentured Chinese Labor: Race Identity in the Recruitment of Unskilled Labor for South Africa's Gold Mining Industry, 1903–1910." *Journal of Chinese Overseas* 4 (1): 51–68.

Huynh, Tu T. 2008b. "Loathing and Love: Postcard Representations of Indentured Chinese Laborers in South Africa's Reconstruction, 1904–10." *Safundi: Journal of South African and American Studies* 9 (4): 395–425.

Huynh, Tu T. 2012. "'We Are Not a Docile People': Chinese Resistance and Exclusion in the Re-imagining of Whiteness in South Africa, 1903–1910." *Journal of Chinese Overseas* 8 (2): 137–68.

Huynh, Tu T., and Yoon Jung Park. 2018. "Reflections on the Role of Race in China-Africa Relations." In *New Directions in Africa-China Studies*, edited by Chris Alden and Daniel Large, 158–72. New York: Routledge.

Huynh, Tu T., Yoon Jung Park, and Anna Ying Chen. 2010. "Faces of China: New Chinese Migrants in South Africa, 1980s to Present." *African and Asian Studies* 9 (3): 286–306.

Innes, Duncan. 1984. *Anglo American and the Rise of Modern South Africa*. New York: Monthly Review Press.

Iqani, Mehita. 2017. "A New Class for a New South Africa? The Discursive Construction of the 'Black Middle Class' in Post-apartheid Media." *Journal of Consumer Culture* 17 (1): 105–21.

Jackson, Mark. 2012. "Visuality, 'China Commodity City,' and the Force of Things." In *Visuality/Materiality: Images, Objects, and Practices*, edited by Gillian Rose and Dibya P. Tolia-Kelly, 39–58. Farnham: Ashgate.

Jaffe, Hosea. 2017. *A History of Africa.* London: Zed Books.

James, Deborah. 2014. *Money from Nothing: Indebtedness and Aspiration in South Africa.* Johannesburg: Wits University Press.

James, Wilmot G. 1992. *Our Precious Metal: African Labour in South Africa's Gold Industry, 1970–1990.* Bloomington: Indiana University Press.

Jenkins, Destin, and Justin Leroy. 2021. "Introduction: The Old History of Capitalism." In *Histories of Racial Capitalism*, edited by Destin Jenkins and Justin Leroy, 1–26. New York: Columbia University Press.

Johnson, Ian. 2014. "The Chinese Invade Africa." *New York Review of Books*, September 25, 2014. https://www.nybooks.com/articles/2014/09/25/chinese-invade-africa/.

Jung, Moon-Ho. 2005. "Outlawing 'Coolies': Race, Nation, and Empire in the Age of Emancipation." *American Quarterly* 57 (3): 677–701.

Kardas-Nelson, Mara. 2013. "The Reef & The City." In *Tales from the City of Gold*, by Jason Larkin, 6–11. Berlin: Kehrer.

Karl, Rebecca E. 2002. *Staging the World: Chinese Nationalism at the Turn of the Twentieth Century.* Durham, NC: Duke University Press.

Karl, Rebecca E. 2020. Remarks in Rebecca Karl, Yige Dong, Eli Friedman, Andrew Liu, Isabella Weber, Jake Werner, and Zhun Xu, "Session 1: Against Capitalism and Imperialism," video, 1:29:33, in *Viral Politics: Left Perspectives on the World and China*, webinar series. Critical China Scholars, June 18, 2020. https://criticalchinascholars.org/webinars/.

Keefe, Patrick Radden. 2009. "Snakeheads and Smuggling: The Dynamics of Illegal Chinese Immigration." *World Policy Journal* 26 (1): 33–44.

Keegan, Timothy. 2001. "Gender, Degeneration and Sexual Danger: Imagining Race and Class in South Africa, ca. 1912." *Journal of Southern African Studies* 27 (3): 459–77.

Kelley, Robin D. G. 2017. "The Rest of Us: Rethinking Settler and Native." *American Quarterly* 69 (2): 267–76.

Kendall, Jane, Bill Maurer, Phillip Machoka, and Clara Veniard. 2012. "An Emerging Platform: From Money Transfer System to Mobile Money Ecosystem." *Innovations* 6 (4): 49–64.

Kihato, Caroline Wanijiku. 2013. *Migrant Women of Johannesburg: Everyday Life in an In-Between City.* New York: Palgrave Macmillan.

Knight, Jasper. n.d. "Development of Palimpsest Landscapes." Vignettes: Key Concepts in Geomorphology. Accessed December 10, 2021. https://serc.carleton.edu/68942.

Kohrman, Matthew. 2021. "Filtered Life: Air Purification, Gender, and Cigarettes in the People's Republic of China." *Public Culture* 33 (2): 161–91.

Koselleck, Reinhart. 2018. *Sediments of Time: On Possible Histories.* Edited by Stefan-Ludwig Hoffmann. Translated by Sean Franzel. Stanford, CA: Stanford University Press.

Koshy, Susan, Lisa Marie Cacho, Jodi A. Byrd, and Brian Jordan Jefferson. 2022. "Introduction." In *Colonial Racial Capitalism*, edited by Susan Koshy, Lisa Marie Cacho, Jodi A. Byrd, and Brian Jordan Jefferson, 1–30. Durham, NC: Duke University Press.

Krige, Detlev. 2011. "'We Are Running for a Living': Work, Leisure and Speculative Accumulation in an Underground Numbers Lottery in Johannesburg." *African Studies* 70 (1): 3–24.

Kynoch, Gary. 2003. "Controlling the Coolies: Chinese Mineworkers and the Struggle for Labor in South Africa, 1904–1910." *The International Journal of African Historical Studies* 36 (2): 309–29.

Kynoch, Gary. 2005. "'Your Petitioners Are in Mortal Terror': The Violent World of Chinese Mineworkers in South Africa, 1904–1910." *Journal of Southern African Studies* 31 (3): 531–46.

Lai, Walton Look. 2004. *Indentured Labor, Caribbean Sugar: Chinese and Indian Migrants to the British West Indies, 1838–1918.* Baltimore: Johns Hopkins University Press.

Lan, Shanshan. 2017. *Mapping the New African Diaspora in China: Race and the Cultural Politics of Belonging.* New York: Routledge.

Landau, Loren B. 2009. "Living within and beyond Johannesburg: Exclusion, Religion, and Emerging Forms of Being." *African Studies* 68 (2): 197–214.

Landau, Loren B., and Iriann Freemantle. 2010. "Tactical Cosmopolitanism and Idioms of Belonging: Insertion and Self-Exclusion in Johannesburg." *Journal of Ethnic and Migration Studies* 36 (3): 375–90.

Lee, Ching Kwan. 2007. *Against the Law: Labor Protests in China's Rustbelt and Sunbelt.* Berkeley: University of California Press.

Lee, Ching Kwan. 2009. "Raw Encounters: Chinese Managers, African Workers, and the Politics of Casualization in Africa's Chinese Enclaves." *China Quarterly* 199: 647–66.

Lee, Ching Kwan. 2017. *The Specter of Global China: Politics, Labor, and Foreign Investment in Africa.* Chicago: University of Chicago Press.

Lee, Christopher J. 2010. "Introduction: Between a Moment and an Era: The Origins and Afterlives of Bandung. In *Making a World after Empire: The Bandung Moment and Its Political Afterlives*, edited by Christopher Lee, 1–42. Athens: Ohio University Press.

Lee, Christopher J. 2021. "Decolonizing 'China-Africa Relations': Toward a New Ethos of Afro-Asianism." *Journal of African Cultural Studies* 33 (2): 230–37.

Legassick, Martin, and David Hemson. 1976. *Foreign Investment and the Reproduction of Racial Capitalism in South Africa.* Foreign Investment in South

Africa: A Discussion Series, no. 2. London: Anti-Apartheid Movement. University of Cape Town Special Collections, BC1150 A2(2).

Letcher, Owen. 1936. *The Gold Mines of Southern Africa: The History, Technology and Statistics of the Gold Industry.* Johannesburg and London: Owen Letcher and Waterlow & Sons Ltd.

Lewis, Mark Edward, and Hsieh Mei-yu. 2017. "Tianxia and the Invention of Empire in East Asia." In *Chinese Visions of World Order: Tianxia, Culture, and World Politics*, edited by Ban Wang, 25–48. Durham, NC: Duke University Press.

Li, Minqi. 2008. *The Rise of China and the Demise of the Capitalist World Economy.* New York: Monthly Review Press.

Lipsitz, George. (1998) 2006. *The Possessive Investment in Whiteness: How White People Profit from Identity Politics, Revised and Expanded Edition.* Philadelphia: Temple University Press.

Liu, Petrus. 2015. *Queer Marxism in Two Chinas.* Durham, NC: Duke University Press.

Liu, Petrus. 2022. *The Specter of Materialism: Queer Theory and Marxism in the Age of the Beijing Consensus.* Durham, NC: Duke University Press.

Liu, Petrus, and Lisa Rofel, eds. 2018. *"Wolf Warrior II": The Rise of China and Gender/Sexual Politics.* Columbus, OH: MCLC Resource Center. https://u.osu.edu/mclc/online-series/liu-rofel/.

Lowe, Lisa. 1996. *Immigrant Acts: On Asian American Cultural Politics.* Durham, NC: Duke University Press.

Lowe, Lisa. 2015. *The Intimacies of Four Continents.* Durham, NC: Duke University Press.

Lowe, Lisa, and Kris Manjapra. 2019. "Comparative Global Humanities after Man: Alternatives to the Coloniality of Knowledge." *Theory, Culture, and Society* 36 (5): 23–48.

Lukasiewicz, Mariusz. 2017. "From Diamonds to Gold: The Making of the Johannesburg Stock Exchange, 1880–1890." *Journal of Southern African Studies* 43 (4): 715–32.

Ly, Linsey. 2020. "Palimpsest Landscapes." Society for Cultural Anthropology, September 22, 2020. https://culanth.org/fieldsights/palimpsest-landscapes.

Lye, Colleen. 2005. *America's Asia: Racial Form and American Literature, 1893–1945.* Princeton, NJ: Princeton University Press.

Madimu, Tapiwa. 2022. "'Illegal' Gold Mining and the Everyday in Post-Apartheid South Africa." *Review of African Political Economy* 49 (173): 436–51.

Maeko, Thando. 2019. "The Ugly Face of Beautiful City." *Mail and Guardian,* November 22, 2019. https://mg.co.za/article/2019-11-22-00-the-ugly-face-of-beautiful-city/.

Magubane, Bernard Makhosezwe. 1979. *The Political Economy of Race and Class in South Africa.* New York: Monthly Review Press.

Magubane, Zine. 2004. *Bringing the Empire Home: Race, Class, and Gender in Britain and Colonial South Africa.* Chicago: University of Chicago Press.

Mail and Guardian. 2005. "Mega-mall to Be Built in Soweto." July 8, 2005. https://mg.co.za/article/2005-07-08-megamall-to-be-built-in-soweto/.

Mail and Guardian. 2006. "Mbeki Warns Africa on Relationship with China." December 13, 2006. http://mg.co.za/article/2006-12-13-mbeki-warns-africa-on-relationship-with-china.

Majova, Zukile. 2005. "Cosatu Berated for 'Made in China' T-Shirts." Independent Online, December 5, 2005. http://www.iol.co.za/news/politics/cosatu-berated-for-made-in-china-t-shirts-260546.

Makina, Daniel. 2010. "Zimbabwe in Johannesburg." In *Zimbabwe's Exodus: Crisis, Migration, Survival,* edited by Jonathan Crush and Daniel Tevera, 225–41. Kingston, ON: Southern African Migration Programme.

Malcomess, Bettina, and Dorothee Kreutzfeld. 2013. *Not No Place: Johannesburg; Spaces and Fragments of Time.* Auckland Park, South Africa: Jacana.

Mamdani, Mahmood. 2001. "Beyond Settler and Native as Political Identities: Overcoming the Political Legacy of Colonialism." *Comparative Studies in Society and History* 43 (4): 651–64.

Manalansan, Martin F. 2014. "The 'Stuff' of Archives: Mess, Migration, and Queer Lives." *Radical History Review* 2014 (120): 94–107.

Manjapra, Kris. 2020. *Colonialism in Global Perspective.* New York: Columbia University Press.

Markovits, Claude. 2007. "Structure and Agency in the World of Asian Commerce during the Era of European Colonial Domination (c. 1750–1950)." *Journal of the Economic and Social History of the Orient* 50 (2–3): 106–23.

Marsh, Jenni. 2014. "Afro-Chinese Marriages Boom in Guangzhou: But Will It Be 'til Death Do Us Part'?" *South China Morning Post,* July 2, 2014. http://www.scmp.com/magazines/post-magazine/article/1521076/afro-chinese-marriages-boom-guangzhou-will-it-be-til-death.

Martin, William G. 2008. "Africa's Futures: From North–South to East–South?" *Third World Quarterly* 29 (2): 339–56.

Marx, Karl. 1976. *Capital: A Critique of Political Economy.* Vol. 1, translated by Ben Fowkes. New York: Penguin Books.

Mashele, Prince. 2017. "Poverty and Protests Will Haunt Us in the Unproductive Age of the Shopping Mall." *Sowetan,* May 15, 2017.

Mashele, Prince. 2018. "The Age of the Shopping Mall Is upon Us . . . and White Men Still Rule." *Sowetan,* October 1, 2018.

Matthews, Charlotte. 2008. "South Africa: Booming China Is World's New Egoli." AllAfrica, January 18, 2008. https://allafrica.com/stories/200801180517.html.

Maurer, Bill. 2012. "Regulation as Retrospective Ethnography: Mobile Money and the Arts of Cash." *Banking and Finance Law Review* 27 (2): 299–313.

Mawani, Renisa. 2009. *Colonial Proximities: Crossracial Encounters and Juridical Truths in British Colombia, 1871–1921.* Vancouver: University of British Columbia Press.

Mbembe, Achille. 2017. *Critique of Black Reason.* Translated by Laurent Dubois. Durham, NC: Duke University Press.

Mbembe, Achille. 2021. *Out of the Dark Night: Essays on Decolonization.* New York: Columbia University Press.

Mbembe, Achille, and Sarah Nuttall. 2008. "Introduction: Afropolis." In *Johannesburg: The Elusive Metropolis*, edited by Achille Mbembe and Sarah Nuttall, 1–33. Durham, NC: Duke University Press.

McClintock, Anne. 1995. *Imperial Leather: Race, Gender, and Sexuality in the Colonial Contest.* New York: Routledge.

McNamee, Terence, with Greg Mills, Sebabatso Manoeli, Masana Mulaudzi, Stuart Doran, and Emma Chen. 2012. "Africa in Their Words: A Study of Chinese Traders in South Africa, Lesotho, Botswana, Zambia and Angola." Brenthurst Foundation Discussion Paper 03, Johannesburg.

Meer, Fatima. 1985. "Indentured Labour and Group Formations in Apartheid Society." *Race and Class* 26 (4): 45–60.

Melamed, Jodi. 2015. "Racial Capitalism." *Critical Ethnic Studies* 1 (1): 76–85.

Meredith, Martin. 1998. *Mandela: A Biography.* New York: St. Martin's.

Michel, Serge, and Michel Beuret. 2009. *China Safari: On the Trail of Beijing's Expansion in Africa.* Translated by Raymond Valley. New York: Nation Books.

Mlambo, Alois S. 2010. "A History of Zimbabwean Migration to 1990." In *Zimbabwe's Exodus: Crisis, Migration, Survival*, edited by Jonathan Crush and Daniel Tevera, 52–76. Kingston, ON: Southern African Migration Programme.

Modderfontein Reserve. n.d. *History and Heritage.* Modderfontein, South Africa: Modderfontein Reserve. Accessed February 2, 2024. https://modderfonteinreserve.co.za/wp-content/uploads/2021/03/Modderfontein-Reserve-History-and-Heritage-Last-FINAL-2021-003.pdf.

Mohan, Giles, and May Tan-Mullins. 2009. "Chinese Migrants in Africa as New Agents of Development? An Analytical Framework." *European Journal of Development Research* 21 (4): 588–605.

Monson, Jamie. 2013. "Historicizing Difference Construction of Race Identity in China-Africa Relations." Social Science Research Council. https://www.ssrc.org/publications/historicizing-difference/.

Monson, Jamie, and Stephanie Rupp. 2013. "Introduction: Africa and China: New Engagements, New Research." In "ASR Forum on Africa and China," edited by Jamie Monson and Stephanie Rupp, special section, *African Studies Review* 56 (1): 21–44.

Moodie, T. Dunbar, with Vivienne Ndatshe. 1994. *Going for Gold: Men, Mines, and Migration.* Berkeley: University of California Press.

Moore, Mick, Wilson Prichard, and Odd-Helge Fjeldstad. 2018. *Taxing Africa: Coercion, Reform and Development.* London: Zed Books.

Moreton-Robinson, Aileen. 2015. *The White Possessive: Property, Power, and Indigenous Sovereignty.* Minneapolis: University of Minnesota Press.

Morrell, Robert. 1998. "Of Boys and Men: Masculinity and Gender in Southern African Studies." *Journal of Southern African Studies* 24 (4): 605–30.

Msiska, Mpalive-Hangson. 2017. "Kujoni: South Africa in Malawi's National Imaginary." *Journal of Southern African Studies* 43 (5): 1011–29.

Mulaudzi, Shandukani. 2014. "Chinese Mall Overhaul." Wits Centre for Journalism Africa-China Reporting Project, March 4, 2014. https://africachinareporting .com/chinese-mall-overhaul/.

Muller, Joan. 2015. "Mall Mania: Why the Boom Is Losing Steam." BusinessLIVE, October 22, 2015. https://www.businesslive.co.za/archive/2015-10-22-mall -mania-why-the-boom-is-losing-steam/.

Muñoz, José Esteban. 1996. "Ephemera as Evidence: Introductory Notes to Queer Acts." *Women and Performance: A Journal of Feminist Theory* 8 (2): 5–16.

Murray, Martin J. 2011. *City of Extremes: The Spatial Politics of Johannesburg.* Durham, NC: Duke University Press.

Murray, Martin J. 2020. *Panic City: Crime and the Fear Industries in Johannesburg.* Stanford, CA: Stanford University Press.

Nanfei 365 南非365 [South Africa 365]. 2015a. "*Ziyou Zhou Fujian Tongxiang Hui tiqian fabu tonggao jinzao ge bumen jiang zhankai lianhe da soucha!*" 自由州福建同乡会提前发布通告 今早各部门将展开联合大搜查！[The Free State Fujian Association Issued an Announcement in Advance that Various Departments Will Launch a Joint Search this Morning!]. Weixin 微信 [WeChat], May 19, 2015. https://mp.weixin.qq.com/s?__biz=MjM5MTA0MjIoMg==&mid =206544040&idx=1&sn=4a4dae1d6336c4c0d7c952b3dae1f7bc#rd.

Nanfei 365 南非365 [South Africa 365]. 2015b. "*Qiaobao fa gongzi zao yuangong qiangjie yuhai, ying jinliang bimian fafang xianjin!*" 侨胞发工资遭员工抢劫遇害，应尽量避免发放现金！[Overseas Chinese Were Robbed and Killed by Employees While Paying Wages. We Should Avoid Using Cash as Much as Possible!]. May 30, 2015. https://mp.weixin.qq.com/s?__biz=MjM5MTA0MjIoMg ==&mid=206979486&idx=1&sn=d99c2002ac551477d8866e8c234a7463#rd.

News.com.au. 2016. "Is This the Most Racist Commercial Ever Made?" May 27, 2016. https://www.news.com.au/entertainment/tv/is-this-the-most-racist -commercial-ever-made/news-story/b7c1a0895364c79b32b9efb48302ed5f.

Ngai, Mae M. 2017. "Trouble on the Rand: The Chinese Question in South Africa and the Apogee of White Settlerism." *International Labor and Working Class History* 91:59–78.

Ngai, Mae M. 2021. *The Chinese Question: The Gold Rushes and Global Politics.* New York: W. W. Norton.

Ngai, Pun. 1999. "Becoming Dagongmei (Working Girls): The Politics of Identity and Difference in Reform China." *China Journal* 42 (18): 1–18.

Ngai, Pun. 2007. "Gendering the Dormitory Labor System: Production, Re-production, and Migrant Labor in South China." *Feminist Economics* 13 (3–4): 239–58.

Nguyen, Mimi Thi. 2014. "The Hoodie as Sign, Screen, Expectation, and Force." *Signs* 40 (4): 791–816.

Nichols, Robert. 2020. *Theft Is Property! Dispossession and Critical Theory*. Durham, NC: Duke University Press.

Niemann, Michael. 2003. "Migration and the Lived Spaces of Southern Africa." *Alternatives* 28 (1): 115–40.

Nixon, Rob. 2011. *Slow Violence and the Environmentalism of the Poor*. Cambridge, MA: Harvard University Press.

Nyamnjoh, Francis B. 2017. "Incompleteness: Frontier Africa and the Currency of Conviviality." *Journal of Asian and African Studies* 52 (3): 253–70.

Nyíri, Pál. 2006. "The Yellow Man's Burden: Chinese Migrants on a Civilizing Mission." *China Quarterly* 56:83–106.

Okeowo, Alexis. 2014. "The Settlers." *New York Times*, July 10, 2014. https://www.nytimes.com/2014/07/13/books/review/chinas-second-continent-by-howard-w-french.html.

Olalde, Mark. 2015. "The Haunting Legacy of South Africa's Gold Mines." *Yale Environment 360*, November 12, 2015. https://e360.yale.edu/features/the_haunting_legacy_of_south_africas_gold_mines.

Olaloku-Teriba, Annie. 2018. "Afro-Pessimism and the (Un)logic of Anti-Blackness." *Historical Materialism* 26 (2): 96–122.

Ong, Aihwa. 1999. *Flexible Citizenship: The Cultural Logics of Transnationality*. Durham, NC: Duke University Press.

Ong, Aihwa, and Donald Nonini. 1997. "Chinese Transnationalism as an Alternative Modernity." In *Ungrounded Empires: The Cultural Politics of Modern Chinese Transnationalism*, edited by Aihwa Ong and Donald Nonini, 3–38. New York: Routledge.

Oonk, Gijsbert. 2013. *Settled Strangers: Asian Business Elites in East Africa (1800–2000)*. New Delhi: Sage India.

Ozynski, Joyce. 1980. "Home Was a Small Piece of Paradise." *Rand Daily Mail*. May 8, 1980.

Palumbo-Liu, David. 1994. "Los Angeles, Asians, and Perverse Ventriloquisms: On the Functions of Asian America in the Recent American Imaginary." *Public Culture* 6 (2): 365–81.

Park, Yoon Jung. 2009. *A Matter of Honour: Being Chinese in South Africa*. Lanham, MD: Lexington Books.

Park, Yoon Jung. 2012. "Living In Between: The Chinese in South Africa." *Migration Policy Institute*, January 4, 2012. https://www.migrationpolicy.org/article/living-between-chinese-south-africa.

Peberdy, Sally. 2001. "Imagining Immigration: Inclusive Identities and Exclusive Policies in Post-1994 South Africa." *Africa Today* 48 (3): 15–32.

Peebles, Gustav. 2008. "Inverting the Panopticon: Money and the Nationalization of the Future." *Public Culture* 20 (2): 233–65.

Pegues, Juliana Hu. 2021. *Space-Time Colonialism: Alaska's Indigenous and Asian Entanglements*. Chapel Hill: University of North Carolina Press.

Penvenne, Jeanne Marie. 1995. *African Workers and Colonial Racism: Mozambican Strategies and Struggles in Lourenço Marques, 1877–1962*. Portsmouth, NH: Heinemann.

Pfafman, Tessa M., Christopher J. Carpenter, and Yong Tang. 2015. "The Politics of Racism: Constructions of African Immigrants in China on China-SMACK." *Communication, Culture, and Critique* 8 (4): 540–56.

Pieke, Frank N. 2014. "Anthropology, China, and the Chinese Century." *Annual Review of Anthropology* 43:123–38.

Pieke, Frank N., Pál Nyíri, Mette Thunø, and Antonella Ceccagno. 2004. *Transnational Chinese: Fujianese Migrants in Europe*. Stanford, CA: Stanford University Press.

Pierre, Jemima. 2012. *The Predicament of Blackness: Postcolonial Ghana and the Politics of Race*. Chicago: University of Chicago Press.

Pierre, Jemima. 2013. "Race in Africa Today." *Cultural Anthropology* 28 (3): 547–51.

Pierre, Jemima. 2020. "The Racial Vernaculars of Development: A View from West Africa." *American Anthropologist* 122 (1): 86–98.

Pillay, Kathryn. 2017. "'The Coolies Here': Exploring the Construction of an Indian 'Race' in South Africa." *Journal of Global South Studies* 34 (1): 22–49.

Posel, Deborah. 2001. "What's in a Name? Racial Categorisations under Apartheid and Their Afterlife." *Transformation—Durban* 2001: 50–74.

Posel, Deborah. 2010. "Races to Consume: Revisiting South Africa's History of Race, Consumption and the Struggle for Freedom." *Ethnic and Racial Studies* 33 (2): 157–75.

Posel, Deborah. 2019. "Changes in the Order of Things: Department Stores and the Making of Modern Cape Town." In *Conspicuous Consumption in Africa*, edited by Deborah Posel and Ilana van Wyk, 25–44. Johannesburg: Wits University Press.

Potts, Deborah. 2010. "Internal Migration in Zimbabwe: The Impact of Livelihood Destruction in Rural and Urban Areas." In *Zimbabwe's Exodus: Crisis, Migration, Survival*, edited by Jonathan Crush and Daniel Tevera, 79–109. Kingston, ON: Southern African Migration Programme.

Pratt, Mary Louise. 1991. *Imperial Eyes: Travel Writing and Transculturation*. New York: Routledge.

Rand Daily Mail. 1904a. "Asiatic Question." November 11, 1904.

Rand Daily Mail. 1904b. "Asiatic Trading." August 30, 1904.

Rand Daily Mail. 1904c. "The Black Peril." April 9, 1904.

Rand Daily Mail. 1904d. "Chinese Recruiting." September 20, 1904.

Rand Daily Mail. 1904e. "Labour Politics." February 5, 1904.

Rand Daily Mail. 1904f. "Native Location." September 30, 1904.

Rand Daily Mail. 1905a. "Asiatic Traders." June 26, 1905.

Rand Daily Mail. 1905b. "Chinese Labour." March 17, 1905.

Rand Daily Mail. 1905c. "Mine Managers." February 14, 1905.

Rand Daily Mail. 1907a. "Chinese Efficiency." March 1, 1907.

Rand Daily Mail. 1907b. "The Elections." February 18, 1907.

Rand Daily Mail. 1907c. "Parliament." June 18, 1907.

Rand Daily Mail. 1913. "Boycott the Coolie! An Appeal from the Pulpit." August 11, 1913.

Rand Daily Mail. 1937. "Cyrildene as an Ideal Suburb for Expanding Johannesburg." November 22, 1937.

Rand Daily Mail. 1956. "The Immigrants Oust Afrikaners: Fighting the 'Coolie.'" January 31, 1956.

Rand Daily Mail. 1974a. "Meeting the Demands of the Indian." July 3, 1974.

Rand Daily Mail. 1974b. "Windfall at Amalgam . . . and Some Gold Too." August 28, 1974.

Rand Daily Mail. 1976. "Browse About for Bargains" and "You'd Think They Eat in an All-Race Place Every Day." August 5, 1976.

Rankin, Elizabeth, and Leoni Schmidt. 2009. "The Apartheid Museum: Performing a Spatial Dialectics." *Journal of Visual Culture* 8 (1): 76–102.

Raya, Rajat Kanta. 1995. "Asian Capital in the Age of European Domination: The Rise of the Bazaar, 1800–1914." *Modern Asian Studies* 29 (3): 449–554.

Reboredo, Ricardo. 2021. "Modderfontein New City." The People's Map of Global China, last updated July 24, 2021. https://thepeoplesmap.net/project/modderfontein-new-city/.

Remi. 2014. "Michael Soi's 'China Loves Africa' Paintings." OkayAfrica, January 30, 2014. http://www.okayafrica.com/culture-2/art/michael-soi-china-loves-africa.

Richardson, Peter. 1982. *Chinese Mine Labour in the Transvaal.* London: Macmillan.

Robinson, Cedric J. (1983) 2000. *Black Marxism: The Making of the Black Radical Tradition.* Chapel Hill: University of North Carolina Press.

Rodney, Walter. (1972) 1981. *How Europe Underdeveloped Africa, revised edition.* Washington, DC: Howard University Press.

Rofel, Lisa. 2007. *Desiring China: Experiments in Neoliberalism, Sexuality, and Public Culture.* Durham, NC: Duke University Press.

Rofel, Lisa, and Carlos Rojas. 2022. "Introduction: Contact, Communication, Imagination, and Strategies of Worldmaking." In *New World Orders: China and the Global South,* edited by Lisa Rofel and Carlos Rojas, 1–18. Durham, NC: Duke University Press.

Rofel, Lisa, and Sylvia J. Yanagisako. 2019. *Fabricating Transnational Capitalism: A Collaborative Ethnography of Italian-Chinese Global Fashion.* Durham, NC: Duke University Press.

Roitman, Janet. 2005. *Fiscal Disobedience: An Anthropology of Economic Regulation in Central Africa*. Princeton, NJ: Princeton University Press.

Rojas, Carlos. 2016. "Introduction: 'Specters of Marx, Shades of Mao, and the Ghosts of Global Capital.'" In *Ghost Protocol: Development and Displacement in Global China*, edited by Carlos Rojas and Ralph A. Litzinger, 1–12. Durham, NC: Duke University Press.

Sadouni, Samadia. 2013. "Somalis in Johannesburg: Muslim Transformations of the City." In *Topographies of Faith: Religion in Urban Spaces*, edited by Irene Becci, Marian Burchardt, and Jose Casanova, 45–59. Leiden and Boston: Brill.

Saranillio, Dean Itsuji. 2013. "Why Asian Settler Colonialism Matters: A Thought Piece on Critiques, Debates, and Indigenous Difference." *Settler Colonial Studies* 3 (3–4): 280–94.

Saranillio, Dean Itsuji. 2018. *Unsustainable Empire: Alternative Histories of Hawai'i Statehood*. Durham, NC: Duke University Press.

Saul, John S., and Stephen Gelb. 1981. *The Crisis in South Africa: Class Defense, Class Revolution*. New York: Monthly Review Press.

Sautman, Barry. 1994. "Anti-Black Racism in Post-Mao China." *China Quarterly* 138: 413–37.

Sautman, Barry, and Yan Hairong. 2016. "The Discourse of Racialization of Labour and Chinese Enterprises in Africa." *Ethnic and Racial Studies* 39 (12): 2149–68.

Schafer, Peter. 1971. "Crown Mines Was a Mining Wonder of the World: A Golden Era Is to Close Next Month." *Rand Daily Mail*, June 7, 1971.

Schein, Louisa. 2000. *Minority Rules: The Miao and the Feminine in China's Cultural Politics*. Durham, NC: Duke University Press.

Schumaker, Lyn. 2001. *Africanizing Anthropology: Fieldwork, Networks, and the Making of Cultural Knowledge in Central Africa*. Durham, NC: Duke University Press.

Sexton, Jared. 2010. "People-of-Color-Blindness: Notes on the Afterlife of Slavery." *Social Text* 28 (2): 31–56.

Shah, Nayan. 2001. *Contagious Divides: Epidemics and Race in San Francisco's Chinatown*. Berkeley: University of California Press.

Sharpe, Christina. 2016. *In the Wake: On Blackness and Being*. Durham, NC: Duke University Press.

Shen Hu. 沈乎. 2011. "*Nanfei huaren dixia jinrong*" 南非华人地下金融 [South African Chinese Underground Finance], 沈乎的财新博客 [Shen Hu's Caixin blog], October 10, 2011. http://shenhu.blog.caixin.com/archives/25438.

Sheridan, Derek. 2023. "The Semiotics of Heiren (黑人): Race, Everyday Language, and Discursive Complicities in a Chinese Migrant Community." *Journal of Ethnic and Migration Studies* 49 (13): 3308–26.

Shih, Shu-mei. 2011. "The Concept of the Sinophone." *PMLA* 126 (3): 709–18.

Shih, Shu-mei. 2013. "Race and Revolution: Blackness in China's Long Twentieth Century." *PMLA* 128 (1): 156–62.

Shih, Shu-mei, and Françoise Lionnet. 2005. "Introduction: Thinking through the Minor, Transnationally." In *Minor Transnationalism*, edited by Shu-mei Shih and Françoise Lionnet, 1–23. Durham, NC: Duke University Press.

Simone, AbdouMaliq. 2004. "People as Infrastructure: Intersecting Fragments in Johannesburg." *Public Culture* 16 (3): 407–29.

Simone, AbdouMaliq. 2022. *The Surrounds: Urban Life within and beyond Capture*. Durham, NC: Duke University Press.

Smith, Anna H. 1971. *Johannesburg Street Names: A Dictionary of Street, Suburb and Other Place-Names Compiled to the End of 1968*. Cape Town, South Africa: Juta.

Snow, Philip. 1988. *The Star Raft: China's Encounter with Africa*. Ithaca, NY: Cornell University Press.

Sohu. 2019. "'*Sanfei heiren' de mafan lai le, zhongfang chutai xin zhengce, daliang heiren yi tiqian likai*" 三非黑人" 的麻烦来了，中方出台新政策，大量黑人已提前离开 ["Triple Illegals" Are in Trouble, Chinese Government Introduced a New Policy, Many Black People Have Left Early]. October 11, 2019. Accessed August 15, 2021. https://www.sohu.com/a/346305150_120098002.

Solinger, Dorothy J. 2002. "Labour Market Reform and the Plight of the Laid-off Proletariat." *China Quarterly* 170:304–26.

Sosibo, Kwanele. 2010. "Fong Kong Hits a Chord." *Mail and Guardian*, July 16, 2010. http://mg.co.za/article/2010-07-16-fong-kong-hits-a-chord/.

Srinivas, Smriti, Bettina Ng'weno, and Neelima Jeychandran. 2020. "Introduction: Many Worlds, Many Oceans." In *Reimagining Indian Ocean Worlds*, edited by Smriti Srinivas, Bettina Ng'weno, and Neelima Jeychandran, 1–22. Abingdon, UK: Routledge.

Steinberg, Jonny. 2002. *Midlands*. Johannesburg: Jonathan Ball Publishers.

Stiglitz, Joseph E. 2015. "The Chinese Century." *Vanity Fair*, January 2015. https://archive .vanityfair.com/article/2015/1/the-chinese-century.

Stoler, Ann Laura. 1995. *Race and the Education of Desire: Foucault's "History of Sexuality" and the Colonial Order of Things*. Durham, NC: Duke University Press.

Stoler, Ann Laura. 2006. "Intimidations of Empire: Predicaments of the Tactile and Unseen." In *Haunted by Empire: Geographies of Intimacy in North American History*, edited by Ann Laura Stoler, 1–22. Durham, NC: Duke University Press.

Stoler, Ann Laura. 2008. *Along the Archival Grain: Epistemic Anxieties and Colonial Common Sense*. Princeton, NJ: Princeton University Press.

Stoler, Ann Laura. 2017. *Duress: Imperial Durabilities in Our Times*. Durham, NC: Duke University Press.

Sudhakar, Anantha, and Vanita Reddy. 2018. "Introduction: Feminist and Queer Afro-Asian Formations." In "Feminist and Queer Afro-Asian Formations," edited by Vanita Reddy and Anantha Sudhakar, special issue, *Scholar and Feminist*

Online 14 (3), http://sfonline.barnard.edu/feminist-and-queer-afro-asian-formations/introduction-feminist-and-queer-afro-asian-formations.

Swanson, Maynard W. 1977. "The Sanitation Syndrome: Bubonic Plague and Urban Native Policy in the Cape Colony, 1900–1909." *Journal of African History* 18 (3): 387–410.

Swart, Sandra. 2001. "'Man, Gun, and Horse': Hard Right Afrikaner Masculine Identity in Post-apartheid South Africa." In *Changing Men in Southern Africa*, edited by Robert Morrell, 75–89. Pietermaritzburg and London: University of Natal Press / Zed Books.

Sylvain, Renee. 2001. "Bushmen, Boers and Baasskap: Patriarchy and Paternalism on Afrikaner Farms in the Omaheke Region, Namibia." *Journal of Southern African Studies* 27 (4): 717–37.

Sylvanus, Nina. 2013. "Chinese Devils, the Global Market, and the Declining Power of Togo's Nana-Benzes." *African Studies Review* 56 (1): 65–80.

Tax Justice Network of Africa. n.d. "Our Organisation." Accessed February 25, 2024. https://taxjusticeafrica.net/about-us/our-organisation.

Templeton, Alameen, and Solly Maphumulo. 2005. "Immigrants Are Getting a Raw Deal." Independent Online, June 20, 2005. https://www.iol.co.za/news/south-africa/immigrants-are-getting-a-raw-deal-244225.

Thomas, Lynn M. 2020. *Beneath the Surface: A Transnational History of Skin Lighteners.* Durham, NC: Duke University Press.

Tomlinson, Richard, Robert A. Beauregard, Lindsay Bremner, and Xolela Mangcu. 2003. "Introduction." In *Emerging Johannesburg: Perspectives on the Postapartheid City*, edited by Richard Tomlinson, Robert A. Beauregard, Lindsay Bremner, and Xolela Mangcu, ix–xv. New York: Routledge.

Tompkins, Kyla Wazana. 2012. *Racial Indigestion: Eating Bodies in the 19th Century.* New York: New York University Press.

Tsai, Kellee S. 2000. "Banquet Banking: Gender and Rotating Savings and Credit Associations in South China." *China Quarterly* 161: 142–70.

Tsai, Kellee S. 2002. *Back Alley Banking: Private Entrepreneurs in China.* Ithaca, NY: Cornell University Press.

Tsing, Anna Lowenhaupt. 2000. "Inside the Economy of Appearances." *Public Culture* 12 (1): 115–44.

Tsing, Anna Lowenhaupt. 2005. *Friction: An Ethnography of Global Connection.* Princeton, NJ: Princeton University Press.

Tsing, Anna Lowenhaupt. 2015. *The Mushroom and the End of the World: On the Possibility of Life in Capitalist Ruins.* Princeton, NJ: Princeton University Press.

Van Mead, Nick. 2019. "The Quiet Failure of a Chinese Developer's 'Manhattan in Africa.'" *Guardian*, October 24, 2019. https://www.theguardian.com/cities/2019/oct/24/failure-chinese-developer-manhattan-in-africa-johannesburg-modderfontein.

Van Onselen, Charles. (1982) 2001. *New Babylon, New Nineveh: Everyday Life on the Witwatersrand, 1886–1914*. Johannesburg: Jonathan Ball.

Van Vleet, Krista. 2003. "Partial Theories: Gossip, Envy and Ethnography in the Andes." *Ethnography* 4 (4): 491–519.

Verdery, Katherine. 2014. *Secrets and Truths: Ethnography in the Archive of Romania's Secret Police*. Budapest: Central European University Press.

Verhoef, Grietjie. 2001. "Informal Financial Service Institutions for Survival: African Women and Stokvels in Urban South Africa, 1930–1998." *Enterprise and Society* 2 (2): 259–96.

Vimalassery, Manu, Juliana Hu Pegues, and Alyosha Goldstein. 2016. "Introduction: On Colonial Unknowing." In "On Colonial Unknowing," edited by Juliana Hu Pegues, Alyosha Goldstein, and Manu Vimalassery, special issue, *Theory and Event* 19 (4): muse.jhu.edu/article/633283.

Vimalassery, Manu, Juliana Hu Pegues, and Alyosha Goldstein. 2017. "Colonial Unknowing and Relations of Study." *Theory and Event* 20 (4): 1042–54.

Volkmar, Barbara. 2000. "The Concept of Contagion in Chinese Medical Thought: Empirical Knowledge versus Cosmological Order." *History and Philosophy of the Life Sciences* 22 (2): 147–65.

Vorster, Hendrik. 1986. "New Golden Age of Gold Prospecting." *South African Mining, Coal, Gold and Base Minerals*, September 1986.

Voyles, Traci Brynne. 2015. *Wastelanding: Legacies of Uranium Mining in Navajo Country*. Minneapolis: University of Minnesota Press.

Vukovich, Daniel F. 2019. *Illiberal China: The Ideological Challenge of the People's Republic of China*. Singapore: Palgrave Macmillan.

Wang, Fei-Ling. 2004. "Reformed Migration Control and New Targeted People: China's Hukou System in the 2000s." *China Quarterly* 177: 115–32.

Welz, Martin, and Karen Schoonbee. 2012. "Howzit China?" *Noseweek*, November 27, 2012. https://noseweek.co.za/wp/article/howzit-china/.

White, Hylton. 2020. "How Is Capitalism Racial? Fanon, Critical Theory and the Fetish of Antiblackness." *Social Dynamics* 46 (1): 22–35.

White, Hylton. 2022. "Race, Capital and Culture: Learning from South Africa." Paper presented at the Annual Meeting of the American Studies Association, New Orleans, LA, November 5, 2022.

Wilderson, Frank B., III. 2020. *Afropessimism*. New York: Liveright.

Wilderson, Frank B., III. 2021. "Afropessimism and the Ruse of Analogy: Violence, Freedom Struggles, and the Death of Black Desire." In *Antiblackness*, edited by Moon-Kie Jung and João H. Costa Vargas, 37–59. Durham, NC: Duke University Press.

Wilson, Ara. 2004. *The Intimate Economies of Bangkok: Tomboys, Tycoons, and Avon Ladies in the Global City*. Berkeley: University of California Press.

Wilson, Francis. 1972. *Labour in the South African Gold Mines, 1911–1969*. Cambridge: Cambridge University Press.

Wilson, Francis. 2001. "Minerals and Migrants: How the Mining Industry Has Shaped South Africa." *Daedalus* 130 (1): 99–121.

Wolfe, Patrick. 2006. "Settler Colonialism and the Elimination of the Native." *Journal of Genocide Research* 8 (4): 387–409.

Wolpe, Harold. 1972. "Capitalism and Cheap Labour-Power in South Africa: From Segregation to Apartheid." *Economy and Society* 1 (4): 425–56.

Woods, Paolo. 2019. Chinafrica. Accessed February 10, 2024. https://www.paolowoods.com/the-desert.

Worden, Nigel. 1995. *The Making of Modern South Africa: Conquest, Segregation and Apartheid*. 2nd ed. Oxford: Blackwell.

Wright, Melissa W. 2011. "Necropolitics, Narcopolitics, and Femicide: Gendered Violence on the Mexico-US Border." *Signs* 36 (3): 707–31.

Wu, Di. 2021. *Affective Encounters: Everyday Life among Chinese Migrants in Zambia*. Abingdon, UK: Routledge.

Wyatt, Don J. 2010. *The Blacks of Premodern China*. Philadelphia: University of Pennsylvania Press.

Xiang, Biao. 2014. "The Would-Be Migrant: Post-socialist Primitive Accumulation, Potential Transnational Mobility, and the Displacement of the Present in Northeast China." *TRaNS: Trans-Regional and -National Studies of Southeast Asia* 2 (2): 183–99.

Xiang, Biao. 2017. "Hundreds of Millions in Suspension." *Transitions: Journal of Transient Migration* 1 (1): 3–5.

Xing 星星 and Xiao Z 小Z. 2021. "*Zhuwai san nian huiguo hou, wo zai ye bu hui qu Feizhou le*" 驻外3年回国后，我再也不会去非洲了 [After 3 Years Abroad, I Will Never Go to Africa Again.] Weixin 微信 [WeChat], September 14, 2021. https://mp.weixin.qq.com/s/gNs6aTeMVubmpJepzWANyw.

Yan, Abigail. 2019. "*Rui Hou Wei: Bangzhu Feizhou chuangye zhe 'linbao ruzhu'*" 芮后伟: 帮助非洲创业者 "拎包入住" [Rui Hou Wei: Making Africa "Ready to Move In" for Entrepreneurs]. Weixin 微信 [WeChat], September 16, 2019. https://mp.weixin.qq.com/s?__biz=Mzg2ODE4MTY4OQ==&mid=2247485966&idx=1&sn=a9c58b24deaoc7ae670ae1c8c9a17aff&chksm=ceb179d8f9c6f0cee450bedfb230cc002286d655d3ee01ed77a68fe9ea812e393d7c64305805&scene=21#wechat_redirect.

Yan, Hairong. 2003. "Neoliberal Governmentality and Neohumanism: Organizing Suzhi / Value Flow through Labor Recruitment Networks." *Cultural Anthropology* 18 (4): 493–523.

Yan, Hairong. 2008. *New Masters, New Servants: Migration, Development, and Women Workers in China*. Durham, NC: Duke University Press.

Yan, Yunxiang. 2012. "Food Safety and Social Risk in Contemporary China." *Journal of Asian Studies* 71 (3): 705–29.

Yanagisako, Sylvia J. 2002. *Producing Culture and Capital: Family Firms in Italy.* Princeton, NJ: Princeton University Press.

Yanagisako, Sylvia J. 2019. "On Generation." In *Fabricating Transnational Capitalism: A Collaborative Ethnography of Italian-Chinese Global Fashion,* by Lisa Rofel and Sylvia J. Yanagisako, 227–63. Durham, NC: Duke University Press.

Yang, Jie. 2013. "'Fake Happiness': Counseling, Potentiality, and Psycho-Politics in China." *Ethos* 41 (3): 292–312.

Yap, Melanie, and Dianne Leong Man. 1996. *Colour, Confusion and Concessions: The History of the Chinese in South Africa.* Hong Kong: Hong Kong University Press.

Yeh, Emily T., and Elizabeth Wharton. 2016. "Going West and Going Out: Discourses, Migrants, and Models in Chinese Development." *Eurasian Geography and Economics* 57 (3): 286–315.

Yoon, Duncan M. 2022. "A South African Imaginary of Maoist China: The Curious Case of Dennis Brutus's China Poems (1975)." *Verge* 8 (1): 141–66.

Yoon, Duncan M. 2023. *China in Twentieth- and Twenty-First-Century African Literature.* Cambridge: Cambridge University Press.

Yue, Gang. 1999. *The Mouth That Begs: Hunger, Cannibalism, and the Politics of Eating in Modern China.* Durham, NC: Duke University Press.

Yun, Lisa. 2007. *The Coolie Speaks: Chinese Indentured Laborers and African Slaves in Cuba.* Philadelphia: Temple University Press.

Zack, Tanya, and Mark Lewis. 2022. *Wake Up, This Is Joburg.* Durham, NC: Duke University Press.

Zee, Jerry C. 2022. *Continent in Dust: Experiments in a Chinese Weather System.* Berkeley: University of California Press.

Zhan, Mei. 2009. *Other-Worldly: Making Chinese Medicine through Transnational Frames.* Durham, NC: Duke University Press.

Zhang, Charlie Yi. 2022. *Dreadful Desires: The Uses of Love in Neoliberal China.* Durham, NC: Duke University Press.

Zhang, Everett Yeuhong. 2011. "China's Sexual Revolution." In *Deep China: The Moral Life of the Person; What Anthropology and Psychiatry Tell Us about China Today,* edited by Arthur Kleinman, Yunxiang Yan, Jing Jun, Sing Lee, Everett Zhang, Pan Tianshu, Wu Fei, and Guo Jinhua, 106–51. Berkeley: University of California Press.

Zhang, Li. 2001. *Strangers in the City: Reconfigurations of Space, Power, and Social Networks within China's Floating Population.* Stanford, CA: Stanford University Press.

Zhang, Li, and Aihwa Ong. 2008. "Introduction: Privatizing China: Powers of the Self, Socialism from Afar." In *Privatizing China: Socialism from Afar,* edited by Li Zhang and Aihwa Ong, 1–9. Ithaca, NY: Cornell University Press.

Zhang, Sheldon X., Ko-Lin Chin, and Jody Miller. 2007. "Women's Participation in Chinese Transnational Human Smuggling: A Gendered Market Perspective." *Criminology* 45 (3): 699–733.

Zhao, Linda Shuo. 2012. "Chinese Underground Banks and Their Connections with Crime: A Review and an Appraisal." *International Criminal Justice Review* 22 (1): 5–23.

Zhihu. 2021. "*Diaocha yixia gewei dui zaihua heiren de taidu, xiwang peihe yixia*" 调查一下各位对在华黑人的态度，希望配合一下 [Surveying Everyone's Attitude toward Black People in China. Please Be Harmonious.] August 16, 2021, https://zhuanlan.zhihu.com/p/392926813 (accessed September 31, 2021).

Italicized page numbers refer to figures.

anti-Asian exclusion laws, 56–57, 91,
99–100, 112
anti-Blackness, 15, 30, 141, 185, 247;
Chinese, 186–88, 190–93, 200–202,
204–8, 211, 214–15, 248–50, 258n1,
259n5; globality of, 17
anticolonialism, 11–12, 129
antiextradition, 47
antimiscegenation, 202, 207
apartheid, 64, 85–86, 93–94, 106, 113,
118, 122, 249, 253n2, 253n4; antiapartheid, 50, 54, 246; apartheid
city, 43–45; and colonialism, 12,
29, 51, 96; consumption under, 49,
96; credit apartheid, 49, 233; and
gold, 129–30; and interracial
mixing, 206–7, 212–13, 215; and
the palimpsest city, 38, 47, 57–58;
racial, 3–4, 49; state, 7, 11, 58.
See also postapartheid era
Apartheid Museum, 40, 50
Appel, Hannah, 166, 222, 233,
259n1
archives, 20, 29, 38, 55, 94–96, 98, 171,
250, 255n1; ephemeral, 193
Argentina, 12, 52, 63
Arrighi, Giovanni, 10, 12, 20
Asia, 4, 9–11, 64, 86, 97, 109, 122, 221,
241, 253n9. *See also* East Asia;
Southeast Asia
Asian American studies, 6
Asian ascendance, 18, 29, 69, 192, 245.
See also New Asian Age
Asian capitalism, 7, 29, 94–96, 104,
110, 240
Asian Financial Crisis (1997), 47
Asian labor, 95, 97–98, 104, 121,
141
Asiatic, figure of, 16, 29, 92, 94–100,
105–6, 113, 122, 226, 246, 259n2
Asiatic bazaars, 57, 94, 105
Asiatic invasion, 96, 98, 104
Asiatic Question, 95, 98–99, 104,
107, 121
asylum, 48, 130, 137, 149
Atlantic Ocean, xi, 6, 10, 63, 125
Australia, 39, 55–56, 58, 63, 97, 99, 105,
206

baas, figure of, 143–44, 154, 160, 176,
178, 181
baasskap, 176
Baijia (One Hundred Households), 46
Bald, Vivek, 112
Banda, Hastings, 129
Bandung Conference, ix, 11–12, 120
Bangladeshi people, 13, 113
Bania people, 96
banking, 2, 26, 44, 88–89, 166, 222,
225–26, 228–30, 246, 260n3; Chinese, 220, 233; underground, 21,
135, 223, 227, 232, 235–39. *See also*
dixia qianzhuang; *individual banks*
Bank of China, 220–21
Bantu people, 16, 52, 64, 130
barcodes, 87–90
bartering, 50, 114, 118
Baudrillard, Jean, 237
bazaars, 104, 114–22; Asiatic, 57, 94,
105, 112
BBC, 206
Beautiful City, 245–46
Belt and Road Initiative, 9, 68, 79, 90,
221–22
Bendor Properties, 51–52
Beuret, Michel, 63
Biao Xiang, 63, 254n3
biopolitics, 30, 192, 209, 214–16, 249
black devil (heigui), figure of, 28, 141,
161–62, 186, 211, 245
Black diamond, 50
Black labor, 17, 122, 125–28, 141, 147,
160–61, 177, 212, 257n4; devaluation
of, 30, 130–31, 153, 249. *See also*
heigong
Black Peril, 101, 104, 206
Black Radical Tradition, 145
Black retaliation, 173. *See also* white
paranoia
Black studies, 6
blogs, 67, 163–64, 227
borders, 119, 131, 136–37, 163, 182, 192,
204–5, 223, 254n5, 257n5; capital
moving across, 233, 237, 239; cross-
border operators, 22; crossing of,
66, 73, 83, 85–86, 90, 154, 231; mining belt as, 43; US-Mexican, 85–86

Group Areas Act (1950), 43, 51, 58, 115

Guangdong-Hong Kong-Macau Greater Bay Area, 70

Hall, Stuart, 161

Han Chinese identity, 14, 16, 19, 162, 186, 258n1; and racial nationalism, 30, 125, 141, 191–93, 199–202, 215

Harris (Lord), 99

Harris, Karen, 98, 100

Harrison, George, 39

Haugen, Heidi Østbø, 71

hawala, 237, 260n3

Hecht, Gabrielle, 41

hegemony, 9–10, 12, 14, 20, 248, 250

hei, 17, 125, 140–41, 188, 192, 248; significance of, 161–62

heigong, 14, 17, 30, 122, 125, 140–41, 153, 162, 177, 186. *See also* Black labor

heigui (black devil), 28, 140–41, 161–62, 183, 186, 211, 245

heipo, 140, 177, 181, 186

Hemson, David, 239. *See also* Legassick, Martin

heteropatriarchy, 30, 79–80, 190, 192, 199, 201–2, 249

Highway M1, 41, *45*

Highway M2, 158

HIV/AIDS, 193, 200, 211, 259n4

Ho, Ufrieda, 85, 234

Hoang, Kimberly Kay, 19, 239

hoarding, 107, 226–27, 259–60n2

Holland, Sharon, 192, 214

homelands, 64, 130

homogeneities, 147, 192, 204

Hong, Grace, 233

Hong Kong, 4, 38, 44, 47–48, 58, 60, 63, 70, 110, 118; Hong Kongese, 55, 59, 84; and PRC, 10, 12

Hood, Johanna, 200, 259n4

household registrations (hukou), 70, 88

Hudson, Peter, 238

Huffington Post, 206

huiguo, 63, 88

humanitarian workers, 67–68

human rights, 17

Hunger Boyz, 110. *See also* Senyaka

Huynh, Tu, 100

hygiene, 183–84, 205–7, 210, 213, 259n5

iGoli2010, 44

iGoli2030, 44

illegality, 17, 83–84, 89, 140–41, 188, 221, 223, 229–30, 233–37, 240; illegalization, 136, 182; and immigrants, 14, 59, 70, 87, 88, 245, 259; triple illegal, 161–65, 192

immigrants, 96, 108, 109, 206, 210, 245, 254n1; settled, 4, 60, 64–65

immigration, 63, 73, 89, 100, 138, 201, 203, 228, 231; Chinese, 84–85; illegal, 14, 59; immigration authorities, 132, 139; immigration lawyers, 26, 88; laws, 87, 136, 254n6; restrictions on, 13, 57, 76, 105, 137

imperialism, 14–15, 64, 192, 206, 248–49, 252, 255n2, 255n4; anti-, 12, 215; British, 98–101, 122; capitalist, 18, 95–96, 222–23, 234, 238–39, 241, 246; Chinese, 10, 30, 65–68, 211; and development, 221, 231; economic, 63, 70; Euro-American, 4, 9; imperial circuits, 98, 112; imperial formations, 4–5, 20–21, 38, 191; Japanese, 16, 19; Western, 14, 16, 19, 205, 247. *See also* decoloniality; empire

indenture, 18, 29, 95–101, 112, 122, 153, 255n2, 255n4; indentured labor, 64, 96, 112, 124, 142

India, 12, 98, 120, 122, 239; Bihar, 96; Gujarat, 93, 96, 104, 106, 112; Madras, 96; Punjab, 93; United Provinces, 96. *See also* BRICS

Indian Ocean, 10, 67, 85, 96–97, 121, 255n2

Indian Ocean methodologies, 96

Indian people, 3, 13, 46, 50, 57, 59, 128, 206, 254n1, 256n5; "Asiatics," 16, 29, 103–8, 110–15, 226; laborers, 93–100, 118–21, 122, 204, 236, 255n2, 255n4, 256n7

Indigenous land, 95

pollution, 202, 205–14
Ponte City Apartments, 58
porosity, 16, 58, 98, 205–15, 223, 230
Port of Durban, 22
Portuguese people, 39, 58, 97, 190, 255n2
Posel, Deborah, 49, 253n1
possession, 211; Chinese, 187–88, 192, 249; white, 161, 174–75
postabolition era, 97
postapartheid era, 16, 20, 87, 91, 104, 108, 110, 126, 136; and palimpsest city, 49, 52–53, 59–61, 223; and crime, 163–65, 174
postcolonialism, 6, 17, 19, 121, 175, 191, 239, 250, 254n1, 259n5
poverty, 2, 66, 74, 148, 165, 180, 182, 221, 232
private security, 59, 148, 165, 173, 175, 230–31, 258n2
privatization, 4, 69, 76, 82, 90, 165
proletarianization, 128–29
public health, 200, 259n4
purity, 121, 192, 202, 205, 213–14

Qiaobi detergent, 205–7, 259n5
Qing era, 10, 16, 19, 99, 258n1
queerness, 151, 173
Quinn, Leung, 99

racial capitalism, x–xi, 19–20, 193, 215, 221, 223, 234; definition of, 6–8; and settler colonialism, 65; in Sino-African context, 125–26, 142, 152–54; in South Africa, 41, 101, 127–28, 241, 246. See also colonial racial capitalism
racial contagion, 30, 105, 188, 205–6, 208–12
racial fictions, 163, 171, 185, 215
racial formations, 5, 97, 104–12, 122, 142, 193, 249–50; Chinese, 20, 30, 125–27, 160, 188, 215; globality of, 8, 188
racial hierarchies, 74, 77, 91, 139–41, 179–80, 183, 200–201, 213, 231, 249
racial ideologies, 4, 8, 17, 179, 199, 214, 250

racial imaginaries, 30, 103, 114, 160–63, 182, 192, 215
racialization, 6–8, 19–20, 141, 192–93, 200, 208, 231–34, 252n6, 253n1, 260n7; Asian, 29, 94–98, 100–101, 255n2; Chinese, 102–4, 111, 121–22; colonial racialization, 96–107; of contagion, 211–12, 214; and crime, 159, 164, 172, 174, 182; and labor, 30, 71, 137–39, 161, 240, 247–49, 251n3, 259n1; of migrants, 13–15, 71, 91, 95, 128, 159; within the Rand, 4, 105, 124
racial violence, 43, 175
racism, 6–7, 27, 53, 109, 124, 137, 162–63, 175, 180, 252n6; anti-Blackness, 15, 30, 141, 185, 247–50, 258n1, 259n5; Chinese, 186–88, 190–93, 200–202, 204–8, 211, 214–15, 248–50, 258n1, 259n5; globality of, 17; without whiteness, 12–21
railways, 52, 77, 222
Rainbow Nation, 50
Rand, the. See Witwatersrand
Rand Daily Mail (RDM), 94, 98, 103, 105–7
Rand Mines Property (RMP), 43–45, 51
recruitment, 102, 127, 129–30, 134, 257n6
recursion, 20–21, 29, 38, 126, 237, 246, 248
refugees, 48, 136–37
regulation, 91, 191, 209, 214, 223–25, 230, 237–38, 240, 253n1, 260n3; of Black people, 49, 52, 130, 257n4; disregulation, 228; state, 71, 82, 108, 231
relocation, 43, 58, 76, 88, 98, 105, 113, 115, 135
remittances, 22, 74, 132, 224, 229, 232, 236, 238–39, 250, 260n3; overseas, 70, 106
reproductive futurism, 80, 90, 214
Republican era (China), 16
revenge killings, 172, 174, 176
riots, 13, 44, 103
rise of China, 4, 9, 11, 19, 94–95, 108

taxis, 22, 25, 138; taxi drivers, 21, 26, 36–37, 135, 224

Tax Justice Network of Africa, 240

theft/stealing, 104, 134–35, 142, 150–51, 157, 165, 173, 176, 178–80, 204, 224; contested meaning of, 147–49, 159–60, 162, 169, 181–85, 240; of land, 64. *See also* criminalization

Tibet, 19

toudu, 84–87. *See also* snakeheads

tourism, 2, 68, 105, 196, 220

townships, 13, 22, 37, 41, 43, 49–52, 57, 82, 112–13, 118, 136, 232

trade unions, 40, 43, 50–51, 109–10, 139, 159. *See also individual trade unions*

Transvaal Chinese Association (TCA). *See* Chinese Association (TCA)

Transvaal United Chinese Club, 54

triangulation: evolving, 95; racial, 15, 29–30, 95–97, 121, 247

triple illegal (sanfei), figure of, 161, 163–64, 192

Tsing, Anna Lowenhaupt, 41, 237

Tutu, Desmond, 50

Uber, 50, 208

underground banking in China, 21, 27, 223, 227, 231–32, 235–38. *See also* dixia qianzhuang

undocumented people, 17, 89, 137, 153, 163, 227, 231, 254n5; workers, 14, 135, 139, 141, 145

unemployment, 22, 51, 108–9, 111–12, 165, 232–33, 254n4, 258n2

Union of South Africa, 11, 97, 124

Urban Areas Act (1924), 43

urbanization, 51, 70, 79, 258n2

urban/nonpeasant class in China, 70

Uruguay, 52

Uyghurs, xi, 19

Victorian period, 205

Vietnam, 19, 239

Village Deep Gold Mine, 246

Vimalassery, Manu, 65

violence, 37, 41, 54, 64, 87, 103, 105, 149, 181, 211; colonial, 171, 173; and crime, 149, 169; domestic, 231; police, 27; political, 132; racial, 43–44, 175–76, 250; xenophobic, 4, 12–13, 109, 135–36, 138

visas, 67, 80–81, 89–90, 196, 198, 201, 223; regime of, 138–39, 163–64; visitor, 84–85, 87, 130, 137; work, 76, 88, 184

Voyles, Traci Brynne, 41

Vredefort asteroid, 39

Vries, Fred De, 50

War on Terror, 9

wastelanding, 41

WeChat, 13, 67, 158–59

West, the, 62–63, 67, 91, 94, 115, 122, 141, 164, 193, 215–16; China's triumph over, 12, 68; and whiteness, 5, 8, 10, 13–29, 205–7, 221, 245, 247, 249

white flight, 43, 45

white genocide, 174

whiteness, 5, 8, 29–30, 125, 154, 183, 202, 247, 249, 259n5; and cleanliness, 205–6, 213; as ideal, 215–16, 245; as power, 160, 174–75, 188; racism without, 12–21

white paranoia, 160, 173, 175–76. *See also* Black retaliation

white possession, 174

white settlement, 3, 54, 99

white supremacy, 6, 10, 17–18, 97, 100, 160, 174, 176, 188, 241; global, 8, 15, 20–21, 121, 192, 216, 247, 251n3

wholesale malls, 22, 35, 73, 75, 96, 104, 114–15, 203, 246; Chinese, 2–3, 38, 45–47, 93–94, 134–35, 152

Witwatersrand, 2, 4, 11, 30, 39–40, 97, 124, 137; Chinese labor in, 99, 122, 124; the mines of, 126, 130–31

Witwatersrand Native Labour Association (WNLA), 129, 131

Wolfe, Patrick, 63

Wolf Warrior 2, 66–67

Woods, Paolo, 63

Workers' Museum, 40

work permits, 86–88, 130, 137, 149

world-making, 9, 38, 248–49
World Trade Organization, 9
World War II, 106, 112
Wu, Di, 179, 187

xenophobia, 4, 12–15, 27, 51, 91, 109, 135–38, 163, 246, 253n9. *See also* Sinophobia
Xhosa people, 64
xiaosan, 194, 196–97, 203
"Xiaosan" (song), 197
Xi Jinping, 12, 79, 194, 222
Xinhua, 162

Yao people, 136
Yap, Melanie, 58
Yellow Emperor, 192
Yellow Peril, 94, 100–104, 109, 113, 226
Yoon, Duncan M., 18
yuan currency, 47, 220, 223, 225, 233, 238

Yun, Lisa, 101, 225n2

Zack, Tanya, 36
zama zamas, 37
Zambia, 187
Zendai Group, 243
Zhang, Charlie Yi, 80
Zhang, Everett, 193
zhongzu, 16
Zimbabwe, 27, 110, 125, 127, 130–31, 178, 186; Beitbridge, 137; Bulawayo, 132; Harare, 132; Plum Tree, 132
Zimbabwean people, 2–3, 12–13, 129, 142, 144, 147, 149, 162, 224, 246; hawkers, 21–22, 37; workers, 52, 75, 88, 93, 111, 119–20, 132, 136–37, 187, 212–13
Zulu language, 82, 253n9; isiZulu language, 2, 36, 55
Zulu people, 64, 96, 114, 255n3